CROWBAR GOVERNOR

A *Driftless Connecticut Series Book*
This book is a 2011 selection in the
Driftless Connecticut Series, for an
outstanding book in any field on a
Connecticut topic or written by a
Connecticut author.

KEVIN MURPHY

CROWBAR GOVERNOR
THE LIFE AND TIMES OF MORGAN GARDNER BULKELEY

WESLEYAN UNIVERSITY PRESS MIDDLETOWN, CONNECTICUT

Wesleyan University Press
Middletown CT 06459
www.wesleyan.edu/wespress
© 2010 Kevin Murphy
Manufactured in the United States of America

The Driftless Connecticut Series is funded by the
Beatrice Fox Auerbach Foundation Fund
at the Hartford Foundation for Public Giving.

Wesleyan University Press is a member of the
Green Press Initiative. The paper used in this book meets
their minimum requirement for recycled paper.

Library of Congress Cataloging-in-Publication Data
Murphy, Kevin (Kevin J.), 1949–
Crowbar governor : the life and times of Morgan Gardner
Bulkeley / Kevin Murphy.
p. cm.
Includes bibliographical references and index.
ISBN 978-0-8195-7074-1 (cloth : alk. paper)
1. Bulkeley, Morgan G. (Morgan Gardner), 1837–1922.
2. Governors—Connecticut—Biography. 3. United States.
Congress. Senate—Biography. 4. Statesmen—
Connecticut—Biography. 5. Connecticut—Biography.
I. Title.
F100.M87 2010
974.6'04092—dc22
[B]   2010020786

5 4 3 2 1

Dedicated to

ROBERT D. MURPHY, M.D.

&

MARY C. MURPHY, R.N.

Two hearts cast together in a war-torn world.

CONTENTS

Gathered illustrations follow page 116

PREFACE

In 1911, when Morgan Bulkeley finished his only term in the U.S. Senate, the *Hartford Courant* printed this summary: "To some he's 'Senator' Bulkeley; To many, he's 'President' Bulkeley; Then again, he's the 'Honorable' Mr. Bulkeley. But his close friends, those who know him well, call him by the title he likes best, 'Governor' Bulkeley, and when they do, he does not feel the least slighted because they did not use the term 'Senator.' To a few intimate friends, he is 'Morgan G.,' but they are the inner circle" ("The Grill Room," *Hartford Courant*, November 23, 1913, 8).

Crowbar Governor considers the years when Morgan Bulkeley was in his political prime and the undisputed boss of Connecticut's Republican Party. This was the Gilded Age—a fascinating time for the country and for Connecticut in particular. Hartford led the country in infrastructure, wealth, and beauty—and Bulkeley came into his political prime just in time to shape it and to savor it.

Morgan Bulkeley's name has been attached to many of Hartford's landmarks, but he remains one of the most controversial politicians the Charter Oak City has ever produced. Early in his political career, Bulkeley realized that almost every candidate he faced turned in a superior resume. In order to win, Bulkeley would adopt increasingly unpopular and corrupt election practices. His antics were all but ignored, and he accomplished a great deal for Hartford and for Connecticut. Morgan enjoyed the political arena, but politics was only an avocation at first. His whole political career emerged as a great surprise.

He started late. Bulkeley wasn't elected to Hartford's common council until he was thirty-seven. At forty-one, he settled into his life's work, and he didn't marry until he was forty-seven. However, during his eighty-four years, he knew everyone of prominence in the United States including each president from Ulysses Grant to Warren Harding. He easily traveled all over the United States forging relationships that would help him and the Connecticut governments he served.

Born the middle son and later expected to become a dry goods clerk, Morgan Bulkeley assumed the role of eldest son when his brother Charlie died in uniform. This slated Morgan to take Judge Bulkeley's place at the helm of Aetna Life Insurance Company after the Civil War. He neither chose nor necessarily wanted the job, but he would build the business of Aetna Life eightfold, and would use his position to serve his constituency and his country.

He was shrewd, pragmatic, sometimes wildly vindictive—but he was also courteous, loyal, and even kind. He wasn't a "man for all seasons," but he accomplished an enormous amount without receiving even a high school diploma. In the pantheon of Connecticut politics, he has his own special place. Love him or hate him, he remains one of the most interesting and complex politicians Connecticut has ever produced.

CROWBAR GOVERNOR

THE BULKELEY GENEALOGY

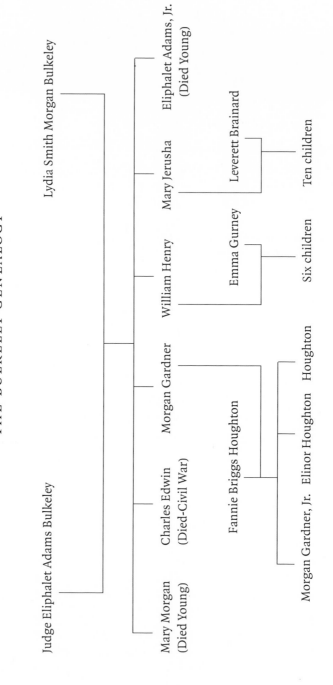

Judge Eliphalet Adams Bulkeley — Lydia Smith Morgan Bulkeley

Mary Morgan (Died Young)

Charles Edwin (Died-Civil War)

Morgan Gardner — Fannie Briggs Houghton

William Henry — Emma Gurney — Six children

Mary Jerusha — Leverett Brainard — Ten children

Eliphalet Adams, Jr. (Died Young)

Morgan Gardner, Jr. Elinor Houghton Houghton

Chapter One

THE MAN

On a Saturday morning in early June 1922, a trim, eighty-four-year-old man stepped out onto the white-columned porch of Beaumaris, his sprawling waterfront cottage in the borough of Fenwick. Beaumaris, a mammoth structure of weathered timbers and shingles, sat forty yards west of Fenwick Avenue. On a clear day, its owners espied an unobstructed southern view across Long Island Sound to Orient Point. Beaumaris was more than just the largest cottage at Fenwick, and more than just the finest work of Hartford architect Willis E. Becker.[1] Beaumaris was the home of the benevolent ruler of this wealthy summer barony by the sea—Senator Morgan Gardner Bulkeley.[2]

Though it didn't appear so from the outside, Beaumaris buzzed with activity. The Bulkeleys employed a large staff of servants. When Bulkeley built Beaumaris in 1900, he installed indoor plumbing, eliminating the need for *pots de chambre*, but the place wasn't electrified until 1915, and the list of new-age labor-saving devices was a short one.[3]

Their longtime cook, Julie Morhan, required her own staff to cut, peel, dice, filet, and churn. (In 1917, Bulkeley also purchased Arrowhead Farm—about three miles away—so that his family would have plenty of fresh fruits, vegetables, and dairy products.)[4]

Two helpers waited tables, while two maids cleaned the house. At one time, a separate nursemaid doted on each of the Bulkeleys' three children—Morgan Jr., Elinor, and Houghton. However, by 1922, the young people were just visitors and had long since outgrown nannies.[5]

A houseman-gardener and a chauffeur completed this cast of servants. The first maintained Beaumaris's lush lawns and colorful flowerbeds, and the latter, longtime employee Arthur Stone, drove and maintained the Bulkeleys' Pierce-Arrow limousine.[6] Together, this swarm of servants kept the massive cottage running smoothly.

Beaumaris was the perfect retreat for a rare man. Beyond the dreams of most men—and for the greater part of his long life—he completely controlled his world. With courage and political savvy, Morgan Bulkeley hopscotched from great success in business and laudable accomplishments in community affairs to the realization of some rather robust political dreams. He rubbed shoulders with people of every station—from destitute immigrants in the Charter Oak City's river wards to presidents of the United States.[7]

Morgan Bulkeley waged some legendary battles in his life as he gracefully negotiated the corridors of power—from councilman to alderman, Hartford mayor to Connecticut governor, and finally United States senator. All the while, as president of the Aetna Life Insurance Company, he increased the size of the firm's total assets eightfold.[8]

Even at eighty-four, Bulkeley projected great physical grace. Standing at about five foot nine and weighing nearly 160 pounds, Bulkeley's erect bearing and aristocratic features made him seem much larger. Bulkeley dressed nattily even while spending time at Fenwick. He preferred a white shirt and bow tie to the increasingly more casual dress sweeping the land after the Great War.

Slow to anger and quick to warm to strangers, Bulkeley had the even temperament of a natural politician, instilling confidence in voters and fellow businessmen alike.[9] His classic bearing was perfectly fitting for a patrician's son, striving as he always did for the grand gesture. When Bulkeley was on top of his game, few men had his élan.

Now, in 1922, Bulkeley hid a full head of white hair beneath the Boston-style baseball cap he preferred to wear around Fenwick. As he puffed on his trademark, big black cigar, his fingers brushed casually against his permanently nicotine-stained white mustache, a little wilder now than when he was in his political prime. He drank sparingly all his life, so cigars were more or less his only vice.[10]

Standing there soaking up the warm sunlight, Bulkeley nonchalantly surveyed the cottages around him for signs of activity. His younger sister, Mary Brainard, who passed away the summer before, had lived right next door to him. Her husband, Leverett—arguably the most ambitious man ever to leave a rural Connecticut farm for a business career in Hartford—was sixteen years older than Mary and died right after the turn of the century. Mary and Leverett birthed ten children, but only five made it to adulthood. So said, Mary always wore black, claiming that the deaths in her family kept her in perpetual mourning.[11] Now their bachelor son, Newton, owned the Brainard cottage, and later shared it with his widowed sister, Lucy. Their three siblings—Morgan B. Brainard, Edith Davis, and Ruth Cutler—maintained Fenwick cottages of their own.[12]

Bulkeley owned more undeveloped building lots than anyone else at Fenwick, and he liked to think he could choose his neighbors. His brother, Billy, who passed away in 1902, had lived in a waterfront cottage just to the west of Beaumaris. As families go, the Bulkeleys were extremely close. In Hartford, they lived side by side at the northern end of Washington Street, near the state capitol, in what could almost be described as a family compound. Morgan's and Billy's homes were cheek by jowl on the east side of the street, while their sister Mary and her brood were just across the way. In the summertime, everyone migrated to Fenwick, where they spent the warm months packed together neatly at the water's edge.[13]

Looking west, Bulkeley could see some of the Goodwins cleaning up the windblown branches left by the winter winds as they prepared their cottage for the season. Bulkeley had known Frankie Goodwin since they were children. Goodwin was two years younger than Bulkeley, but they had both attended the small Centre School on Market Street in Hartford, the finest of the Charter Oak City's eleven common schools.[14] The feelings between the two men were, to be sure, mixed. They could get along when they needed to, but generally their sensibilities swung between cautious tolerance and unbridled contempt. They were both conservative Republicans, but any similarities between them ended there. As far as Bulkeley was concerned, if Frankie Goodwin's first cousin, J. P. Morgan, would chase a dollar to hell, the former wouldn't be far behind. The Morgans, but more particularly the Goodwins, were just too avaricious for Bulkeley's tastes. He wasn't against making money, but neither did he see it as an end in itself—an important distinction in his mind.

To the east, Bulkeley enjoyed an unobstructed view all the way to the inner lighthouse at the mouth of the Connecticut River. Barge and boat traffic constantly plied the waters around the silted bar at the river's delta, where the shifting sands made navigation difficult. In 1874, two parallel stone jetties were constructed at the mouth of the river, which encouraged a deep channel and eliminated the need for an annual dredge. A lighthouse sat on shore and another was erected at the end of the westernmost jetty.[15]

About a quarter mile down the beach, Bulkeley spotted Dr. Tom Hepburn out in the yard with some of his children. He needed to present the forty-two-year-old surgeon with an unpleasant bill and planned to use the opportunity to get to know his new neighbor.[16]

The bill in question represented carpentry repairs done on the three-foot-high wooden breakwaters protecting the waterfront cottages from the ravages of winter storms. Periodically, bad weather destroyed sections of these barriers, and with most of the cottages sitting only a few feet above sea level, the bulkheads had to be rebuilt regularly—and quickly. Typically, Morgan Bulkeley ordered the repairs as needed and settled finances later. Experience taught him that few people balked when presented with his bill. Bulkeley was one of the most powerful politicians Connecticut ever produced, and a refusal to accept his bill was to court trouble. In addition, Bulkeley, a likeable man, rarely encountered a person who did not want him for a friend.[17]

Since now was as good a time as any, Bulkeley eased down the wooden stairs in front of Beaumaris, walked across the luxurious lawn and then down another small set of steps to Beach Road. As he walked along, he waved to friends and neighbors. Everyone knew Senator Bulkeley. For his part, he loved people. His whole life was people. In a life spanning eight and a half decades, it would be difficult to find Bulkeley alone, even for a few hours.

As he walked on the now-abandoned gravel road, Bulkeley no doubt chuckled to himself, for he was the one who had closed it down. This rutted lane, along with the 2,800-foot rickety, wooden bridge across South Cove served, until recently, as the main artery for all of the Old Saybrook traffic, skirting Fenwick on the south and traversing South Cove to Saybrook Point. When Beaumaris was first built, the occasional horse and wagon were welcome reminders of the rural nature of the beach community, and Bulkeley enjoyed the sight of the farmers hauling hay and produce along the shore road. When the automobile exploded onto the scene, the pleasant novelty of Beach Road ended abruptly. Oddly enough, it was one of Bulkeley's neighbors at Fenwick who had ruined the pleasant reverie.[18]

A decade earlier, while Morgan Bulkeley sat quietly on the front porch of Beaumaris enjoying the scenery and a cigar, his neighbor, George Day—who manufactured the new gas-powered automobiles for Col. Albert Pope—blithely motored along Beach Road in the latest Pope-Hartford automobile. Unlike the previous electric models produced by Pope, this contraption made an ungodly racket and stunk up the whole neighborhood. Even as Bulkeley waved politely to George Day, he decided the time had arrived for traffic to find a new route to Saybrook Point. Soon thereafter, he hatched a plan to close down Beach Road.

In hindsight, his solution was simplicity itself, but only for someone with a wide circle of business and political allies. Bulkeley knew the principals of the Shore Line Railroad—J. P. Morgan & Co., as it turned out. He also knew they were unhappy with the spur across the causeway from Saybrook Point to Fenwick. It made sense back in the 1870s when it was first built, but as the wealthy families of Fenwick bought automobiles and stopped using the train, the spur—with its expensive causeway—became an irksome money loser.

He also knew that the shaky wooden bridge across the cove—a little farther east—was a source of endless friction between the people of Fenwick and the Town of Old Saybrook. Its maintenance costs were astronomical and out of all proportion to its worth.[19]

With these two facts in mind, Bulkeley saw an opportunity. By getting the railroad to cede its spur across South Cove, the causeway could accommodate automobiles. In this way, traffic would be routed from the southern side of

Fenwick to a northern route, leaving the small beach community pleasantly isolated from Old Saybrook. By 1918, all traffic abandoned Beach Road and Beaumaris once again bathed in blessed tranquility and salty breezes. Bulkeley loved these little puzzles and reveled in his ability to solve them with alacrity.[20]

Bulkeley looked forward to meeting Dr. Hepburn. Much like his own father, Judge Eliphalet Bulkeley, Morgan possessed an uncanny ability to remember the family trees of an unlimited number of people as well as important events in each of their lives. Though Morgan Bulkeley was a rather mediocre student, and never much of a reader, he had an astounding ability to remember names and faces and was a veritable treasure trove of information.[21]

Making his way eastward on Beach Road, Fenwick's little hummocks of progress registered in his mind like the hachures on a cartographer's map. Golfers dotted the little nine-hole golf course that snaked its way between the cottages, and tennis players rallied on the well-used courts.

Less than ten minutes later, Bulkeley was shaking hands with Tom Hepburn at the surgeon's cottage—the fourth from Fenwick Avenue. Bulkeley and the doctor exchanged the usual pleasantries, and rather than tendering the bill for rebuilding the wooden bulkheads right off, Bulkeley first took the opportunity to explain his plans for the small beach community.[22]

Though he did not have a particularly mellifluous speaking voice or the fast-and-easy banter of an old-time ward politician, Bulkeley was a good conversationalist. His voluminous record of achievement coupled with his boyish charm made others pay heed to him, and with what might be considered the genetically inherited logic of his father, he could assemble the most compelling arguments to buttress his causes.

From his earliest days in politics, Morgan Bulkeley had learned the value of action. Typically when there was a job to do, he whistled up the men and materials needed to get it done with no mention of finances. The money could always be sorted out later. This one small preference won him plenty of hearts and minds over the years, and not without good reason. When people were in trouble, the last thing they needed was a committee to study the problem. In truth, Bulkeley could feather his own nest better than most men, but he was smart enough to keep his machinations out of the public eye.

Bulkeley liked Dr. Hepburn. The two men had much in common; moreover, they were both products of small-town America. Tom Hepburn was from Beaver Dam, Virginia, a dusty Scottish-American farming crossroads twenty miles north of Richmond. Bulkeley, with his deep Anglo-American roots, was originally from East Haddam—fifteen miles upriver.

Bulkeley and Hepburn were both ambitious, competitive men, who rose to positions of prominence in their chosen fields. The younger man fulfilled his residency requirements at Hartford Hospital and began his career as a general practitioner. He quickly advanced to surgeon, specializing in urology.

Beyond their professional achievements, both men were married to Houghton women. This last point could just as easily be described as a place where similarities ceased, for their wives were as different as buttons and bows. Bulkeley's wife, Fannie Briggs Houghton Bulkeley, distantly related to Hepburn's wife, was the doyenne of Fenwick—bright, charming and steadfastly loyal to her husband. She was born to one of the most prominent families in San Francisco, went to the finest finishing schools in the Bay Area, and was goddaughter to Governor Leland Stanford and Jane Lathrop Stanford, founders of Stanford University.[23]

Conversely, Dr. Hepburn's wife, Katharine Houghton (Kit)—and her two sisters, Edith and Marion—had all the manners and breeding of Fannie Bulkeley but displayed willful, independent spirits that could really get under the skin of a dyed-in-the-wool conservative like Morgan Bulkeley. Kit Hepburn championed the entire spectrum of the cutting-edge feminist issues of her time, from family planning to women's suffrage.[24]

Nevertheless, Bulkeley went out of his way to get along with her. Kit and her two sisters were born in the Buffalo area, where their engineer father, Alfred Houghton, worked in the family business—Corning Glass Works. When the girls were sixteen, fourteen, and twelve, respectively, Alfred committed suicide. Caroline, their mother, died two years later. Their rich and socially prominent uncle, Amory Bigelow Houghton, came to the rescue. With the help of Uncle Amery, Kit Houghton was able to attend Bryn Mawr and then earn an MA in art history from Radcliffe College.[25] It was through her sister Edith that Kit met a likable—albeit cash-strapped—Johns Hopkins medical student, Tom Hepburn. They were married in 1904—just after Dr. Hepburn started his internship at Hartford Hospital. In November 1906, their first child arrived, followed by five more, each given the middle name Houghton.[26]

The cottage that the Hepburns bought in 1921 was not the property out by the lighthouse where a decade and a half later, Tom and Kit's daughter Katharine, the actress, sought privacy. The Hepburns had been renting cottages at Fenwick since 1912, but the first cottage they owned was a small affair sold to them by Donald and Edith Hooker (Kit's sister), who purchased the cottage in 1918 from Morgan Bulkeley's nephew, Morgan Brainard.[27]

Tom and Kit had recently endured one of the worst years of their lives. The previous spring, their daughter Katharine discovered her older brother's body hanging behind a bedroom door.

Dr. Hepburn first told reporters that his son Tom's death may have been the result of a moment of "morbid depression," but later allowed that it could have been a stunt gone wrong. The boy had suffered earlier from Saint Vitus' dance (Sydenham's chorea), a streptococcal infection associated with rheumatic fever and causing unpredictable movements. While the details of the incident will never be completely known, the fact remained that Tom and Kit Hepburn's oldest child was gone.[28] Just two days later, Dr. Hepburn's older brother, Sewell Hepburn, a forty-seven-year-old physician, died of a massive coronary.[29]

The Hepburns purchased the Hooker cottage in September 1921, thereby assuring themselves that their children's summers would be happily cluttered periods of golf, tennis, swimming, fishing, and sailing, rather than empty stretches where the gloom of recent events might fester.[30]

After the two men chatted, Morgan Bulkeley handed Tom Hepburn the bill representing his portion of the carpentry work on the bulkheads—$500. Considering that the Hepburns had paid only $3,636 for their waterfront cottage on an acre of land, the bill was proportionately shocking. Unlike Bulkeley, who paid cash for everything, including Beaumaris, Tom Hepburn took a mortgage on every property he ever owned. A typical early-twentieth-century doctor, Tom worked his way through Johns Hopkins, labored through a long internship and residency for a pittance and then, with almost superhuman frugality, managed to start a family and buy a home. Five hundred dollars was a fortune to him at the time. However, Dr. Hepburn was copiously endowed with an important character trait—pride. He would do whatever it took to get the money before he would let Senator Bulkeley know he didn't have it.[31]

When Morgan Bulkeley named his cottage Beaumaris, he did so in the mistaken belief that he and the rest of his American ancestors descended from Sir Richard Bulkeley of Beaumaris, the lusty, larger-than-life, sixteenth-century high sheriff of Beaumaris Castle on the island of Anglesey, located off the coast of Northern Wales. This belief was so widespread in the Bulkeley clan that Morgan's younger brother, Billy, named his sixth and youngest child Richard Beaumaris Bulkeley.[32]

Sir Richard had two wives, Margaret Savage and Agnes Needham, and many children, including the fourth Richard, whose birthright was to reign over Beaumaris after his father's death. Sadly, Sir Thomas Cheadle poisoned Sir Richard's son in order that the former might steal the younger Bulkeley's wife.[33] Those were treacherous times in Northern Wales, accompanied by great intrigue, endless conflict, murder, cuckoldry, bastardy, and attendant perfidies of the most titillating sort. What politician wouldn't want this excitement in his portfolio?

Unfortunately (or fortunately) for the American Bulkeleys, none of the Welsh affairs pertained directly to them. Easily their most important ancestor was Rev. Peter Bulkeley, who brought the name to the Massachusetts Bay Colony in 1635 and shortly thereafter founded the town of Concord. Peter Bulkeley's grand-father, Thomas Bulkeley of Woore, Shropshire, England, was born in 1515—the same year as Sir Richard of Beaumaris. So if Peter Bulkeley did not descend from Sir Richard—and he did not—then neither did Senator Morgan Bulkeley of Connecticut.[34]

In the ensuing decades after Rev. Bulkeley founded Concord, many genera-tions of Bulkeleys fanned out across New England. The Bulkeleys were notable for their intellectual gifts, as many of them became clerics, physicians, and lawyers, and they dutifully served in the young nation's wars.[35]

In 1798, Morgan Bulkeley's grandfather, John Charles Bulkeley, married a Connecticut farm girl, Sarah "Sally" Taintor, and settled in Colchester, where John followed in his father's footsteps as a landowner and businessman. The couple had three children, all boys—Charles Edwin, John Taintor, and Eliphalet Adams Bulkeley. The youngest of the Bulkeley's three sons, Eliphalet, would one day become a prominent attorney, powerful state legislator, far-sighted insur-ance executive, and the father of Morgan Gardner Bulkeley.[36]

Though Morgan Bulkeley became a household name in Connecticut, with a high school, a stadium, a street, a bridge, and a park named after him, this was only possible because he began life on the shoulders of a giant.[37] As we shall see, Morgan Bulkeley's charmed life and outsized achievements would never have been possible without the genius, industry, and providence of his father, Judge Eliphalet Adams Bulkeley.

Chapter Two

THE JUDGE'S WORLD

Eliphalet Bulkeley was born in Colchester, Connecticut, in the summer of 1803. At the time of Eliphalet's birth, the Bulkeleys, now five generations strong, were one of the leading families of Colchester. During those years, Colchester grew steadily as a manufacturing town, and with this industrial growth came the demand for labor. By the time Eliphalet graduated from the local Bacon Academy and left for Yale College in 1820, Colchester's population was over 2,000.[1] Judge William P. Williams accepted Bulkeley to study law in Williams's Lebanon, Connecticut, offices after Bulkeley received his Yale degree.[2]

While in Lebanon, Eliphalet began to court a local girl, Lydia Smith Morgan. Lydia could trace her roots back two centuries to three brothers who left England for the Massachusetts Bay Colony in 1636.[3] The oldest of the three brothers, John, went directly to Virginia. The second brother, Miles—the foundation for the J. P. Morgan line—settled in West Springfield (Holyoke), Massachusetts, and some of his descendants later migrated to Hartford. The last of the brothers, James, put down roots in New London and started a third branch of the Morgan family tree in America. This third line was the one from which Lydia Smith Morgan descended. Her parents, Avery and Jerusha Morgan, lived in Bozrah, where young Lydia was born and raised. The family later moved to Colchester.[4]

Six years out of Yale, Eliphalet Bulkeley married Lydia Morgan and the couple soon settled in East Haddam, one of over 200 small manufacturing villages scattered throughout Connecticut. Other than the great ports of Hartford and Middletown, East Haddam was the busiest Connecticut River town.[5] The land, formerly an underdeveloped section of Haddam known as "thirty-mile plantation," became accessible in 1670 when two highways, Creek Row and Town Street, were laid out. Fifteen years later, the first homesteads took shape.

In 1695, a ferry service began operating between Hayden's Shipyard in East Haddam—later Goodspeed's—and what is now Tylerville in Haddam. In the first half of the nineteenth century, there were three landings in East Haddam—the Lower Landing at Hayden's Shipyard; the Upper Landing, which was the principal dock used by arriving and departing travelers; and farther north, a commercial landing near East Haddam Island. It was at the Upper Landing—off Old

East Haddam Road—where a counting house was erected to collect tolls from passing ships. By the time the Bulkeleys arrived in East Haddam in 1830, two ferries equipped with horse treadmills shuttled passengers and farm equipment to Haddam.[6] The passage across the river was a quick and fairly routine affair.[7]

East Haddam differed from other successful waterpower manufacturing towns, like Whitneyville, where Eli Whitney manufactured guns; Gaylordsville, where William Gaylord ran sawmills; or Terryville and Collinsville where Eli Terry and the Collins brothers made clocks and axes respectively. True, East Haddam nurtured manufactories and mills that employed tanners, coopers, cabinetmakers, wagon builders, cobblers, milliners, distillers, and malt makers. Nonetheless, East Haddam also supported shipbuilding. On the waterfront, a succession of yard owners including James Greene, Daniel Warner, Horace Hayden, and Joseph Goodspeed and his two sons George and William honed their craft. The low-lying waterfront in the southern end of town and East Haddam's deep channel favored the Connecticut River shipbuilding trade.[8]

Besides the legal work these abundant businesses threw off, this bustling river port suited the Bulkeleys on several scores. First, East Haddam was only ten miles from Colchester, so the couple did not feel completely cut off from family and friends. Second, there were already a few Bulkeleys and Morgans living in East Haddam, making the move less wrenching.[9] Lastly, East Haddam fell almost equidistant from Connecticut's two capital cities—Hartford and New Haven—crucial since Bulkeley aspired to enter politics.

In 1832, after practicing law for little more than a year, Eliphalet Bulkeley was appointed judge of the court of probate for East Haddam. Thereafter, folks referred to Eliphalet as Judge Bulkeley, or simply "the Judge."[10]

The Judge's 1832 daybook lists clients in Chester, Colchester, Hebron, Westbrook, Middletown, Haddam, and Old Saybrook. Generally he received two dollars for a property conveyance and one dollar for simple legal advice. He entered a ten-dollar charge for "William Coe/Negro/Defend you on a charge of assault" and noted seven dollars defending Curtin Holmes on a "charge of bastardry."[11]

By all accounts, Judge Bulkeley successfully practiced law and confidently assumed a place of respect in Middlesex County; but he grew restless. His clients in East Haddam and surrounding towns brought business opportunities, and Bulkeley was quick to recognize the merits of these propositions. Bulkeley's first serious venture beyond his legal business involved banking. Sensing a necessity, he organized the East Haddam Bank and installed himself as president.[12]

The Judge dabbled in many businesses and became an early stockholder in some of the companies he helped to organize. Work for Willimantic Linen Company and its peripatetic founder, Austin Dunham, for example, resulted in quite a few shares. Dunham, a prickly Hartford Yankee, began his manufactory in a rundown shed in 1825. Almost immediately driven to the brink of insolvency by the fiercely competitive New England linen industry, Dunham compensated Bulkeley with shares in Willimantic Linen as opposed to hard cash. In the inventory compiled to probate Judge Bulkeley's estate after his death in 1872, there were 1,400 shares of the original Willimantic Linen Company stock that he held for over forty years.[13]

During his early law and banking career in East Haddam, Judge Bulkeley established the work habits of a lifetime. He dressed impeccably and arrived for all of his engagements with unfailing punctuality.

Politically, Judge Bulkeley was from a long line of Federalists and Whigs. Later in life—when the Whig Party was in the throws of its 1850s death spiral—Judge Bulkeley helped organize the Republican Party of Connecticut.[14]

Religiously, the Judge was a Congregationalist, as were most of the successful men in the Northeast. This church was so powerfully intertwined with politics that tax revenues subsidized operations until Connecticut's Constitution of 1818 took effect.[15]

Life in the first half of the nineteenth century was harsh, and the Bulkeleys were not spared its adversities. The year 1835 ushered great happiness, and at the same time, overwhelming sorrow. When they first arrived in East Haddam, Eliphalet and Lydia rented a house. Then, in the spring of 1835, Lydia became pregnant with their second child, and pressed by the obvious need for more space, the couple purchased a home. They remained there for the rest of their seventeen years in town.[16]

The house, an aged colonial dwelling with a horse barn, occupied a three-quarter-acre lot on Old East Haddam Road, diagonally across from the spot where Champion Hall hostelry (later Hotel Champion) opened in 1840. It sat atop a hill facing west and offered a six-mile view up the Connecticut River. A three-acre woodlot sweetened the $950 purchase.[17]

Sadly, in June of that year, twenty-month-old Mary Morgan Bulkeley died in a fall. She was laid to rest in the small cemetery next to the First Congregational Church. The heartbroken couple went home to grieve and to await the birth of their new baby, Charles Edwin. Mary's death marked the first of many losses Eliphalet and Lydia Bulkeley would suffer during their marriage, but their firstborn's accident cut especially deeply. In December, Charles Edwin Bulkeley was born.[18]

Morgan Gardner Bulkeley, now the second child, was born the day after Christmas in 1837, a Tuesday. In a two-story colonial home, such as that of the Bulkeleys, children were usually birthed in a small room off the kitchen—for warmth, and for convenience.[19]

Since the law did not require registration of births in the first half of the nineteenth century, Eliphalet Bulkeley simply didn't bother. No birth records exist for any of the Bulkeley children. This educated and socially prominent family periodically dispensed with life's customary paperwork, as we shall see.

After Morgan, there were three more children, but of the three only William Henry and Mary Jerusha survived. The sixth and youngest child, Eliphalet Adams Bulkeley Jr. was born in Hartford in 1847, but died a year later. In short, only four of the Bulkeleys' six children made it to adulthood, and these four were all born in East Haddam.[20]

By 1835, there were nineteen school districts in East Haddam. The first, Nathan Hale schoolhouse, was abandoned in 1799 when residents built the Second Landing District School. Charlie, Morgan, and Billy attended Second Landing; however, Mary did not start school until after the family moved to Hartford in 1847.[21]

Judge Bulkeley continued investing in East Haddam property, purchasing twenty-three acres of woodland along the river and south of Hayden's Shipyard. This property boasted a dwelling house, store, and wharf at the town's lower landing.[22]

In 1834, the Judge ran on the Whig ticket and was elected to the lower house of the General Assembly, representing East Haddam. He followed this position with the post of clerk to the state House of Representatives, state's attorney for Middlesex County, and two-terms as state senator in 1838 and 1840.[23]

Throughout the early 1840s, the Judge practiced law, but he soon realized that although East Haddam provided a good beginning, opportunities were greater in the Port of Hartford. Nevertheless, with a family of six to feed and clothe—and most of his money tied up in real estate—he was reluctant to pull up stakes and leave East Haddam with nothing in hand but a collection of law books. To ease this transition, Bulkeley prevailed upon friends in the General Assembly to invent a position for him in Hartford. During the spring session of 1845, legislators created the post of assistant commissioner of the School Fund, which offered an annual salary of $1,000 plus expenses.[24]

With a secure position in Hartford, Eliphalet and Lydia made plans to leave East Haddam. The Judge went to Hartford alone in 1846, fulfilling his duties at the School Fund and making important contacts in the legal community.[25]

The following year, the whole Bulkeley family—including a very pregnant Lydia—took a steamship from the Upper Landing in East Haddam to the municipal wharf at the foot of State Street in Hartford, thereby using the Connecticut River as the important commercial highway it was. Stepping off the steamboat at the town wharf, the Bulkeleys—Eliphalet, Lydia, Charlie, Morgan, Billy, and Mary—walked up the hill to the Aetna Fire Insurance Company building at

58 State Street—on the north side of the State House—and took up residence on the second floor.[26] The Bulkeleys remained in these cramped quarters above Aetna Fire for three long years until 1850, when they purchased a home at 38 Church Street.[27]

Perhaps owing to the list of high-powered communicants at the First Congregational Church, the new neighbors originally worshipped at the slightly younger South Church on the corner of Main and Buckingham Streets, making the mile-long trek each Sunday morning. Later, they switched to the Pearl Street Congregational Church, a little closer to home.[28]

Judge Eliphalet Bulkeley entered into a legal partnership with Judge Henry Perkins under the business name of Bulkeley & Perkins, and beginning in 1846, he acted as director and general council for Aetna Fire Insurance Company. His daybook lists an 1849 entry describing a trip to Boston in order to settle a claim for Aetna. He billed the company $13.50 for two days time plus expenses.[29]

This legal work supplemented his salary as assistant commissioner of the School Fund nicely, but Bulkeley still longed to become more involved in business ventures. When another young attorney, Edwin Goodwin, teamed up with Dr. Guy Phelps to form Connecticut Mutual Life Insurance Company, a great opportunity presented itself. As the process of organization pushed forward in 1846, the Judge—now in his early forties—was asked by the board to be president of the firm.[30] He quickly agreed.

The Goodwins, one of Hartford's founding families, constituted a collection of ubiquitous Federalist tavern owners and land speculators who prospered mightily in the intervening two centuries. At first glance, Bulkeley's decision to take the helm of this nascent insurance company was an important step forward, yet an unfortunate episode developed.

Connecticut Mutual's charter bestowed "many other privileges not granted to any other company; and being established on the *mutual benefit system*, each person insured is a member, participating in the profits of the accumulating funds."[31] Judge Bulkeley's business expertise lay with simple stock companies, in which profits accrued to shareholders. Bulkeley did not know, or chose to overlook—due to his enthusiasm for the new post at Connecticut Mutual—that his business ideals were quite different from those of Goodwin, Phelps, and others within the firm.[32] In all probability, the gimlet-eyed principals of Connecticut Mutual intended to increase profits over a stock company by overcharging for policies and then returning only a small fraction of the gain to policyholders.[33] Altruistic, they were not.

As a start-up, Connecticut Mutual bore considerable pressure to register sales quickly. If nothing else, the partners determined to simply pay the $1,000 salary

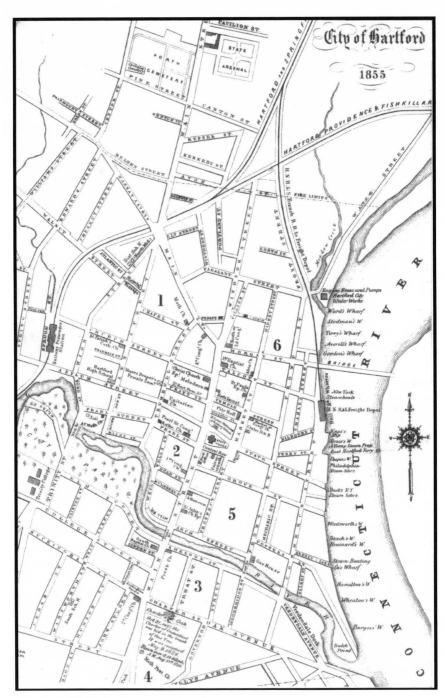

Street Map of Hartford, 1855

of Dr. Phelps and the $500 salary of Judge Bulkeley. Further eroding morale within the firm, Dr. Phelps constantly "tried to talk new agents into working for lower commissions."[34]

All through 1847, grievances accumulated until the Boston agent, and director, Elisha Pratt decided to do something about it. Besides the differing philosophies about the structure of the company, Pratt was convinced Judge Bulkeley "lacked practical knowledge of the problems of selling life insurance."[35] He also named the man he wanted to take Judge Bulkeley's place—James M. Goodwin, a Hartford insurance agent and entrepreneur. Goodwin was the brother-in-law of Junius Morgan—another man of finance and the father of J. P. Morgan. Some believe "it was [Junius] Morgan himself who put the name of his brother-in-law forward as a candidate [to replace Judge Bulkeley]."[36]

At the annual meeting on January 5, 1848, Elisha Pratt "appeared armed with sixty-eight proxies that he had collected from Boston policyholders."[37] Other directors quickly fell into line, and Judge Bulkeley was voted out in favor of James M. Goodwin.[38] Though a similar story could be told of many young companies, the long months of disagreements had done great damage to the relationships between all the parties involved, thus creating lifelong enmity between the Bulkeleys and the Goodwins.

The Goodwins were a clannish and money-hungry bunch, and were related by marriage to an equally clutching family—the Morgans.[39] To say that the Goodwins and the Morgans were ruthless in business is to understate the case significantly. When asked to state his occupation by a census taker, James M. Goodwin responded, "Capitalist."[40]

Unlike the Goodwins, whose roots were solidly in Hartford, the Morgans were from West Springfield (Holyoke), Massachusetts. Toward the end of November 1816, Joseph Morgan purchased a tavern at 33 State Street and subsequently brought his family to Hartford. Amos Ransom had started this business when he bought the brick dwelling house of the merchant Jacob Ogden sometime before 1800 and converted it into a tavern-coffee house.[41] Morgan's Tavern became a great gathering place for businessmen and served as Hartford's busiest stagecoach depot for people traveling to and from New York, Albany, and Boston.[42] Eventually, Joseph Morgan bought the stagecoach line too. Arguably, Morgan's greatest success was as an original incorporator of the Aetna Fire Insurance Company in 1819.[43]

Joseph Morgan had a razor-sharp mind for business and was at the center of most business ventures of note. Convenience, no doubt, had much to do with this, because one of the lower rooms of Morgan's Tavern doubled as a coffee house. Morgan's Coffee-House—later Exchange Coffee-House—enabled Hartford's marine insurance business to thrive and its fire insurance industry to spawn.[44] Merchants with vessels involved in the West Indies trade would lay off some of their risk by selling shares to other merchants, just as the ship owners at Edward Lloyd's Coffee-House in London did in 1688. By the time the Hartford Fire Insurance Company was organized at Morgan's Coffee-House in 1810, a primitive marine insurance industry was well established.[45]

Not only was Aetna Fire Insurance Company born in Joseph Morgan's front room, its founders used Morgan's Coffee-House—33 State Street—as the company's headquarters until around 1835, when they bought the property next to the coffeehouse and built their own headquarters.[46] In the meantime, clients accessed Aetna's tiny office in Morgan's Coffee-House through the coffin door on the east side of the building.[47]

On the home front, Joseph Morgan fathered three children—Mary, Lucy, and Junius. In 1832, Lucy married Maj. James M. Goodwin, and cemented the bloodlines between the two families. This marriage made Maj. Goodwin's sons, James and Francis "Frankie" Goodwin first cousins to Junius's son, J. Pierpont Morgan.[48]

Another important point was that the Goodwins and the Morgans were Episcopalians, while the overwhelming majority of Hartford's merchant-banker denizens, including the Bulkeleys, were Congregationalists.[49]

In the autumn of 1847, Judge Bulkeley's three sons, Charlie, Morgan, and Billy—twelve, ten, and eight years old, respectively—enrolled in the same schoolhouse that James and Francis Goodwin attended.[50] Children can be cruel, and one can only imagine the taunts heaped on the Bulkeley children—newcomers to the city—by the headstrong, rich, and overbearing Goodwin boys. As it turned out, the Bulkeleys carried their father's scabrous treatment with them the rest of their lives.[51]

The Connecticut Mutual mess chastened Judge Bulkeley, but he was not a man given to brooding. Instead, while he continued with his legal practice, he began laying the groundwork for an independent life insurance company to compete with Connecticut Mutual.[52]

Life insurance was one of the new enterprises much on entrepreneurs' minds, although it couldn't compare with the 1849 California gold rush for raw excitement. Convinced an insurance business had considerably better odds of success if it were wed to an existing company with a solid reputation, Bulkeley approached Thomas Brace of Aetna Fire.[53]

Brace was an extremely likable man, a former Hartford mayor and an able administrator. He liked the Judge's idea immediately, but could not make any quick promises.

Foremost among Brace's concerns was the public perception of life insurance at midcentury. Insuring personal property against "acts of God" was accepted, but "to ensure one's life seemed to many Congregationalists to be a substitution of a human commercial agency for trust in Divine Providence."[54] In short: Wasn't your life in the hands of the Lord? That said, the 1850s framed a time of enormous change. Just as society's sensibilities shifted with regard to streetlights, circuses, billiard parlors and indoor plumbing, a philosophical receptiveness toward life insurance began to grow. Eventually, what had once been a controversial concept gained credence.[55]

Thomas Brace pitched Judge Bulkeley's plan for a life insurance company paired with Aetna Fire to the board of directors. To a man, they wanted nothing to do with the new business on the grounds that it was a needless adventure into unexplored territory.[56]

Judge Bulkeley was not so easily dissuaded. Instead, he recommended the new venture be a separately incorporated subsidiary of Aetna Fire with its own capital and board of managers. As such, the new company would gain instant credibility, yet put none of the existing company's assets in jeopardy. The board found this approach acceptable and arrangements got underway.[57]

On June 6, 1850, Governor Thomas Seymour signed the legislature's bill expanding the powers of Aetna Fire to sell life insurance.[58] Later the same day, Aetna's stockholders voted to accept the change as passed. Thomas Brace then appointed Judge Bulkeley the head of a new Annuity Fund, which was capitalized with $150,000 and governed by Aetna Fire overseers.[59]

Interestingly, the question of whether the new company should be a mutual company or a joint stock company surfaced. Judge Bulkeley went to great lengths to explain what he perceived to be the two major flaws with the mutual-ownership insurance model. First, the Judge questioned the necessarily speculative nature of the dividends promised to mutual policyholders. More important—at least as Judge Bulkeley saw it—was the weakness of entrusting important management decisions to policyholders. The directors were, of course, well aware of the Judge's demeaning experience at Connecticut Mutual and voted for a stock ownership format.[60] While the Annuity Fund began life on the second floor of the Aetna Fire building at 58 State Street, the Judge maintained a law office in a building at 274 Main Street, close to the State House.[61]

In the early days of the Annuity Fund, business was not exactly robust. Almost two months after the firm opened its doors, Judge Bulkeley himself sold policy number one. The transaction was a by-product of a coal syndicate Bulkeley was organizing in West Virginia. One of the principals, George F. Tyler of Philadelphia, was in Hartford representing coal-mining interests in the negotiations when the subject of life insurance surfaced. The Judge, a born salesman, convinced Tyler to buy a $5,000 policy.[62]

In May 1853, Governor Seymour signed a resolution changing the charter of

Aetna Fire Insurance Company and effectively establishing Aetna Life Insurance Company. Judge Bulkeley continued as president.[63] It was a position the Judge held the rest of his life. While this new insurance company grew, Bulkeley was involved in all of Aetna's moneyed corporations, banking and insurance. He was also one of the busiest men in Hartford, serving in a variety of public offices and taking great interest in all of the social, political, mercantile, and religious activities of his adopted home.[64]

The history of Aetna is a fabulous success story, but it did have some unsavory moments. During its early years, Aetna sometimes insured the lives of slaves, as in 1854, when Thomas Murphy of New Orleans took out a $1,000 policy on his twenty-two-year-old slave, Reuben, for an annual premium of $35. Reuben was valued at $1,400.[65] Some of the policies on slaves were written as late as 1860, but they all "continued to appear on forms for the 'Annuity Fund,' which folded in 1853 when the Aetna Life Insurance Company was incorporated."[66] Thus, slaves were regarded as property, rather than lives.

From the scraps of information available, Eliphalet Bulkeley appeared to be a first-rate father. He doted on his children, enjoyed their small successes and suffered with them when they came up short. He did, however, insist that they develop a certain level of dignity in the way they conducted their affairs, and he infused in them a great sense of duty, an obligation to contribute something to the world.

In return, the Judge's children idolized him. When he served in the General Assembly, they snuck in the back door of the State House, climbed up into the balcony, and watched him meet with other legislators, pass laws, and address his fellow members of the state's highest governing body.[67] When Gen. Zachary Taylor, a hero of the Mexican War, ran for the presidency on the Whig ticket in 1848, legend has it that ten-year-old Morgan Bulkeley campaigned for him, to the secret delight of the Judge.[68]

Strict though he was, Judge Bulkeley could be an incredibly soft touch. For example, when the Bulkeley boys were still in grade school, the Judge paid them a dollar a week to sweep out the offices at Aetna Fire on State Street.[69] When they began high school, he raised their salaries. At a time when a mechanic at Colt's Patent Fire-Arms earned $6 a week, the Judge compensated his sons $5 a week "for services at [the] office . . . at different times."[70] Keeping in mind that Aetna's building was tiny, the workload on his sons was miniscule, while the pay proved spectacular.

In their early years in Hartford, the Bulkeley children had no reason to feel superior to anyone. Truth be told, the reverse might have been the case, inasmuch as they lived in rented rooms above the Aetna Fire Insurance Company, and later in a simple brick house on the north side of Church Street. This is an important point, considering Morgan Bulkeley's later success in politics. The people of Hartford always felt warmly toward him. He attended grade school with their children and played in the neighborhood around State House Square. Even though his father was Judge Bulkeley—a lawyer and successful businessman—they never held it against Morgan. The people of Hartford always considered Bulkeley one of their own.[71]

Morgan Bulkeley lived in the shadow of his older brother, Charlie, whom he adored. Charlie, Morgan, and Billy spent their free time around State House Square, where the old meetinghouse sat on a huge lawn completely surrounded by wrought iron fencing. When the Hartford Water Works went into operation in October 1855, an ornate fountain was erected in the middle of the State House's east lawn.[72] State House Square offered a commanding view of the riverfront, and the young boys watched steady processions of steamboats coming and going.

The first luxurious passenger steamer, the 227-ton *Oliver Ellsworth*, began making regular runs between Hartford and New York in 1851. It was the first ship to furnish separate cabins for ladies and gentlemen, staterooms, and novel amenities. Later, many new steamers made the run to Hartford, most notably the *Granite State* (1852) and the *City of Hartford* (1853).[73] Watching passengers disembark and dockhands offload cargo was a diversion that never lost its appeal for young Morgan Bulkeley.

In the summertime, young boys—and less often young girls—swam in the river, north of the wharves and warehouses. In the wintertime, games of "war" were a constant diversion, with snowballs flying everywhere. Down the hill from Ann Street—west toward the railroad tracks and Gully Brook at the base of Lord's Hill—children used sleds "with runners sawed out by a carpenter and shod with iron hoops."[74] Not until 1853 did the common council set aside land for City Park (later Bushnell Park), space more conducive to recreation than midcentury cow pastures.

Each time the youngsters passed "one-armed Billy," the public well at the northwest corner of State House Square, they gave the handle a quick pump. There was the occasional apple or peach stolen from one of the open-air vendors on Market Street, but if anything, Morgan Bulkeley's childhood was notable for its simplicity.[75]

Morgan's one brush with delinquency involved the bell atop the State House. The clanging of this bell was the town's only fire alarm. Upon hearing this signal, horse-drawn pumpers stampeded out of firehouses all over the city and people followed to form bucket brigades. Young boys dared each other to sneak up into the building and ring the bell, a much tougher assignment than imagined.

First, it had to be done when the State House was empty and locked up tight.

Secondly, it required a certain amount of climbing skill. The front portico, facing the river, had twelve-foot-high wrought iron gates locked with a huge padlock. However, a small boy like Morgan could squirm between the tops of the gates and the ceiling of the portico to gain entrance to the building. Moving quickly, the intruder would then run up the stairs to the second floor, grab the bell rope and ring the bejesus out of the bronze bell before beating a hasty retreat. Sounding a false alarm was, of course, against the law.[76]

On Sundays, everyone stayed close to home, as church and a big dinner in the afternoon dominated the day. Everything was closed on Sundays save the Wadsworth Atheneum, where books could be checked out and natural history exhibits and paintings could be viewed. In a word, Sundays were dull for young boys in the late 1840s and early 1850s.[77]

It was clear from the very start that Morgan and Billy Bulkeley were not great students, at least not compared to their older brother, Charlie. Very little correspondence of Morgan's still exists, but enough to conclude he was not dyslexic or learning impaired.[78] More likely, he was an overactive child and not easily given to long hours of study. Later, an overcrowded work schedule concealed a lifelong aversion to reading and scholarship.[79]

When it came to the educations of his sons, the Judge sent Charlie to Hartford Grammar School (private), then Bacon Academy, followed by two years at Trinity College and finally Yale College, where he received his degree in 1856.[80] Bacon Academy was founded in 1803 using a $35,000 bequest from a local farmer, Pierpont Bacon. Originally, the price of tuition was six dollars a term for Latin and Greek; four dollars for mathematics, grammar, geography, and arithmetic; and three dollars for elementary English studies. Obviously, these fees were slightly higher by midcentury.[81] Morgan and Billy attended Centre School (common), nicknamed the "Old Stone Jug," and Morgan subsequently studied at the Judge's alma mater, Bacon Academy, while Billy attended Hartford Public High School.[82]

Charlie worked hard and earned good grades. Morgan and Billy were Charlie's polar opposites, inasmuch as they preferred high jinks, social activities, and sports to studying.

Actually, Morgan Bulkeley's secondary education remains a bit of a puzzle. In later life, he gave an interview to a newspaper reporter in which he alluded to his early education but never mentioned Bacon Academy.[83] At the same time, he claimed that he started working in his Uncle Henry's dry goods store in Brooklyn Heights when he was fourteen.[84] This is unlikely because at that age he would have been fresh out of grade school.

Most important, when Bacon Academy held its 100th anniversary in 1903, the school listed its most distinguished alumni as Senator Lyman Trumbull of Illinois, Governor William Buckingham of Connecticut, and Morrison Waite, chief justice of the United States. Governor Morgan Bulkeley was not mentioned, even though he was a nonresident trustee of the school at the time.[85] What are we to think when Morgan Bulkeley refused to mention Bacon Academy and the school declined to embrace him?

Many decades later, Bulkeley delivered a few remarks to the young scholars at the Centre (Brown) School and claimed "he had only attended high school for a few years and hence his attendance at what now is the Brown School was his principal school experience."[86] Lastly, at Bacon Academy's 150th anniversary celebration in 1953, a reporter for the *Courant* did state that Morgan Bulkeley attended the school, being careful not to use any form of the word "graduate."[87]

Unfortunately, the school does not have records back that far. However, a preponderance of the evidence suggests that Morgan attended Bacon Academy for a time, but did not graduate. Morgan probably left Bacon Academy after a couple of years, and then kicked around Hartford for a while.[88] With his future a complete blank—and undoubtedly of great concern to Judge and Lydia Bulkeley—Morgan had more options than most by dint of his father's position at Aetna Life and the Judge's contacts. Sadly, Morgan, perhaps shrunk a tad by his brother Charlie's success, could not find his way.

Taking into consideration his great success in later life, it is difficult to envision Morgan Bulkeley as a slow starter, but that's exactly what he was. As Morgan knocked around Hartford, going nowhere, a solution to his dilemma emerged in far off Brooklyn Heights, New York. In the spring of 1854, a dry goods merchant, Henry P. Morgan, ran the following ad in the Brooklyn Daily Eagle:

Dry Goods

H. P. Morgan, No. 111 Fulton Street . . . Wanted: An intelligent young man, 16 or 18 years of age. Apply as above with references.[89]

Henry Morgan was Lydia Bulkeley's youngest brother. Eighteen years her junior, he was in the dry goods business in Brooklyn Heights and was looking for help at exactly the same time Morgan Bulkeley needed to learn a trade. Henry was only thirty-four and a great favorite of the Bulkeley children, particularly Morgan and Billy. They especially liked his wife, Aunt Eunie, only twenty-one at the time.[90]

To the great relief of the Judge and Lydia, Uncle Henry agreed to take sixteen-year-old Morgan into his home in Brooklyn Heights and teach him the dry goods business. This proved the perfect solution to the problem. The dry goods business had made some of Hartford's residents, like Calvin and Albert Day, wealthy men. The Day brothers had come to Hartford in their teens from a farm in Westfield, Massachusetts.[91] If the dry goods business could provide a substantial living for a couple of boys right off the farm, imagine what it could do for Morgan Bulkeley.

Chapter Three

BROOKLYN HEIGHTS

When Morgan Bulkeley arrived in Brooklyn Heights in 1854, Greater Brooklyn was in the process of absorbing Williamsburgh.[1] The final incorporation produced a city with a population of 205,000—ten times that of Hartford. Still, less than 17,000 inhabitants lived in the small village of Brooklyn Heights where Morgan's aunt and uncle lived.[2] For the next eighteen years, Morgan Bulkeley's life would be centered in this wealthy little hamlet.

Considered New York's first suburb, Brooklyn Heights got its start as local landowners subdivided their farms and sold off building lots of 25 × 100 feet to Manhattanites. By 1814, a steam ferry shuttled more than half of the borough's residents from the Fulton Street Ferry Terminal to Manhattan each day.[3] As implausible as it sounds, Morgan Bulkeley once said, "When the tide came in and jammed the ice into the channel, you would find a stream of fool-hearted men crossing on the temporary highway, risking death in order to save a half hour of time."[4]

Brooklyn Heights, perched on a bluff seventy feet above the waters of the East River—and opposite Manhattan's South Street Seaport—offered a commanding view across New York Harbor. Even though the Heights became famous for some of the grandest residential houses in the New York metropolitan area, most of the homes were brick row houses like Henry and Eunice Morgan's home on Joralemon Street. Besides the stately addresses, Brooklyn Heights displayed neat granite-paved streets, magnificent churches, and several lovely hostelries.

Nonetheless, when Morgan Bulkeley arrived, the village lagged slightly behind Hartford in amenities. While Hartford's municipal water works was about a year from completion, Brooklyn's Well & Pump Commission maintained a growing number of public wells on street corners.[5] A municipal waterworks bill finally passed in 1859.[6] Again, in the area of infrastructure, Hartford's streets were completely illuminated by gaslights at midcentury, while Brooklyn waited another decade for light. Early sewers were often just open trenches designed to drain water from wet parts of town. Most cities had rudimentary sewers well before 1840. Hartford's common council established a Board of Sewer Commissioners in 1847, while Brooklyn didn't form one until more than a decade later.[7]

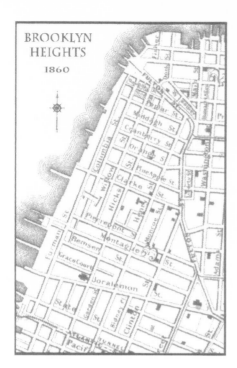

BROOKLYN
HEIGHTS
1860

*Street Map of Brooklyn Heights, 1860
(Brooklyn Collection, Brooklyn Public Library)*

Brooklyn Heights, like Hartford, published a great many newspapers—the *Brooklyn Citizen, Brooklyn Daily Times, Brooklyn Standard Union,* and *Brooklyn Daily Eagle*—just to name a few. Manhattan papers numbered about twenty.[8] Manhattan's newspaper readership was divided among so many different papers that the *Brooklyn Daily Eagle* actually boasted the largest circulation of any evening paper in the United States.[9] Still, only a few groceries, dry goods stores, and taverns conducted business in Brooklyn.[10]

Uncle Henry and Aunt Eunie lived in a brick, three-story Greek Revival row house—86 Joralemon Street—close to the southern end of the Heights. The couple purchased their home around the time of their marriage in April 1850.[11]

Henry and Eunice Morgan were not Morgan Bulkeley's only Brooklyn Heights kin. The Judge's older brother, Charles Edwin Bulkeley, worked as an insurance agent and served as clerk of the King's County Board of Supervisors. Sadly, he collapsed at one of the board's meetings in September 1853. His son Charles happened to be present and tried to assist him, but the older man's heart had given out and all attempts to resuscitate him failed. His wife, Julia, continued to reside on Livingston Street for many years thereafter.[12]

Morgan Bulkeley and his aunt Eunice developed a close, lifelong bond.[13] Eunice Hicks was the daughter of George Hicks, proprietor of the grocery store Schoomaker & Hicks. The firm did business on Fulton Street, and by contemporary accounts attracted a larger than average following, affording its two owners upscale lifestyles.[14] Eunice met Henry Morgan in Brooklyn Heights, and the two were married probably right after Eunice turned eighteen.[15] Aunt Eunie was twelve years younger than Uncle Henry, and only five years older than Morgan Bulkeley.

Life was comfortable for Henry and Eunice Morgan and their two daughters, Carolyn and Elizabeth. (A third daughter, Sarah, came later.) The family lived in a decidedly upscale neighborhood, and employed five Irish servants and a coachman.[16]

Uncle Henry established his dry goods firm, H. P. Morgan & Co., in a small storefront at 111 Fulton Street, between Johnson and Tillary Streets. Most Brooklyn Heights' businesses resided on Fulton between Clark Street and the Fulton Street Ferry, but H. P. Morgan & Co. conducted business about a block south of this congestion.[17] Uncle Henry's goods included fancy dresses, quilts, towels, draperies, flannels, blankets, linens, mourning apparel, and housekeeping goods, all of which were sent to customers homes for examination upon request.[18]

Owning a business had many rewards for Uncle Henry—and at least one huge drawback. At midcentury, merchants worked long hours. Typically a retail merchant worked until after eight in the evening, and these hours were punishing for Uncle Henry. Thus, in April 1854, Uncle Henry Morgan decided to take on a helper, his nephew Morgan. In the early 1860s, an Early Closing Association took wing, dividing merchants into two groups—those who would agree to close by 7:30 in the evening and others who insisted upon staying open until 8:00. Henry, of course, lobbied to close early.[19] As wet behind the ears as a teenager could be, Morgan was originally paid to run errands and to sweep floors. While Henry Morgan certainly needed someone to mind the store if he ever wanted to have dinner with his family, the fact is that he also hungered for new business challenges. This urge to expand into new areas probably developed from the tedium of selling fabric for thirteen cents a yard, sunup to sundown, six days a week. In any event, Uncle Henry involved himself in a number of Brooklyn organizations along with many of his fellow storeowners and businessmen.[20]

For Morgan Bulkeley, the dry goods business, while not exactly romantic, served as a step toward learning a trade and acquiring the business skills that he would need regardless of where his interests eventually took him. As with all clerks at midcentury, Bulkeley had to work long hours Monday through Saturday.

As young Morgan's customer skills grew, he graduated from sweeping the floors to waiting on women who came in to buy fabric, clothing, and household goods. Eventually, he "became successively a salesman, confidential clerk and finally partner" in the firm.[21]

Life in the late 1850s wasn't as comfortable as it might have been. Owing to the national debate over slavery and the nagging possibility of war with the slave-owning states, business everywhere slowed to a crawl.[22]

In spite of the tensions that grew daily in the late 1850s, no one could actually contemplate the fact that the South would secede and the North would be forced to bear arms against its countrymen. Instead, reasonable people expected the South to reluctantly stay with the Union.

In 1856, Rev. Henry Ward Beecher—one of Harriet Beecher Stowe's seven cleric brothers and arguably the most influential minister of his time—gave a sermon at his Plymouth Church of the Pilgrims in Brooklyn Heights, asserting, "Better civil war than universal slavery. Civil war would be a blessing did it but lift us one plane higher in spiritual being."[23]

Beecher's provocative stance is not all that shocking considering he had a reputation as a rousing speaker and invited controversy wherever he went. Rev. Beecher was a handsome man with deep, soulful eyes, making him absolutely irresistible to women. As a result, rumors of adultery, not without basis, followed him relentlessly. Later, in 1875, Rev. Beecher was actually brought to trial on charges of adultery with a married member of his Brooklyn parish, Mrs. Elizabeth Tilton.[24] In court, Beecher was acquitted but, for the remainder of his life, the whiff of scandal followed him like the stink of manure in Brooklyn's streets.

In 1857, Morgan Bulkeley's brother, Billy, arrived in Brooklyn Heights after arrangements were made for Uncle Henry to teach him the dry goods business too. Billy graduated from Hartford High School, accepted a job with Thacher, Goodrich & Stillman, a Hartford dry goods firm, but felt he could learn more from Uncle Henry.[25] So, he too moved into 86 Joralemon with his uncle and aunt and their three daughters. Morgan and Billy were close. They shared similar interests and ambitions. At the time, a good bet might have been that the two would eventually return to Hartford and become partners in a dry goods business. Still, even if the two were the quickest of studies—and all accounts suggests otherwise—the late 1850s would prove a terrible time for entrepreneurship. The economy was declining, and all the talk was of slavery, the South's secession, and war.

Then, in the fall of 1857, a full-blown financial panic engulfed the nation when disclosures of massive embezzlement generated the collapse of New York's branch of the Ohio Life Insurance and Trust Co. Hard on the heels of this bankruptcy, English investors pulled their money out of the United States, and manufactured goods piled up on the docks. Unemployment rose, and within a year of the Panic of 1857, over five thousand businesses failed.[26]

Two years later, things turned uglier still. A slave insurrection at Harper's

Ferry, Virginia (West Virginia now), shocked everyone. On Sunday, October 14, 1859, John Brown and some of his followers seized a government arsenal. They held out until marines, under the command of Col. Robert E. Lee, put down the insurrection. The final firefight cost the lives of ten men, including two of Brown's sons. In early December, Brown was tried for treason against the Commonwealth of Virginia, found guilty, and hanged.[27]

In Connecticut, the first Republican Party organizational meeting commenced on February 4, 1856, in the law office of the fervent abolitionist Joe Hawley.[28] As the Whig Party died, a new Republican Party formed around a collection of diverse political philosophies. In the North, the party was "an amalgam of former Whigs, free-soilers, business leaders who wanted a central government that would protect industry, and ordinary folks who wanted a homestead act that would provide free farms in the West."[29]

John Hooker (also a fierce abolitionist), Nathaniel Shipman (Hawley's close friend and antislavery idealist), and other free-soil men—Gideon Welles, Calvin Day, James Bunce, Mark Howard, and David Robinson—joined Joe Hawley for this first meeting at Hooker & Hawley on Main Street opposite Hartford's State House. Gideon Welles, Calvin Day, and Mark Howard were frequent visitors in the offices of the free-soil *Hartford Evening Press*. With the personal beliefs of these men, it is clear that the nascent Republican Party of Connecticut harbored a strong antislavery predisposition from the start.[30] Though Brooklyn had citizens who took an antislavery stance—including Rev. Henry Ward Beecher—according to Morgan Bulkeley, Greater Brooklyn usually voted Democratic while he lived there.[31] As war drew near, the Democratic Party steadfastly asserted its states' rights stance, believing that the Southern states were free to do as they pleased. The war disgraced the party. After the war, the few remaining Democrats of the merchant-banker class defected to the Republican Party, and Irish American laborers became the backbone of the Democratic Party.

In the 1860 presidential race, the Republicans ran an Illinois lawyer, Abraham Lincoln, a dark horse to be sure. He was such an unknown quantity that newspapers sometimes referred to him as "Abram" Lincoln.[32] When it came to the issue of slavery, the gangly Lincoln was guarded. He once wrote to Horace Greeley, "If I could save the Union without freeing *any* slave I would do it; and if I could save it by freeing *all* the slaves I would do it; and if I could save it by freeing *some* and leaving others alone I would also do that."[33] Lincoln's foremost concern was holding the country together. If the Southern states tried to secede from the Union, he was determined to subvert such a move with force.

In the November presidential elections, Lincoln received less than 40 percent of the popular vote—about 1,865,000 votes—winning only the Northern states. The Northern Democrat, Stephen Douglas, received "about 1,000,000 votes plus a large but indeterminate share of nearly 600,000 fusion votes, nearly all of which were concentrated in the free states."[34] Of the other two candidates in the race, the Southern Democrat, John C. Breckenridge, finished third and the Constitutional Union candidate, John Bell, finished fourth.[35] In spite of this split, Lincoln managed to corral enough electoral votes to become the sixteenth president of the United States.

The new president realized that sending government boats to reprovision Fort Sumter at the mouth of Charleston Harbor would foment war. When shelling actually began, however, Americans were stunned.

Federal steamers evacuated Fort Sumter at noon on April 14, 1861, and the Civil War was underway. Immediately, Lincoln called 75,000 soldiers to serve for ninety days in order to put down the insurrection. Instead of intimidating the Southerners, however, the call to arms caused four more states to secede—Virginia, North Carolina, Arkansas, and Tennessee.[36]

Meanwhile, the North was completely bewildered. Since 90 percent of the country's manufacturing was in the North, it didn't seem possible that the South could fight, no matter how strong their resolve. Beyond that, the North had a population of 22 million, while the South had only 9 million, almost a third of them slaves. Significantly, the North had almost complete control of the arms industry and most of the country's coal, iron ore, and copper mines. Put more succinctly, how would the South mount a campaign against the North without any of the raw materials and manufacturing needed to wage war?[37]

President Lincoln's call to arms sent Brooklyn Heights, and the rest of the North, into frenzy. Great crowds gathered in the streets, and recruiting stations opened overnight. Young men and boys, without any inkling as to the seriousness of the matter, volunteered in huge numbers to fight the rebels.[38]

War fever replaced spring fever. Morgan's brother Billy captured the general mood in Brooklyn Heights when he wrote to his mother back in Hartford after Fort Sumter fell. "We are all full of excitement here. We hate to believe that Fort Sumter has fallen. . . . Isn't it too bad that we should be right in the first fight? . . . P.S. The Herald office will probably be sacked tonight. Great excitement in New York."[39]

The war fever increased daily, with the national flag waving from every building, public and private. The whole city exhibited an unsettling mob spirit. Young men rushed headlong into conflict, giving little thought to the gravity of the matter. With the wonderful gift of hindsight, it is fair to say that Morgan and Billy Bulkeley—along with their friends in Brooklyn Heights—expected their time as soldiers to be a great adventure. Hardship, deprivation, dismemberment, and death were the last things on their minds.[40]

In only a week's time, 1,650 volunteers filled the rolls of four Brooklyn regiments—the Thirteenth, Fourteenth, Twenty-eighth, and Seventieth. These four units constituted a brigade, and they were under orders to be ready to move out on three day's notice.[41]

The three Bulkeley boys—Charlie, Morgan, and Billy—descended from an almost unbroken line of ministers, lawyers, and physicians, going back to the sixteenth century. Yet the Bulkeleys served in almost every war fought on American soil. It was unthinkable that they would not engage.[42]

So said, Morgan and Billy could not both go off to war at the same time and leave Uncle Henry—to whom they owed so much—shorthanded. With so many young men volunteering for duty, clerks could never be found to take their places. Billy, the more dispensable of the two brothers joined the Thirteenth Regiment first.[43] It was expected Morgan would join after Billy's return.

Since everyone, including President Lincoln, thought the war would be over almost before it began, one has to consider the possibility—at least in Morgan Bulkeley's mind—that he might not have had to serve at all. This is not to imply he wouldn't have quickly volunteered had the situation been different, but because his military service would be an important part of his public persona in later life, the details of his service are noteworthy.

When Billy joined the Thirteenth Regiment of the New York Militia—Brooklyn Heights's own unit—Morgan joined the Home Guard, a division of the Thirteenth. The Home Guard, mostly older citizen-soldiers, had no uniforms, didn't march, and didn't carry weapons. Mostly they met to discuss the possibility of a band of misguided Southerners stealing boats, rowing across New York Harbor, and sacking Brooklyn. Obviously, the odds of such an assault were slim.[44]

During his ninety-day hitch, Billy wrote many times to Morgan in Brooklyn, and even more often to his mother in Hartford.[45] Toward the end of Billy's service, Morgan visited Billy in camp.[46] Between the eyewitness accounts of Billy Bulkeley and the elaborate descriptions of the movements of the Thirteenth Regiment in the Brooklyn Daily Eagle, a fairly detailed picture of military life for the young soldiers emerges.

The Thirteenth Regiment—in name only, because there were no official regiments until 1858—was organized in 1847 to march in Fourth of July parades and other ceremonial events.[47] One company dressed in the uniform of the Old Continentals, with the cocked hat, ridiculous looking shad-bellied coats, and yellow knee breeches. Another dressed in red coats and bearskin caps.[48] Young children loved them.

As war approached, a dull-gray uniform replaced their colorful costumes, and the Thirteenth Regiment marched off to war with the dreary sobriquet "the National Grays." Few in Brooklyn Heights thought the Thirteenth could fight.[49] It was frightening for Brooklyn's citizens to imagine the Thirteenth Regiment facing a fierce Southern warrior like Gen. Nathan Bedford Forrest, or any other rebel for that matter.

Volunteer regiments throughout Brooklyn Heights assembled apace. The *Eagle* noted, "The following is given as the strength of the several Brooklyn regiments—13th Regiment, 250 men; 14th Regiment, 150 men; 28th Regiment, 400 men; 70th Regiment, 350 men. There is no doubt but that within a few days the regiments will be filled with the requisite number—700 each. These four regiments . . . are under orders to be ready for service on three days notice."[50]

So-called "volunteer companies" were filling up rapidly too. Men and boys from every conceivable trade and ethnic background were organizing their own units. Brooklyn's journeymen painters formed a unit, and the Irish organized an Irish Brigade. The Metamora Guard, the Hibernian Greens, the Williamsburgh Volunteers—the list is almost endless as former military men opened recruiting offices to ensure themselves a command.[51]

On the morning of Tuesday April 23, just eleven days after the shelling of Fort Sumter, activity in Brooklyn escalated to fever pitch. Pure bedlam ensued at Brooklyn Armory on Cranberry Street. The Thirteenth was stationed there, and police had cordoned off the building to keep wives, girlfriends, and female relatives out while young soldiers tried on uniforms. Nearly all of the recruits found caps, but few were issued knapsacks, pants, or shirts when their muskets arrived at noon.[52]

Curiously, though Hartford was the epicenter of gun manufacturing at the time, it was the fifteen-dollar Springfield muzzle-loader that was the most popular firearm of the war. (In addition to the output at Springfield, about a dozen small Connecticut manufacturers also produced this weapon for the Union army.) That said, Sharps Rifle Manufacturing Co. in Hartford sold breach-loading rifles, which were also popular. The company produced 140,000 units for the Union army.[53] The government awarded Colt's Patent Fire-Arms, also located in Hartford, "contracts for 112,500 arms, all of a type classified as the Model 1861 Special Musket," but received only 75,000.[54]

Finally, on April 23, the soldiers of the eight companies of the Thirteenth, including Billy Bulkeley, marched down to the East River, where they boarded the ferryboat, *Atlantic*. The ferry delivered them to the steamer, *Marion*, at South Street Seaport, and by suppertime they were underway.[55]

The Thirteenth was assigned to guard the railroad depot at Annapolis, Maryland, and then another one at Baltimore. Generally, sleeping arrangements were acceptable, but the food was poor. Because all the young soldiers were from families with servants, none of them knew how to cook.

With tens of thousands of young, poorly trained, raw recruits parading around

CROWBAR GOVERNOR

with loaded muskets, accidents were common, but an incident that occurred in Company D remains absolutely heartrending.

Twelve-year-old Clarence McKenzie and his older brother, William, joined the Thirteenth Regiment as drummer boys in 1860. Now at war, Company D's commander, Capt. Henry Balsdon, looked out for young Clarence, even giving him a bunk in his tent on officers' row. Clarence's brother, William, was never far from Clarence, and both boys wrote home regularly.[56]

In mid-afternoon on June 11, Pvt. William McCormick of Company B borrowed a musket from a friend and began to practice the position of "charge bayonet." The weapon accidentally discharged, and Clarence McKenzie, sitting on the ground nearby reading a book, was shot through the back. Capt. Balsdon cradled Clarence in his arms, but the boy died a short time later. The next morning, Capt. Balsdon, four soldiers, and Clarence's brother William returned to Brooklyn with the little drummer boy's body. (In Brooklyn's Green-Wood Cemetery, a large, ornate plinth topped with a white bronze statue of a drummer boy marching to glory sits on Clarence McKenzie's grave. It is the most popular memorial at Green-Wood.)[57]

Things went downhill from there. The *Eagle* noted, "It appears that the regiment is in an almost complete state of insubordination, the legitimate consequences of a lack of discipline. The men fight amongst themselves, in one case weapons were used [and] one private was cut in his hand. . . . On another occasion a lieutenant was with a sergeant. [A nineteenth century reference to homosexuality.] Intoxication is not uncommon."[58] At times, Col. Abel Smith even failed to provide food for his charges, an infraction for which he was later court-martialed.[59]

Toward the end of July 1861, Morgan paid his brother Billy a visit at Company G's encampment at Baltimore. While he was there, the two turned a piece of paper sideways, put a crease down the center and wrote home to their mother. Morgan's letter is on one side, with Billy's opposite. This double letter is the only Civil War correspondence of Morgan Bulkeley that survives:

Coleman's Eutaw House
Baltimore, Maryland
July 24, 1861
Dear Mother,
I left New York rather unexpected last evening for a trip to the seat of war, and as you will see above, am now at Baltimore. Have spent the whole day with Billy at camp and visiting Mr. Hicks [Aunt Eunie's father] at Fort McHenry. And we both leave tonight for Washington, from which place I

will write you at the earliest moment. Billy's time expires tomorrow. . . . To give yourself easiness about him, you can depend on having him with you, the last of next week. We have yet but little intelligence from the Connecticut regiments. You, I suppose, have heard more than we. Whatever I may learn tomorrow shall be forwarded with dispatch. I was very glad to hear by Frank [Bulkeley, the Judge's cousin, who also lived in Hartford] that you were well, more so nearly restored to your usual good health. And I trust that no undue anxiety will bring on another attack. Be careful of yourself, and believe that all is well.

With much love from both of us. I remain your affectionate son—
Morgan[60]

A few days later, the Thirteenth arrived back in Brooklyn. Billy Bulkeley and his brothers in arms were mustered out at the Cranberry Street Armory. Of the nearly seven hundred men fielded by the Thirteenth Regiment during this period of active duty, six members died—Clarence McKenzie from a musket ball and five others from disease.[61]

None of the excitement and war fever that accompanied the Thirteenth Regiment's first tour in April 1861 prevailed when Morgan Bulkeley committed to a three-month hitch in May 1862.[62] The notion of a short, neat, little war had been violently torn from the minds of Northerners, as the *Eagle* treated its readers to the horrific details of Bull Run (5,000 casualties), Shiloh (23,000 casualties) and a dozen smaller skirmishes in between. In short, any innocent or naive delusions about the war had vanished. Many of the original soldiers of the Thirteenth were off fighting with other units, but those who remained behind joined up for another hitch.[63] The Thirteenth still used the Cranberry Street Armory to outfit its different companies, and uniforms, caps, tents and camp equipment were in much better supply this time around. Except for a shortage of muskets, the soldiers were well equipped.[64]

On May 30, the new commander of the Thirteenth, Col. Robert Clark, informed a reporter for the *Eagle* that the regiment would leave for Washington at eight o'clock that night. The regiment was 728 strong.[65]

A week after arriving in Washington, they proceeded to Fortress Monroe, a Tidewater Virginia military installation at the tip of the peninsula where the James River meets Chesapeake Bay.[66] Only later was it learned that the wife of one of the soldiers had snuck onto the government steamer and arrived at Fortress Monroe before anyone was the wiser. She followed the Thirteenth around, making herself useful by mending uniforms and doing chores.[67]

In due time, the Thirteenth received orders to join the Seventh Army Corp stationed at Suffolk, Virginia. The year before, while Billy was still serving in

Baltimore, Morgan had heard a rumor that this might happen. He immediately dashed off a letter to Billy to see if he knew anything about this unit. Billy responded, "There are several regiments in Washington that are thought more of than the 7th, among them is the 9th and the Rhode Island. The 7th are very nice gentleman, but their fighting qualities haven't been tested."[68]

To put it mildly, the soldiers in the Thirteenth had not exactly distinguished themselves in their 1861 outing. Besides killing their young drummer boy, they proved less than able to feed themselves or to march in formation. To boot, they were ill disciplined and had managed to get their commander, Col. Abel Smith, court-martialed.[69] All of this begs a serious question: What fighting unit would want Brooklyn's Thirteenth guarding its flank in a real battle? Based on the scuttlebutt about the Seventh Army Corps and the reputation of Brooklyn's Thirteenth, one wonders if the Union army wasn't squirreling away all of its questionable units at Suffolk for the duration.[70]

While en route to Suffolk, the Thirteenth traveled in separate steamers, and due to a colossal mix-up, half of the soldiers wound up at Norfolk and half at Portsmouth. Finally, the *Balloon* steamed over to Portsmouth reuniting the regiment.[71]

In the interim, commanders allowed the soldiers a few hours ashore to stretch their legs. This was Morgan Bulkeley's first exposure to Southerners, and it was an awakening. Young girls waved secession flags, and shopkeepers gave soldiers change in Southern script, claiming it was all they had.[72] Maybe so, but "people's eyes fairly sparkled with delight at the sight of greenbacks or coin—gold or silver—bearing the Eagle or the Goddess of Liberty."[73]

After lounging on the curbstones of Crawford Street in Portsmouth for most of the day, the Thirteenth took orders to present themselves at a train siding on the Portsmouth branch of the Norfolk & Petersburg Railroad.

The next forenoon, they crowded into baggage cars and left Portsmouth for Suffolk. Among other things, they passed the "burned barracks of the 29th Alabama and the Louisville Killers. Further along, they saw the burned dwellings, log huts of poor whites, and mansions of the F. F. V.'s [First Families of Virginia] with Negro quarters attached."[74] For the most part though, the view between Portsmouth and Suffolk offered woodland and swamp.

At sundown, Morgan Bulkeley and his fellow soldiers arrived at Suffolk, a sleepy little town almost indistinguishable from hundreds of other small Virginia towns. Two streets crisscrossed with a few houses, stores, and churches sitting near the intersection. Before the war, Suffolk had been a prosperous town of 2,500, doing a thriving business in oysters, roofing shingles, and barrel staves.[75] Now women and old folks populated the town, with few businesses in operation. That first night, the Thirteenth slept in a church.

When twenty-four-year-old Morgan Bulkeley arrived at Suffolk, his regiment was assigned to an encampment area about a mile west of the city. The Twenty-fifth New York State Militia, and a detached battery of the Fourth United States Artillery, including Rev. Henry Ward Beecher's son, Second Lieutenant H. B. Beecher, camped nearby.[76]

Suffolk was first captured by the Union in May 1862, although "captured" may be too strong a word. The rebels heard the Union troops coming and bugged out during the night. The town was of little military importance, but it did sit on a major railroad line to Richmond—the Norfolk & Petersburg Railroad—at a point where a spur line to Portsmouth connected to it. By the summer of 1862, there were about 15,000 Union troops encamped there.[77]

Suffolk was located eighteen miles south of Norfolk and a very important piece of military real estate—the long spit of land between the James and York rivers where General McClellan amassed a huge army for his peninsular campaign. The maneuver envisioned a Union force marching up the whole length of the peninsula and capturing Richmond, using the two rivers to guard its flanks. On paper, the plan was inspired, but McClellan was such a timid commander that Lincoln had to replace him before the campaign got underway.[78]

As for the troops at Suffolk, it was possible that the Seventh Army Corp—along with Brooklyn's Thirteenth—could dissuade the Confederate government and accompanying troops from escaping to the southeast if and when they were dislodged from Richmond. However, Morgan Bulkeley's Suffolk experience involved no hostile military activity whatsoever. The *Eagle* had no misconceptions about the Thirteenth Regiment's battle readiness. On July 3, they wrote, "The men are in good spirits, but feel the necessity of perfecting themselves in the art of war before being called upon to take an active part in the field. They are still, it appears, in the elementary branches of a military education. It is not, therefore, probable that the 13th will be called upon to fight very soon."[79]

By Civil War standards, Morgan Bulkeley's time in Tidewater Virginia was cushy indeed. In camp, the men constructed rustic wooden tables, stools, lounges, chairs and settees.[80] With plenty of good-quality food, and a fresh-water well, these soldiers nourished themselves far better than their 1861 counterparts. The men took turns going into town for toiletries, writing utensils, and other small items.[81] A few stores were filled with customers, and many of the private residents offered hospitality. No longer fearful, the ladies of Suffolk mingled with the soldiers. From the nicer homes, piano music spilled into the streets, and at least some of the women, if asked politely, would answer questions put to them.[82]

In camp, reveille sounded at 5 A.M., followed by roll call and then an hour of company drill.[83] Breakfast was at 6:30, followed by more drilling and target practice. Groups of soldiers charged up to a snake rail fence near the woods surrounding the compound and poured musket balls into it.[84]

From 8 A.M. to 4 P.M., the men cleaned their muskets, took swimming baths, and attended to other personal matters. From 4 to 6 P.M. there was brigade drill, commanded by Gen. Max Weber. Each man was assigned to picket duty—two miles out—once every fifth day. On the day a soldier came off picket duty, he joined the camp clean-up squad. Between guard duty, picket duty, police guard, fatigue duty and drilling, the soldiers' time was fairly well occupied.[85]

Suddenly on July 3, orders came down to break camp and prepare to march. Tents were struck, baggage packed, and unnecessary articles thrown away. Speculation ran high as to where they were headed. Some thought they would be sent back to Norfolk to replace the units heading for the peninsula, or maybe sent directly to join McClellan. Others thought they would be joining Burnside in North Carolina. Spirits soared.[86]

However, as soon as everything was packed and the soldiers were in formation, word arrived that the exercise was only to ascertain how quickly the Thirteenth could be ready to move out. The matter was treated like a joke, as the tents were replaced and camp life returned to normal.

On August 24, things really did change. After three months of endless drilling and ennui, the Thirteenth made preparations to return to Brooklyn.[87] At Suffolk, they had lost only two men—P. P. Dodge, their hospital steward, died of heart disease and Pvt. Guy Holt was killed by friendly fire.[88]

Morgan Bulkeley's regiment left Suffolk on Sunday morning, August 31, first by train to Norfolk and then by the steamer *Baltic* from Fortress Monroe. Their planned seagoing route passed along Virginia's eastern shore, up the Delaware coast, across the mouth of the Delaware River, and followed the length of the New Jersey shoreline to New York Harbor.[89] However, six hours out, the steamer ran aground at Winter Quarter Shoals, just south of Assateague Island in Virginia. Under orders from their commanders, the soldiers threw overboard everything that wasn't nailed down—coal, muskets, backpacks, and other heavy materials. Then they were taken aboard rescue schooners and brought to Baltimore and Philadelphia.[90]

As a result of all this Sturm und Drang, the soldiers arrived back in Brooklyn in waves. The first group of 360 men landed at South Street Seaport on Friday night, September 5, and was immediately ferried across the East River.[91] A reception committee arrived at the Brooklyn ferry slip on Fulton Street and even fired a little six-pound cannon in salute. A parade was anticipated, including a triumphant march from the Fulton Street Ferry to City Hall. The different fire companies placed their pumpers at the cross streets and all were decorated colorfully for the occasion. The crowd was immense.[92]

Unfortunately, the soldiers of the Thirteenth were exhausted and marched only a couple of blocks to the Cranberry Street Armory, where Col. Clark dismissed them. Over the next days, the remaining 400 soldiers landed at the Fulton Street dock almost completely unnoticed. The citizens of Brooklyn meant well, but the war refused to accommodate them. Morgan Bulkeley mustered out on September 28, 1862.

The Thirteenth was called to duty again in mid-June 1863 and sent to Harrisburg, Pennsylvania, but for only thirty days. They shipped out on June 20, swapped musket fire ten days later with a few rebels at Fort Washington, Pennsylvania—just north of Philadelphia—and then proceeded to Harrisburg. A week later, without any further engagement with the rebels, they returned to Brooklyn and were mustered out on July 21, 1863.[93]

Two months later, on a sunny Friday afternoon, September 18, 1863, Morgan's brother, Billy, married a local Brooklyn girl, Emma Gurney, a niece of Henry Morgan.[94] The groom was twenty-three and the bride nineteen. Their first child, Mary Morgan Bulkeley, was born almost exactly nine months later, and five more children followed.[95] Despite the disruptions and butchery of the Civil War, life went on, with the Bulkeleys having ostensibly escaped the worst of it. That was about to change.

At the outbreak of the Civil War, Morgan and Billy's brother, Charlie, joined the First Connecticut Light Artillery, which commenced straightaway to guard Washington.[96] Charlie had studied law with his father and was in the process of building a law practice on Main Street in Hartford.[97] He also had a girlfriend who was crazy about him. In one of Billy Bulkeley's letters to his mother in May 1861, he marveled, "I don't think there is any young lady who cares to hear from me as much [as] Kate does from Charlie."[98]

After ninety days in the First Connecticut Volunteers, Charlie joined the First Connecticut Heavy Artillery and rose to the rank of lieutenant. He participated in McClellan's peninsular campaign and then defended Washington.[99]

The Union army had adopted the custom of naming forts and embattlements after fallen officers, and in mid-1863, they completed Battery Garesche, near Washington. This battery was named after Lt. Col. Julius P. Garesche, who died at Murfreesboro, Tennessee, in the Battle of Stone River. (More precisely, Battery Garesche sat where South Abington Street intersects Thirtieth Road South in Alexandria, Virginia, today.)[100]

Lieut. Charles Bulkeley and the First Connecticut Heavy Artillery took command of Battery Garesche in the summer of 1863. At the beginning of 1864, the army promoted Charlie to captain and adjutant of the fortress.[101] A month later, he came down with typhoid fever and pneumonia. He died on Saturday, February 13, 1864, at the age of twenty-eight.[102]

The news devastated everyone who knew him. It was said that the news hit Judge Bulkeley so hard that it took years off his life.[103] Capt. Charles Bulkeley's body was brought back to Hartford, and his family held a funeral service the following Wednesday at the family home on Church Street. Charlie was interred at Spring Grove Cemetery, and a few years later removed to the Bulkeley family's new plot at Cedar Hill.[104]

The Bulkeleys hid their sorrows and soldiered on. Billy wrote to his mother on March 2, 1864, just two weeks after Charlie's death, and seems to have gone out of his way to talk about frivolous things in order to avoid any mention of that which was most heartfelt.

> Dear Mother,
> . . . Twenty-four today. I can hardly realize it. But when I look back over the past years, it does seem a while. . . . Em and myself have been very busy the past week, buying furniture and carpets for our new home. We're all done now except for buying the crockery, which we will get in a day or two. . . . We hope to get into the house the first of next week. May possibly sleep there Saturday night. Will have to hear from us soon about our progress in getting to housekeeping. It's no small job as I'm sure you are well aware.
> Em is well and sends love to father, Mary and yourself and all the friends. Give my love to all . . . and keep a large share for yourself. From your boy—Billy[105]

Meanwhile, Morgan had returned to his uncle's dry goods business. The death of Charlie made him the oldest of the three remaining Bulkeleys, and he became a far more serious person thereafter.

After the obscenities and savagery of the Civil War, where 620,000 of the nation's youngest and most vibrant citizens lost their lives, Morgan Bulkeley developed a lifelong obsession with martial music and parades. He enjoyed watching soldiers marching in full dress uniform and traveled far and wide to attend musters, outings, campfires and banquets with members of the Grand Army of the Republic (GAR). Though his contribution to the war effort could, with great charity, be called minimal, the Civil War was a major turning point in his life.

The war had just about bankrupted the small towns of the United States. Municipal coffers were exhausted, and a credit crunch descended over the nation.[106] However, Brooklyn did better than most and showed its financial strength by dedicating 585-acre Prospect Park in 1867.[107] Work on the park started in 1860, but halted during the war. Morgan Bulkeley would not necessarily have been interested in Prospect Lake, Brooklyn's only lake—covering sixty acres—but he undoubtedly visited the park's seven baseball diamonds regularly. He played a stick and ball game, one o'cat, in the fields around Brooklyn—a game that had been around since 1856—but after the war, baseball was the rage.[108]

As for politics, Bulkeley began slowly. First, he was elected treasurer of the newly formed Dry Goods Clerks Early Closing Association.[109] Then he became a member of the Republican General Committee of Kings County.[110] These groups were small and parochial, yet they helped Bulkeley form the notion that politics was the way to get things done. Much later, one Brooklynite reminisced about the days after the war when, "the Bulkeley boys ran Republican politics in the [Third Ward]."[111] In 1870, after Billy moved back to Hartford, Morgan Bulkeley was one of Brooklyn's five Third Ward delegates to the Republican City Judiciary Convention.[112]

By 1870, Morgan Bulkeley had served sixteen years behind the counters of H. P. Morgan, and he was getting restless. Thanks to Morgan's hard work, Uncle Henry had been able to spread his time considerably, including serving as a director of the Brooklyn Savings Bank. That same year, Morgan finally got the chance to join Uncle Henry in a banking venture.[113] The Security Bank, however, wasn't a typical commercial or savings bank. Instead it operated as a pawnbroking bank.[114] The Civil War had impoverished almost everyone in the South, but also a goodly number of families in the North. Often a household's chief breadwinner either didn't return from the war or came back unable to provide for his family. Pawnbrokers prospered in this troubled economic climate.[115]

In the bill to incorporate Security Bank, the legislature allowed it "to loan money at rates not to exceed two per cent a month on pledge of goods and chattels and various securities."[116] (An annual rate of 24 percent was shocking, considering that the United States had adopted the English usury rate cap of 6 percent per annum, which stayed in effect until 1950.) There were twenty-eight original incorporators, including Henry P. Morgan and Morgan G. Bulkeley.[117]

≫ Toward the end of Bulkeley's time in Brooklyn Heights, New Yorker's decided to build the East River (Brooklyn) Bridge and the contract was awarded to the finest bridge builder in the United States, John A. Roebling of Trenton, New Jersey. While Roebling was doing some preliminary measurements on the Brooklyn side of the East River, a ferryboat crushed his foot. He was brought to the home of his son, Washington Roebling, at 117 Hicks Street, Brooklyn Heights. Sadly, tetanus set in, and the older man died in a week. The following month, the City of New York awarded the job of finishing the bridge to the younger Roebling, age thirty-one at the time.

Hicks Street intersects Joralemon Street right next to the home of Uncle Henry and Aunt Eunie. Washington Roebling's house was only six blocks to the north.[118]

Washington Roebling, a life-long Republican, and Morgan Bulkeley, now hip-deep in Republican politics, were both born in 1837 and both were Civil War veterans. In an interview with an *Eagle* reporter after Bulkeley had become a United States Senator, Bulkeley offered, "I remember very well when work on the bridge was first begun. . . . I saw the caisson floated into place after the first dock was built on the Brooklyn side. . . . I remember . . . Col. Roebling . . . lived on Columbia Heights [He had moved from 117 Hicks Street to 111 Columbia Heights so he could see the bridge better]. . . . [A]fter losing the use of his limbs, [he] would sit in his room and watch the work on the bridge through a telescope."[119]

≫ On January 6, 1872, a most unusual incident occurred. Though the event and the participants must have seemed a galaxy away for the thirty-four-year-old Morgan Bulkeley, little could he know that the principal scoundrel at the heart of this scandal would play a prominent part in his life twenty-five years later.

On the Saturday in question, wealthy socialite Edward "Ned" Stokes, from old Philadelphia money, shot and killed Wall Street speculator Jubilee Jim Fisk on the elaborate main staircase of the Grand Central Hotel—at Broadway and West Third Street (near Washington Square).

As the *Eagle* wrote, "About six o'clock, it began to be whispered in the stages and streetcars, in the hotels and restaurants, in the cigar stores and barber shops . . . to say that it was whispered is to state the literal truth, for at first the news was thought to be too startling to be true, and nobody wanted to take the risk of communicating the news."[120]

The only other scandal of the Gilded Age to consume as much newsprint was Rev. Henry Ward Beecher's trial for adultery in 1875, but Bulkeley was no longer living in Brooklyn Heights then.

While New York was mesmerized by all the salacious details of Jubilee Jim Fisk's murder—and the actress Josie Mansfield's part in it—Morgan Bulkeley received a telegram with the news of his father's death. He immediately packed a bag and left by train for Hartford. Although he may not have known it at the time, his days in Brooklyn Heights were over.

Chapter Four

RETURN TO HARTFORD

While business and politics kept Morgan Bulkeley active in Brooklyn Heights, back in Hartford his parents had been making some changes. They never got over the death of their son Charlie, and old memories in their home on Church Street proved too much. Thus, at the beginning of February 1870, the Judge and Lydia Bulkeley bought a large, 1835 brick Italianate home at 136 Washington Street. They purchased it from their old friend Thomas Brace, president of Aetna Fire.[1] The north section of Washington Street became known as "Governors' Row" because a number of Connecticut's governors, at one time or another, occupied homes there—William Ellsworth, Marshall Jewell, Richard Hubbard, and later, Morgan Bulkeley.[2] One wonders how many of the city's Gilded Age denizens knew that Governor Street (one block east of South Prospect) was home to five Connecticut governors—Edward Hopkins, George Wyllys, Thomas Welles, John Webster, and Thomas Seymour.[3]

Washington Street was one of the most desirable neighborhoods in the city with its extra-wide boulevard shaded by ancient maples, oaks, and elms. It was one of the city's favorite thoroughfares for Sunday carriage drives in the summertime and sleigh rides in the winter.

From his front yard, the Judge could throw a stone and almost hit the verdant lawns of Trinity College (located where the Capitol is today). There were several barns for horses and carriages, and plenty of room in the house for a seamstress, cook, and nurse. After purchasing the home from Thomas Brace, the Judge bought a small parcel at the back of the property from William Ellsworth. There he built a cottage (facing Cedar Street) for his coachman, John Pegram.[4]

During these years, aside from these personal adjustments, the Judge built up Aetna Life considerably. This was not without struggle, for he was burdened with the never-ending chore of mollifying Aetna Life's shareholders.[5] After the Panic of 1857, many of them were anxious to liquidate their shares and take what profits they could—while they could. Fortunately, Judge Bulkeley was able to win them over with his unshakable belief in the future of life insurance.[6]

By 1867, the company had 15,251 policies in force, representing $91 million of life insurance.[7] Total income grew to $5 million and assets were $7.5 million.[8] In spite of such impressive numbers, there were still only nineteen employees. The company's huge army of sales agents in the field ultimately delivered this fabulous success.[9]

Although Aetna Life had now moved—with Aetna Fire—to a new building at 670 Main Street, the Judge still ran it like a family business. Most of the directors were family members or good friends.

The Panic of 1857 had been particularly tough on Hartford's banks. On October 6, 1857, three Hartford banks temporarily closed their doors and suspended specie payments.[10] Four months later, the treasurer of Hartford County Savings Association, John W. Seymour, fled to Mexico with $115,000 in bank funds.[11] Times were tough, but Judge Bulkeley was undaunted and helped organize Aetna Bank in the fall of 1857. The Judge sat on the original board of directors and oversaw its affairs throughout his life.[12]

༄ Billy and Emma Bulkeley had tired of Brooklyn Heights by 1868 and relocated to Hartford four years ahead of Morgan. Originally, they lived in the old family homestead on Church Street. After Judge Bulkeley's death in 1872, they moved next door to Lydia, into a house that the Judge had bought from Governor Ellsworth's estate.[13]

Despite his background in dry goods, or perhaps because of it, Billy headed in a new direction. He went to work for an art publishing company, Kellogg & Comstock, with offices in downtown Hartford and New York.[14] Billy Bulkeley timed his return to Hartford perfectly, for the firm wanted to expand into the color printmaking business.[15] John Comstock had recently passed away, and Billy saw a great opportunity. By the spring of 1870, the name had been changed to Kellogg & Bulkeley, and this new combination brought out the heretofore unseen financial genius in Billy. With the introduction of color printmaking in 1871, the company enjoyed a huge demand for prints of portraits, cities, and prominent buildings. Kellogg & Bulkeley added state-of-the-art lithographic equipment and landed commercial contracts—including a big chunk of Aetna's work—enabling Kellogg & Bulkeley to grow markedly over time.[16]

༄ As of 1872, the Judge's province, Aetna Life, may have been doing reasonably well, but the man himself was not. For years, Judge Bulkeley's eyesight had been failing, and now he spent hours desperately trying to read letters and interoffice memos. On Tuesday, February 6, he was stricken with paralysis. His coachman quickly drove him home and summoned the Judge's personal physician. For the next two days, the Judge was able to converse a little, but thereafter slipped into unconsciousness. He died at home just before seven o'clock in the evening on Tuesday, February 13. Eerily, Judge Bulkeley passed on the same month and day as his oldest son Charlie—eight years before.[17]

Judge Bulkeley's funeral was held the following Friday at his home on Washington Street, with a large phalanx of businessmen and political leaders in attendance. Rev. William Gage of the Pearl Street Congregational Church conducted the service, and the Judge's remains were at length brought to Cedar Hill Cemetery for burial. His bearers were men associated with Aetna Life and the Pearl Street Congregational Church or its Ecclesiastical Society.[18]

Morgan and his brother Billy were the executors of their father's estate, along with their brother-in-law Leverett Brainard and the Judge's old friends Austin Dunham and Newton Case. Among other things, the Judge left $450,000 in cash and stocks. The equities were in some of Connecticut's finest companies, including Aetna Life, Aetna Fire, Putnam Fire, City Fire, and Willimantic Linen. He also left the home on Washington Street and the old Governor Ellsworth place next door. The value of his entire estate came to roughly $600,000.[19]

To put this in perspective, a quick look at some other Hartford residents is instructive. Judge Bulkeley's fellow Yale graduate and one of Hartford's most prominent attorneys, William Hungerford, then about eighty-five, was worth $332,000. Closer to the top of the scale was Elizabeth Colt, considered the wealthiest woman in Hartford after her husband, Samuel Colt, died in 1862. In 1870, she estimated her net worth at $1.25 million. (This figure was probably on the low side.) At the same time, Hartford's wealthiest citizen, Maj. James M. Goodwin, father of James and Francis Goodwin, estimated the value of his real estate at $300,000 and his other property at $1.2 million.[20]

Though the fortunes of Elizabeth Colt and James M. Goodwin appeared colossal by 1870 standards, Judge Bulkeley's $600,000 wasn't meager by any means. The Judge prospered nicely for a country lawyer turned businessman.

❦ The Judge's passing caused a tectonic shift in Morgan Bulkeley's life. The death of his father following his brother's demise made Morgan the oldest male in the family. Not only would he eventually step into the family business—Aetna Life—and take the office slated for his brother Charlie, but Morgan now became the titular head of the family.

Since neither Morgan nor his brother, Billy, knew anything about insurance, the stewardship of the company fell into the hands of the Judge's alter ego, Thomas Enders. Morgan and Billy served on the board of directors, but initially they had little to do with the day-to-day operations of the company.[21] It was a good thing too.

After the name of the company was changed to Aetna Life back in 1853, Judge

Bulkeley hired Thomas Enders as one of the firm's first employees. While Judge Bulkeley still depended almost entirely on his law practice for subsistence, Thomas Enders ran the company.

Enders was an odd little man but unwavering in his loyalty to the Judge and Aetna Life. Born on a farm in Glen, New York, Enders tried his hand at a half dozen different jobs before traveling to Hartford for an interview with the Judge in 1853. From a simple job as clerk, Enders eventually rose to vice president. A short time after the Judge's death, and just eighteen and a half years after walking in the door, Enders became president of Aetna Life.[22]

Beginning in the late 1860s, insurance companies, banks, railroads, and other financial institutions came under a cloud of suspicion as bad times slowly descended over the country. Questions about solvency became fodder for the nation's newspapers, and their stories exacted a toll. In 1868, six life insurance companies went under, followed by nine more the following year. Another eight closed their doors in 1870, and in the succeeding eight years, seventy-nine more life insurance companies declared insolvency.[23] As for Aetna Life, the total amount of insurance in force fell annually for nearly ten years.[24]

Under these circumstances, it was wise indeed not to insert Morgan or Billy Bulkeley into the upper management of the company. Better to let the battle-hardened Thomas Enders cope with the hard times.

❧ Morgan Bulkeley lived in his mother's home on Washington Street. There were few decent apartments in Hartford at the time—a typical unit comprised two small rooms in a run-down tenement building. The only other option was to board at one of the city's many hotels. Samuel Colt, for example, rented a suite of rooms at the City Hotel on Main Street prior to his marriage in 1856. As an added bonus, the hotel's first-class dining room eliminated the problem of cooking for the busy gun maker.[25]

In Morgan Bulkeley's case, there was an overarching need on Washington Street. His mother, Lydia, now resided in her big house with just a cadre of servants to keep her company. True, her daughter Mary lived right across the street, but Lydia welcomed the idea of her older son moving into her home. Thus, the decision where to live was not a tough one for the returning dry goods salesman.

After the Judge's death his coachman, John Pegram, went into the grocery business, and the Bulkeleys hired Daniel Wallace, the brother of Mary Brainard's coachman, Frank Wallace. The Irish immigrant John Pegram was an anomaly because the Bulkeley servants usually stayed on. Frank Wallace began working for Mary when he was only twelve years old, and stayed with her for seventy years thereafter. Dan Wallace worked with Morgan Bulkeley for thirty-four years until death took the coachman in 1906. Lydia Bulkeley employed the same seamstress, Bridget McCormick, for over forty years.[26]

≋ Hartford had been a city of taverns (hostelries) before the 1870s, where rooms rented for as little as ten cents a night.[27] The upper classes came to prefer the new hotels and restaurants, and the old taverns and saloons became the province of the ever-increasing masses of immigrants.

Kerosene lamps lighted most homes, while wealthier folks availed themselves of the new gaslights. People preferred coal stoves for cooking and heating because they made kitchens toasty warm and at least some heat found its way into the adjoining rooms. Telephones hadn't yet become commonplace, but did ring in a number of homes of the wealthy. Doctors and drug stores were among the first business patrons for telephones. An early newspaper account mentions 1877, when the Capitol Avenue Drug Store was wired to Dr. Campbell's home on Buckingham Street.[28] It is perhaps apocryphal but Samuel Clemens has always been billed as the third telephone subscriber in the city. Meanwhile, Gen. Hawley of the *Courant* was so taken with the invention that fellow workers had a terrible time persuading him "not to invest a couple of his not abundant thousands in the wonderful discovery."[29]

During the Civil War, rails had been laid down the center of Main Street and horse cars trundled between the State House and the center of Wethersfield.[30] These horse cars drove people into the city for six cents and enabled Brown, Thompson & Co. and G. Fox & Co. to become the largest stores in Connecticut over the next century. (The rails eventually hosted the city's trolleys until jitney busses, and then the ubiquitous blue-and-white Connecticut Company buses, replaced them.)[31] By 1866, letterboxes were established throughout the city, making it easier for folks to mail letters to friends, relatives, and business people.[32]

Meanwhile, Hartford had not only developed into a huge manufacturing center but also a large railroad hub. When the river froze in the wintertime, steam ships were effectively out of business, and year by year, railroads solidified their grip on the business of moving freight and passengers in and out of the city. In the decades after the war, "railroad building became almost an article of faith with the American people. Lines were expanding everywhere, whether needed or not."[33]

≋ Like his brother Billy, Morgan Bulkeley returned to Hartford with no interest in remaining in the dry goods business. Eighteen years had proved enough. Morgan's favorable experience with the Security Bank in Brooklyn had given him firsthand knowledge of the enormous profits in banking. Also, Hartford's dismal business environment continued long after the war ended, and it left the city short of banks.

In 1872, before Morgan moved back to Hartford, his brother Billy, along with a dozen other businessmen, organized the United States Trust Company.[34] Morgan was not one of the original incorporators, probably because he had been back in Hartford for less than six months and did not meet the state's residency requirements. However, his brother Billy stood in for him, and Morgan became the bank's first president. It was a small bank, capitalized at only $100,000— Hartford National Bank was capitalized at $1.1 million—but with Morgan as president; another old family friend, Henry Bunce, as treasurer; and a stellar board of directors, the United States Trust Company had enormous potential.[35]

By the 1870s, Hartford's population was riding one very important trend—an exploding immigrant base. In a city with a population of 37,000, fully 27 percent were foreign born, and the Irish made up 72 percent of that number. The flood of immigrants—particularly the Irish—swelled to such numbers that they eventually spilled out of the Fifth and Sixth Wards, north into the Seventh. Still, the Fifth and Sixth Wards boasted the heaviest concentration of the foreign-born Irish. Most of these immigrants worked as day laborers all their lives and were counted among the most socioeconomically marginal members of Hartford society.[36]

Immigrant entrepreneurs were fairly rare, especially among the Irish, but some immigrant-run businesses—mostly saloons, liquor stores, and small groceries—sprung up on the East Side.[37] Besides these businesses, the East Side crawled with pushcarts. These peddlers would make one or two turns a day around the neighborhood, selling meat, fish, bread, coffee, vegetables, fruits, cigars, and anything that would fetch a few cents.[38]

Not surprisingly, as the numbers of immigrants on the East Side swelled, a contentious relationship developed between them and the city's old guard. The poor had to be kept in their place. For example, Maj. James M. Goodwin, a real estate speculator and the city's wealthiest businessman, routinely employed Irish domestics, cooks, maids, gardeners, and coachmen at his home, Goodwin's Castle at 83 Woodland Street, yet he was loath to allow the immigrants to rise above simple servitude.[39]

For many prosperous Yankees, Asylum Hill afforded a sanctuary from the floodtide of aliens in the river wards. Thus, when the Catholic Church agitated to build St. Joseph's Cathedral on Asylum Hill in 1872, James Goodwin refused to sell the land to Bishop McFarland. Quietly McFarland enlisted the help of the Irish attorney Thomas McManus, who approached George Affleck, an Asylum Hill florist and nurseryman. James Goodwin probably trusted Affleck because both men were Episcopalians. However, Affleck apparently was empathetic toward the Irish immigrants because he was an immigrant himself—from Scotland.[40] Affleck bought the land for $70,000 and resold it to McManus, who then turned it over to Bishop McFarland. After all this folderol, when the cathedral was finally completed, its distant location made it practically worthless to the very people it was built to serve.[41]

～ Hartford's post–Civil War politics were much the same as the politics of the nation, which is to say chaotic. For about a dozen years after the war, at the gubernatorial level, Republicans and Democrats each held office half the time. In the state legislature, the Senate swung back and forth, while the Republicans from Connecticut's small towns invariably held a crushing majority in the House.[42]

At the city level, the Republicans slowly reasserted control. Whereas from 1843 until 1864 there were eight Democratic mayors and only two Republicans, after the war, the two parties played leapfrog until 1880, when Morgan Bulkeley's political machine exploded onto the scene. The perception after the war that the Democratic Party represented division (even treason) caused the defection of old-time Yankee Democrats to the Republican Party. East Side Irishmen formed the core of the tarnished Democratic Party.[43]

Republican Marshall Jewell was serving as governor when Morgan Bulkeley first returned to Hartford. Jewell was a fascinating man—talented, wealthy, and charming. He and Bulkeley became fast friends. The son of Pliny Jewell, the founder and patriarch of the largest maker of industrial belting in the world—the fabulous Jewell Belting Company—young Marshall was born into great wealth, yet he worked as a tanner's apprentice in his father's business. Owing to the constant exposure to the steaming vat, all of his life he "was unable to sleep unless his arms were bare."[44] Little wonder he came to hate the industrial belting business. In a move that did not exactly stun his father, Marshall set off for Boston to learn the new field of electricity. For a time, he worked in the telegraph business, traveling all over the eastern United States, and finally superintending the New York and Boston telegraph lines. When he was twenty-five, Marshall received a message from home. His father needed him at Jewell Belting. Marshall obediently returned.[45]

As one might expect, the industrial belting business just couldn't keep Marshall's attention. Politics beckoned, and Jewell served two nonconsecutive terms as Connecticut's governor in 1869–70 and 1871–72. When Jewell left the governor's office, President Grant appointed him United States minister to Russia and later postmaster general. He also served as president of the Jewell Pin Co. and Southern New England Telephone Co. and as chairman of the Republican National Committee.[46]

CROWBAR GOVERNOR

There was a fierce—at times destructive—competition between Marshall Jewell and Gen. Joe Hawley. In fact, Charles Clark of the *Courant* once called it "the first line of division . . . within the Republican [P]arty."[47] Voters throughout the state considered themselves either a Jewell supporter or a Hawley supporter. Since Hawley owned the *Courant*, Marshall Jewell bought a controlling interest in the *Hartford Post*. When one of Connecticut's u.s. Senate seats became available in 1878, Jewell's unwillingness to let Hawley have the seat allowed Meriden's Orville Platt to slip in.[48] Thanks to this superheated competition between Jewell and Hawley, Platt was able to keep the seat until his death, twenty-seven years later. For many politicians like Orville Platt, the General Assembly proved the all-important stepping stone to higher office, but Joe Hawley, Marshall Jewell, and Morgan Bulkeley never served in the statehouse.[49]

Hawley appeared more statesman than politician, and Jewell came across exactly the opposite. For all intents and purposes, they kept getting in each other's way until 1881 when Hawley won the Republican nomination and thence the one available u.s. Senate seat. Gen. Hawley was eventually elected to four terms in the u.s. Senate, but Marshall Jewell never made it to that august body. Sadly, he died in 1883, two years after this showdown with Joe Hawley.[50]

Morgan Bulkeley sided with the Jewell camp.[51] Still, even though Bulkeley engaged in election practices beyond Joe Hawley's abidance, the two men somehow managed to get along. There was no political capital to be made by crossing Hawley. He was too well liked.

❧ It is probably fair to say that a day didn't go by without some sort of political matter occupying a piece of Morgan Bulkeley's life. Nevertheless, he had a bank to run. The Victorian Age was awash with men who ran a number of different companies and still found time for elective politics. This wasn't unusual. However, such an arrangement became difficult when trouble struck.

Just as Bulkeley's United States Trust Company began to win depositors and make solid loans, the economy suffered a severe setback. The trouble began in Philadelphia, where the banking firm of Jay Cooke & Co.—financiers of what aimed to be the second transcontinental railroad, the Northern Pacific—went bankrupt on September 18, 1873. In the aftermath of this shock, it was only a question of time before bankruptcies proliferated and unemployment soared.[52]

The Panic of 1873 was one of the worst economic downturns the United States has ever endured. The collapse of Jay Cooke & Co. sent financial tremors throughout the nation. The New York Stock Exchange closed for ten days. Of the country's 364 railroads, 89 went bankrupt, and a total of 18,000 businesses failed in just the next two years. By 1876, unemployment was 14 percent and the future looked bleak.

It didn't end there. In late summer 1875, the banks in San Francisco began to fail. First it was the National Bank and Trust Company, followed by the Merchants Exchange Bank. Talk on the street rumored that the Bank of California was in trouble. Confusion and canards mounted as fear spiraled out of control. The depression of the 1870s really didn't end until the early 1880s.[53]

The sagacity of Hartford's local businessmen and the city's tremendous wealth partially insulated it from this financial nightmare. One would be hard pressed to name a nineteenth-century instance when a Hartford bank became insolvent. They did have spells where they had to suspend specie payments, but even those instances were rare. So said, if the prosperity of a bank can be gleaned from its share price, then Morgan Bulkeley's United States Trust Company wasn't exactly a blue chip investment. From a price of over $100 a share in 1875, the price plummeted to $60 by 1878, only climbing to $80 by 1881.[54]

Throughout much of the difficult 1870s, Bulkeley's biggest challenge was the United States Trust Company, as he daily battled a business climate that refused to improve. However, this battle didn't stop him from thinking about politics. In his earliest years after returning to Hartford, Morgan Bulkeley yearned to follow up on Brooklyn's political lessons. One New York paper wrote, "[He learned] . . . how to handle a primary and to practice the political prestidigitator's arts, which cause an adverse majority in a ward to become a majority on Election Day. But Brooklyn politics became a bit too rank for [him]."[55]

Hartford's political scene *was* less rank than Brooklyn's, but it wasn't lily white either. Newspaper reporters swore that the Republicans were buying votes like party favors, while the Democrats had more resident aliens voting than all the Irish immigrants who ever came to America.[56]

In the 1870s and 1880s, some of Hartford's political meetings were held at American Hall on the east side of State House Square. One night, as a reporter for the *Courant* relates, a Democratic convention was underway when one delegate asked another man, "Are there any real Americans among the delegates?" The second man answered, "Not enough to do any harm."[57]

Even with the almost overpowering pull of politics, Bulkeley didn't seek election until 1875 when he won a seat on the common council, representing the Fourth Ward. The Democrat, Joseph Sprague, was elected mayor, and most of the aldermen and councilmen were Democrats as well. Thus, Bulkeley's entry into Hartford politics was not exactly well timed, though it offered a start for the thirty-seven-year-old Republican banker. Perhaps the weekly scuffles at council meetings toughened Bulkeley, but butting heads with Democrats convinced Bulkeley that he must work his way up to mayor if he wanted his opinions to count. For that to happen, the Republicans had to retake control of the city. There was work to do.

A year later, in the April city elections of 1876, Bulkeley ran for one of the two aldermen spots in the Fourth Ward.[58] He managed to garner 35 percent more votes than his opponent, Samuel White, treasurer of Charter Oak Life. White, no doubt, lost votes because Charter Oak Life had fallen under a cloud of suspicion and voters tarred White with the same brush they used on the company.[59] Other than a very important friendship Bulkeley formed with another Republican alderman, Gideon Winslow of the Fifth Ward, Bulkeley's two years as alderman passed uneventfully. As we shall see later, this Bulkeley-Winslow friendship was the very beginning of the Bulkeley machine and the glue that held him atop city politics for the next decade.

During this period, the Irish immigrants' influence in Hartford's politics was growing. In the 1876 election, the precise division of the city along class lines was evident. All twelve of the councilmen elected in the Fifth, Sixth, and Seventh Wards were Democrats. In the First, Second, Third, and Fourth Wards, fifteen of the sixteen councilmen elected were Republicans. This dogged immiscibility of the city's two principal classes continued well into the twentieth century.[60]

〰 Bulkeley's entry into mayoral politics wasn't a simple matter. The reigning Republican city boss had to anoint him. In 1878, Judge Arthur Eggleston, even at the tender age of thirty-three, was one of the most prominent trial lawyers in Hartford County and the biggest power broker for the Republicans.[61] Among the inner circle, the odds-on favorite for mayor was the good-looking, charismatic bachelor, Alexander Harbison, a highly successful grocer.[62] Harbison was among the rarest of commodities, a Republican Irish immigrant. His emigration from Ireland as a child allowed him to attend Hartford's common schools and quickly move beyond the circumscribed world of the hapless river ward immigrants. The connection between Harbison and his countrymen in America was not readily apparent. With his brother Hugh, Harbison built Harbison Brothers into the largest retail grocery store in the city. All the same, Judge Eggleston didn't think the tall Irishman was a very strong candidate and was quietly looking for a better choice.

In the end, Eggleston's gaze fell on Morgan Bulkeley, for he felt the forty-year-old alderman was a "bigger and abler" candidate than Harbison.[63] Caucus night results surprised the favorites. For two ballots, Harbison lagged one vote behind the Harvard-educated attorney Maj. John Parsons with no majority for either.[64] On the third ballot, Morgan Bulkeley, a compromise candidate, got twenty-five of the thirty-two votes and was nominated. (Harbison eventually ascended to the mayor's office, but not until 1900. Ignatius Sullivan may have been Hartford's first Irish Democratic mayor when he was elected in 1902, but the Republican Alexander Harbison was Hartford's first Irish immigrant to hold the office.)[65]

A long—albeit friendly—rivalry persisted between Gen. Joe Hawley and Morgan Bulkeley from 1893 forward, simply because Bulkeley lusted after Joe Hawley's U.S. Senate seat. The fact that Hawley presided at this 1878 Republican caucus—and effectively launched the younger man's mayoral career—makes this rivalry all the more interesting.[66]

In the 1878 race, Bulkeley was up against a tough opponent—George Sumner, aptly nicknamed "Genial George."[67] Both men were outsiders, after a fashion. Sumner had been born in Bolton and, of course, Bulkeley in East Haddam. Sumner was a sickly youngster and unable to get a university education. He served as Bolton's town clerk for three years and then studied law with David Calhoun of Manchester. As the Civil War ended, he landed a position with the law firm of Waldo, Hubbard & Hyde in Hartford. Two years later, Sumner was elected to the state House of Representatives, serving his native Bolton. Not long afterward, he settled in Hartford and in 1868 became an alderman. That was followed up with one term as city attorney and a four-year stint as judge of the city court. In 1873–74, he served as chairman of the Democratic State Central Committee. Finally in 1878, he beat Morgan Bulkeley in the city's mayoral race. The capper was that he did all this before his thirty-sixth birthday![68]

There was one last thing that may have made the voters sympathetic toward George Sumner. In 1870, he married Ella Gallup of Plainfield and they had two children—William and Julia. Neither of the children reached the age of two, and then Ella died in 1875, leaving George alone in the world. (At the Wadsworth Atheneum, the Ella Gallup Sumner and Mary Catlin Sumner Collections Fund was founded and named for the wives of George Sumner and his younger brother, Frank.)[69]

In short, Morgan Bulkeley ran against an able attorney, an accomplished politician, and a man with great personal tragedy in his life. And to top it all, Sumner was a consummate stump speaker. Bulkeley exhibited none of these traits.

Besides the issue of portfolio, Bulkeley had only been back in Hartford for six years when he first ran for mayor. Sumner was five years his junior but a better-known quantity. Sure, everyone knew that Bulkeley was the Judge's son and president of the United States Trust Company, but they favored Sumner, who beat Bulkeley by a plurality of 601 votes.[70] Oddly enough, Sumner's 601-vote plurality exactly matched his majority in the river wards.

That 1878 loss to George Sumner really stung Morgan Bulkeley. He had come face-to-face with a harsh reality—if he couldn't find a way to beat men with superior résumés, his career in politics would be brief. As they say, however, adversity can be a great teacher, and after this loss, Bulkeley underwent a huge change. From that point forward, he used a two-pronged attack to win elections. The first prong was above board. He added an *action* component to his enormous native charm, constantly looking for ways to meet the needs of the voters, particularly those in the river wards.

Aside from the obvious appeal of action, Bulkeley's moves seem characteristic of a fun-seeking man who sincerely wanted to be loved—perhaps an early forerunner of New York's Mayor Fiorello LaGuardia. However, as we shall see later, Bulkeley required a tangible reason to explain his soon-to-be-astounding popularity in the river wards on election day. In short, he needed cover.

An important display of Bulkeley's action component can be seen in a public entertainment designed to titillate the crowd at the dedication of Connecticut's new Capitol building in 1879. The city had finally bested New Haven in the race to become the sole capital of the state.[71] This was accomplished when Hartford made the state two extraordinary proposals. First, they offered a stunning thirteen-acre parcel of land overlooking Bushnell Park. Trinity College sat there at the time, but for a price ($600,000), the trustees could be persuaded to relocate the school.[72] Next, Hartford put together a grant of $500,000 toward the construction of the new Capitol. These were truly fantastic numbers to be throwing around in the 1870s, and the state wasted no time in accepting. The building committee hired the architect Richard Upjohn to draw the new Capitol, with an original construction estimate of $900,000. (When it was finally completed in 1879, the cost ran to $3 million.)[73]

In order to dedicate the building properly, the state legislature declared that the anniversary of the Battle of Antietam would be known as Battle Flag Day and planned a full day of festivities.[74] The high point of this celebration on September 17, 1879, involved a grand parade in which military regiments would march from the State Arsenal on Main Street—opposite the old North Cemetery—to the new Capitol, each unit carrying a Civil War battle flag. In all, more than 8,000 veterans carried the flags to the Capitol. These flags were to be installed in permanent holders in the rotunda of the building.[75]

When the day finally arrived, over 100,000 spectators witnessed the parade and, it is estimated, 30,000 remained for the evening's festivities.[76] The highlight of the evening was the "grand illumination" of the new Capitol. Willimantic Linen Company lent six huge arc lights and Colt's Patent Fire-Arms provided an electric generator for the occasion. For three hours, lights played all over the new building and its grounds, while workmen rotated colored filters in front of the lights to amuse the public. Spectators gathered in the park had never seen anything like it and were completely spellbound. Loud "Oooohs" and Ahhhs" were heard throughout the vesperal light show.[77]

Morgan Bulkeley was given credit for the "grand illumination," and some said, erroneously, that this one masterstroke catapulted him into the mayor's office in 1880.[78] People love action, and the "grand illumination" helped; however, this fantastic light show would not have singularly awarded Bulkeley the mayor's office.

The idea for the light display might have come to Bulkeley the year before when he and twenty-five of Hartford's most prominent businessmen were invited to tour Willimantic Linen Company after it had been electrified.[79] Austin Dunham's son, Austin Cornelius "A. C." Dunham, was the first man in Hartford to grasp the industrial value of electric light.[80] His father, Austin Dunham, who passed in 1877, was also a member of the board of Aetna Life since Judge Bulkeley first organized the company.

A. C. Dunham frequently thought way ahead of those around him, and the idea for the "grand illumination" might have been his. It doesn't matter. Fortunately for Bulkeley, A. C. enjoyed the role of a behind-the-scenes man. Like Samuel Colt, James Goodwin, and a dozen other very wealthy businessmen, A. C. Dunham wasn't interested in public office. He remained convinced that his needs could be met by simply helping those who sought the limelight.

The second prong of Bulkeley's election strategy was darker—the outright purchase of votes. Generally speaking, a Republican candidate who was soundly beaten in a mayoral election would not get another chance—at least not for a while. This would hold especially true for a candidate like Bulkeley who ran behind his ticket even in the heavily Republican wards—the First, Second, Third, and Fourth.[81] In order to stay with him, Judge Eggleston and the other members of the Republican Town Committee had to be convinced the result would be different in April 1880. True, Judge Eggleston may have felt voters would warm to Bulkeley in the fullness of time, but a great deal of circumstantial evidence suggests the candidate himself found a more reliable way to win. In any event, the Republican nominating meeting of Saturday, March 27, 1880, "was characterized by entire harmony," with Morgan Bulkeley as their candidate for mayor.[82]

In 1877, the General Assembly passed a very clear statute against bribery, making the buying of votes an offense punishable by a $500 fine and one year in prison.[83] Although conflicting public opinion made enforcement unpopular, Morgan Bulkeley knew about the law. In an appearance before a state Senate corrupt election practices probe, Bulkeley said outright, "Bribery was prohibited by the law."[84]

A little later, in 1884, a Republican operative, Hiram Buckingham, was caught red-handed paying cash for votes in the Fourth Ward. He was arrested, jailed, and bailed out by Billy Bulkeley—a former lieutenant governor by then. Buckingham later benefited from a dismissal due to lack of evidence.[85] The editor-in-chief of the *Courant* wrote, "I know public men have openly declared that a citizen had as much right to sell his vote as to sell his potatoes. . . . The buying of . . . any voters is disgraceful . . . and should be a recognized criminal offense."[86] In this environment, it's easy to see why some politicians weren't particularly bothered by the practice of buying votes and broke with the *ancien régime*.

Much later, in 1910, Norwich mayor Charles Thayer gave another Hartford politician some advice, "If it begins to look smoky as the campaign develops . . . call Bulkeley around the corner where you will not be overheard, and ask him how he carried the river wards back in the good old days when he ran for mayor, and how he worked the racket in Gid Winslow's butcher shop. A few fine points from an expert will surely tide you over."[87] Incidentally, Charles Thayer was given credit for the adage, "Connecticut—corrupt and content."[88]

Thayer's accusation rings true. Gideon Winslow, a pudgy English immigrant, ran G. D. Winslow & Co., a butcher shop and grocery business at 199 State Street (on the corner of Front Street) from 1865 to 1897.[89] State Street was the busiest commercial street in Hartford, running from Main Street down to the warehouses and wharfs at the Connecticut River. The dividing line between the Sixth Ward on the north and the Fifth Ward on the south ran one block north of State, down Temple and then Kilbourne Streets to the river. There wasn't one decent building appropriate for a voting station in the Fifth Ward, so this boundary line was drawn to include Engine House No. 3. Front Street, running parallel to the river, sliced down the middle of both wards. This put Gideon Winslow's butcher shop almost dead center of these all-important districts.

As mentioned earlier, Winslow, the only Republican alderman ever elected from the city's Fifth Ward, had established a strong friendship with Morgan Bulkeley when the two served on the same Board of Aldermen in 1876 and 1877.[90] The two men were also members of St. John's Lodge of Masons. Later, as governor, Bulkeley appointed Winslow head of the state's Dairy and Food Commission.[91] The dairy farmers hated Winslow and recommended he be removed because of his complete lack of interest in the job, but Bulkeley paid no heed, reappointing his friend to a second term regardless of the ruckus.[92] Gideon Winslow was considered Bulkeley's "favorite commissioner."[93]

All evidence suggests that Bulkeley and Winslow initiated a scheme whereby votes in the river wards were bought for five dollars worth of stew meat, flour, and groceries at G. D. Winslow & Co. A family could live for two weeks on this windfall. Five dollars is a good guess, since a few years later, Bulkeley claimed, "[A]ccording to common rumor, $5 would influence men in many other ways besides voting."[94] There were Republican households on the western edge of the river wards—on Prospect and Market Streets and the east side of Main—but the Democrats held a decisive majority. Without chicanery, how could Bulkeley have done so well there in 1880, 1882, 1884, and 1886? The answer is, of course, he could not have.

All through the 1860s and 1870s, the city's newspapers, particularly the *Hart-*

ford Daily Times, claimed there was vote buying during elections.[95] As if to prove the *Times* right, the *Courant* hired a private detective to ferret out the toughs who planned to rig the statewide elections of 1878.[96] By printing the detective's diary in the paper the day before the election, the fixers had no choice but to lay low that year.[97]

However, most city vote fixing was penny-ante stuff. After all, it was Judge Bulkeley who secured a court injunction against the city's water commissioners in 1865, enjoining them from taking the waters of Trout Brook in West Hartford.[98] If the Judge wanted to buy votes, he certainly had the money and the political contacts to do it. Despite the *Times*'s assertions of vote buying, the fact that the Judge's position was soundly defeated at the polls evidences the contrary.[99]

By the same token, if the Republicans had a scheme in place to routinely buy votes, Morgan Bulkeley never would have lost to George Sumner in 1878. Hartford's politics actually *was* less corrupt than many of the larger cities in the country.

Bulkeley's loss to George Sumner ushered in a whole new era in Hartford politics. In 1878, Bulkeley accepted the proposition that Hartford elections were different from those in Brooklyn Heights—more refined perhaps. Many years later, Bulkeley talked of his early days in New York. "Brooklyn was normally Democratic by about 30,000 in those days, and the Republicans had a hard time making headway, but the campaigns were always red hot affairs."[100] This hardly describes an honest canvas and a fair election.

In Hartford, Bulkeley learned the hard way that he couldn't take control of city hall with his winning personality alone. Now he would employ different methods to win.[101] The enfant terrible had entered the arena.

Why did Bulkeley do it? For the money? Not hardly. Bulkeley always earned a handsome living but was never overly motivated by money. The simple answer is he *had* to—if he wanted to win.

Comparing the results of the 1878 and 1880 mayoral elections, an important difference emerges. In 1878, since Bulkeley ran behind his own ticket even in the Republican wards, it appears he was reluctant to employ the corrupt election practices he'd learned in Brooklyn. Let's not forget Bulkeley had been a member of the Republican General Committee of King's County. If there had been any vote buying, he would have known about it. Moreover, remember that Aunt Eunie's father, George Hicks, was a partner in Shoomaker & Hicks, one of the largest grocery stores in Brooklyn. Bulkeley's visit to "Mr. Hicks at Fort McHenry," leaves little doubt that he cultivated a kinship with Aunt Eunie's father.[102] If a food-for-votes scheme existed at election time in Brooklyn, Morgan Bulkeley would have known about that too.

On a deeper level, the introduction of the corrupt election practices of Brooklyn into Hartford politics calls into question Bulkeley's sense of himself. The men who invariably rose to the top of Connecticut government during the second half of the nineteenth century were men with superb educations, admirable professional achievements, exemplary war records—and very often, all three. Bulkeley would have been less than human if he didn't feel a certain Adlerian inferiority when compared to such men. He hadn't finished high school and his war record was hardly worth mentioning. True, he was president of a small bank, and in July 1879, became president of Aetna Life—when he basically swapped jobs with Thomas Enders—but this position was the result of lineage, not his razor sharp business acumen.[103] In sum, Bulkeley had something to prove.

One last point: Other men, like Col. Samuel Colt, for example, had grateful governors bestow spurious titles on them. These titles uplifted their public image at a time when men were fanatic about titles and honoraria. In much the same way, politics bestowed the titles and the power that Morgan Bulkeley craved. To be blunt, Bulkeley lusted after the grandeur of political office.

≫ In 1879, while Bulkeley set the stage for his triumphant mayoral race, he became the state legislature's star witness in a corrupt voting practices probe.[104] The General Assembly summoned Bulkeley to a series of appearances over the next two decades. In this probe, the state Senate was all fired up about the alleged bribery used in an effort to get Bulkeley's friend, Joseph L. Barbour, elected clerk of Hartford's Common Council.[105] There is no evidence that Bulkeley bought votes for Barbour. In truth, since Bulkeley lost so badly to George Sumner in 1878, it seems unlikely that he was in a position to help Barbour or anyone else.

This logic notwithstanding, Bulkeley was asked in every conceivable way if he had given anyone money to vote for Barbour; and Bulkeley simply answered "No Sir" over and over again. This occurred early in Bulkeley's career, and his answers to these questions barely made headlines. As he became increasingly self-possessed, he learned to give answers that were provocative—even troubling. At times his answers were so controversial they were reprinted in newspapers all over the Northeast.[106] Nonetheless, he never admitted buying votes or bribing anyone, nor did he mention observing anyone else doing so. Over the years, Bulkeley repeated a number of false statements before the General Assembly and even Connecticut's Supreme Court related to voting irregularities in which he was involved. Newspapers, such as the *New York Sun*, openly asserted, "[He] is believed to have no convictions as to the potency of cash in politics as a persuasive argument in the way of thorough organization."[107] All through the 1880s, the *Times* spelled out exactly how much money he was spending for votes in each ward.[108] Bulkeley either wasn't troubled by this or kept his qualms to himself because his feelings with regard to these matters was never publicly discussed or recorded.

Wrongdoing aside, in the summer of 1879, things changed dramatically on the business side of Morgan Bulkeley's ledger. The Judge's handpicked successor at Aetna Life, Thomas Enders, effectuated a marvelous job of steering a steady course for the company through the miserable downturn following the Panic of 1873—but at a terrible price. Professionally, Enders was at the top of his game, but the stress took a toll on his health. He was only forty-six, but sorely in need of rest.[109] To help, Morgan Bulkeley left most of the work at the United States Trust Company to his secretary-treasurer, Henry Bunce, and in July 1879, Bulkeley became the third president of Aetna Life.[110]

It was not a smooth transition. There were men at Aetna Life who questioned Bulkeley's knowledge of the insurance business and his executive abilities in general.[111] After all, Hartford was a small city, and the United States Trust Company's uncomfortably high level of bad loans probably wasn't kept secret any more than the firm's sagging stock price. In addition, Bulkeley had lost the mayoral race to George Sumner the year before. Were these workers wrong to consider that perhaps Morgan Bulkeley was not the man to lead Aetna Life to higher ground?

Winning over recalcitrant voters seemed like a snap compared to the task confronting Bulkeley now. The rank and file at Aetna Life couldn't be won with empty promises. Though he had been sitting on Aetna Life's board since 1872, most of the organization's members were convinced that Bulkeley would just "rattle around" in the job.[112] It was time for Morgan Bulkeley to prove his worth.

There would be no honeymoon period, since Morgan's continued interest in politics and his determination to become Hartford's mayor would constantly bring out the naysayers, mudslingers, and political tricksters. On the bright side, while mixed up in Brooklyn politics, Bulkeley had learned to take a punch. Maybe things would work out.

Morgan Bulkeley was so busy with business and politics, one would think he would have no time for other pursuits, but such was not the case. Bulkeley always found time for fun. While out of office, Bulkeley devoted hours to his two favorite pastimes—baseball and horse racing. As a new member of the Home Circle Club—a small social organization with rooms in the Putnam Building, a few doors north of his office in the Charter Oak Life building—Bulkeley enjoyed watching baseball up close.[113] The Home Circle's baseball team played other clubs from all over New England.

Soon enough, watching other people's baseball teams play lost its charm. Early in 1874, a Middletown, Connecticut, native, Ben Douglas, gathered together some of Hartford's businessmen, including Morgan Bulkeley, and pitched them on the idea of starting a professional baseball team.[114] They liked the idea enough to put up $5,000 to equip their new team, the Hartford Dark Blues, and elect Morgan Bulkeley president.[115] This was fortuitous because Bulkeley had learned a thing or two about winning while in Brooklyn, and he did something that was "audacious and costly, but very characteristic of [him]. He went to New York and captured the famous Mutual "nine," Bob Furgeson and all, and brought them to Hartford."[116]

The Dark Blues baseball club was the city's first professional sports team and a member of the National Association—a player's group. A plot of land on the corner of Wyllys Street and Hendricxsen Avenue—adjacent to the Church of the Good Shepherd—served as home field. (The owners of the team did not have the money to buy land in the city, and since programs stated, "All games played at Colt Meadows," the land was undoubtedly leased from Elizabeth Colt.)[117] Many years later, Bulkeley claimed he "had seen 10,000 and even 15,000 people on the grounds, at a time when the horse cars were few and none ran nearer . . . than Main Street."[118]

Baseball was a much tougher game then. The players refused to wear gloves, or in the case of the catcher, protective gear. Pitches were delivered underhand, and then sidearm. Finally this delivery morphed into an overhand throw in the 1880s. Arthur "Candy" Cummings, who played for the Dark Blues, was credited with inventing the curveball after he watched a clamshell sail through the air. The pugnacious players were infamous for their drinking, gambling, and foul language.[119]

In 1875, under the weight of economic and behavioral problems, the National Association collapsed. The following year, William Hulbert and Albert Spalding, both of Chicago, organized a more financially stable professional baseball league —the National League—and invited Hartford to join.[120] There were only eight teams in the original league—the Boston Red Stockings, Hartford Dark Blues, Chicago White Sox, Cincinnati Red Stockings, Louisville Grays, St. Louis Brown Stockings, New York Mutuals (Brooklyn) and the Athletics (Philadelphia). Hartford was the smallest city in the league.[121]

To kick off the new National League, members attended a large luncheon at New York's Grand Central Hotel in February 1876. (In one of those coincidences speckling the pages of history, this was the same hotel where Ned Stokes had murdered Jubilee Jim Fisk four years earlier.)

Hulbert's plan called for four teams from the West and four from the East. Since he and Spalding were from Chicago, he felt that the president of the newly formed National League should be an easterner, so he approached Morgan Bulkeley. Inasmuch as Bulkeley was then up to his ears in the affairs of the United States Trust Company and matters related to his position on the common council, he agreed to serve a single year, with Hulbert doing most of the work. After Bulkeley's year was up, Hulbert was elected National League president by the other owners and held the position until his death five years later.[122]

Bulkeley knew he needed to curb the drinking and gambling, not to mention the fighting and cussing, so he turned to Bob Ferguson, the teetotaler player-captain of the team. Not only did Ferguson know nothing about managing men, he was a despot with a violent streak to boot. He did curb the players' bad habits, but a landslide of bickering and backbiting filled the void. Finally, the Dark Blues best pitcher, Tommy Bond, told Bulkeley he was through playing for the Dark Blues while Ferguson was captain. Cavalierly, Bulkeley voided the remaining portion of Bond's 1876 contract and released him from his 1877 commitment.[123]

Despite their success on the diamond, the Dark Blues struggled financially. Bulkeley tried everything he could think of to boost attendance, but his efforts bore little fruit. Ultimately, he sold the Dark Blues to the New York Mutuals' owner William Cammeyer, whose luck was no better. The 1877 season was their swan song.[124]

After selling the Dark Blues, Bulkeley lost interest in baseball, although he stayed in contact with friends in the game. Often he attended testimonial dinners in New York—for William Hulbert, Albert Spalding and others. Even after Bulkeley's Senate years, Arthur "Candy" Cummings occasionally came down from Athol, Massachusetts, to visit and it was always "How are you, Arthur?" "Feeling very fit, Morgan."[125] Bulkeley and Cummings were the only two men from the Dark Blues organization to make it to the Baseball Hall of Fame.[126]

≈ Even more than baseball, Morgan Bulkeley loved horses, something he probably inherited from the Judge. The family stabled the finest horses in the city in their Washington Street barns, and their "driving pairs were conspicuous."[127] Coachman Dan Wallace babied them like they were his own children.

One can just imagine it warming Bulkeley's heart to hear of Burdett Loomis's new Charter Oak Trotting Park in the Parkville section of West Hartford. Loomis acquired 135 acres of nice flat land between 1871 and 1873.[128] Oakwood Avenue bounded it on the east, Flatbush on the north, and East Street (now South Quaker Lane) on the west. A one-mile track was laid out, paddocks and grandstands constructed, and in short order, the gates opened and races were on at Charter Oak Park.

Eventually, horse-car service extended to Parkville and ran to the track every two hours all day long. Admission for a bleacher seat cost seventy-five cents, and the Hartford police assumed the responsibility for maintaining order. Despite roof collapses, sanitary problems and other issues, Charter Oak Park prevailed until the 1930s, when Chase National Bank foreclosed on the property. The land was eventually sold piecemeal, and factories and other commercial buildings replaced the park.[129]

In the 1870s though, Charter Oak Park represented a godsend for Morgan Bulkeley. The trotters ran about as often as the horse cars down Main Street, and Bulkeley was a regular attendee. He even served as a director of Charter Oak Park for many years. So many men in Hartford owned "speedsters" and "roadsters" that Bulkeley seems like a natural to have purchased a few racehorses of his own, but he never did. Apparently he was content to bet on the horses of others.

Morgan Bulkeley was thirty-four when he returned to Hartford upon the death of his father. The years in Brooklyn Heights had taught him the value of hard work, the minutiae of the dry goods business, and something about politics. Yet, when he assumed the presidency of the United States Trust Company, his plans for the future were no better than when he was selling fabric to fancy ladies in New York. For whatever reason, he had little in the way of aspirations, and simply did not plan well.

That said, politics performed an odd service for Morgan. He originally indulged in politics for fun. As he said, the elections in Brooklyn were "red-hot affairs." Yet, politics in Hartford offered him many things. First, public affairs gave him a sense of self that was plainly lacking. Secondly, they gave him goals. He wasn't quick to grab the reins at Aetna Life, but he did become a councilman and alderman, which kept him moving up in the community. Lastly—although he might not have understood it completely at the time—politics eventually gave him the means to control his world, both in business and pleasure. True, his methods raised eyebrows then as they do now, but apparently it was a Faustian bargain he proved willing to make.

Chapter Five

MAYOR BULKELEY: PART ONE

By 1880, Hartford had burgeoned into an industrial powerhouse. There were 800 manufactories churning out a prodigious variety of consumer goods. Hartford's work force, now 20,951 strong, brought home $8.45 million a year, amounting to an average annual income of more than $400.[1] The stunning variety of goods produced in Hartford made the city fairly unique, as single companies—Du Pont de Nemours in Wilmington, Delaware, for example—tended to dominate American cities.

Hartford's largest business, Colt's Patent Fire-Arms, produced the finest pistols and rifles money could buy and was the most prolific private armory in the world. During the Civil War, Colt's production peaked—only to slump once hostilities ceased. However, Colt's survived the temporary downturn and continued manufacturing firearms into the twenty-first century.[2]

Weed Sewing Machine Company ranked as the second-largest company in Hartford, producing their ubiquitous sewing machines. Beginning in 1878, this firm began manufacturing Col. Albert Pope's Columbia high-wheeled velocipede (a bicycle with a small wheel in back and a very big wheel in front). These "ordinaries" were treacherous beasts and not for the faint of heart. They required enormous skill to operate and caused so many problems in Hartford that the common council eventually forced velocipede proponents into indoor arenas. In 1891, Col. Pope bought out Weed and merged Weed Sewing Machine Company with Pope Manufacturing Company. The composite firm soon unveiled their Columbia Safety Bicycle, resembling the two-wheelers of six decades hence. With this new model, sales increased markedly, and by the time the bicycle craze hit its peak in 1896, there were 300 different manufacturers in the nation building 1.2 million bicycles a year. Pope Manufacturing Company wasn't always the largest bicycle maker in America, but Col. Pope's human-pedaled vehicles were never surpassed in quality.[3]

Pratt & Whitney, another successful Hartford manufactory, made precision machine tools. Not to be confused with the aircraft engine manufacturer, Francis Pratt and Amos Whitney—erstwhile Colt's machinists—combined forces in 1860 to incorporate this highly specialized business.

Hartford supported many other businesses: For industrial belting, there was none bigger or better in the world than Jewell Belting Company. It is believed that Samuel Colt introduced drop forgings to the United States, but Billings & Spenser brought the business to the level of an art form. Christopher Spencer invented the single-spindle automatic screw machine, and operated Hartford Machine Screw for George Fairfield, who was also president of Weed Sewing Machine. Hartford Woven Wire Mattress manufactured the first spring mattresses, and Plimpton Manufacturing Company ranked among the biggest office suppliers in the country, with government contracts augmenting its tremendous volume of commercial work.[4]

Hartford's biggest bookbinder, Case, Lockwood & Co. printed and bound dictionaries, schoolbooks, Bibles, as well as annual reports for hundreds of different companies. Morgan Bulkeley's brother-in-law, Leverett Brainard, became a partner in this firm and the name was changed to Case, Lockwood & Brainard in 1868.[5]

Due to this crush of industry, Hartford served as a prime destination for highly skilled craftsmen, native and foreign born, as these businesses combined to transform the city into an industrial Mecca. More than 500 steam vessels and 270 barges dumped thousands of tons of coal, lumber, iron, cement, lime, fertilizer, potatoes, and other commodities on Hartford's docks.[6] Meanwhile, Hartford had also become a financial center, with twenty major insurance companies and a like number of banks. By the nineteenth century, Hartford's financial clout, combined with its manufacturing prowess, turned it into one of the wealthiest cities per-capita in the country.[7]

Despite all of this industry and daily commerce, Hartford was a gorgeous city priding its residents with a forty-acre park in its center, boulevards lined with heavily bowered trees, and a large shopping district. The streets were watered four times a day—to damp the dust—and swept by city workers using push brooms. No less an authority than Mark Twain wrote of Hartford, "Of all the beautiful towns it has been my fortune to see, this is the chief . . . . Each house sits in the midst of about an acre of green grass, or flowerbeds or ornamental shrubbery . . . . You do not know what beauty is if you have not been here."[8]

During this period, life was good for all the Bulkeleys and Brainards of Washington Street. Their houses were full of domestic servants, cooks, and coachmen, and the families attended an endless whirlwind of political receptions and social gatherings.

Despite the familiar merriment, sibling rivalry persisted between Morgan and his younger brother, Billy. One might call it a genteel rivalry. They helped each other in their business ventures and in their political forays, and lived within close proximity all their lives. Yet they still maintained a healthy competitiveness. Perhaps this was possible because the two men had such completely different personalities, much like the tortoise and the hare.

Although he was more than two years younger than Morgan, Billy had been the first to enlist in the Civil War and had finagled a commission as captain when he re-upped. Not to be forgotten, Billy was the first to wed, marrying Emma Gurney a full twenty-two years before Morgan met and married Fannie Briggs Houghton of San Francisco.[9] Billy entered elective politics first, preceding Morgan's entry by several years. Of course, Billy returned to Hartford four years earlier than his older brother. While Morgan was serving on Brooklyn's Republican General Committee, Billy was reestablishing himself in Hartford and running for a seat on the common council.

That said, it was Morgan who stepped into his father's shoes at Aetna Life in 1879 and turned the company into the financial juggernaut it became. Along the way, Morgan reaped the benefits that the presidency of Aetna Life afforded, both at the local level and on the national stage. Billy was commissary general and lieutenant governor before he ran unsuccessfully for governor in 1882. It was Morgan who served four terms as Hartford's mayor, two-terms as governor of Connecticut, and then a term in the U.S. Senate. Billy was a fast starter, but it was Morgan who invariably won the biggest prizes.

Not surprisingly, history remembers Morgan best. Besides the aforementioned stadium, street, high school, bridge, and park, Bulkeley had an oil portrait of his majestic countenance on permanent display in the Capitol.[10]

Thanks to Bulkeley's two-pronged election strategy, the mayoral race of 1880 was not a replay of his 1878 loss. Charles R. Chapman got the Democratic nod, which inadvertently helped Bulkeley.[11]

Chapman, ten years Bulkeley's senior, hailed from one of the oldest families in Connecticut and had already served three terms as mayor—1866 to 1872. He acted as city attorney for three years and sat in both the upper and lower chambers of the General Assembly.[12] Thus, Bulkeley would be battling another lawyer with a fabulous résumé. However, Chapman personified the bitter partisan. For example, he refused a "charter amendment establishing a board of street commissioners, under which a superintendent shall be appointed and be able to do his work without partisan interference."[13] The Democrats should have stayed with George Sumner, who, in the eyes of the press, "administer[ed] the affairs of the city with becoming discretion, [and made] judicious appointments."[14] Instead, the Democratic bosses chose "a candidate who would stand the best chance of conciliating the 'bummers.' "[15]

Although Morgan Bulkeley was squeezed out of elective office for two years, he stayed involved by participating in Republican Town Committee and city ward working groups. That was the least of it. He also made sure that he was invited to every occasion of any importance. For instance, when the Knights of St. Patrick held their annual banquet at the Hotel Capitol, only a dozen non-Irish-American guests attended, and Morgan Bulkeley was one of them.[16]

Just as the political pundits called it, in the mayoral election of 1880, Morgan Bulkeley beat Charles R. Chapman in a walk. Chapman's record of bitter partisanship sat poorly with voters, and they gave him short shrift.[17]

As far as the overwhelmingly Democratic river wards were concerned, Bulkeley should have gotten very few votes. Together, the Fifth and Sixth Wards elected two aldermen and eight councilmen—all Democrats. Yet, Bulkeley eked out a win in the Fifth Ward and took 60 percent of the votes in the Sixth.[18]

Bulkeley didn't always win the river wards, but he got far more votes than he should have. His four triumphant mayoral campaigns in the 1880s revealed four opportunities to win the Fifth Ward and four to win the Sixth Ward. Bulkeley was successful only three out of the eight times. On average though, he always managed to get about 45 percent of the vote.

When he won both of the river wards in 1880, it caused him more trouble than it was worth. Straight-laced Republicans abandoned him. However, by disguising the vote buying—and losing the river wards by small margins—he was able to win back some of those precious Republican votes.

Mayoral races were sometimes very close—as was Bulkeley's 229-vote squeaker in 1882. Contrast that with the 1880 race—before honest Republicans realized Morgan bought votes—when Bulkeley won all eight wards and enjoyed a majority of 1,369.[19]

To understand how poorly the elections were run in the river wards, it is worth considering that men in the Fifth Ward voted at Engine House No. 3, which was located with reasonable neutrality at 124 Front Street (just north of State Street).[20] Meanwhile, in the Sixth Ward, ballot boxes were set up at Hezekiah Gaylord's grocery store on Front Street (corner of Morgan). Gaylord was a Democrat and represented the Sixth Ward at Democratic City Committee meetings, making his grocery store a poor place for a voting station.[21] Since Bulkeley took 60 percent of the Sixth Ward in 1880, one suspects that Hezekiah Gaylord might have helped for a price.

Gaylord had left Windsor for Hartford at eighteen to work in Nehemiah Rice's grocery store on the corner of Morgan and Front Streets. After some years, he bought Rice out. Because of the paltry incomes of the people in the river wards, the margins—and thus the profits—could not compare with grocers in slightly wealthier districts like those on Exchange Corner (State Street at Main) for example. Nevertheless, soon after Bulkeley's last mayoral campaign in 1886, Gaylord, then fifty-seven, retired to Girard Avenue, an affluent neighborhood just south of what later became Elizabeth Park, and idled away the last twenty-two years of his life.[22] Since retirement in the Gilded Age was an option only for the financially independent, one suspects Gaylord landed a lucrative deal with someone—perhaps Morgan Bulkeley.

Naturally, since the Democratic river wards went completely Republican, it attracted—to put it mildly—headlines. It would not even be outrageous to say that the election results beggared belief. The Hartford Daily Courant, however, seemed unaware of these earth-shaking changes in long-standing voting patterns.[23] The Hartford Daily Times, conversely, more than made up for the Courant's embarrassing silence by writing, "The opening of the purse strings to the extent of $8,000 to secure this one election . . . is something for Republicans themselves to consider. It is inconsistent for honest men . . . to give their support to a ticket, which originates in and is supported wholly by Tweedism."[24] Nor did they let it go at that. In the days ahead, they chided, "There has been shameless purchase of votes at the polls. The men were followed to the ballot boxes by the [men] employed to bribe them, and then taken to . . . some other place [to be] paid for selling their votes. . . . Some of the purchased men peddled tickets with Morgan G. Bulkeley's name at the head, followed by Democratic names for other city offices."[25] And what was the result of all this tub-thumping? Absolutely nothing, except to waste a bunch of newsprint. Few people cared and Morgan Bulkeley became mayor.

By this time, members of the Connecticut General Assembly were ensconced in the new Capitol, and city hall had been relocated to the old State House building in what would later be called City Hall Square. In the very chambers where he had, in his youth, watched his father debate issues and hold court as Speaker of the House, Mayor Bulkeley now ran the city. Typically, the mayors of Connecticut's largest cities were paid $1,000 annually and Bulkeley was paid roughly the same.[26] This was a pittance compared to his Aetna Life compensation. Just after the turn of the century, the heads of Hartford's largest insurance companies were paid $30,000 a year.[27] A quick comparison of dry goods and commodity prices fixes Bulkeley's 1880 annual salary to about $20,000—while the average worker in one of the city's many manufactories was making $400.[28] As one can imagine, giving away his mayoral salary to charities and other worthy causes imposed no hardship on the new mayor.

Even though Bulkeley had been living and working in Hartford for the past eight years, when he became mayor in 1880, it was as if he had sprung full-blown from the brow of Mercury. With an astounding energy level and the money to do things right, he was especially good at making the office his own. The fact that he was still single afforded him time in the evenings and on weekends to attend political gatherings, parades, veterans' reunions, and social affairs. As the president of Aetna Life, Morgan allowed plenty of time to attend city functions at all hours.

One fine morning, the mayor and a few other gentlemen, including Hartford's water commissioner, Edward Murphy, crowded into Morgan's carriage, and asked Dan Wallace to drive them out to Hartford Water Works' new Reservoir No. 4 in Farmington (later Batterson Park).[29] This reservoir was about half full, but upon completion it would hold 600 million gallons, more than the other three reservoirs at Trout Brook combined.[30]

Edward Murphy acted as interim president of the Board of Water Commissioners, really only taking up space until Ezra Clark, erstwhile Board of Water Commissioners president, could once again be favored by the caprice of the electorate. Bulkeley had mixed feelings about Murphy because he had been the secretary and treasurer of Hartford Foundry, a firm that had thrust the city into a water famine in September 1873 with its inexplicably poor performance on a contract for new pumps at the Connecticut River Pumping Station. Because of its elevation, one of the first areas of the city to lose drinking water was Washington Street.[31]

For the same reason, Bulkeley had misgivings about Ezra Clark as well. This may have been unfair, because it had been Clark's predecessor, Hiram Bissell, who gave the contract to Hunter & Sanford, the forerunner of Hartford Foundry. Clark, the proverbial man in the wrong place at the wrong time, did everything he could to exact a performance from John Hunter, Edwin Sanford, and Edward Murphy—to no avail.[32]

Some others matters about Clark must be considered. In the parlance of the old merchant-banker class, Ezra Clark—although a Congregationalist and a Whig (later a Republican)—was considered a "commoner," born in Brattleboro, Vermont, without serious wealth or higher education. In addition, Bulkeley considered himself first, last, and always a conservative Republican, but Ezra Clark operated more as a middle-of-the-road man. During one dispute with his fellow party members in 1854, Clark ran for Congress on the controversial American (Know-Nothing) Party ticket—and won.[33] Although Bulkeley bolted on fellow party members at times, he held others to a higher standard and disapproved of Clark's actions in 1854.

Clark had one last strike against him. Twenty years earlier, as a result of signing some notes for a friend who later defaulted, Clark was forced to declare bankruptcy. He was such an honorable man that he paid back all of his discharged debts in full, and with interest![34] But failure was failure in Bulkeley's eyes, and this gave him one more reason to dislike Clark.

When voters turned on the Republicans, Ezra Clark found himself on the street too, but people generally liked Clark. He was a very courteous man and a first-rate water commissioner, regularly delivering clean, potable water. For this reason, Bulkeley forced himself to get along with Clark, although he didn't try very hard to hide his true feelings. Ultimately, Morgan Bulkeley would live to regret his harsh words toward Ezra Clark at council meetings.

In the same vein, Bulkeley had to find a way to get along with Francis Goodwin. It seems all politicians have a Brutus they must find a way to pigeonhole, and for Bulkeley, it was Francis Goodwin.

James M. Goodwin's sons, James J. and Francis, were chips off the old block, as they were hardnosed capitalists like their father. James J. had little to do with Hartford over the years, inasmuch as he worked in New York with his cousin, J. P. Morgan. Conversely, Francis remained in Hartford and helped his father with the family's real estate empire.[35]

Neither of the two brothers had served in the Civil War, undoubtedly one of the reasons why Bulkeley didn't like the Goodwins. Avoidance of service might not have been so meaningful if Morgan's brother Charlie had not died in uniform.

The older Goodwin brother, James J., worked in J. P. Morgan's financial house during the Civil War. J. P. Morgan paid a substitute to take his own place in the war and James J. Goodwin probably did the same.[36] In a city the size of New York, such a move would have gone completely unnoticed. Francis Goodwin had a different problem because he had chosen to stay in Hartford, where people knew almost everything about their neighbors. Not to worry. A few months before the shelling of Fort Sumter, Francis Goodwin suddenly had a religious calling and enrolled in the Berkeley Divinity School in Middletown.[37] This gave him a deferment for the duration of the war. The Goodwin genealogy is conspicuous for its lack of clerics. Family members were typically farmers, tavern-keepers, tailors, cabinetmakers, saddlers, sea captains, coffee importers, and real estate speculators.[38]

Bulkeley had another reason to dislike Francis Goodwin. His degrees—at least the ones received after he graduated from Berkeley Divinity School—were suspect. For example, Goodwin left divinity school in May 1863 and was awarded a master of arts degree by Trinity College in July of the same year. Since he got married and honeymooned in that same two-month period, how much work could he possibly have done to earn this master's degree? In June 1902, while Francis was a trustee of the school, Trinity recognized him with an honorary doctor of divinity degree and he was thereafter referred to as the Rev. Dr. Francis Goodwin.[39]

When it came time for Goodwin to actually take the pulpit in May 1866, he became rector of Trinity Church on Sigourney Street in Hartford. Yet in 1871, at the age of thirty-one, he resigned "because of a weak heart, but somehow managed to do the work of ten healthy men for the rest of his life."[40] He was always called Rev. Goodwin, or later, Rev. Dr. Goodwin, even though he only performed just enough masses, weddings, and funerals to give the title credence.

The reality in 1880 was that Goodwin was devoting almost all his time to the family's real estate interests. Apart from this, or rather because of it, he was intensely interested in the city's park system and spent time persuading elderly friends to leave their estates to the city. Goodwin was good at it too, for he could talk a starving dog off a meat wagon.[41] The parks, of course, were merely a way to boost the value of the Goodwins' building lots. Francis Goodwin could fairly be described as the poster child for enlightened self-interest.

Fortunately for Bulkeley, Goodwin couldn't be bothered with elective office. He may have thought it unseemly for a man of the cloth to sit on the common council, or perhaps he just didn't want to waste energy on something he perceived lesser men could do for him. Whatever the reason, it was good news for Bulkeley, making it easier to pigeonhole the man.

Goodwin fancied himself as very creative. It was said he drew the plans for his father's Anglo-Norman Castle at the northwest corner of Asylum and Woodland Streets. In reality, the plans "were made by a thorough student of the antique, the beautiful and the practical, and who had carte blanche to make all perfect without restrictions as to cost." The New York architect Frederick C. Withers, in fact, planned the home.[42] Francis Goodwin may have had some input, but to say that he designed the dwelling—without any architectural training—is a bit fanciful.

Goodwin also thought he knew quite a bit about landscape architecture. This delusion took wing because he knew Hartford native Frederick Law Olmsted, considered the father of landscape architecture in the Unites States. Olmsted was seventeen years older than Goodwin. Somewhere along the way the two had talked informally about a few "park ideas" for Hartford. It was Olmstead who told the city to hire the Swiss-born architect, engineer, and landscape designer Jacob Weidenmann, to plan the city's central park—later renamed Bushnell Park.[43]

With real estate all over the city and hundreds of building lots to sell, Francis Goodwin developed a self-interest in making the city more attractive and family friendly. Logically, he could do that best by heading the city's Parks Commission, which Bulkeley readily agreed to. Even though Bulkeley didn't like or trust Goodwin, he was a force to reckon with because of the Goodwins' vast wealth and real estate holdings. Francis Goodwin and his wife, Mary, had seven children by this time, and would have another child in 1884, so the family would be a permanent fixture in Hartford for the remainder of Bulkeley's life—and probably far beyond.[44]

On the flip side, as Morgan Bulkeley's political power grew, Francis Goodwin practiced affording Bulkeley a wide berth.[45] It was not uncommon to see both men at any number of functions—Republican Committee meetings, sessions of the General Assembly, governor's balls, funerals of friends—but they rarely stood together. And then, of course, there was Fenwick, where three cottages separated their waterfront homes. Nevertheless, the distrust between the two men was palpable.

～ Morgan Bulkeley once said, "speaking from personal experience . . . the position of mayor of Hartford [is] more attractive than even that of governor."[46] Maybe so, but it didn't stop him from making the necessary moves to rise higher in politics in 1880. After he and his cousin Frank Bulkeley visited Hartford City Coal in West Virginia—one of the Judge's old business interests—they traveled to Chicago in time for the Republican National Convention.[47] The narrow escape from a Democratic president in 1876 and the loss of both congressional houses were blamed on Rutherford Hayes, a bumbling president in the eyes of many Republicans. The thrust of the whole 1880 convention was to make sure the Republicans were better represented the next time around. Many favored the idea of Ulysses Grant running for a third term after four years out of office, but this gained no traction. All told, it took six days and thirty-six ballots before James Garfield was finally chosen as the party's standard-bearer.[48]

A few weeks later, colored fires and torches brightly illuminated Washington Street in the vicinity of Mayor Bulkeley's house, where 3,000 people gathered to congratulate Billy Bulkeley on his nomination for lieutenant governor.[49] Weed's band played while the Bulkeleys' parlors filled with guests. Gen. Hawley, a congressman at the time and always a garrulous visitor, announced, "I'm happy that the Republicans [are] doing so well. I have known [James] Garfield in Congress and out, and respect him deeply. To use an old slang expression from the western steamboats, Garfield is 'a man you can drink with in the dark.' "[50] Mayor Bulkeley followed up with a few eminently forgettable remarks of his own. Hawley was a tough act to follow.

One of the hallmarks of Morgan Bulkeley's political life was his ability to take something that already existed, improve it, and make it his own. Such was the case with what the city indelicately called, "The Excursion for the Poor of Hartford." Beginning two years before Bulkeley took office, the city decided to hold a summer excursion for Hartford's poor children. In 1878, about 100 urchins rode down the river on a steamboat, and the following year, the city crammed almost 1,000 kids onto a Valley Railroad train that brought them to Fenwick Grove for a swim and a clambake. These junkets marked the highpoint of the year for Hartford's inner-city kids.[51]

The city's charities expected this to be paid for by donations dropped in collection boxes around town. However, the city's wealthiest families were off on vacation at the very time these donations were needed, and the collection boxes remained disappointingly light.

Mayor Bulkeley had a better idea. He would pay for "the Excursion" out of his own pocket. This eliminated the problem of scrambling for donations and benefited him far more than $500 dollars worth of good will. Maj. Woods of the YMCA acted as general manager of the whole affair, and Frank Oakes, the proprietor of the Oakes' Place, a boarding house at Fenwick, took responsibility for serving a memorable meal to a thousand inner-city children and their chaperones.[52] Among invited dignitaries, Mayor Bulkeley included a local physician, Dr. Knight, who traveled along in a professional capacity. The doctor "had four patients on the trip down and applied lively doses of Williams's Jamaica ginger, two quarts of which were sent by the manufacturers for the purpose."[53]

Sure enough, early on the morning of Saturday, August 30, 1880, a band of 250 newsboys, shoeshiners, and other poor boys assembled on Main Street near the YMCA. From there, they marched to the mayor's office at City Hall. Bulkeley and an assortment of councilmen and aldermen joined the boys and whistled their way down to the State Street Depot where a special train was already half-filled with young girls and women. When the boys crowded onto the train, there were so many of them that they had to sit five to a seat. Bulkeley squeezed in too, and rode the train to Fenwick with the kids.[54]

The trip to Fenwick meant so much to Hartford's poor, that there were even "several cripples and aged or unfortunate men and women from the hospital of the town house [almshouse]."[55]

At eight o'clock, the train finally chuffed and snorted its way out of the station and was quickly up to speed. When it arrived at Fenwick two hours later, Mayor Bulkeley gave a quick explanation of the facilities and turned everyone loose. Just before noon, 500 women and girls were served dinner—clam chowder, oyster stew, blue fish, clam fritters, and young lobsters. When the women were done, the men and boys were fed. In the afternoon, the children played on the swings and walked around the grove. From two o'clock on, they swam in the cove, with the girls changing in the bathhouses and the boys just stripping down on the beach.[56]

By 7 p.m., it was time to go home. There were all sorts of problems reloading the train—inaccurate headcounts, lost clothing, and special situations—so they didn't start back until 9:30 p.m. A snack of sandwiches, donuts, and milk was served on the train, and everyone returned to the State Street Depot by 11 p.m. Mayor Bulkeley traveled with the poor kids only as far north as Essex, where Dan Wallace and his carriage waited to return him to Fenwick.[57]

Mayor Bulkeley's "Excursion for Hartford's Poor" lasted for only a few years. In 1883, bad weather forced Bulkeley to push the trip to the second week in September, when few children were able to attend. The following year, he was so busy chasing his future bride around Europe that the trip never materialized. Soon, it was a no more than a dream remembered.

Obviously, Bulkeley used the city's poor kids for his own political purposes. One way or another, he had to explain his popularity in the river wards, to clarify the amazing new voting patterns, and to demonstrate why the Fifth and Sixth Wards were so amenable to Morgan Bulkeley's reign as mayor.

In fairness, a considerably more complex problem doomed the excursion. The average person, much less a wealthy first-time mayor, does not always appreciate the specialized nature of charity work. These inner-city kids were poor—diphtheria and tuberculosis poor—and they each had special needs. The idea of cramming them like baggage onto a train bound for Fenwick Grove wasn't terribly realistic. Even Hartford's longtime social workers, like Miss Josephine Griswold and Mrs. Virginia Thrall Smith of the City Mission Society, never took more than 125 kids at a time when they traveled to Sunrise Cottage, Bartlett's Tower, White Oaks Grove, Cottage Grove, Rainbow Park, or any of the other facilities available to the charity.[58]

~~~ Each September, Mayor Bulkeley attended a Union Veterans meeting at Whittlesey's Hall in Hartford.[59] The Civil War was the defining event for many generations of Americans. Not counting the huge celebrations on Veterans Day, the Fourth of July, and Battle Flag Day, it would be almost impossible to catalog all of the different associations, reunions, and meetings held annually thereafter. Morgan Bulkeley traveled widely just to meet other veterans and to march in their parades—good politics, and a kick for the proud soldier from Brooklyn's Thirteenth Regiment.

~~~ While Connecticut's fall colors ascended to their mid-October peak in 1880, word got around that Gen. Ulysses Grant intended to make a brief stop in Hartford on his way from Boston to New York.[60] Grant was the nation's First Soldier and a former u.s. president, but Hartford rarely encountered trouble enticing important people like Grant to visit. Men running for higher office depended on East Coast money to finance their campaigns. Owing to its fabulous wealth, Hartford's citizens—including Morgan Bulkeley—gave enormous sums toward these elections.[61]

After receiving word of Grant's proposed visit, Mayor Bulkeley and his staff quickly made plans whereby they would escort Grant to Hartford. Together with

Sam Clemens and a few other men, Bulkeley left Hartford for Boston on the afternoon of Friday, October 15.[62]

The following morning, a special train of palace cars left Boston carrying Gen. Grant, his family and staff, and all of the principal characters of the Hartford welcoming committee. At Putnam, crowds waited to see Grant, and a few dignitaries boarded the train. At Willimantic, an even larger throng waited to see the general, and an even bigger pile of dignitaries hopped aboard, including Gen. Joe Hawley, former governor Marshall Jewell, Samuel Dunham of Willimantic Linen, Charles Dudley Warner of the *Courant*, James Batterson of Travelers Insurance, and at least a dozen others.[63]

Gen. Grant, and his ever-increasing entourage arrived at Union Station a little before noon, and thousands of spectators gave them a rousing welcome. An elegant barouche drawn by four magnificent horses quickly whisked the general and his party off to the Allyn House (hotel and popular Republican Party hangout) for lunch. Meanwhile 20,000 people waited expectantly in Bushnell Park. After a suitable repast, Grant boarded his carriage and, accompanied by James Batterson and Gen. Joe Hawley, traversed the city to greet the crowd at the park.[64]

On a reviewing stand at the corner of Elm and Trinity Streets (facing the Capitol), James Batterson, Gen. Hawley, and Sam Clemens gave speeches before the massive assembly on the hillside. Then Grant delivered a short speech to thunderous applause. (Bear in mind, Sam Clemens's publishing house, Webster & Co., aspired to issue Grant's memoirs, which they did in 1886 to marvelous reviews.)[65]

Later, Grant and his party, along with the most important dignitaries present, drove to the elegant home of James G. Batterson on Albany Avenue for dinner. The guests spent considerable time milling about Batterson's parlors, admiring his large collection of paintings and his huge library—the largest private library in Hartford. Then they dined in casual comfort until around eight o'clock when they were expected on Washington Street at the home of Billy Bulkeley, candidate for lieutenant governor. Never before had the City of Hartford been so fabulously decorated. People jammed tightly into the streets, and Grant's carriage had trouble getting through. Thanks to Billy and Emma Bulkeley's thoughtfulness, more Hartford citizens and Civil War veterans got to meet Gen. Grant than anyone could possibly have imagined. For his part, Grant was graciousness personified.[66]

At about ten in the evening, preparations got underway to return Gen. Grant and his party to Union Station. Civil War veterans, their families, and spectators of all ages lined the general's route. Torchlights, Roman candles, fireworks, and electric lights lit the way to the depot. With Mayor Bulkeley and a half-dozen other dignitaries on board, Gen. Grant and his family finally left Union Station at 10:30 P.M. bound for New York.[67]

Grant's visit excited Hartford's inhabitants so much that people must have had a hard time returning to their everyday activities. The visit was certainly the highpoint of Mayor Bulkeley's first term in office, what with newspaper reporters writing glowing articles about his city's hospitality toward the country's First Soldier and former president—heady stuff for the forty-two-year-old mayor.

After Gen. Grant materialized safely in New York, the people of Hartford presented Bulkeley with a less sanguine chore. His schizophrenic sentiment with his constituents could rear its ugly head now and then, and this was one of those occasions. The Hartford and Wethersfield Horse Railroad Company wanted to extend service to the people in the southwestern corner of the city by laying tracks down Washington Street—directly in front of Morgan Bulkeley's home.[68] At a December meeting of the city's aldermen, the pros and cons of this petition were heard. Bulkeley and the city's aldermen never used the horse cars, but had to tread lightly because of the thousands of voters who depended on the smelly, unheated trolleys to get back and forth to work. It was for this reason that Bulkeley chose to express his opposition to the Washington Street route in the semiprivacy of the aldermen's chambers, where his remarks might not gain wide exposure.

In short, the mayor did not want the unwashed masses trundling by his home every hour on the hour, which constituted the proposed schedule. Accordingly, he gave an impassioned plea to have the horse cars use Lafayette Street—fifty yards to the west—instead. Contrarily, when the mayor's wealthy friends used Washington Street for sleigh races in the wintertime, nothing could have pleased him more.

By May of the following year, the principals of the Hartford and Wethersfield Horse Car Company realized that they had hit a brick wall at city hall—Morgan Bulkeley.[69] Unless they could accommodate him, they wouldn't be laying tracks anywhere. Sure enough, when the horse car company finally got the green light, Washington Street was spared. The tracks ran on Lafayette Street behind Mary Brainard's house.[70]

Between the city's business, the never-ending meetings of the common council, Civil War reunions, military parades, and campfires, together with attending as many Republican meetings as possible—both in Connecticut and as far away as San Francisco—it's a wonder that Bulkeley was able to manage so much. And this doesn't even address his responsibilities as president of Aetna Life. While Aetna was advancing slowly at the time of Judge Bulkeley's death, the pace had picked up considerably. Aetna Life's total assets in 1872 were around

$13 million and, in the intervening eight years, they had doubled.[71] How was Bulkeley able to do so much?

Bulkeley knew how to delegate. He knew how to break a job into small pieces and assign the work accordingly. Without any worries that he might not be doing enough himself, Bulkeley diced up projects and doled out work to others. Just as with the "Excursion of Hartford's Poor," all he had to do was make a few decisions and then leave the heavy lifting to others. Bulkeley surrounded himself with the most talented people he could find and then simply got out of the way. Effectively, good decision making became the sum and substance of his work.

In politics especially, Bulkeley attracted some incredibly talented organizers and election assistants. Besides the corpulent—and exceedingly useful—Gideon Winslow, he had the good fortune to win the loyalty of another immigrant, Pat McGovern. By dint of his ancestry, Patrick McGovern, was the least likely man to ever rub shoulders with Morgan Bulkeley, yet the two became inseparable in political matters.

McGovern was born in County Cavan, Ireland, in October 1849—one of fourteen McGovern children—birthed smack in the middle of the Great Famine. By some miracle, his family got through the famine, but Pat left for America when he was fifteen years old anyway. In the steerage section of an ocean steamer, he met some Hartford-bound Irishmen from Tipperary and decided to tag along with them.[72]

Upon arriving in Hartford, McGovern first went to work for Colt's. Generally, an Irish immigrant without much education was destined to live in the river wards, work as a laborer, and vote Democratic. McGovern got lucky, though. He caught the eye of Hugh and Alexander Harbison and quickly joined their grocery firm as a clerk. McGovern had a skimpy education but was an absolute whiz with figures. His idea of fun was to spend the evening playing games with numbers, which he did all his life. Pat started with Harbison Brothers at twelve dollars a week, and in no time advanced to almost thirty-five dollars—making him the highest paid clerk in the city. His skill with numbers was so extraordinary that an actuary from Connecticut Mutual Life hired him within moments of their first meeting.[73]

Then McGovern met Morgan Bulkeley. The two had been on the common council in the 1870s, so they had a passing friendship. In July 1879, Bulkeley just walked into McGovern's office at Connecticut Mutual and said, "Get your hat and coat and come for a ride with me."[74] McGovern protested, saying he wasn't with Aetna Life, and besides, he had work to do. "Tell them to go to hell," Bulkeley said, "I've just been made president of Aetna Life today and I want you to come with me."[75]

McGovern didn't hesitate again. He went to work for Morgan Bulkeley at

Aetna Life—and in the political trenches—securing his own future in the process. Many times in later life, Pat credited his extraordinary financial successes to Morgan Bulkeley. (On the eve of the 1929 stock market crash, McGovern was worth $30 million.)[76]

An Irish immigrant who joined the wealthy Republicans would usually be shunned, but McGovern had an easy charm and was never an object of scorn. He lived on Buckingham Street in the Third Ward, which bordered the river wards, and was helpful to Bulkeley on many levels. First, having the Irishman at his side was good for Bulkeley's image in the Irish wards. How could the immigrants accuse him of giving them the "high hat" if he was joined at the-hip with one of their own? Secondly, Gideon Winslow ran the food end of the food-for-votes scheme, but Bulkeley badly needed men who could go down into the river wards to ferret out the purchasable votes, and more important, to recruit poll operatives. Pat McGovern was one of these men. This strong-willed Irishman could travel freely in the densely populated Irish wards without attracting attention. Lastly, McGovern was a powerful presence in his own Buckingham Street neighborhood and faithfully delivered the Third Ward to the Republicans.

McGovern eventually became the Republican Town Committee boss, but was considered a little too uppity by the far right of the party. For that reason, he was never nominated for mayor, although he longed for the job. In August of 1902, his wife, Vitaline, died suddenly at forty-eight.[77] As a token of their respect for a friend in pain, the Republicans nominated him for the state Senate and the red-faced, balding Irishman was elected. Still, McGovern never gave up on his city hall dream. Try as he did though, and even with Morgan Bulkeley's help, he just couldn't make it happen. There were men in the party who did not want Pat McGovern running Hartford.

McGovern eventually remarried and bought his new wife, Julia, a house located just a few doors away from the Bulkeleys on Washington Street (corner of Park).[78] The two men remained close political friends almost to the end of their lives. Even as the Democrats managed to increase their voting base each year, it was Pat McGovern who kept the city in Republican hands.

〜 While the Bulkeley political machine increased its prehensile grasp on the Charter Oak City, Morgan Bulkeley amused himself with the distractions of the Gilded Age. All things related to the new field of electricity fascinated him. In the first week of February 1881, A. C. Dunham, led the Arkwright Club of Boston on a tour of Willimantic Linen—now completely wired with electric lights. Arkwright Club membership consisted of treasurers and agents for textile mills owned by the Everetts, Lowells, and Saltonstalls. The mills in question were household names at the time—Pepperill, Laconia, Merrimac, Great Falls, and Amoskeag.[79]

Governor Bigelow, Lt. Governor Billy Bulkeley, ex-Governor Marshall Jewell, Mayor Morgan Bulkeley, Sam Clemens, Rev. Joe Twichell, and many others took the train from Hartford to Willimantic to join this group of visiting dignitaries.[80]

Bulkeley and Clemens had known each other since the humorist first came to Hartford, as he attended many of the Hartford Dark Blues' baseball games when Bulkeley owned the team. Their paths crossed regularly at The Hartford Club, where both men were members during the two decades that Clemens lived in Hartford. However, it is unlikely that Bulkeley read even a single book by Clemens, because he just wasn't a reader. He read newspapers, but everything else bored him.[81]

It seems unlikely that Morgan Bulkeley could warm up to the author of *The Gilded Age*, Clemens's satirical look at politics in the second half of the nineteenth century. But the graft, materialism, and corruption detailed in the book would mean nothing to Bulkeley anyway, since Bulkeley probably never even looked at the book. Even if he did, the book was published in 1873 before Bulkeley even became a councilman, so he would be safe in assuming he wasn't Clemens's satirical inspiration. Besides, it was common knowledge at the time that Clemens based the thoroughly corrupt Senator Abner Dilworthy on Senator Samuel Pomeroy of Kansas, and given the age difference, Bulkeley probably didn't even know Pomeroy.[82]

Like Bulkeley, Clemens was fascinated with new technology. He was delighted with the complex manufactories in and around Hartford and wrote humorous pieces about his visits to them. Sam toured Colt's Patent Fire-Arms in 1868, just before he moved to Hartford, and wrote in *Alta California* magazine, "On every floor is a dense wilderness of strange iron machines . . . a tangled forest of rods, bars, pulleys, wheels, and all the imaginable and unimaginable forms of mechanism."[83] He was completely taken by the whirring machines and the whole mesmerizing world of manufacturing. Perhaps the real reason Clemens was so interested in technology was that he was a great speculator, constantly on the lookout for the one big invention to make him rich beyond the dreams of avarice. Was the electric light his own personal El Dorado?

When the men from Hartford arrived at Dunham's textile mills, they were ushered into the plant's library, where they met the men from Boston. After exchanging pleasantries, they all sat down to a nice lunch catered by Merrill's Café of Central Row in City Hall Square. They then toured the mill, staying until about six o'clock when the lights came on. After witnessing the miracle of electric light, writ large, they repaired to the library for another sumptuous feast.[84]

～ While Morgan Bulkeley was busy with his new responsibilities at Aetna Life and about to begin his second year as mayor of Hartford, he wrought one of his most impressive coups—the creation of Hartford Electric Light Company. The General Assembly granted the charter for Hartford Electric Light in the spring of 1881, but of course the labyrinthine persuasions and maneuverings engaged a considerable swath of time.[85]

Hartford's oldest utility was the Hartford Gas Light Company, in operation since 1849. Because it supplied all of the city's street lighting, it seemed logical to some that the gas company would become the producer and distributor of electricity.[86] The use of electricity was still a novelty all over the United States. By the middle of 1881, the lobby of Hartford's Allyn House was electrically lit. A little later, a single arc light was hung outside the American Theatre, a variety house on Market Street. But that was it.[87]

A number of different electric companies desperately tried to persuade the common council to allow electric poles and overhead wiring throughout the city. For their part, the members of the council were not easily won over to electric wires dangling above the streets, and naturally the gas company was bitterly opposed to any changes for obvious reasons.[88]

Still, Morgan Bulkeley was one of the men who thought the electric franchise should be in the hands of a single utility. It was with this in mind that he championed Hartford Electric Light Company and did what he could to thwart the efforts of its would-be competitors. One such rival was ex-mayor George Sumner—Bulkeley's old opponent in the mayoral election of 1878—who organized Capital City Electric Light Company.[89]

Bulkeley really had his work cut out for him, but in short order he (1) had his friends at the Capitol refuse to grant a charter to George Sumner's Capital City Electric Light Company, (2) convinced the principals of Hartford Steam Heating Company and Hartford Gas Light Company to drop their petitions to supply electricity to the city, and (3) got everyone aboard the Hartford Electric Light Company bandwagon. The details of this scheme are not important, but the fact Bulkeley was able to pull it off is. His ability to persuade others to do things his way was astounding. Sure enough, on April 12, 1881, the state legislature awarded a charter to Hartford Electric Light Company.[90]

Nevertheless, the individual incorporators of the new utility had their own businesses to run and spared no time for this new venture. As long as the franchise was secure, there wasn't any pressure to get the company up and running. Thus, the charter for the new electric company sat in a safe deposit box at the Connecticut Trust and Safe Deposit Company on Main Street for the next nine months.[91]

It probably would have sat there much longer if American Lighting Company hadn't forced the issue. American Lighting was like a mosquito that wouldn't go away, constantly trying to expand in the new business of providing electricity.

With Bulkeley and his Republican friends running City Hall, every single attempt by American Lighting Company to install street poles, wires, and lights met with defeat. Nonetheless, pressure was building on the incorporators of Hartford Electric Light Company to do something, and finally they were forced to act.[92]

A. C. Dunham took charge. He turned everything at Willimantic Linen over to his brother Samuel—now an Aetna Life director—in order to assume the presidency of the nascent electric company. Dunham accepted it as the full-time job it was, but the utility still got off to a painfully slow start.[93]

The charter awarded by the General Assembly had designated George Gilman, Henry Judd, and Sylvester Dunham (A. C. Dunham's distant cousin) as commissioners to receive subscriptions to the capital stock and to call the first meeting of the shareholders. On January 12, 1882, these men opened the subscription books for Hartford Electric Light Company and Morgan Bulkeley quickly subscribed to 60 shares at $100 apiece, ostensibly acting on behalf of several banks and insurance companies. The original incorporators taken together only subscribed to another 60 shares. Meanwhile, American Electric Company, who had practically done cartwheels at council meetings for the right to put up poles and string wires in the city, took 200 shares. When one considers that electric utilities in other cities were capitalized to the tune of $1 million or more, this initial $32,000 was embarrassingly small.[94]

At the company's first official meeting, Morgan Bulkeley was elected to preside over matters, while Sylvester Dunham—Hartford's city attorney at the time—acted as secretary. When they elected their board of directors, Mayor Bulkeley was excluded so as to remove the suspicion of conflict of interest. These conflicts were as common as cabbage during the second half of the nineteenth century, and businessmen usually didn't go to extremes to hide them. In this case though, Morgan Bulkeley, perhaps because of his other dubious political activities, did.[95]

By June 1881, Mayor Bulkeley recommended fun matters by chairing the planning sessions for a huge reunion of the Civil War veterans of the Army of the Potomac. Gen. William Tecumseh Sherman was scheduled to review the troops in Hartford on June 8, 1881. Following the parade and celebration in Hartford, Sherman hastily left for West Point, where he was expected the following day at the United States Military Academy graduation ceremonies. Morgan Bulkeley became close friends with all of the most important generals of the Civil War as the Grand Army of the Republic held regular reunions, encampments, parades and campfires.[96]

The mention of Gen. Sherman brings up a funny story. Like Bulkeley, Sherman was a horse lover, so one year the mayor brought the general to the National Trotting Association gathering at the Murray Hill Hotel in New York. Naturally, Sherman was asked to say a few words. At the time, Bulkeley was actively seeking the National Commandery of the Grand Army of the Republic. In the course of the general's remarks, he looked at his friend and said, "What uplifts the spirit [is] that each of you exemplifies the fact that being an American is to be self-forgetful, self-assessing. . . .Your Vice-President [Bulkeley]—I speak from long affectionate acquaintance—reaches the utmost ideal. Can any man think of Bulkeley as a seeker of self-glorification? Impossible!"[97]

Bulkeley turned beet red and smiled sheepishly as applause filled the room. He then slipped out of the hall and sent a telegram back to Hartford's Grand Army Post, "Cut my name out. Let's get busy, all of us for the Order, not for the man."[98]

On September 19, 1881, President Garfield—who had been shot in July by disgruntled attorney, Charles Guiteau—passed away. In the summer, Garfield reposed at the New Jersey shore away from Washington's oppressive heat. At first, the move invigorated the president, but he later died from an infection and internal hemorrhaging.[99]

When he heard of Garfield's death, Mayor Bulkeley quickly called Hartford's clergymen to his office at City Hall to arrange for memorial services. Sixteen clerics and rabbis from all of the city's major houses of worship showed up, although the Courant mentions no one from Rev. Francis Goodwin's Trinity Episcopal Church on Sigourney Street. Apparently, Goodwin himself was not there either. Francis Goodwin would crawl on his belly over broken glass for a dollar, but he wouldn't travel a few blocks to honor a fallen president—not even a Republican one.[100]

Bulkeley and the clerics agreed on an orchestrated program for the day. Public offices would be closed and bells would toll for one hour beginning at 2 P.M. Religious services in places of worship would commence at 2 P.M. and continue for an hour. Then the bells would toll again from 4 to 4:30 P.M., during which time a presidential salute of twenty-one guns would be fired.[101]

Lastly, Mayor Bulkeley, Alderman Henry Taintor (another Bulkeley relative), and Councilmen Frank Kellogg and John Brocklesby would leave on Saturday night for the funeral in Cleveland Ohio.[102]

Deeper into in the fall of 1881, Mayor Bulkeley departed the city for some more fun, as he and Maj. William Barrows, the treasurer at Willimantic Linen Company, attended a big military gathering in Atlanta.[103] Connecticut's governor, Hobart Bigelow, and his staff took part too. Governor Bigelow was one of Connecticut's most forgettable chief executives, even claiming in his inaugural address that he saw "very little to criticize in [the state's] affairs, much to praise in all the state's institutions, and very few changes to recommend." The keynote of the whole address was to "Leave well enough alone."[104] One out-of-town newspaper called Bigelow "the thinnest and weakest governor Connecticut has had in years."[105] The only bright spot in an otherwise lackluster two-year term was Bigelow's signature on a bill in 1881, creating the Storrs Agricultural School (later the University of Connecticut).[106] True, Bulkeley knew how to have fun, but these short interludes didn't last long due to Hartford's vibrancy.

A little after two in the morning on January 24, 1882, a fire broke out in the furnace room at Hartford High School on Hopkins Street—a quarter mile south-west of Union Station. In no time at all, the whole building was in flames. A general alarm was sounded and firemen fought the blaze all night long.[107] Mayor Bulkeley got to the fire during the night, but first made arrangements with the Park Central Hotel to keep plenty of coffee, food, and other comforts coming to the exhausted firemen, as they in turn kept a dozen fire hoses on the burning building. The temperature was ten below zero, and some of the firemen suffered frostbitten fingers.[108]

The building opened to 450 students in December 1869 and an addition was added ten years later in order to house an extra 150, but now it accounted for a total loss. This was a situation the city could not abide for long. Sure enough, only a few weeks after the fire, the common council voted to spend $200,000 to build the new high school.[109]

≥ Mayor Bulkeley's reelection in April 1882 was a bit of a letdown after his victory in 1880, but it did bring to light one worrisome development. Bulkeley's vote count suffered from opposition in the Republican wards with his majority reduced far below the numbers he enjoyed two years earlier. Of course, his vote buying was common knowledge by 1882, and many Republicans of integrity refused to vote for him. This was especially true of the Nook Farm crowd, virtually all of whom were related to clerics.[110] Bulkeley had something to think about before the next election rolled around. Still, he had a Republican majority among the aldermen and councilmen, so he could expect clear sailing for the next two years.[111]

True, this election was a bit on the dull side, but it did have its moments. Once again, the *Courant* was embarrassingly silent on the irregularities at the polls, while the *Times* heaped scorn on the Republicans by printing: "A large number of Democrats were bought like sheep by Mr. Bulkeley." They bore down, "Mr. Bulkeley declined to close the liquor saloons, as he was authorized to do, and they were generally run in his interest." The city had eight wards and it was the contention of the *Times* that the election cost Bulkeley $1,000 per ward. One Irish-born voter returned home from the polls and exclaimed, "Oh my God. You never did see such work—rum and money—how they have bought it."[112] (On election day, "the first single order . . . for either side was to get the moderator drunk.")[113]

In a separate incident, the *New Haven Register* asserted that Bulkeley's popularity with the liquor interests in Hartford had made him mayor. The *Register* further noted that, "the [growing] prohibition element of the Republican party will oppose Bulkeley's political aspirations."[114] As the mayor's complete indifference to the state's bribery statutes became common knowledge, he lost some Republican votes, so he could ill afford to alienate the prohibition faction of the party too. To convince this group that he wasn't in league with the liquor dealers, he brought a $25,000 libel suit against the *New Haven Register*.[115]

Bulkeley never sued the *Hartford Times* for claiming he was buying votes en masse, but he did sue the Osborne brothers, publishers of the *New Haven Register* for exposing his close ties with Hartford's rum dealers. Later, Bulkeley relented, claiming the alleged libel was printed during the heat of a partisan campaign, and dropped the lawsuit.[116]

⬗ By the middle of June 1882, there was tremendous agitation for some kind of a Fourth of July celebration. Owing to the poor economy following the Civil War and the general economic malaise that continued into the 1880s, the city hadn't properly celebrated Independence Day since 1866.[117]

In that year, Hartford spent $2,000 for the festivities, which brought more than 5,000 people from the surrounding towns by train and carriage to join the fun. The program included the usual parade, food, and fireworks, but the real highpoint was Professor Bassett and his balloon ascent from State House Square. At 3:30 in the afternoon, the enigmatic Professor Bassett took off, but he completely misjudged the wind and got caught in a tree. As the professor clung to the tree, the balloon departed for places unknown. The crowd, of course, roared as if schadenfreude were some magic elixir ladled out on such occasions for their pleasure. All in all, it was a Fourth of July to remember.[118]

Mayor Bulkeley's 1882 Independence Day celebration aimed to be better, bigger, grander, and more exciting. As the big day drew near, more and more features were added until Bulkeley's Fourth of July celebration was one that could never be topped—even by him. In addition to the usual colorful parades, floats, barbecues, and fireworks, there were also huge crowds of visitors who enjoyed baseball games in Bushnell Park and horse-racing all afternoon at Charter Oak Park. Thoroughly pleased with himself, Mayor Bulkeley proclaimed it a huge success.[119]

⬗ Since so many Republican businessmen aspired to the state's highest office during the Gilded Age, Republicans had adopted a quaint—though unwritten—rule, effectively limiting each man to a single two-year term. Therefore, as Governor Bigelow's term wound down toward January 1883, Lt. Governor Billy Bulkeley sought the office. Thomas Waller—Connecticut's "Little Giant"—a man whose life was not exactly a path strewn with roses, ran against Billy. Waller was orphaned at the age of eight and still managed to study law and serve both as Connecticut's secretary of state and Speaker of the state House of Representatives, in short, an inspiring story.[120]

Offering an alternative point of view, Gen. Hawley once moaned, "Why, oh why, [does] the *Courant* persist in helping . . . Waller, who is upon the lowest possible plain as a politician? He is an arrant demagogue. . . . I have felt deeply the friendship of the *Courant* for this cheap man."[121]

The Republican candidate, Billy Bulkeley, was characterized by the *New York Sun* as "a most genial, companionable and cultivated man, but wholly at sea in politics."[122]

On election day, Waller took 59,180 votes, almost 52 percent of the 114,165 votes cast.[123] However, 7,000 Democratic "black ballots" were tallied in New Haven.[124] (State law required plain white paper ballots.)[125] Six weeks after the election, Chief Justice Park of the Connecticut Supreme Court ruled these ballots "palpably unlawful."[126] A re-tally left Waller with only about 46 percent of the vote to Billy Bulkeley's 48 percent. Neither of the men won a majority, but since both houses of the General Assembly were Republican, the office was Billy's for the asking. Instead, Billy chose "not to use a technicality to take office when . . . it was the intent of the voters to elect another."[127] The *Courant* wrote ruefully, "[I]f Thomas M. Waller takes the 'gubernatorial cockade,' he may find satisfaction in remembering that he owes it to the magnanimity of William H. Bulkeley."[128] Billy's self-realization that he lacked the killer instinct necessary for politics finished him. Thereafter, he invested his time more judiciously at Kellogg & Bulkeley.

~ Billy's brother Morgan, a man involved in many different businesses, entertained conflict-of-interest issues all of the time. While voters understood the only way to elect public officials without these conflicts was to recruit leaders from the flophouses and whorehouses on Ferry Street, they stopped short of advocating this. Still, the calculus of personal gain with regard to Hartford Electric Light Company constituted a delicate problem that just would not go away. Year by year, Hartford Electric Light effectively became the elephant in the room. As the 1880s progressed, Mayor Bulkeley regularly used his office to keep electric competitors at bay, while at the same time favoring a utility in which he was a major stockholder.[129]

The company's early progress was positively glacial. In April 1883 the company had just six customers with a total of only twenty-one lights.[130] In January 1884, the council finally agreed to the installation of six arc lights around City

Hall Square on a six-month trial basis.[131] A big surprise to everyone, public opinion was so favorable that in early May the council allowed Hartford Electric Light to place twenty-six more lights along Main Street. These lights eliminated the need for 163 gaslights, and they were placed where their glow would shine down the side streets. Judging by the abbreviated trial period, Hartford readily accepted illumination.

With the wonderful gift of hindsight, we can now see the "tangled web" Bulkeley wove for himself with his vote buying. At first blush, winning with a majority of 1,369, and taking all eight wards in 1880 seems like a spectacular way to take control of city hall. The *Courant* taunted Democrats by dubbing this election "The Waterloo." Yet to win the Fifth and Sixth Wards by 51 and 60 percent, when the most recent Republican mayor—the popular Henry Robinson in 1872—had managed only 34 and 31 percent, was actually a risky miscalculation. Republicans understood the situation instantly, each treating Bulkeley according to the dictates of his own conscience.[132]

Thanks to Bulkeley's overeagerness in 1880, all future elections had to be corrupted with exquisite care, otherwise he could never hope to win the votes of more straight-laced Republicans. Settling for an average of 45 percent of the ballots in the river wards, brought some of them back into the fold. Happily for Bulkeley, this fine-tuning eliminated any serious impediments to a long tenure as mayor.

Chapter Six

WEDDING BELLS

Considering that Morgan Bulkeley didn't get married until he was forty-seven, it is quite possible that he considered business, politics, horse racing and baseball, more important than attracting a wife and starting a family. Or maybe, as they say, he just hadn't met the right woman.

In truth, Bulkeley was shy around women. Billy, the younger brother, was a hail-fellow-well-met extrovert, while Morgan was more reserved. As if the mustaches were the measure of the men, Billy usually brandished a "fixed-bayonet" variety, while Morgan favored the more conservative walrus style.[1]

Morgan Bulkeley might have become a pear-shaped, tobacco-chewing Tammany Hall politician, bursting with base instincts, but he did not. There were plenty of temptations surrounding City Hall, not the least being of the sexual variety. Like all cities of the second half of the nineteenth century, Hartford swarmed with prostitutes. There were a dozen brothels within shouting distance of City Hall Square alone, on State and Market Streets, and more particularly down by the river, on Front and Ferry Streets. At least 300 women worked at these houses of ill-repute—plus an additional 100 streetwalkers, whose numbers could shoot up wildly when the General Assembly was in session or when a Civil War reunion gathered.[2] Could Morgan Bulkeley have been a regular customer? Not likely.

Although he was not an especially spiritual man, Morgan was raised in a fairly religious home. Judge Bulkeley attended the Pearl Street Congregational Church every Sunday, and as one source noted, "[He] never failed . . . to attend, and preside over the meetings of the Pearl Street Ecclesiastical Society, to which he belonged."[3]

With this type of upbringing, it is unlikely Morgan Bulkeley was a "rounder" who frequented roadhouses when the urge was upon him. In matters associated with life's underbelly, he was actually a bit of a prude—not just concerning sex, but the whole universe of criminality. At least in his mind, dirty tricks went with the territory in politics, but when it came to sin of the wickedest kind, it just wasn't his style.[4]

So said, Cupid stormed into his life in 1884 and Morgan Bulkeley was never the same. A gamine, lovely young woman, Fannie Briggs Houghton of San

Francisco, California, came to Hartford with her mother, Carrie, to visit some old friends.[5] The wealthy Protestants of the Gilded Age traveled widely to find suitable mates for their children, and so the possibility that Carrie Houghton had matchmaking on her mind when she planned this trip to Hartford cannot be discounted. Nevertheless, Morgan Bulkeley was smitten from the moment he first set eyes on the gorgeous Fannie Briggs Houghton.

Morgan faced a little problem though. Fannie and her mother were headed to Europe after a short visit in Hartford, and Morgan needed to work fast. Not only did he have to convince Fannie that relocating to Hartford was a sound idea, but he had to sell her on a far bigger proposition—that he was her man. Lord only knows where Bulkeley came up with the fortitude to attempt this merger, but let's just say, he found it.

As tall an order as all of this sounds, Bulkeley caught an enormous break because the Houghtons were a peripatetic bunch themselves. Fannie's father, Gen. James F. Houghton—a rough-and-tumble man with the square-block face of a prizefighter—was born in Cambridge, Massachusetts, in 1827, studied engineering at Rensselaer Polytechnic Institute, and earned his degree in 1848.[6] Boston Water Works gave him his first job, but gold fever got the better of him, and in 1849 he and some friends chartered the Richmond, stocked her with supplies, and sailed around Cape Horn to California. He was twenty-two when the boat pulled into San Francisco.[7]

Right off, James could see panning for gold was dicey at best, so he took a job with the commission house of B. T. Baxter & Co., receivers of consignments from the Otis Rich Line of Boston and California packets. Then in 1852, he purchased a lumber business in Benicia—where the state capital had been moved from Vallejo (for exactly one year)—a business he later sold to his brother.[8]

The following year, James partnered with a friend in Pine & Houghton, the lumber firm that "became one of the best known and most powerful on the Pacific Coast."[9] In later life, he became president of the South San Francisco Dock Company and the Central Land Company of Oakland.[10]

When Leland Stanford was elected governor of California in 1861, James Houghton was elected surveyor general on the same ticket.[11] Governor Stanford and James Houghton became close friends.

Undoubtedly, when the owners of the Central Pacific Railroad—Leland Stanford, Charles Crocker, Colis Huntington, and Mark Hopkins ("The Big Four")—needed railroad ties and trestle timbers to complete their end of the transcontinental railroad, Pine & Houghton received at least some of the business. The work from the Pacific side of the transcontinental railroad was completed as far east as Promontory Point, Utah, where the tracks of the Central Pacific joined those of the Union Pacific on May 10, 1869.[12]

In 1874, Gen. Houghton became the president of the Home Mutual Insurance Company of San Francisco, giving him some common ground with Morgan Bulkeley. At the tail end of his business career, Houghton was appointed a regent of the University of California.[13]

When it came time for James Houghton to take a wife, he traveled back to Massachusetts and married Caroline (Carrie) Sparhawk of Newton.[14] James enticed Carrie back to California; however the family spent so much time traveling between the two states that their four children were born in alternating venues. The oldest, Charles, was born in California, followed by Harry in Massachusetts, then Fannie in California, and Minnie in Massachusetts.[15] Thus the concept of crisscrossing the country was not exactly new to the Houghtons. But unlike James and Carrie Houghton—who traveled by steamship from California to Panama, then by donkey across the Isthmus and finally to Boston on another steamer—Morgan and Fannie Bulkeley would have the benefit of the new transcontinental railroad.[16] Comparatively speaking, life would be a dream.

When Fannie was old enough for high school, the family lived in Oakland. Owing to its excellent private schools, the city was once known as "the Athens of the Pacific." The private schools of Oakland attracted boarding pupils from all over the West—even Hawaii. None of these fine schools have records back to the nineteenth century, but using exclusivity as a guide, Fannie Houghton most likely attended "The Oaks."[17]

In any event, after their children were educated, the general moved his family to a spectacular mansion at 2018 Franklin Street in the shadow of Leland and Jane Stanford's home on Nob Hill.[18]

As a hobby, Stanford built the Palo Alto Stock Farm, where he raised and trained 600 of the finest trotters in the world. By the time Leland Stanford was finished adding land to his horse farm, it consisted of more than 8,000 acres.[19]

When Fannie and Minnie desired a small vacation, they simply asked the family coachman to drive them the thirty-five miles down the peninsula to "Uncle Leland's" Palo Alto Stock Farm, where they, no doubt, stayed as long as they liked and rode their favorite horses.

The transcontinental nature of the union of Fannie and Morgan apparently did not pose an insurmountable obstacle; however, she was twenty-four and he was forty-six. A problem? Could it possibly work? Morgan didn't look forty-six. He aged well—a saving grace perhaps. No matter, they made an attractive couple.

Still, in the early summer of 1884, time was the enemy. Fannie Houghton set off for Europe before Morgan could even suggest that they might make a good team. What could he do? Why, follow her of course.

Bulkeley wrapped up every piece of business he could at Aetna Life and at City Hall, and booked a first-class stateroom aboard the SS *Servia*, one of Cunard's newest and fastest steamships.[20] On July 18, close to the eve of his departure for Europe, Morgan's brother Billy, along with other relatives and friends, gave him a going away dinner at Merrill's Café in City Hall Square. It was another of those "hollow leg" affairs. The menu included littleneck clams, consommé Julien, veal à la financiere, reis petits pois, banana frites, Ponchello Romane, woodcock au natural, pommes de terre frites, salade Russe, crème de politan, frommage, fruits, berries, Chablis, amontillado, St. Julien, Mumms Extra Dry Champagne, Sazerac, cafés, cigars, and cigarettes.[21]

The *Servia* was built in 1881 and was the first merchant steamer to be built entirely of Siemens mild steel instead of iron. It was also the first steamship to be lighted electrically. The vessel's three boilers generated a massive 10,300 horsepower, enabling the *Servia* to make almost eighteen knots. This was extraordinary for a single-screw steamer.[22]

Morgan Bulkeley didn't exactly suffer while crossing the Atlantic. For first-class passengers, the *Servia* furnished a music room, a men's smoking room, a huge ladies' drawing room, and of course, a grand staircase leading to the main saloon. All of these rooms were fitted with paneling of polished Hungarian ash and maple. Additionally, there were beautifully polished inlaid panels of fancy woods, and the saloon was upholstered in morocco leather.[23]

Bulkeley left Hartford on the New York train late in the afternoon on Tuesday, July 22, accompanied by a large group of friends. That night, they threw a bachelor party for him in New York, and made sure he safely boarded the *Servia*, bound for Liverpool, the following morning. His return trip was booked on the same vessel for Wednesday, September 10. The voyage to and from Europe would consume two of his eight weeks of vacation.

Unfortunately, Morgan Bulkeley did not choose to share the details of his efforts to win Fannie Houghton's hand in Europe. Completely understandable. What if the young lady said no? We know that Bulkeley landed in Liverpool and went immediately to London. Since J. P. Morgan was a fellow director of Aetna Fire, simple courtesy dictated that the mayor pay a visit to the financier's father, Junius, at his 32 Old Broad Street office.[24]

Remember, Junius Morgan might well have been the man who suggested that his brother-in-law James M. Goodwin take Judge Bulkeley's place as the president of Connecticut Mutual in the late 1840s, but for some reason, Morgan Bulkeley never harbored the enmity for Junius Morgan or Junius's son that he felt for James Goodwin and his sons. There are several possible reasons for this.

First, J. P. Morgan did not go to the same elementary school in Hartford as the Bulkeleys and the Goodwins. The Morgans lived on Asylum Hill, and young John Pierpont went to the West Middle (Lord's Hill) schoolhouse.[25] This almost completely forecloses the possibility that J. P. Morgan had ridiculed the Bulkeley boys about their father's dismissal at Connecticut Mutual, while the cool feelings between Morgan Bulkeley and the Goodwins suggest that Frankie and his brother James probably did engage in taunting.

Secondly, Bulkeley's mother, Lydia, was a Morgan, and distantly related to Junius and J. P. Morgan. Granted, this didn't have to mean anything in the Anglo Saxon Protestant world of nineteenth-century New England because so many people were related to one another. Nonetheless, it might have.[26]

Lastly, Junius Morgan left Hartford in 1851 to enter the financial house of George Peabody & Co. when he was only forty-two. His son, J. P. Morgan, left Hartford for all of his secondary and advanced schooling, and in 1859, started his business in New York. Therefore, the Morgans never represented the constant burr under Bulkeley's saddle that the Goodwins did. Frankie Goodwin was a constant reminder of the ugliness of avarice. Even though J. P. Morgan and Mayor Bulkeley both sat on Aetna Fire's board of directors, it was an honorary post for Morgan, and Bulkeley saw him so infrequently that he was genuinely glad to see him when he did.[27]

Beyond this obvious port of call, Bulkeley did send a letter back to his friends in Hartford from the Grand Hotel in Paris, dated August 10. Enclosed was a page from the *Grand Hotel News* listing the comings and goings of the hotel's guests, including several families from Hartford.[28]

Rather than return to the United States on the *Servia* as he had planned, Bulkeley exchanged his ticket for a cabin on the SS *Alaska*, of the Guion Line, the ship on which Carrie and Fannie Houghton were traveling.[29] Logically, he needed all the time with Fannie he could get. A few extra days together could, and did, make all the difference in the world.

The twin-screw *Alaska* was built the same year as the *Servia*, but all comparisons ended there. Thanks to her tremendous speed, the *Alaska* became the first ship to make the Atlantic passage in less than seven days, knocking a full half-day off the voyage. With this fantastic speed, she was dubbed "the Greyhound of the Atlantic."[30] In fact, on this passage the *Alaska* skipped from Queenstown, Ireland, to New York in six days, twenty-two hours, and seven minutes—coming within twenty-seven minutes of beating her own record for the run.[31] Bulkeley undoubtedly would have preferred the *Alaska* to move a bit slower, but was powerless to do much about it. On a happier note, the more luxurious *Alaska* made the *Servia* look like a tramp steamer.

A humorous sidebar to Morgan Bulkeley traveling with the Houghtons involves the *Alaska*'s social director and print shop. The steamship's printers rolled off colorful programs listing all of their first-class guests—just as the most exclusive hotels on the Continent did. Since Morgan Bulkeley and Caroline Houghton were fairly close in age—much closer than Morgan and Fannie—the ship's social director mistook Morgan and Carrie for husband and wife, while ignoring Fannie altogether. The *Alaska*'s leaflet lists Mr. Morgan G. Bulkeley and Mrs. Morgan G. Bulkeley, but no Fannie Houghton.[32] This misprint must have caused the height of embarrassment, for it highlighted the fact that Mr. Bulkeley was about to marry a woman who could easily pass for his daughter. Despite the social director's egregious faux pas, the *Alaska* docked in New York on September 21, and most important, by the time the spring lines were wrapped on the cleats, Fannie Briggs Houghton had agreed to become Mrs. Morgan Gardner Bulkeley.[33]

An eight-week absence from Aetna Life and City Hall seemed long, even in the summertime. To celebrate his return, Mayor Bulkeley's friends planned a reception for him at The Hartford Club, but eighty-one-year-old Lydia Bulkeley fell ill. All extracurricular activities were scotched.[34]

The couple planned a society wedding for the first week in February 1885, and colossal preparations lay ahead. In the months before the wedding, Fannie Houghton traveled east to visit Morgan at Thanksgiving. On the Saturday prior, Emma Bulkeley arranged a women's reception in Fannie's honor, where Emma introduced her future sister-in-law to members of Hartford society.[35] A few days after Thanksgiving, the bride-to-be returned to California.

The first telephone call from New York to San Francisco wasn't made until 1914, so in December and January, Morgan and Fannie had to rely on letters and telegrams to keep in touch.

Finally the big day drew near. On Monday morning, January 26, 1885, Mayor Bulkeley, Lydia Bulkeley, and Billy and Emma with their daughter Mary Morgan Bulkeley left Hartford in a private railroad car attached to the back of the morning train bound for New York.[36] There, they picked up Uncle Henry Morgan, Aunt Eunie, and another Morgan cousin, and headed for San Francisco. The private parlor car, or in railroad slang, the "private varnish," generally had an observation platform and included a full kitchen, dining room, four state rooms, a secretary's room, a parlor room, and even servants' quarters. These cars allowed the wealthy to travel in splendidly upholstered privacy. Counting stops and reconnections along the way, the cross-country train excursion usually took seven days.[37]

The Bulkeleys' and the Morgans' private railroad car pulled up at the Great Overland Railway terminus, a block from the Palace Hotel in San Francisco.[38] The hotel's management sent a carriage to collect the travelers and their baggage. The Palace—now booked for the Bulkeley-Houghton wedding reception—engulfed the entire block at Market and New Montgomery Streets. It was a fabulous seven-story monarch and easily San Francisco's most elegant hotel. Designed in the shape of a quadrangle, it featured an extraordinary crystal-roofed garden court. This magnificent central court acted as a circular drive for carriages and promenaders arriving from New Montgomery Street.

The hotel's private orchestra played in a nearby room, so arriving guests disembarked from their carriages to a stream of music caressing their ears. At the same time, they were treated to the delicate scents of exotic flowers and tropical plants growing between the statuary and artistic fountains around the court like memories of lost Eden.[39]

On the big day, Wednesday, February 11, a large crowd gathered at Trinity Church on Powell Street. Guests entered through the Post Street entrance, as prearranged, leaving the front entrance for the wedding party.[40]

As early as seven in the evening, a crowd of mostly women, gathered in front of the guest entrance to Trinity Church. The usual enticements were offered, but the door attendants firmly refused admission to anyone without an engraved invitation. As it was, the guests completely filled the pews of the church's nave and many of the outer rows too, making the invitation check a necessary precaution. It was "one of the largest and most fashionable assemblages of society people ever seen in Trinity Church."[41]

Christmas evergreens still bathed the church's interior, and special plants and flowers were added to make the whole scene inordinately festive and bright. Trinity was a cruciform church, and the transepts at each side were covered with heavy festoons of evergreens. A large Norfolk Cross of pine boughs was mounted atop the baptismal font.[42]

Ushers William Crocker, Joseph D. Grant, Henry Reddington, William Hamilton, James Dyer, Osgood Hooker, and Frank Carolan, all sporting their groomsmen gifts—butterfly-shaped diamond stickpins—in their lapels, seated the guests.[43] The groom, accompanied by his best man, Harry Houghton, brother of the bride, and Gen. James Houghton entered from the vestry and took up their positions in front of the altar. Just before eight o'clock, as the organist began playing the first bars of the bridal chorus from *Lohengrin*, two small children, Master Alexander Rutherford and Miss Birdie Rutherford—Charles Crocker's grandchildren—entered the church and processed up the aisle. The bride, Fannie Houghton, plus her sister and maid-of-honor, Minnie, followed. Walking side by side, they slowly glided to the altar steps. The other bridesmaids followed—Mrs. Charles Crocker, Minnie Corbett, Gertrude Gordon, Mrs. Hewlett Morgan of New York and Mary Morgan Bulkeley of Hartford. (Leland and Jane Stanford were not in the wedding party, probably because their only child, Leland Jr., died March 13, 1884, in Venice. Victorian society strictly observed a traditional one-year period of mourning.)[44]

As the bride reached the side of the groom, the young children opened the floral gates and the bride and groom entered the sacred precincts. Morgan and Fannie knelt on the pink and white satin pillow that became something of a good luck talisman for the Bulkeleys. Five other family weddings, including those of Billy and Emma Bulkeley's three girls—Mary Morgan, Grace Chetwood, and Sally Taintor—featured the pillow.[45]

Rt. Rev. William Kip, the first Episcopalian bishop of California, and Rev. Dr. Beers, rector of Trinity Church, approached the couple and proceeded to read the service. The organist's energetic playing and the cavernous size of the church permitted the wedding guests to hear very little of the ceremony.[46]

At the conclusion of the minister's nuptial blessing, Minnie Houghton approached the bride, lifted her veil, and presented Fannie to Morgan for the traditional kiss. A few minutes later, the bride and groom strode down the aisle to the strains of Mendelssohn's "Wedding March" and were off to the reception.[47]

Carriages transported the guests to the Palace Hotel, where an elaborate party commenced. As the papers declared, "the preparations there were made upon the most liberal and elaborate scale, fully in keeping with the importance of the affair and the distinguished company present." The reception, which was held in one of the Palace Hotel's many parlors, was scheduled to last from nine until midnight, but the merriment carried on into the wee hours of the morning.[48]

The Palace Hotel had been completed a decade before Morgan Bulkeley married Fannie Houghton, and it was the very last word in luxury. In addition to 755 guest rooms, three of these parlors were decorated in Louis Quinze style and easily accommodated several hundred guests.[49]

One paper gushed, "For weeks past, society of San Francisco and Oakland, where the bride formerly resided, had been in a state of expectation and excitement, anticipating the affair that proved to be the most notable event of the season. . . . Seldom has any occasion called forth such an array of wealth, beauty and fashion, the company embracing as it did a full representation of the best people of San Francisco."[50]

The following day, Morgan and Fannie Bulkeley left for the New Orleans Exposition.[51] One has to wonder if Morgan Bulkeley's interest in electricity and his stock holdings in Hartford Electric Light Company attracted him to the fair. The New Orleans Exposition was laid out on a 425-acre parcel of land along the Mississippi River, four and a half miles from downtown New Orleans. Above these grounds, "a huge electric light of 100,000 candlepower rose on a standpipe sending rays a considerable distance. Five other lights, placed on 125-foot-tall towers, boasted 36,000 candlepower, enhancing the illumination. Fifty additional Jenny arc lights were placed at various points around the fair."[52]

From New Orleans, the Bulkeleys traveled to Chicago and then on to Hartford, arriving on Wednesday, February 25. Accompanying the newlyweds on their honeymoon was Fannie's sister, Minnie, who had been quietly enrolled at Miss Porter's School in Farmington.[53] This was an ingenious way to keep at least one family member close to Fannie while she adjusted to her new life as the wife of an insurance executive and mayor. Not that it was necessarily expected, but Minnie stayed at Miss Porter's only a short time and then returned to California.

Another ritual to keep Fannie from getting too homesick began at the same time. Every other year, Morgan, Fannie, and their children, as they arrived, hired a private parlor car and headed west to see the Houghtons in San Francisco.[54] Since Leland Stanford, and many other Bulkeley cronies owned "private varnishes," borrowing or renting a luxurious railroad car never posed a problem.

🌊 Fannie Bulkeley did not have an overly hard time adjusting to life in Hartford. She couldn't have felt alone, because she lived in the Washington Street house with her new husband; his eighty-one-year-old mother, Lydia; and a half dozen maids, servants and cooks. Dan Wallace would take her wherever she wanted to go, and Hartford easily compared with San Francisco when it came to fine stores and restaurants. Fannie's new sister-in-law, Emma Bulkeley, lived right next-door, and Fannie's other sister-in-law, Mary Brainard, occupied the home across the street.

Fannie could talk to her sister Minnie at Miss Porter's School with just a quick word to the telephone operator running the switchboard on Main Street. However, the best news of all made itself known within ten weeks of the wedding— she was pregnant with her first child, Morgan, Jr., who was born on December 25, 1885. Fannie birthed a second child, Elinor Houghton Bulkeley, in 1893 and a third, Houghton Bulkeley, in 1896, while the family was vacationing at Fenwick.[55]

The Bulkeley children never wanted for anything and attended the finest schools, but by the time "Houghtie" was born, Morgan Bulkeley was almost fifty-nine, so a generational distance added to the challenges in their relationship. This is not to suggest that Morgan wasn't a good father, but between Aetna Life, politics, and his other duties, he left little time for parenting.

Fannie was like many other women of the Gilded Age. In public, she was the perfect mother and politician's wife—warm, charming, bright, engaging, and, of course, immaculately and elegantly dressed. Then at night she would sit by the fire in the bedchamber with Morgan and smoke cigarettes as they talked about business, politics, their social life, and the children.[56]

Even though she was young, and forced to move in with her aging mother-in-law, Fannie excelled as the wife of a public man. In 1893, after Bulkeley left the governor's office, a magazine reporter visited the couple's home and had this to say, "The rich antiques in the house, which the governor and his wife have collected, would excite the envy of the oldest connoisseurs. Mrs. Bulkeley is an exceptional collector of china and art works and has some of the most interesting specimens in the state. The souvenir plates, with which the walls of the dining room are decorated, cannot be surpassed in Connecticut. The governor himself has a cultivated taste in this direction and has recently acquired one of the most valuable specimens in the United States. The most elegant specimen in the governor's collection is an invaluable plate that was owned by Governor Saltonstall [1708–1724]. It is a unique work of art in itself. With this magnificent piece is a fragment of the dress worn by the wife of Governor Saltonstall when she was presented to the queen. But the Bulkeleys' special interest is in old furniture. He's the owner of some of the most valuable specimens to be found in New England. One set of superbly carved mahogany chairs in his possession can be traced back for 175 years [1720]. Tables and chairs of rare association and interest occupy the parlor and reception rooms, and the house throughout is rich in art and evidences of culture."[57]

Chapter Seven

MAYOR BULKELEY: PART TWO

Just before Morgan Bulkeley dashed off to Europe to win the hand of the enchanting Fannie Houghton, the voters of Hartford once again passed judgment on the job the mayor was doing at city hall. If Bulkeley had gained a reputation as a vote buyer in the 1880 and 1882 elections, he cemented it forever in the 1884 race. The *Hartford Times* wrote, "At noon, the appearance at the polls indicated that the Democrats in a number of wards had sold out. It appears as if [there were] 200 Democrats working for Mayor Bulkeley in the 6th ward. . . . They were paid of course. . . . From our reports, it appears that Mayor Bulkeley will carry every ward in the city."[1]

The mayor's slippage at the polls in 1882 had grabbed his attention, and he took the requisite action. As Bulkeley spread money madly about the city's wards, the *Times* continued to scold, "Many of these vote sellers are accustomed to talking loudly about the 'power of monopolies,' and the 'hardships for the poor man.' They had better 'dry up'. . . . A $5 greenback held close to the eyes obscures all the horizons of the future with its legacy of evils for laboring men especially."[2]

Despite the *Times*'s taunts, voters elected Bulkeley by an 830 majority over Col. Charles Joslyn, who was fast becoming the Democrats' sacrificial lamb.[3] Moreover, the Republicans kept a solid majority among the aldermen and councilmen. This foretold clear sailing for the city's chief executive.

Marriage put a fire under Morgan Bulkeley as he delivered his annual message in April 1885. Hardly a shock, Bulkeley announced that he "would not again be a candidate for mayor."[4] Morgan clearly had gubernatorial ambitions, and by publicly announcing his intentions, he was in effect asking the delegates to the Republican State Committee to give him the gubernatorial nod. As we shall see, they weren't exactly in agreement.

Through spring and summer, Mr. and Mrs. Morgan Bulkeley frequented a more polished side of Hartford. Before marriage, Morgan's cultural preferences were in line with those of the common man—baseball and horse racing. Rarely did he attend any of the city's artistic activities. Now, however, Fannie's influence even brought them to the opera. On Friday night, May 14, 1886, for example, the operatic audience at Robert's Opera House on Main Street might have spied Morgan and Fannie seated in one of the boxes. The Eggleston English Opera Company performed Michael William Balfe's *The Bohemian Girl*, scheduled to benefit the Police Mutual Aid Society.[5] Many of the cast members were amateurs, but the performance received the most favorable reviews. An American actor, however, once described this opera's most famous aria, "I Dreamt I Dwelt in Marble Halls,", as "deadly dull and grandiose."[6] How might the under-educated musical ear of Mayor Bulkeley have appreciated this piece?

As the hot summer months baked the city, bad news came calling. On July 23, 1885, Gen. Grant died. Just five years earlier, the people of Hartford had turned out in huge numbers just to catch a glimpse of the great man, and now he was gone. As soon as the news reached Mayor Bulkeley, he ordered sixty-three rings on the city's Pearl Street fire alarm bell.[7] Three thousand of the city's leaders and former military men gathered at the State Arsenal for a solemn service honoring the late president. Mayor Bulkeley arranged with Western Union and the quartermaster general's office to have word sent to Hartford at the exact moment when Grant's body was interred in the kiosk on Riverside Drive in New York City. At that precise time, soldiers fired a thirty-eight-gun salute on the west side of Bushnell Park.[8] Though his presidency was marred by scandals involving the men around him, the people in the North never lost their love and respect for Ulysses S. Grant.

Mayor Bulkeley's clear expression of his decision not to run for a fourth term as mayor nevertheless went unheeded by the Republican City Committee. Meeting at Allyn Hall the following April, they overwhelmingly nominated Morgan Bulkeley. "No other names were heard."[9] Since Bulkeley accepted the nomination, he must have received word from the higher-ups in state Republican politics that he would not be their choice for governor in September.

Even though he was as popular as ever among most of Hartford's Republicans for his ability to get the job done, resistance to the Bulkeley machine was growing in the poorer sections of the city.[10]

Bulkeley's final mayoral campaign in April 1886 introduced a whole new element in city politics. Hartford was caught up in a nationwide maelstrom, represented by the labor movement. In this mayoral election, there were the usual Democratic and Republican tickets, but also a Prohibition ticket and a Union (Labor) ticket. Ultimately, a Citizen ticket was added at the last minute—Morgan Bulkeley's attempt to hoodwink voters into supporting him and his followers.[11] By printing "Citizen" at the top of the ballot and then including all of his hand-picked candidates—mostly Republicans with a few friendly Democrats—Bulkeley won a few extra votes.

Bulkeley's biggest competitor was Col. Edward Graves, popular among the working class and running on the Union (Labor) ticket.[12] The newly founded Labor League—said to represent 1,500 workers—sought to pit the rich against the poor.[13] Bulkeley of course represented the rich, while Col. Graves campaigned as a poor man. As usual, the *Courant* praised the Republican candidates for their businesslike approach to running the city, but the *Times* went after Bulkeley's corrupt practices with renewed vigor, "The necessities of poor men, who are out of coal and have no flour in their dwellings and little of anything to satisfy the hunger of children, are relied upon by the purchasers of votes to aid them in their corrupt work."[14]

Journalists for the *Times* frequently exposed the outrageous level of corruption at the polls, but after Bulkeley sued the *New Haven Register* in 1882, the *Times* editors were cautious. Thus, much of their reporting had a contradictory quality to it: "As usual in our city elections, more votes were bought outright by the Republicans than are counted in the majority for Mayor Bulkeley. . . . Had no votes been bought, Col. Graves would have been elected . . . [still] we do not believe that Mayor Bulkeley and the council elected with him would sanction corrupt practices."[15]

In the end, Bulkeley was reelected by only 328 votes—24 percent of the majority he enjoyed in his 1880 victory, when he took all eight wards.[16] It could not be denied; the mayor's ability to recruit workers and purchase votes in the river wards was on the wane. The rise of the labor movement was troublesome for the Republicans, yet Bulkeley's connection with the Hartford Electric Light Company (Helco) was an even bigger predicament.

By July 1884, the principal ownership of Helco had been transferred from American Electric & Illuminating of Boston to Morgan Bulkeley, Billy Bulkeley, Thomas Enders, A. C. Dunham and three other Hartford men.[17] As things stood, 940 streetlights illuminated the city. Gas fired 650 of them, only 101 used an electric supply, and 190 relied on naphtha, a flammable hydrocarbon mixture, for flame.[18] The gas company delayed the switchover by lowering the price of gas, but such a strategy had limits.[19] As the conversion process sped up, Morgan Bulkeley's preferential treatment of the Hartford Electric Light Company at council meetings did not go unnoticed.[20] Bulkeley, however, had already convinced himself that his mayorship would soon be over, as it was his turn to receive the Republican nomination for governor in 1888.

≈ The Morgan Bulkeleys slipped away for a quick vacation to Virginia's Fortress Monroe in April 1886, where Fannie surveyed her husband's wartime way station.[21] Soon, they returned to Hartford and Morgan Bulkeley was back to work at Aetna Life and City Hall. Besides the long—and often tedious—council meetings on Monday nights, Mayor Bulkeley's duties were limited to mostly ceremonial events like marching in the Memorial Day Parade and touring the city's reservoirs at Trout Brook in West Hartford with other interested politicians and businessmen.[22]

However, a little mischief loomed in what could otherwise be considered routine city business. In one case, a lone citizen, John Garvie, sought to keep the common council from giving money to its different committees.[23] Oddly enough, Mayor Bulkeley also thought the bleeding was illegal and refused to sign the appropriations bills. The council passed them over his veto. A final resolution of the case wasn't forthcoming until February 1887, when the Connecticut Supreme Court sustained the Garvie injunction.[24] In the meantime, the lower court wanted the common council to pay its share of the court costs—$50.42. The council balked, so the court issued a *writ of attachment* with Sheriff Chapman ordering him "to take possession of some of the city's property, at once."[25] Chapman's first choice was to impound the council's furniture; but later he decided to attach a police paddy wagon, the Black Maria (pronounced Mar-î-ah), instead. To settle the common council's bill, an auction was arranged at ten o'clock on the morning of Wednesday, July 21. The auctioneer, Peter Lux, started the bidding at $50, and in due time, it was gaveled down to Mayor Bulkeley for $111.[26] He paid up and then quietly gave the Black Maria back to the police. The matter was soon forgotten. This was Bulkeley's idea of running the city smoothly—do what had to be done, and worry about the money later.

When Bulkeley went to the Republican State Convention at Hartford's Allyn Hall in early September 1886, he and Phineas Lounsbury of Ridgefield were the two favorites.[27] Even Bulkeley knew Lounsbury was the committee's choice, yet at the same time, he may have entertained the idea of an upset thanks to the political friendships he had nurtured over the years. After all, just prior to the convention, he campaigned all out at Camp Smith, the brigade campgrounds in Niantic. The *Springfield Republican* noted, "The brigade campgrounds is becoming a favorite field for the political campaigners. . . . Mayor Bulkeley's genial manner and his lively style of circulating among the boys gives him a decided advantage. . . . It is no drawback to him that his charming wife is also on the field."[28]

Lounsbury was in the shoe business, but he was a lot like Morgan Bulkeley in that he too had only a rudimentary education.[29] Unlike Bulkeley, though, Lounsbury served on the Connecticut General Assembly from 1874 to 1876, and had plenty of loyal friends in state government. Too, "many delegates felt that it ought to be Lounsbury this time in view of the fact that he was rather shabbily treated two years [earlier]," when the nomination went to Henry Harrison.[30] (It was important to seek candidates from all over the state for the top job before giving the nod to the favorite.) On just a single ballot, Lounsbury got more than twice as many votes as Bulkeley.[31]

Bulkeley's loss of the Republican nomination to Phineas Lounsbury in 1886 is easily explained, but there is another matter that deserves consideration—Mayor Bulkeley's less than honorable practice of buying votes. At the Republican Convention, there were many highly principled men who knew all about Bulkeley's corrupt election practices. For example, Senator Joe Hawley was there, and it was said that he "hated a mean trick or a dishonest act."[32] Senator Orville Platt was cut from the same bolt. Since the vote was secret, one can only wonder whether either of these men voted for Morgan Bulkeley.

The Republicans were suitably impressed with the way Bulkeley accepted this loss to Phineas Lounsbury. As one paper put it, "he showed no inclination to sulk."[33] To the contrary, the Bulkeleys threw a big reception for Phineas Lounsbury at their residence that Thursday night.[34] In January, after the new governor's inauguration, they gave an even bigger reception for Governor and Mrs. Lounsbury at their home on Washington Street.[35] The Lounsburys did not live in Hartford, although they rented the late Lucius Barbour's residence at 130 Washington Street in early 1887, and Senator Dixon's place on Farmington Avenue during the winter of 1887–88.[36] (Governor Raymond Baldwin, 1939–41 and 1943–46, was the first to use the executive mansion on Prospect Avenue.)[37]

Politics aside, the highpoint of 1886 was the September 17 dedication of Hartford's new memorial arch to the veterans and fallen heroes of the War Between the States. Hartford was the first city in the United States to build a permanent triumphal arch after the Civil War.[38] The Soldiers and Sailors Memorial Arch predated both the Grand Army Plaza Arch in Brooklyn's Prospect Park (1888) and Stanford White's Washington Memorial Arch at the foot of Fifth Avenue in New York (1889).

On a cloudy and damp Friday in the middle of September 1886, Mayor Bulkeley and a large collection of dignitaries assembled in Bushnell Park to dedicate the new arch.[39] About 5,000 Civil War veterans gathered for the ceremony, and several thousand spectators joined them. The veterans paraded in their uniforms, singing "Marching through Georgia." Volunteers served coffee and sandwiches from large tents pitched in the park.

Col. George Bissell, on behalf of the building committee, presented the memorial to the town, and Gen. Joe Hawley—now u.s. Senator Hawley—on behalf of Hartford, accepted it. When it was his turn at the podium, Hawley mesmerized the crowd with a truly unforgettable speech in which he humanized the brownstone arch with a haunting voice that whispered, "Remember! Remember!" In the company of such high-powered Civil War heroes and officers, Mayor Bulkeley was only peripherally involved in the ceremony.[40]

The soldier's monument committee assembled in May 1882 and consisted of Col. George P. Bissell (chairman, Civil War veteran, Twenty-fifth Connecticut Volunteers), Hon. Charles R. Chapman (former mayor), Dr. John O'Flaherty (Civil War surgeon), Hon. Richard D. Hubbard (former governor), Gen. Thomas McManus (Civil War veteran), Rev. Joseph Twichell (Civil War chaplain, Seventy-first New York "Excelsior Brigade"), Mayor Morgan Bulkeley (Civil War veteran, Thirteenth Regiment, New York Militia), Henry C. Robinson (former mayor), Judge Sherman W. Adams (Civil War veteran, u.s. Navy) and Rev. Francis Goodwin.[41]

Even though he had nothing to do with the Civil War—and his timing in enrolling in divinity school was deemed suspect—as chairman of the city's Parks Commission, Francis Goodwin more or less had to be included in this group. Even before the committee formed, city planners envisioned the monument somewhere in Bushnell Park. All the same, Goodwin's participation in the creation and placement of this monument to Army and Navy Civil War veterans must have been awkward for everyone.[42]

One can only imagine what other members of the committee thought, particularly someone like Rev. Joe Twichell, who volunteered to be chaplain to New York's Seventy-first Volunteers, a regiment of poor Irish kids, 168 of whom died in the war. These tough New York street kids were little more than cannon fodder to the Union Army brass.[43] While Francis Goodwin attended divinity school, got married, and helped his father scoop up more real estate in Hartford, Joe Twichell served three long and hard years at the seat of war. Twichell administered last rites to young kids wounded or killed at Bull Run, Fair Oaks, Kettle Run, Oak Grove, Fredericksburg, Chancellorsville, Gettysburg, Spotsylvania, Cold Harbor, and Petersburg. Rev. Joe Twichell was one rugged cleric.

Originally, the Little (Park) River wound around just south of the monument, and a bridge carried the roadway over the river and thence under the arch. Later, when the river was moved into large concrete conduits beneath the park, the roadway and the arch stood alone.

The brownstone arch has staunchly dignified Bushnell Park for well over a century—outlasting many of Hartford's finest buildings. Besides the Old State House and the Center Church, the Soldiers and Sailors Memorial Arch has become an important symbol of Hartford itself; and it was completed and dedicated during Morgan Bulkeley's final term as mayor.

In March of 1887, Bulkeley addressed a long-standing transportation dilemma. Ever since the railroad came to Hartford in 1839, trains rumbled across Asylum Street. This worked fine for a couple of decades, but now the crossing presented a problem of frightening proportions. The regular traffic on Asylum Street—horses, wagons, omnibuses, people, and of course the horse cars—rendered the whole intersection perilous, and serious accidents occurred regularly.[44]

Finally, Mayor Bulkeley assigned a delegation to look into the matter. The commission unanimously recommended that the tracks be raised to a height of sixteen feet. This wouldn't be easy. A temporary depot would be constructed in Union Place, rerouting trains while the construction work continued.[45] The project was consummated just after Morgan Bulkeley left the mayor's office.

In the early years of their marriage, the Bulkeleys traveled to California often. As the buds formed on Hartford's trees in the spring of 1887, the family traveled by private parlor car as far as Omaha.[46] There, Fannie and her baby, Morgan, Jr., continued west while Mayor Bulkeley went on to Chicago for a meeting of the National Trotting Association. Once again the club elected Bulkeley treasurer and sent him back to Hartford to wrap up business at Aetna Life and City Hall. Come June, he boarded another westbound train and caught up with his wife and child in San Francisco.[47]

Thanks to Gen. Houghton's position in San Francisco society, whenever Morgan Bulkeley visited, he was given passes to the city's exclusive clubs including the Pacific Club, the Bohemian Club, and the Union Club at the Palace Hotel.[48] The wealthiest and most influential men in San Francisco patronized these clubs. Bulkeley, of course, wasn't exactly a stranger to posh old boys' haunts. Just after he returned from New York in 1872, Morgan joined the Home Circle Club. Later, he served as president and effected a merger with The Hartford Club, the city's most luxurious and prestigious men's society.[49] In a Georgian Revival clubhouse on Prospect Street, members assembled for lunch each day, entertained out-of-town visitors, and socialized. As an interesting sidebar, The Hartford Club was originally headquartered in what had been the home of Governor Joseph Trumbull, arguably the state's most inept chief executive. As Trumbull's one-year term came to an end, his friends hustled him out of office before he could do any serious damage.[50]

In Bulkeley's fourth term, papers from all around the state began to expose his self-dealing in the matter of Hartford's street lighting. The New Haven Union wrote, "For years past, the company of which Mayor Bulkeley is one of the principal stockholders has had the contract for lighting the streets, and a handsome profit too."[51]

Indeed, on January 23, 1888, as his city hall tenure fast drew to a close, Mayor Bulkeley tried to ramrod through the legislation necessary to convert the whole city to electric lights.[52] This would have reduced the revenues of the Hartford Gas Light Company markedly. The members of the council, at least for the moment, insisted on the cheapest supplier of street lighting and left Bulkeley's effort foundering. In the years ahead, the Hartford Electric Light Company nevertheless consolidated its power and took complete control of the city's electric needs, ultimately benefiting Morgan Bulkeley and all those who financed Helco back in 1881.

The last event of any consequence in Morgan Bulkeley's eight years as mayor had nothing at all to do with politics. Rather, it had to do with a snowstorm. The Great Blizzard of '88 struck on Monday, March 12, 1888, and blew for three days, piling thirty inches of snow into ten-foot drifts. Few council members made it to City Hall for their weekly Monday night meeting while the storm raged. Shy of a quorum, those present declared the storm the worst in memory, and adjourned.[53]

Early on Wednesday of that week, Mayor Bulkeley enlisted Mrs. Elizabeth Sluyter of the Union for Home Work and Mrs. Virginia Thrall Smith of the City Mission Society to make food and fuel arrangements for the poor. Bulkeley insisted that the women spare no efforts in finding and assisting the suffering, and he instructed them to send him the bills.[54]

~~~ In the April mayoral election, Capt. John G. Root, chosen by Bulkeley, represented the Republicans and Col. Charles M. Joslyn, once again, represented the Democrats. Most Republicans regarded Col. Joslyn, an attorney, as a weak candidate because of votes he cast while in the state legislature. The Republicans squeaked out a narrow victory, even though Root lost the river wards convincingly.[55]

Capt. Root served in the Civil War as part of the Army of the Potomac, presided over the Farmers & Mechanics National Bank and was a thirty-second-degree mason.[56] The election results don't lie; Root would not stoop to buy votes. His successor in 1890, the Republican Henry Dwight, also lost the river wards badly.[57] Going back a few years, the three Republican mayors before Bulkeley— Timothy Allyn (1858), Allyn Stillman (1864), and Henry Robinson (1872)—all lost the river wards convincingly.[58] This suggests strongly that Morgan Bulkeley's election practices, in the four mayoral races from 1880 to 1886, were an aberration, an island of corruption in an otherwise fairly honest ocean of political commerce. Other Republican candidates could win the mayoral race even though they lost the river wards, but once Bulkeley started buying votes, he made the winning process more difficult for himself than he could have imagined.

At five o'clock on the afternoon of April 3, 1888, Mayor Bulkeley invited fifty prominent citizens to his office. As soon as everyone was assembled, he announced that they had been invited to witness John G. Root take the oath of office and become the city's next mayor.[59]

But first, Mayor Bulkeley did an unusual thing. He was a collector of antiques and political paraphernalia, and now he announced that he was gifting his Hartford-mayor portrait collection to the city.[60] Bulkeley spent eight years assembling this fabulous 100-year series and exhibited it on the walls of his City Hall office. (Actually there were three portraits missing, but one of those was being shipped even as he spoke.)

The oath of office was given to Capt. Root, and in an instant, Bulkeley was the ex-mayor of Hartford. Root made a few simple remarks and Morgan Bulkeley stepped into his own future.

After politics and horses, collecting antiques ranked among Bulkeley's passions. He acquired curios, books, bound sermons, antique furniture, and a number of other antiquities. He even owned a rare hornbook, an academic implement of colonial America. The hornbook Bulkeley owned was found in Guilford, and had belonged to John Hart, the second graduate of Yale College.[61] In the furniture department, Bulkeley was particularly proud of a richly carved mahogany table that once belonged to Thomas Jefferson. He kept it in his office at Aetna Life on Main Street, where he occasionally posed for photographs.[62]

꙳ Of course, Bulkeley's primary passion played out in the political arena. There, Bulkeley could command, send his troops into action, maneuver his operatives, and rally the ward bosses. Winning was even more exciting when there was a little chicanery involved. The expression, "There nothing more exciting than a dishonest dollar," comes to mind.

Not to be forgotten is the fact that Bulkeley concerned himself with Aetna Life too. Politics bestowed personal glory—and allowed winners the ability to fashion laws that would benefit them financially—but it didn't pay the bills. There wasn't an office in the land that could keep the Bulkeleys' lifestyle. Therefore, Bulkeley wisely treated Aetna Life as the golden goose it was. At the moment, it was a golden goose in need of a bigger nest, and a rare opportunity presented itself.

During the railroad expansion after the Civil War, the president of Charter Oak Life—another one of Hartford's insurance companies—wanted in on the boom. Charter Oak was a fairly young company, founded in 1850, but its president, James C. Walkley, had big dreams. Undaunted by the fact that Judge Bulkeley of Aetna Life or James Goodwin of Connecticut Mutual had no interest in such dicey ventures, Walkley not only agreed to build the Valley Railroad from Hartford to Old Saybrook, but also to finance an upscale beach community with a massive hotel, Fenwick Hall.[63] It was hoped that together these projects would attract the finest families in Hartford to the Connecticut shore.

Milton Clyde of Springfield began the actual construction work in 1870.[64] This railroad builder was the same man who built the faulty dam for Hartford's Water Works at Trout Brook.[65] Not exactly a good omen.

With no big bridges or tunnels, the line was completed quickly and Clyde declared the Valley Railroad ready for paying customers and freight by mid-summer 1871. As a harbinger of trouble, the railroad's test runs included rock slides that buried the tracks under two feet of stone. Moreover, as the new locomotive, the James C. Walkley, with six cars in tow, thundered along at fifty-five miles an hour on its maiden voyage up from Saybrook, laborers were laying the last hundred feet of track in Cromwell. Luckily, the last spike was set in time to avoid a catastrophe—barely.[66]

Connecticut's biggest shoreline hotel, Fenwick Hall, began accepting guests just as the tracks were set. Naturally, the hotel's first guests should have arrived by train, but instead the steamship Sunshine delivered vacationers to Saybrook Point, from whence they were whisked over to Fenwick by sailboat. Bad omen number three.[67]

If Charter Oak Life could convince Hartford's leading citizens to build cottages at Fenwick, the beach community might ensure the success of both the Valley Railroad and Fenwick Hall. In an effort to spur land sales, a new causeway was built with a new spur of track across South Cove to Lynde's Neck. The shiny new railroad station at Fenwick was like the cherry atop the project.[68]

As Hartford's finest families bought building lots, it looked for a time like Charter Oak Life was onto a good thing. Unfortunately, the Panic of 1873 intervened. The 1870s became the "Long Depression" and money was tight even for Hartford's elite. A short five years after its maiden run, the Valley Railroad defaulted on its bonds and was placed in receivership. Proprietary rights to the railroad changed hands a few times, but by 1892 it became part of the New Haven Railroad, and eventually plopped into J. P. Morgan's lap. Even with injections of cash from Morgan, the Valley Railroad never achieved lasting success. The implosion of the Valley Railroad felled Fenwick Hall at the same time. While Charter Oak Life gasped for life, a pair of wreckers from out of state, Edwin R. Wiggin of Boston and Henry J. Furber of New York, descended on the ailing insurer. The company stumbled along for over a decade, but ultimately went belly up.[69]

Enter Morgan Bulkeley. On Saturday, April 7, 1888, the Charter Oak building on Main Street slipped under the auctioneer's gavel. Easily one of the city's most beautiful buildings, it graced the perfect downtown location. The structure was completed in the fall of 1870, and "the land and building cost nearly $1,000,000."[70] Aetna Life held a first mortgage of $200,000.[71]

However, when the time came for bids, the room fell silent and the auctioneer began to sweat. For several minutes, there were no bids at all. At length, a bid of ten dollars was voiced. More silence. Finally the right of redemption was sold to Mr. William C. Russell, an insurance agent, for fifty dollars. Russell declined to say for whom he was bidding, although people suspected it was Morgan Bulkeley.[72] As it turned out, Russell spent fifty dollars in the hopes he could interest someone else in the building before May 1, 1888. He was unable to accomplish this, and the building went to the first mortgage holder, Aetna Life.[73]

The Charter Oak building was a magnificent six-story polished Concord granite edifice on the east side of Main Street, just north of the Wadsworth Atheneum. The building was of the "wedding cake school of architecture" and practically a virgin, having been completed only eighteen years earlier.[74] True, the effects of the Panic of 1873 were still fresh in people's minds and could have dissuaded some buyers, but Hartford was full of smart—and wealthy—speculators. Therefore, why was ex-Mayor Morgan Bulkeley permitted to scoop up one of the city's most prized commercial properties for about a quarter of its value?

The answer to the puzzle is really quite simple. Although the Republicans wouldn't announce their nominee for governor until the fall, it was common knowledge that Bulkeley would become the next governor of the state. Add to this the fact that governors had infinitely more power in Bulkeley's time. The Civil War notwithstanding, states' rights were still important. An all-powerful central government would not rob the individual states of their power until they gladly relinquished it in the face of dire and unrelenting financial problems during the Great Depression of the 1930s. Once the individual states turned to Washington for help, they inadvertently surrendered their power.[75]

Not only was Morgan Bulkeley likely to be the next governor of Connecticut, word on the street foretold refitting the Charter Oak building for Aetna Life. Holding back a bid on the Charter Oak building must have driven Francis Goodwin—Hartford's preeminent real estate mogul—to the brink of madness. Watching his old Centre School classmate steal such a gem likely played havoc with Francis Goodwin's "weak heart."

But what kind of a businessman would Goodwin have been if he had chosen to cross the next governor of the state, a governor who might very well have half the state legislature in his pocket? He would have been a fool. So, J. P. Morgan's first cousin, Frankie Goodwin, a man who knew the ownership, history, and value of every building in the city, had to stand down while Morgan Bulkeley completed the shrewdest real estate transaction in Hartford's history. Including the defaulted interest payments, Aetna Life took the marble gingerbread wonder for about $230,000.[76] As for Frankie Goodwin, some days it doesn't pay to gnaw through the restraints.

⁂ When one evaluates Morgan Bulkeley's years as mayor of Hartford, there are of course high notes and low notes. True, he was an able administrator and the city ran like a fine watch from 1880 to 1888. It is also true Bulkeley introduced a shortcut to power, understandably unacceptable to many. However, more than one small anecdote—such as this one—casts sympathetic light on the man. While retold here not to exonerate Bulkeley, it does lower the level of opprobrium a bit.

One night, a drunken saloonkeeper killed his wife and then himself, and left six children behind. Mayor Bulkeley went to the scene and took charge. Unfortunately, the woman he summoned to care for the orphans didn't arrive until five o'clock in the morning, so Morgan stayed up all night comforting the children. Bulkeley wasn't a perfect human being. As usual, folks had to take the good with the bad, but at the end of the day, it was difficult to hate him.[77]

Chapter Eight

CROWBAR GOVERNOR

Since Bulkeley's sights were set on the governorship, he wasted no time wining and dining the men who controlled his fate. In March 1888, he hosted an eight-course dinner at The Hartford Club for the Republican State Central Committee.

The men of the Gilded Age were world-class trenchermen. Rather than grab a quick bite on the way to some other extravaganza, they enjoyed a whole evening of food and drink, often entertaining each other with short speeches, humorous raillery, and verbal badinage between dishes.

Although Bulkeley served Connecticut River shad as the main course for this particular Republican dinner, a typical feast would consist of oysters on the half shell, followed by consommé. Then, fried smelts, stewed terrapin, fillet of beef larded with mushroom sauce and finished with a side of vegetables, cheese soufflé, canvas-back duck with black cherry sauce, lemon ice, fruits, cakes, and coffee would be served. Port accompanied the oysters and soup; claret complemented the fish; Chablis was paired with the terrapin; champagne offset the roast; and liqueurs, of course, were matched with dessert.[1]

By the end of the evening, a stuffed Bulkeley felt reasonably certain he would be the next governor of Connecticut. Although implausible, his certainty rings true for a curious reason: Since the legislature was overwhelmingly Republican, as long as neither candidate got a majority of the popular vote, the General Assembly would hand the governorship to Morgan Bulkeley. This was exactly how the two preceding Republican governors, Henry Harrison and Phineas Lounsbury, found their way into office.[2] As we saw earlier, the governor right before Henry Harrison would have been Billy Bulkeley had he been of the same mind as his successors.

In the 1880s, the gubernatorial races were so close that almost any third party candidate could easily scrub off enough votes to prevent a majority. Moreover, during this period, the third party was always the Prohibitionist Party, the one group with whom the Democratic Party could never form a fusion ticket. Their ranks included so many hard-drinking Irish immigrants, that any combination with the Prohibitionists was unthinkable.[3]

So said, this "third party as spoiler" scheme of winning elections deserves a closer look. While the Prohibition Party worked like a charm for three Republicans in a row—Henry Harrison, Phineas Lounsbury, and later, Morgan Bulkeley—the *Courant* claimed "[T]his vote is almost exclusively taken from Republican votes."[4] Presumably, the Prohibitionists got their votes from people who knew the evils of liquor firsthand. Was this more likely to be Republican voters or Democratic voters? A good guess is the latter, making the "third party as spoiler scheme" something Republicans would have encouraged. In any event, because of the unchanging makeup of the lower chamber of the General Assembly, this little quirk in Connecticut's election laws made it a wonderful time to be a Republican.[5]

Other than speeches given in a few towns around Hartford, campaigning was a very muted affair in 1888. The state's newspapers carried little or no political advertising. Once again Bulkeley was up against a far more accomplished man, and though this 1888 race for the governor's office didn't present any obstacles he hadn't encountered before, it turned out to be one of the most irritating races of his life.

The agent of all this vexation was Judge Daniel C. Birdsall of Westport. How Birdsall ever became a judge is a great mystery, for his behavior was eccentric—even bizarre. To begin, he was arrested in 1874, along with Mrs. Ada Troubee, on a charge of adultery. Once the enchanting Ada was free of her husband, Birdsall married her.[6] On the business side of the ledger, by 1883 Birdsall's heart had abandoned the law and he was itching to start a newspaper. He moved to Hartford, and in November, the first edition of the Democratic-leaning *Hartford Telegram* hit the streets.[7]

Originally, Birdsall took the high road, turning out honest, high-quality journalism, but since the city already had a matched set of Democratic and Republican mouthpieces—the *Times* and the *Courant*, respectively—the *Telegram* had trouble attracting an audience. That's an understatement. In no time at all, the paper sank $20,000 into debt. Birdsall quickly abandoned the high road and began to crank out the most salacious lies that three cents could buy.[8]

The "yellow journalism" produced during New York's great newspaper wars between Joseph Pulitzer's *New York World* and William Randolph Hearst's *New York Journal* did not surface until the mid-1890s. As such, Birdsall's gutter journalism was ahead of its time—not necessarily a big consolation for those he chose to slander.[9]

His extraordinarily trashy stories and outright lies befuddled the public completely. No one knew what to do about the *Telegram*, if anything. Since Birdsall's dream slid in and out of insolvency with remarkable regularity, allowing nature to take its course seemed logical. All well and good, but the *Telegram* had the resilience of an alley cat. Each time creditors silenced the editor, the paper somehow sprang back to life. Even after Daniel Birdsall was arrested for nine different counts of embezzlement, the paper continued to publish.[10] Birdsall was such a madman that he even chewed the finger of his Meriden correspondent, J. M. Fletcher, in a dispute over pay—an errant bit of cannibalism for which he was promptly arrested.[11]

After each brush with the middens of history, the *Telegram* went right back to attacking the city's top business and political leaders—and their families. Morgan Bulkeley was a special fixation for Birdsall, as he heaped abuse on the mayor in almost every edition of the paper. Hardly a day went by without one of Birdsall's baseless charges soiling the air on Washington Street. At one point, Bulkeley even threatened to horsewhip Birdsall, but regained his composure in enough time to avoid serious trouble—just.[12]

One interesting sidebar—Col. Edward Graves, the man Bulkeley beat in the mayoral election of 1886, worked for Birdsall at the *Telegram*. If Birdsall needed moral support to go after Morgan Bulkeley, he didn't have to look far.

Finally, on Monday, July 2, 1888, Birdsall made the mistake of attacking Aetna Life. The *Telegram* wrote, "[I]t is only a question of time, and evidently a short time at best, that its affairs will be placed in the hands of a receiver."[13] Birdsall accepted claims as losses, disregarding the fact that claims are just one of the routine costs of doing business for a life insurance company.

It was one thing for Birdsall to call Bulkeley names, but when he printed outright lies about the financial health of Aetna Life, his slandering went beyond the pale. With an order of attachment signed by Judge Charles Perkins, the city marshal went to the offices of the *Telegram* and removed everything—desks, chairs, tables, type, and even the printing presses.[14] When the marshal's men were done, the rooms stood bare. Birdsall tried to bribe the marshal, making cash offers for the equipment, but the lawman simply replied, " I have orders from Morgan G. Bulkeley to remove everything from the place, and I just did."[15] Bulkeley placed the furniture and machinery in the basement of Aetna Life.

The next day, the city's prosecuting attorney issued a warrant for Birdsall's arrest for publishing "offensive, indecent or abusive matter," and Officer Gunn (later the chief) apprehended him on Asylum Street.[16]

The complaint actually charged two distinct offenses—abusive language concerning Aetna Life and the same offense against ex-Mayor Bulkeley. Judge Henney set bail at $500, which Birdsall quickly met.[17]

An ordinary man might be chastened by this arrest, but it had exactly the opposite effect on Birdsall. The following day, he rolled off a six-by-nine handbill, under the masthead of the *Telegram*, reprinting the whole libelous article against Bulkeley and Aetna Life that got him arrested twenty-four hours earlier! A competing newspaper wrote ruefully, "It is likely that a new criminal suit will be brought, if the offender should remain in Hartford."[18]

When Birdsall was brought into court, the presiding judge increased his bail from $500 to $1,500 and the case was continued until July 18. Then, to Birdsall's own surprise, he was quickly rearrested for reprinting the article the second time and his bond was increased to $2,000.[19]

On October 5, Birdsall was arrested again following a civil action for $25,000 damages brought by Aetna Life.[20] The difference between the two motions was that the first—back in July—constituted a criminal motion against Birdsall and the *Telegram*, and under it, the paper's property was attached. The second brought a civil suit for damages against Birdsall personally as the author of the libelous articles, and under it, his body was attached. Seeing no options, Birdsall was forced to retract the story about Aetna Life and reluctantly Bulkeley returned Birdsall's printing presses and office furnishings.[21]

Surely, Birdsall would lay low now, wouldn't he? Not hardly. Near the end of October, Birdsall wrote an editorial in the *Telegram* calling on Austin Brainard, the city's prosecuting attorney, to charge an alleged violator of the Sunday liquor laws. The article averred, "Morgan Bulkeley entered a saloon on Albany Avenue one Sunday, threw down a $10 bill, and paid for the 'drinks' for nil, and gave the bartender the change."[22] Birdsall claimed to have affidavits from the witnesses, however, he never produced them.

To the relief of Hartford's fact-appreciating public, the *Telegram* masthead disappeared a few years later. Judge Birdsall retreated to his law practice and died in 1891 at the age of fifty-seven.[23]

The *New York Sun* summed up Morgan Bulkeley's political persona succinctly when a journalist penned these words, "He is a strategist in politics; he is no mugwump. He is no stump speaker, but he is a manager of primaries, a master in war manipulation, an organizer and does not embarrass those who vote for him by chilling dignity. He does not put on [airs] and does not allow himself to have a big head. He can never be a megalomaniac, but he is believed to have no convictions as to the potency of cash in politics as a persuasive argument in the way of thorough organization."[24] Since *The Sun* was a New York paper, it is reasonable to assume that everyone in the Northeast knew about Bulkeley's penchant for buying votes, but this statement needs a qualifier. Though Bulkeley's practices may have been common knowledge, proving that he ever bought a single vote was another matter. Bulkeley insulated himself behind a wall of Republican fixers, and even some Democrats who were willing to help for a price.

Morgan Bulkeley's opponent in 1888 was a well-respected jurist and a man whose personal life was without scandal. Judge Luzon Morris was born in Newtown, Connecticut, and graduated from Yale in 1854, after which time he read the law for three years. He began his law practice in New Haven and while still a young man served as a probate judge. In 1874, the people of Connecticut elected him to a single term in the state Senate.[25] Despite this sparkling resume, Morris was not considered a particularly charismatic politician. Nevertheless, he proved a tough opponent for Morgan Bulkeley.

In an effort to blunt Judge Morris's clout in the southern part of the state, and at the same time make the people of the Elm City feel they wouldn't be left out of his administration, Bulkeley chose Gen. Samuel Merwin of New Haven for his lieutenant governor.[26] Just as in national politics, the governor's running mate was of little consequence except as a gesture to the electorate.

On Tuesday, November 6, 1888, the men of Hartford headed to their local fire stations to cast their ballots. The election results were nastily tangled. Judge Morris received 75,074 votes to Mayor Bulkeley's 73,659—a plurality of 1,415 for Morris.[27] The problem was that the third-party candidate, David Camp of the Prohibition Party, skimmed off 4,631 votes. Add this to a few "scattered" ballots, and neither Morris nor Bulkeley had the 76,819 votes necessary for a majority of the 153,637 votes cast. As usual, the matter was thrown into the General Assembly for a resolution, and the legislators gave it to Bulkeley. In the wake of Bulkeley's win, the Times wrote, "The Republicans spent a fund of $200,000 in their vile work of corrupting the ballot and trying to secure the sturdy old state by purchase. . . . But Connecticut . . . gives to Judge Morris a plurality of nearly 1600 over the representative of 'Boodle.' The Senate stands—Democrats 8, Republicans 16; the House—Democrats 105, Republicans 144; a majority no part of which could have been secured in an honest election."[28]

At eight the following morning, a crowd of men gathered on the north side of City Hall Square in front of the United States Hotel and shouted for Bulkeley to come out.[29] A moment later, he appeared on a balcony and issued a few remarks about the election of President Benjamin Harrison and the Republican sweep of the U.S. House and Senate.[30] The Republicans completely controlled the nation's government. The crowd cheered wildly at this news as the governor-elect waved and then reentered the hotel.[31]

A rag-tag parade followed. Hartford had done away with formal election parades almost three decades before, but a spontaneous crowd moving through the streets wasn't unheard of. The employees of Pratt & Whitney (machine tools) and Billings & Spencer, headed by the bands from Colt's and Weed's, formed the nucleus of a procession on foot, on horseback, and on bicycles. Approximately 5,000 men marched up Main Street and then doubled back to City Hall.[32]

On January 10, Governor Bulkeley announced his staff, which was composed of able operatives from all over the state.[33] For his personal secretary, he chose Samuel O. Prentice. A North Stonington native, Prentice was a Yale-educated lawyer, a former city attorney, and a man who proved an able guardian of all confidences large and small. Prentice later became chief justice of the state in 1901.[34] Bulkeley could spot talent.

Another appointment of interest was that of Col. Lucius Barbour, an old Bulkeley political ally, who became his adjutant-general. Barbour was nine years younger than Bulkeley, and in fact came to Hartford from Madison, Illinois, as an infant at the same time the Bulkeleys were planning their move from East Haddam in 1846. Barber was affiliated with Charter Oak Bank and was now treasurer and president of Willimantic Linen Company.[35] Bulkeley always kept the Dunhams in the loop.

At noon on Thursday, January 10, 1889, the First Companies of the Governor's Foot Guard and Horse Guard escorted Governor Morgan G. Bulkeley from his home on Washington Street to the Capitol—a distance of about a quarter mile. They wore their "gilded uniforms and rattling swords," and the whole ceremony was conducted with great solemnity.[36] In days gone by, this exercise had all the trappings of a British coronation, but a winter session of the General Assembly— with no state officers other than members of the legislature to be sworn in—was a dull affair. The great pomp and circumstance of the ceremony had fallen by the wayside. No longer did huge crowds descend on the city, nor were there venders selling oyster stew and other refreshments on street corners.[37]

This first day commenced with the new governor's opening message to a joint session of the General Assembly.[38] The state's finances called for "the reduction of the direct tax . . . and its final abolition altogether," the governor announced. He also recommended "paying off the whole state debt by creating a sinking fund . . . out of the surplus receipts."[39] The Republicans, and especially Morgan Bulkeley, prided themselves on running the state better than the Democrats—and for less money. In the late nineteenth century, there was a considerable difference between the parties in fiscal matters.[40]

Next, Bulkeley called for the state to "pension judges after long service. . . . We draw them away from their practices, use the best part of their lives, on only moderate pay, and then drop them. We want the best men and we should offer the best inducements."[41] This initiative raises questions. Since Connecticut's judges were not included in any of the state's disability or pension statutes until 1919—and then only with a minimum of twenty-five years service—Bulkeley's proposal was more than three decades ahead of its time.[42] Moreover, since most judges probably didn't meet the rules of qualification until fifty years later, Bulkeley's proposal was *profoundly* ahead of its time. Is it possible, given his complete disregard for the 1877 state law against bribery, that Bulkeley felt the need to curry favor with the state's judiciary? Was he, or perhaps Sam Prentice, that clever? Unfortunately, Governor Morgan Bulkeley's interest in Connecticut judges' well-being will forever remain one of history's little imponderables.

In the evening of inauguration day, the First Company of the Governor's Foot Guard threw the new governor and his wife a magnificent ball.[43] Foot Guard Hall, the red brick, Romanesque Revival structure on High Street was technically an armory, but all the city's major social functions were held there until Bushnell Hall was completed in 1930.

That night, the foremost families of the city attended—the whole Bulkeley clan, the Brainards, Dunhams, Robinsons, Jewells, Shipmans, Jarvises, Bunces, Sumners, and Elizabeth Colt. Yes, even Francis Goodwin was there, although his wife, for some reason, was not. The guest list shows 2,500 people packed into the Armory for dancing, drinks, and hors d'oeuvres. The biggest hit of the evening was Fannie Bulkeley, only twenty-eight and radiant. She wore "a white satin dress with trimmings of pink satin, myrtle green, and white brocade velvet. Her ornaments were diamonds and pearls."[44]

≫ Even while he spent most of each day working at Aetna Life, Governor Bulkeley spent January and February sifting through large mounds of mail in his office at the Capitol. He received a great many letters from commissioners and businessmen hoping to influence his decision on certain bills or to thank him for one thing or another—the agricultural commissioner, Connecticut Humane Society, state chemist, Connecticut Hospital for the Insane, Connecticut Association of Farmers and Sportsmen—the list goes on and on.[45]

Clubs and organizations also wrote to offer him honorary membership in their groups. Others wrote to request that he give a speech or hand out diplomas or even to recommend a friend for a job. State senators and representatives dropped quick notes to enlist his help in steering legislation in the General Assembly.[46] In short, everyone wanted something, and the new governor had the power to make it happen—or not.

These letters cast a glaring light on election practices of the nineteenth century. Routinely, appointees thanked the governor by including a check made out to him personally. A simple example is the letter from Frederick Burnham of New York City. In it, he scrawled:

> Dear Sir,
> Your favor of . . . informing me of my commission as Commissioner
> of Deeds for the State of Connecticut in the State of New York . . . was
> duly received. I hereby respectfully apply for reappointment and enclose

herein my check of $3 payable to your order. His Excellency, Governor Bulkeley, will perhaps remember that I am a personal acquaintance . . . having crossed from Liverpool to New York on the steamer, *Alaska*, with him in September 1884.[47]

Typewriters were common in business offices by 1889, but typewritten letters were considered rude. Almost all of the correspondence received by Bulkeley arrived written in long hand. Bulkeley earmarked letters to be answered by his staff using quick scribbles on the pages' lower-left-hand corners: "Acknowledge receipt, MGB" or "Acknowledge and decline, MGB."[48] If the letter included a formal invitation he wished to refuse, he wrote "Acknowledge and decline engagements, official, MGB."[49] Sam Prentice, the governor's secretary, or Frank Rood, executive clerk, answered these letters.

Some correspondence Bulkeley chose to answer personally. In these official letters—the few still extant—his handwriting is bold and expansive. The loops hang low below the words and the crossing of the t's is quite pronounced. The writing is done with a thick-nibbed fountain pen and is almost completely illegible.[50]

In early February, the annual banquet of the Yale alumni club of Hartford booked Foot Guard Hall. There were 150 guests seated at a U-shaped table, and only about a half dozen were not actually Yale graduates, including Governor Bulkeley, Lt. Governor Samuel Merwin, and Sam Clemens. The people of Hartford loved Sam Clemens and often invited him to say a few words at gatherings around the city. At this particular banquet, he was introduced as "Marcus Aurelius Twain." He had just returned from Washington, where he had been working to get the nation's copyright laws toughened, without any luck. He ruminated, "It would have brought us a national principle—that old commandment 'Thou shalt not steal.' "[51]

Next, Governor Bulkeley took the podium and joked that he really didn't belong there, but was pleased to dine with so many distinguished men of Hartford who were Yale alumni.[52]

The new governor's days were full as he juggled the presidency of Aetna Life with his duties as Connecticut's top executive. Bulkeley's schedule included all sorts of meetings, even some he considered great fun. For instance, Charter Oak Park's annual meeting was a bright spot for him. As one of the directors of the track, Governor Bulkeley joined Hartford's other horse fanciers for an afternoon of agreeable turf talk. Among the members of the board were his brother-in-law Leverett Brainard and Henry Keney, another horse lover. Envisioning great bridle paths through the northern part of the city, Keney bequeathed money for Hartford's Keney Park.[53]

When the General Assembly met on February 15, Democratic state senator Edward Cleveland of Hartford introduced a resolution to have an official oil portrait of the governor placed in the Capitol.[54] By 1889, the General Assembly had commissioned about a dozen portraits of former governors, so Senator Cleveland's resolution might simply have been the proverbial extending of the olive branch.

Bulkeley was a little on the vain side, inasmuch as five likenesses of him were eventually painted by the artist Charles Noel Flagg (four are still extant).[55] Because previous portraits of governors cost the state a little under $500, the House decided this amount should be the maximum the state would pay.[56] The Senate balked, stripping this stipulation out and sending it back to the House. The final version had no financial limit on it, although Flagg was able to complete the final painting for $500 anyway. Oddly enough, when the legislature commissioned a portrait of Lt. Governor Merwin a few months later, the committee budgeted only $60.[57] Europeans have always accused Americans of measuring art with a yardstick. Nonetheless, one has to wonder what the state got for such a paltry sum.

At the beginning of March 1889, a special Pullman parlor car was attached to the 8:29 A.M. express train to Washington so that the governor and his party could attend President Benjamin Harrison's inauguration. Accompanying the governor were Fannie Bulkeley, Miss Minnie Houghton, Mr. Harry Houghton (Fannie's brother), Billy Bulkeley, Executive Secretary Samuel Prentice, Adjutant-General Lucius Barbour, and a dozen others. After a connection in Jersey City at 1 P.M., the party left in another parlor car and arrived in Washington at 8:45 P.M. They then settled into their headquarters at the Arlington Hotel.[58]

Benjamin Harrison and Morgan Bulkeley found some common ground. Not only were they both Republicans, but the new president hadn't won the popular vote either. As a point of divergence, Harrison himself was a small, cold man with a handshake "like a wilted petunia."[59] To the consternation of all the party animals in the nation's capital, Benjamin Harrison and his wife plunged all of Washington into the social equivalent of the dark ages because they were so unpopular—even with fellow Republicans.[60]

In the evening of inauguration day, Governor Bulkeley and his party held a reception in the Arlington's ballroom. The parlors were crowded with people from Connecticut offering their congratulations. The Wide Awakes—a young men's Republican group formed in 1860—arrived at 3 P.M. and paid their respects to the governor, who received them cordially.[61]

Arrangements were made for the Wide Awakes to visit the president on Tuesday morning between ten o'clock and noon and they received fifty tickets to the inaugural ball. The Wide Awakes were the only organization from Connecticut to march in the inaugural parade, and also the only group from the state to attend the ball.[62]

In the morning, the Wide Awakes gathered at the west gate of the White House and were met by a cadre of policemen. With the help of Senator Joe Hawley, they were eventually admitted to the grounds. Hawley brought them through the gates and up to the steps of the White House. Soon they were inside shaking hands with President Harrison in one of the anterooms. Col. Wilson, the president's master of ceremonies, introduced each member of the Wide Awakes by name and they each greeted the president.[63]

Later in the day, the Wide Awakes called on Senator and Mrs. Hawley at their home on C Street and were warmly received. Joe Hawley's first wife, Harriet ("Hattie"), died of pneumonia three years earlier.[64] The widowed senator remarried, this time to an English nurse, Edith Anne Horner, a nun in the Episcopal Church working at the Blockley Almshouse in Philadelphia.[65] Earlier, she had served with the British Red Cross in the Anglo-Zulu War, where she received the South African campaign medal and the Royal Red Cross. At the time of their marriage in Philadelphia on November 15, 1887, the groom was sixty-one and the bride thirty-six. There remains one interesting note regarding the guests at Senator Hawley's second wedding. Since Joe Hawley had such high moral standards, one can assume the guests he invited would be men of similar character. From his military days, Hawley invited Generals Sheridan and McCook.[66] Gen. Sherman was invited but sent a long letter with his regrets, explaining that he had to be in Saint Louis.[67] Another close friend, Gen. Grant, had died in 1885. Hawley's friends in Connecticut were represented by Stephen Hubbard and Charles Hopkins Clark of the Courant, his Senate colleague Orville Platt, and Rev. Joe Twichell. Although the wedding made the front page in the New York Times, it was buried on page eight of Hawley's paper, the Courant, presumably so hometown folks would not feel slighted.[68] Since Morgan Bulkeley would have walked on hot coals from Hartford to Philadelphia to attend, one assumes he was not invited. Perhaps this highlights the great divide between the two men.

Before Morgan Bulkeley and his family left for Benjamin Harrison's inauguration in Washington, the new governor initiated a few actions. Now that all the parades and speeches were over, it was time to get down to business, passing legislation to shape the insurance industry to his tastes, and give Aetna Life some advantages in the process. The first item in this category was "An Act Relating to Taxes on Foreign Insurance Companies" (raise them); followed by "Liability of Officers of Insurance Companies" (limiting it, of course); and this gem, "Investments of Insurance Companies" (limiting them, which in a complicated way gave Aetna Life an advantage).[69]

The insurance committee of the General Assembly chose to move quickly on behalf of the governor because the work of the legislature often slowed down dramatically in the second year of a chief executive's term. Better to ram legislation through while there's plenty of smoke on the battlefield. Effectively, they had from February until July to conclude all the serious legislative work.[70]

〜 Without question, the wheels of justice ground quickly in 1889, and it is informative to examine Governor Bulkeley's position on the death penalty. Lawyers representing John Swift, a man who had killed his wife, appealed to the state legislature to have Swift's death sentence commuted. Bulkeley issued a ten-day reprieve.[71] A tumultuous debate followed in both houses, with commutation seemingly the preferred course, but Governor Bulkeley vetoed it. In the end, the House decided to go with Bulkeley's decision and refused to override the veto. Swift's fate was completely in Bulkeley's hands. After much thought, he decided to let justice proceed exactly as the judge and the jury had ordered.[72]

The New York World reported that Bulkeley's decision to give Swift a reprieve was influenced by his brother and his mother. When a local reporter mentioned this to Bulkeley, he was quick to set the record straight: "[No] living person knew how he was going to act; that he had conversed to no one about it; that his brother was in Dakota and had been for some time; and that his mother was ill in bed."[73] At eighteen minutes past ten on the morning of April 18, 1889, the murderer, John Swift, was hanged by the neck until dead.[74]

Charles Flagg was painting the likeness of Bulkeley during this sordid ordeal. He destroyed the first portrait because "it was during this time that the unfortunate mother and sister of John Swift . . . were pleading with the governor for the life of their erring relative, and the governor, who has never been noted for his hardness of heart, was under a great strain during these sittings."[75]

〜 By the end of April 1889, all of Connecticut's soldiers—the Governor's Foot Guard, the Governor's Horse Guard, and the Fourth Regiment—were in New York for the centennial observance of George Washington's inauguration. The highlight of the gathering was a parade from the Battery to Central Park. Governor Bulkeley, followed by his staff, headed the troops.

About a third of the 100,000 spectators at the parade were from Brooklyn and some of them remembered Bulkeley and cheered him wildly. He smiled broadly, acknowledging old friends as he rode up Broadway, bowing and hat-tipping.[76]

The following month, Fannie and Morgan Bulkeley received the members of the General Assembly, state officers, and officials of the various departments of the state government.[77] Governor Bulkeley no doubt had a wonderful time showing his appreciation to those who had helped him fine-tune the state's insurance laws to benefit Aetna Life.[78]

↪ The Secret Ballot Bill was a new piece of legislation designed to do away with secret ballots in the General Assembly and thus curtail the constant bribery of senators and representatives. It was of intense interest to Bulkeley. Remember, the Republicans had always been well served by secret ballots, and to be blunt, Bulkeley's administration would never have existed without the secret ballot. Naturally, he vetoed the bill.[79]

Bulkeley was clever. Rather than just vetoing the bill and give cause for everyone in the state to brand him a skunk, he put his decision in writing and had the *Courant* and the *Times* publish it. He claimed to favor any bill eliminating bribery and bringing transparency to the voting process, but he did not see how the bill presented to him would do that. The bill was "so experimental in its character, so cumbersome in its details, so burdensome to the voter in its operation, so expensive in its machinery, so unharmonious with existing laws, that it can only prove a burden and a failure."[80] His detractors could say what they liked, Bulkeley knew how to stir doubt.

In June 1889, one of Bulkeley's pet projects finally passed the legislature—the elimination of the toll on the bridge to East Hartford. In the process of offering businessmen and visitors a free bridge across the Connecticut River, the eighty-year-old Morgan Street Bridge charter had to be purchased, and funds had to be collected to pay for the bridge itself. The state would buy the charter for $84,000, and Hartford, East Hartford, Glastonbury, South Windsor, and Manchester would provide an additional $126,000 to purchase the bridge itself—a total of $210,000. The bill passed the General Assembly, and Bulkeley signed it into law on June 10, 1889. Allowing time for the necessary financial transfers, the toll would be eliminated by the middle of September.[81]

That same month, just before the graduation exercises at Yale College, the school conferred an honorary master's degree on the governor. (Trinity College gave him one a few years later.) A little earlier, Yale had given a similar degree to Samuel Clemens and an honorary doctor of laws degree to Senator Joe Hawley. With the governor, both men attended the commencement on June 26 for the first time since receiving their degrees.[82]

In a 1906 interview, after he had become a U.S. senator, Bulkeley mentioned that he didn't go to college, and commented quickly in passing, "We didn't get much education in those days."[83] That was bunk, because his older brother Charlie graduated from Yale in 1856 and Morgan certainly could have attended too, had he applied himself at Bacon Academy. Bulkeley often portrayed himself as uneducated by circumstances rather than character.

With a vast knowledge of genealogy, Judge Bulkeley delighted in telling people stories about their ancestors in bygone days. (Connecticut Historical Society, Hartford, Connecticut)

Unlike Morgan and Billy, Charlie Bulkeley applied himself in school, graduated from Yale College in 1856, and became an attorney. His death in the Civil War was the catalyst for Morgan Bulkeley's later success. (Connecticut Historical Society, Hartford, Connecticut)

Morgan's mother, Lydia, was active in charity work and served as president of Hartford's Orphan Asylum. (Connecticut Historical Society, Hartford, Connecticut)

When Billy Bulkeley ran for governor in 1882, he had enough votes to win without any illegalities. Instead, he handed the office to the Democrat, Thomas Waller. (Bulkeley Collection, Connecticut State Library)

Morgan's sister, Mary Brainard, always wore black. Five of her ten children died young, including Helen, who expired after an emergency appendectomy on the family's kitchen table. Mary claimed she was in a state of perpetual mourning. (Connecticut Historical Society, Hartford, Connecticut)

Thanks to his willingness to purchase votes, Bulkeley won every ward in the city and became Hartford's mayor in 1880. He married five years later, and remained mayor until 1888. (Bulkeley Collection, Connecticut State Library)

Fannie Briggs Houghton at the time of her marriage. When Morgan Bulkeley was in the U.S. Senate, President Teddy Roosevelt took a shine to Fannie. Is it possible she reminded him of his ill-fated first wife, Alice Hathaway Lee? (Connecticut Historical Society, Hartford, Connecticut)

In 1898, the Bulkeleys wanted a summer cottage, so Morgan bought Fenwick from the murderer Ned Stokes. (Bulkeley Collection, Connecticut State Library)

During World War I—
with her two sons fighting
in Europe—Fannie (left)
was state chair of the Women's
Liberty Bond Campaign. Her
counterpart in Hartford was
Mrs. Richard M. Bissell
(right), whose husband
was president of Hartford
Fire Insurance Co.
(Bulkeley Collection,
Connecticut State Library)

During the day, Fannie sold
Liberty Bonds and was the
perfect politician's wife—bright
and charming. At night she
smoked cigarettes by the fire in
her bedchamber.
(Bulkeley Collection,
Connecticut State Library)

Mary Brainard's cottage is at the far left, and at the top of Fenwick Avenue is Fenwick Hall (far right). The children standing where Fenwick Avenue meets Beach Road are Edith Brainard, Ruth Brainard, Morgan Bulkeley Jr., and Marjorie Matson. This picture was taken about 1890. (Connecticut Historical Society, Hartford, Connecticut)

The Bulkeleys' coachman, Dan Wallace, waits outside the Bulkeley residence at 136 Washington Street. (Connecticut Historical Society, Hartford, Connecticut)

The Charter Oak Life building at 650 Main Street, which Morgan Bulkeley
bought for Aetna Life in 1888—for about a quarter of its value. The Wadsworth Atheneum
can be seen through the trees on the right.
(Connecticut Historical Society, Hartford, Connecticut)

Although no provenance exists for this lock and hasp, it was donated to the Connecticut State Library
by Houghton Bulkeley—the governor's younger son—in the 1940s. There are three patent dates on the
back of the Yale lock, ranging from 1876 to 1878. The hasp (with lock) was pried off one of the doors
leading to the governor's rooms at the Capitol on March 21, 1891.
(Bulkeley Collection, Connecticut State Library—Photograph by Dave Corrigan.)

In later years, Bulkeley loved to be photographed sitting at this
richly carved mahogany table, which once belonged to Thomas Jefferson.
(Hartford History Center, Hartford Public Library)

Soon thereafter, Governor Bulkeley received an invitation in the mail. It read:

Mr. & Mrs. Henry C. Bowen request the pleasure of your company at the celebration of the 113th anniversary of American Independence in Roseland Park, Woodstock, Connecticut on Thursday morning July the 4th 1889 at 10:00 A.M.[84]

Since Henry Bowen was the executive secretary to President Benjamin Harrison, naturally Bulkeley planned to attend. However, Bulkeley wasn't about to let the president of the United States bypass Hartford on his way to Woodstock on the biggest holiday of the year. He quickly wired an invitation to President Harrison suggesting a visit to Hartford on his way to Woodstock. He also suggested to Senator Joe Hawley that he send his own message, seconding the motion.

In return he received the following telegram: "The President will leave Washington on Wednesday morning as scheduled, and he would be glad to spend an hour in Hartford en route if it could be arranged. He will not be able to do so on his return."[85]

An hour? Was Bowen joking? An hour wouldn't be long enough for a parade and a few speeches, much less a nice luncheon. The cables flew back and forth until it was agreed the president would leave an hour earlier, giving them a two-hour window in Hartford. Bulkeley then assigned his adjutant-general, Lucius Barbour, to go to New York to meet the president's train and ensure that Harrison didn't dillydally in New York and wind up with less than two hours in Hartford. Barbour would accompany the president into Connecticut, where Governor Bulkeley, Senators Hawley and Platt, most of Connecticut's representatives, and a host of other dignitaries would board the presidential train at Stamford, the first stop in Connecticut.

At 2:02 P.M. on July 3, the presidential train—complete with a baggage car, two drawing cars, and a private parlor car—lumbered into Union Station.[86] President Harrison's party was comprised of the man himself, his wife, several cabinet officers, a Supreme Court justice, and his personal staff, including Henry Bowen. Marching bands and the First Regiment of the Governor's Foot Guard greeted the train, and the parade began from there.[87]

Horses and carriages went up Church Street to Main; down Main to Park; from Park onto Washington and finally to the Capitol. A reception was held in the senate chambers with lunch for the president in one of the anterooms. Then the carriages headed back to Union Station via Trinity Street, under the Soldiers and Sailors Memorial Arch and thence to Union Station.

The train left Hartford a little after four o'clock, and arrived in Woodstock by five. Putnam and other towns made extensive preparations for the president's visit to Roseland Park—on the shores of Woodstock Lake—but the elements had not been consulted. Through a steady rain and heavy fog, President Harrison, along with hundreds of invited guests, found their way to Henry Bowen's residence for a huge reception.[88]

The following morning as the rain continued, the Grand Army of the Republic soldiers escorted the party to Roseland Park. Among the speakers on the platform with President Harrison were Governor Morgan Bulkeley, Senator Joseph Hawley, and Associate Justice Samuel Miller.[89]

As governor of the state, Bulkeley made the first speech and introduced the president. Senator Hawley and the other dignitaries from Woodstock followed. Later, almost every veteran in attendance met and spoke with President Harrison and the hours passed quickly.[90]

After a relaxing couple of days at Henry Bowen's place in Woodstock, the president rose at 5 A.M. on July 5—a bright and clear morning—and planted a tree in the garden in front of the Bowen's home. Governor Bulkeley and Senator Hawley assisted him.[91]

After breakfast, a carriage delivered the president to Putnam station, where a private railroad car and baggage car were waiting to whisk him to New London. Still, he took the time to shake hands with about 200 people before he left the platform.[92]

The president's party arrived at New London at about 9:30 A.M., and the handshaking and speeches started all over again. From New London, President Harrison left Newport on an overnight cruise back to Washington aboard the U.S. Navy steamer *Despatch*. One suspects that this sort of thing got tiresome, yet spending time with presidents, riding in parades and making speeches were Bulkeley's stock and trade—and he was getting especially good at it.[93]

≫ By the first week of March 1890, Bulkeley, Fannie, and young Morgan, Jr. were back in California visiting the Houghtons and traveling about. Bulkeley indulged his passion for horses by attending stock sales.[94] One particular sale took place at Count Ginlio Valensin's famous Pleasanton Stock Ranch in Alameda County. The Pleasanton racetrack was well known to horsemen all over the United States and Canada. The stables were of high grade, and horse lovers prized the thoroughbred animals raised and trained there.[95] Bulkeley's brother-in-law Leverett Brainard and Burdett Loomis, the first owner of Charter Oak Park, accompanied him.[96] (A few years later, the Oakland Race Track, a tad more upscale, replaced the Pleasanton Track.)

Many of the fastest horses had their beginnings at Pleasanton, and the sale attracted some of the most skillful drivers in the country. At this auction in 1890, many of the colts went for $20,000, while one proven animal went for $27,000, though experienced horsemen placed the true value closer to $75,000. Also at this sale, a sportsman from Boston, J. Malcolm Forbes, paid $8,100 for the colt Nellie May. Later, Forbes Farm became the outstanding stud farm in the East, and Forbes made headlines by paying Leland Stanford the incredible sum of $125,000 for his stallion Arion.[97]

These trips to California served Bulkeley well as a politician, but even more so as president of Aetna Life. He never missed an opportunity to add talented people to the company's ranks. By this time, Fannie's brother, Charles, was working for Aetna Life, running all of the firm's California sales offices.[98] Brother Billy and his children, sister Mary's kids, nephews, nieces, cousins, in-laws—almost all of them worked for Aetna Life at one time or another. Most spent their whole lives with the firm.

By 1890, Leland Stanford, Fannie Bulkeley's godfather, was the junior senator from California, which coincided nicely with the passage of the Sherman Anti-trust Act, signed into law by President Benjamin Harrison on July 2, 1890.[99]

In the 1869 case of *Paul v. Virginia*, the Supreme Court held that "insurance was not commerce within the meaning of the Commerce Clause in the Constitution, and therefore, states held exclusive regulatory authority over the business of insurance."[100] However, such an extraordinary exclusion required constant vigilance. Thanks to Senator Leland Stanford and Connecticut senators Orville Platt and Joe Hawley, Aetna Life was well protected when Republican senator John Sherman of Ohio shepherded through his antitrust legislation. (Later, the Clayton Act of 1914, the Robinson-Patman Anti-Discrimination Act of 1936 and the McCarran-Ferguson Act of 1945 further cut into the Insurance Industry's antitrust exemption, but it still enjoys exclusions that other industries do not.)[101]

✒ Back in Hartford, probably the most humorous chapter of Bulkeley's political life began. In May 1890, he was called before the Connecticut Supreme Court as a witness in an unusual case—*Talcott v. Philbrick*. This case developed out of the race for aldermen in the Seventh Ward during the city elections the month before. Republican Halsey Philbrick defeated William Talcott, the Democrat, by one vote, though not exactly on the up and up. Rank and file Republicans were always coming up with new ways to inveigle voters, but they were sorcerer's apprentices compared to Morgan Bulkeley. In this particular election, he and Pat McGovern resurrected the "Citizen" ballot, which they placed alongside the "Republican" and "Democrat" offerings. This proved an effective tactic in snookering people into voting for the Republican, Halsey Philbrick.[102]

Bulkeley wasn't a bit shy about this deceit, nor was he concerned with public condemnation. When asked in court why he and McGovern did this, he replied, "It was in response to a demand. We intended to have them available in every ward. A good many people don't like to vote tickets that say 'Republican' or

'Democrat.' "[103] This was utter nonsense, and the judge undoubtedly had a hard time containing his laughter. Clearly, there were no voters anywhere, at any time, who requested such ballots.

Of course the only thing William Talcott and Halsey Philbrick cared about was which one of them would become alderman in the Seventh Ward. In an October ruling, the court held that the "Citizen" ballots were void and therefore the Democrat, William Talcott, was the new alderman from the Seventh Ward.[104]

Morgan Bulkeley didn't win them all, but neither did he ever stop trying to invent new ways to rig the game. This is a fine but important point—politics was great fun in the Gilded Age and practically cried out for such outrageous abuses. No one ever went to prison in Connecticut for stuffing ballot boxes, buying votes, or stealing elections. It was just part of the great blood sport of politics. Actually, things had gotten so crooked that shameless schemes—like the Bulkeley-McGovern "Citizen" ballots—were begrudgingly admired. There was no reason for a politician to hang his head if his play was exposed and disallowed. He simply needed to try a little harder next time.

Since the Republicans adopted the quaint practice of giving everyone a chance at the governor's office, a governor rarely stayed in office more than two years. As a result, no matter how much a man wanted to keep the job, the party bosses always said no. Bulkeley knew the unwritten rule as well as the next man, but he insisted on going before the state convention for renomination. In effect, he forced the party bosses to turn him down—which they did.[105]

Based on this rejection, Morgan Bulkeley's name was not on the ballot in the November 1890 election. Instead, the race pitted Republican Samuel E. Merwin of New Haven against his fellow townsman Judge Luzon B. Morris.[106]

However, just as in 1888, there was a third-party candidate who took precious votes from the total. In this case, it was another member of the Connecticut State Temperance Union, Edwin Augur, who represented the Prohibition Party. Auger garnered 3,413 votes, and in a very tight race, that was more than enough to cause trouble.[107] After the first count, it looked like Judge Morris had a majority of 27 votes. That was on Tuesday. By Thursday, the ballots had been recounted several times, and instead of having a slight majority, Judge Morris was 53 votes short of the mark. The race would have to be decided by the General Assembly.[108]

It appeared to be a case of "same song, fourth verse," but the composition of the legislature had changed in the intervening two years. The Republicans still held an overwhelming majority in the House of Representatives, but the Senate was now top-heavy with Democrats.[109]

Governor Bulkeley had few enemies and plenty of friends, and as one newspaper put it, "He deserves all the friends he has, because there is no man . . . who is more . . . loyal to his friends. And these friends are not [only] among the rich and powerful. Mr. Bulkeley has been . . . generous . . . to many who have been much in need of his friendship."[110]

This is where Governor Bulkeley's loyalty to his Republican friends in the House paid off. There were 167 cities and towns in Connecticut at the time, and by making sure that the big cities—the now-blossoming Democratic strongholds —still had just the same two votes in the House allotted to the smaller towns, the tight-fisted, old swamp Yankees from the rural crossroads of the state could scotch the ambitious city spending programs. In effect, Hartford's immigrants traded their votes to the Democratic Party for good city jobs and better schools for their children. But under this "rotten boroughs" system of government— where all 167 cities and towns got the same two votes in the House of Represen- tatives—the money for these jobs and schools could be doled out by the small- town Republicans of the House in the most cheeseparing way, if at all.[111]

Through November and December, the state Senate tried to get the House to back their efforts to seat Judge Morris, but no soap. Governor Bulkeley's friends in the House simply refused to agree to anything. All the while, Bulkeley claimed, by law, he couldn't leave office until his successor was certified and duly sworn in by the *entire* legislature.[112]

The newspapers had a field day with this. Even out-of-state papers like the *Springfield Republican* took to calling the governor, Brer Rabbit Bulkeley, and of- fered the following explanation of the mess in Connecticut, "There seems to be only one man . . . calm and undisturbed during all the muddle and that man is Morgan G. Bulkeley . . . and this becomes amusing [since] his party had no further use for [him]. . . . He 'lay low' and . . . demonstrated the soundness of Brer Rabbit's philosophy."[113]

Finally on the bitter cold morning of January 13, 1891, the state Senate met to take action. They appointed a committee to notify the Democratic candidates that they should come to the Capitol to be sworn in.[114] But, when the newly elected state comptroller, Nicholas Staub, was sworn in by the Senate and tried to take over the comptroller's office, Governor Bulkeley walked in with several friends. "A big staff you have, Governor," observed Staub. "Yes," replied Bulkeley. "Every citizen of Connecticut is my staff."[115]

At this point, Staub insisted he had won the race for comptroller by a majority, and the state Senate had duly sworn him in. Thus, he was determined to take office. Bulkeley quickly informed him that no declaration by one branch of the General Assembly was valid. Furthermore, he let it be known that if assistance were needed to maintain order, he would be happy to supply it. Shocked by the implied threat, Staub asked if the governor intended to call out the military. Bulkeley shot back, "Yes, if necessary."[116]

There was stunned silence and Staub finally sought to diffuse the issue with humor, "Governor, if you order out the militia, be sure to get out the cavalry, for I'm a very fast runner." To which Bulkeley fired back, "If you start to run Mr. Staub, we won't hunt for you long."[117] If a resolution wasn't forthcoming, everyone could see Bulkeley would steal another two years in office without a second thought. The state Senate was completely impotent and, all day long, kept introducing one bill after another in a futile effort to assert their power.[118]

Just before four o'clock, Judge Morris was brought forth, and the Democratic senators announced they would do their duty and swear him in as governor. To howls of laughter, they passed a resolution inviting "the retiring governor" to the "inauguration." Meanwhile, a group was sent to Bulkeley's office to deliver the "invitation." As the *Courant* reported later, the following conversation took place:

"We are a committee appointed by the Senate to invite you to . . . the inauguration of the governor at four o'clock," said John Seymour of Norwalk.

"What?" said Bulkeley in a surprised tone. "By what authority does the Senate take this action?"

"We are unable to answer that question, as the Senate in its vote did not give us instructions," said Seymour lamely.

"I give you notice that I regard such action as revolutionary and unauthorized. No person that they inaugurate will be recognized by the state officials now in office. I regard these proceedings by one branch of the General Assembly as revolutionary. I desire you also to say to the Senate that they do it at the peril of each individual member."

"Will you give us your reply in writing, that we may submit it in the Senate?" asked Seymour meekly.

"I think you can remember it," said Bulkeley stone-faced.[119]

Just to make sure everyone understood the issue, Governor Bulkeley composed a proclamation which he had printed in all the city's newspapers a few days later. It read in part, "It having come to my knowledge that certain persons . . . have combined to . . . hold the chief executive offices of this state . . . by authority vested in me by the constitution. . . . [I] do hereby command all such persons to desist from their unlawful acts."[120]

Bulkeley may not have thought up the idea of calling out the military on his own. In the 1872 gubernatorial race, his friend and mentor, Marshall Jewell, had been the victim of some rather clumsy ballot box stuffing by the Democrats in New Haven's Fourth Ward.[121] When it was exposed, they didn't even bother to deny the fraud and, led by future governor Charles Ingersoll, demanded that the governor-elect on the "face" of the returns [Marshall Jewell] be seated and that the case then be adjudicated by the courts. With that, Hartford's ultraconservative future U.S. senator William Eaton, a Democrat, "expressed his fire-eating regret that the governor [James English] had not called out the militia to prevent this outrage and defy the legislature."[122] Jewell's election stood.

The stalemate at the General Assembly continued all through the spring of 1891 with neither side giving an inch. In some ways the situation went beyond bizarre. For example, even though the Democrats hated what Bulkeley was doing, on their own time they still liked him and socialized with him. Some members of the legislature declared Luzon Morris the governor, but then paid Bulkeley two dollars for commissions as notary publics bearing his signature as "governor."[123]

A special House election committee reported that all the Democratic candidates, except Nicholas Staub for comptroller, lacked overall majorities. At this, Comptroller Wright (outgoing) relinquished his office to Nicholas Staub. Having his nose under the tent, Staub thought he could forge a solution. He received word that a Democratic committee sought the use of a retiring room that was between the great Representatives' Hall and the governor's apartments. Never before had the members of the House used this room. When Staub asked about it, Governor Bulkeley said they could use the room, but he reserved the right to pass through it to access the great Hall of the House.[124]

It is not clear whether Staub thought he could really accomplish anything or was simply being obnoxious, but he persuaded superintendent Fred Goebell to attach a hasp—with a sturdy Yale padlock—on the door connecting this retiring room to the great Hall of the House.[125]

On Saturday morning, March 21, 1891, Governor Bulkeley walked from his home on Washington Street over to the Capitol and found the door padlocked from the opposite side. Immediately, he sent a staff member to the maintenance rooms in the basement for a crowbar.[126]

The man who actually wielded the crowbar was James Price, a deputy sheriff working under Sheriffs Spalding and Smith, all three responsible for guarding the governor's rooms at the Capitol. (Legend holds that Bulkeley had the actual crowbar recast into miniature "crowbar watch fobs," although no collector has ever seen one.)[127]

In a matter of seconds, the crowbar had done its work and the iron hasp and Yale lock were in Morgan Bulkeley's pocket. Before leaving the Capitol, he called Fred Goebell to explain that the governor of Connecticut would pass through any and all doors of the Capitol at his pleasure, and he (Goebell) was to ignore any future lock-down requests from the comptroller, or anyone else.[128]

Word of Bulkeley's method of dealing with the padlocked door spread wildly over the next few days and he was dubbed Connecticut's "Crowbar Governor." He loved it.

That same month, in an effort to force Governor Bulkeley out of office, Judge Luzon Morris brought *quo warranto* proceedings against Bulkeley in New Haven

Superior Court.[129] This initiative was a bit late because the matter had already become a cause célèbre. Besides, when did any court act in a timely fashion?

Meanwhile, the state Senate took a diabolical tack. As appropriations bills came up—earmarking funds to run the different departments of the state—they simply refused to pass them. Connecticut was soon out of money. The Democrats in the state Senate even went so far as to refuse to pay Governor Bulkeley's travel expenses.[130]

⬅ While running Aetna Life and serving as governor, a side of Bulkeley emerged that very few people were aware of. Routinely talented lawyers surrounded Bulkeley. Judging by comments he made before the state Senate, Bulkeley availed himself of this legal aptitude on a regular basis. When the 1879 General Assembly questioned him, Atty. Thomas Perkins asked, "Have you been to anyone's house within the past forty-eight hours to get anyone to go and see a member of the common council?" Bulkeley replied, "I presume I have conversed with an attorney." Perkins then asked, "With what attorney?" To which Bulkeley replied, "With several."[131]

There it was. While others went off to consult the law books for precedent, Bulkeley was way ahead of them. He knew exactly where he stood and proceeded accordingly. Bulkeley wasn't a cowboy. He had the best legal advice that money could buy, and lest it be forgotten, he was the one who suggested Connecticut give pensions to judges. Therefore, as the matter wound its way through the courts—and since judges are, after all, only human beings—one might say Bulkeley had an edge.

Even so, the state Senate backed him into a corner. That same month he met with officials of the finance committee for the state insane asylum at Middletown. Their funds were scheduled to run out August 1, 1891. Bulkeley told them "it was his duty to see that the institutions of the state were not left without sufficient funds. Furthermore, if the trustees gave him twenty-four hours notice, he would furnish whatever funds were needed."[132]

Governor Bulkeley pledged his entire fortune as a guarantee and arranged with Aetna Life to advance the necessary funds to run the state. Over the next eighteen months, Aetna Life advanced nearly $300,000. This was a whopping sum of money, but the cost to run the state for 1891 and 1892 was $3.9 million (actually for twenty-seven months owing to a change in fiscal year). Simple math shows that Governor Bulkeley, with the help of Aetna Life, was able to furnish less than 8 percent of the money required to pay all the state's bills for two years.[133] Clearly suppliers had to wait for their money, and salaries probably were not paid either. Somehow most got through the fiasco.

At about this same time, it became apparent that even the Republican organ, the *Courant*, wasn't backing Governor Bulkeley in his effort to steal a second term. The editor-in-chief, Charles Clark, was the son of Ezra Clark, who Bulkeley treated badly at council meetings back in the late 1870s and early 1880s. The jousting between Clark and Bulkeley forged an enmity that lasted for decades. Bulkeley claimed Gen. Hawley's paper, the *Courant*, was a "weak sister" when the fighting was on. This so vexed Charles Clark he was said to have "taken an oath to show Bulkeley that his paper [was] more of a 'singed cat' than a 'weak sister.' "[134]

These tussles often caused politicos to talk of a Bulkeley camp and a *Courant* camp, but this doesn't entirely explain the situation. Since 1867, there had been four—and for a time five—owners of the paper. Senator Joe Hawley and Charles Dudley Warner were long-standing part owners and both were considered elements of the Nook Farm crowd. In short, Morgan Bulkeley's battles with the *Courant* really amounted to an offshoot of the Nook Farmers' dislike of him, and more particularly, his political practices.[135]

In January 1892, the Supreme Court took up Judge Morris's *quo warranto* petition. After hearing from both sides, it handed down a unanimous decision that "Governor Bulkeley, in the absence of a constitutionally chosen successor, remained the de jure as well as de facto governor of Connecticut."[136]

This was an important hurdle for Bulkeley because the governors in neighboring states, like Governor David Hill of New York, for example, refused to recognize Bulkeley as the governor of Connecticut, and as such, would honor nothing with his name on it—not even a simple extradition order. Things weren't just coming to a halt in Connecticut, but in some of the neighboring states as well. However, once Bulkeley was declared governor, Comptroller Staub began to pay some of the state's bills, and a badly needed change in tenor took hold.[137]

As Connecticut citizens looked forward to the gubernatorial election in November 1892, they fostered high hopes that another election hitch wouldn't shut down the state again. The race pitted the long-suffering Judge Luzon Morris of New Haven against Morgan Bulkeley's Lieutenant Governor Sam Merwin.

Despite the longing for a clear winner, things looked bad because there were an ungainly five candidates in the race. Besides the Republican and Democratic candidates, there were three other entries—Edwin Auger of the Prohibition ticket, Edwin Ripley of the People's ticket, and a fifth-party candidate, Morris Reithor. To the great surprise of everyone, Judge Luzon Morris was able to win a simple majority, and in the process, became the next governor of the state.[138]

Voters in Connecticut may have admired Morgan Bulkeley's guts in refusing to relinquish the governor's office on principal, yet since suppliers and state workers didn't get paid for eighteen months, there had been the nagging possibility of violence. True, the state managed to get through it without any blood-shed, but things could easily have gotten out of hand.

Governor Bulkeley carried on the state's business until January 3, 1893, when he presented the following declaration to the General Assembly:

> To the honorable General Assembly . . .
>
> I have the honor to transmit herewith an exhibit of the financial trans-actions of the executive department for period commencing July 1, 1891 and ending Jan 3, 1893. Together with the vouchers of the same and the certificate of the state auditors as to its correctness.
>
> The disbursement through this department of nearly $300,000 during the period named was rendered necessary by the failure of the preceding General Assembly to make the customary appropriations for the conduct of the gov-ernment, and has been done without expense to the state, even in the way of interest, as the requisite funds were obtained at the same rate of interest the state was receiving on its bank deposits. I deemed it my duty under the provisions of the constitution "to take care that the laws be faithfully exe-cuted" and my oath of office of the government should fail or be impeded in the duties imposed upon it by law and for reasons unnecessary to repeat here, already familiar to the people of this state.
>
> I sincerely trust that the action of the department will receive your approval.
>
> Morgan G. Bulkeley, Governor[139]

The General Assembly declared all the acts of Governor Bulkeley valid, repaid Aetna Life $299,379.50 and got the state off to a fresh start.[140]

About five months later, Morgan Bulkeley was again called to the General Assembly to give testimony as the state Senate mulled over another Corrupt Election Practices Act.[141] One small detail is worthy of mention here. The man conducting the questioning, Democratic state Senator Edward S. Cleveland, was the very same man who introduced a resolution to have Governor Bulkeley's portrait painted about a month after he first took office in January 1889. Cleve-land was an odd duck with a stentorian voice and who was said to have resembled George Washington. However, when he was the Democratic nominee for gover-nor in 1886, newspapers around the state couldn't say enough bad things about him. The *Bridgeport Standard* tagged him "a political lightweight," while the *New London Telegraph*, a Democratic paper, regarded him as "inferior." Republican papers like the *Courant* considered him "a demagogue"—and worse.[142]

In any event, Bulkeley delivered some of the most controversial testimony ever heard in the General Assembly. To wit:

SENATOR CLEVELAND: Which is the greatest criminal, governor, he who buys or sells a vote?

GOVERNOR BULKELEY: There are a lot of voters who are devoid of principles themselves. . . . You cannot influence them by argument, and I believe that they should be influenced by those who know what is right. . . . I don't believe that there is a more honest man in Connecticut than he who for a day's work goes to the polls and votes as you want him to.

SENATOR CLEVELAND: Do I infer that it is right and lawful for a candidate for office to buy a vote that is for sale?

GOVERNOR BULKELEY: I think it is right for you as a candidate to secure that man's vote. If he is a man without principle and ignorant, by any means you can use. . . . I believe it to be proper for a man, acting in the interests of his party, his state and country, to influence in any way the unintelligent, ignorant and unprincipled voter to vote his party ticket, believing that the interests of his state and country were best served by the success of his party."[143]

These words of Bulkeleys were quoted far and wide by fair-minded journalists and muckrakers alike. Many believed Governor Bulkeley was rotten to the core. Maybe he was, but he considered himself a practical politician who insisted on getting things done. In Bulkeley's mind, sometimes rules had to be broken for good things to happen. It just didn't trouble him.

Governor Bulkeley's extra term in office has been discussed and debated at great length. In quizzes of Connecticut state history, a question sometimes surfaces regarding the governor who served from 1891 to 1893 without his name even appearing on the ballot. That said, a larger question looms. After the Republican State Committee refused him a second term, did Bulkeley then decide to steal a second term?

Like all politicians, Bulkeley was an opportunist. When the election of 1890 did not produce a majority for either candidate and Bulkeley had the chance to stay in office on a technicality, unlike his brother Billy, he took it. However, he could not possibly have seen the opportunity in advance. So said, no candidate had achieved a majority in the previous three elections—1884, 1886, and 1888. Bulkeley realized it could happen again, but he had no specific knowledge before the 1890 election. Nevertheless, when Judge Luzon Morris came up short, Bulkeley happily stepped into the breech.

Chapter Nine

ON THE SIDELINES

Shortly after the New Year's holiday in 1894, Morgan Bulkeley hosted a dinner at The Hartford Club for all of his former staff members. Since there had been many personnel changes, the club was packed. The party coincided with the fifth anniversary of Bulkeley's inauguration as governor in 1888. Since he had no idea how long he would have to wait for Joe Hawley's Senate seat, and was not entirely sure about his political future, there were no speeches, just warm comments and well-wishes all around.[1]

There surfaced one little oddity in the wake of Morgan Bulkeley's theft of a second term as governor. He became something of a folk hero in Connecticut. People admired his guts. However, as one newspaper noted many years later, "[T]he party was nearly wrecked by it and at the next election lost everything—hook, bob and sinker."[2] The Democrat, Judge Luzon Morris of New Haven, was elected with a comfortable majority of 1,800.[3] However, from 1879 to 1911, only two of sixteen governors were Democrats—Thomas Waller and Luzon Morris. (Incidentally, the Republicans added a prohibition plank to their platform, eliminating the need for the Prohibition Party.)[4] Did the voters choose Judge Morris out of sympathy, or were they determined to avoid more gridlock? Probably both.

Morgan Bulkeley's future in politics was perhaps more circumscribed than one might imagine. Although Gen. Joe Hawley entered the United States House of Representatives after his gubernatorial service, this was really quite unusual. Most politicians looked toward the U.S. Senate or the presidency as the next step. Including territorial, military, and protectorate governors, there have been twenty U.S. presidents who were governors before their years in the White House.[5]

Unlike Joe Hawley, Morgan Bulkeley had no interest in the U.S. House of Representatives, and with good reason. When he ran for governor, he didn't win the popular vote. Fortunately, he didn't have to. If he decided to run for U.S. senator, he wouldn't have to worry about the popular vote either because his friends in the Connecticut General Assembly—with or without their constituents' consent—would use secret ballots to put him in office. But things would be different if he ran for a seat in the U.S. House of Representatives. Bulkeley, by trickery or not, would have to carry the popular vote.

Bulkeley's choice to become a "holdover" governor on a technicality caused the kind of political flap he liked. He flexed his muscles, exhibited his political power, and earned the nickname "Crowbar Governor." James G. Batterson, the president of Travelers Insurance, started calling him "Caesar." Bulkeley loved all of it. The newspapers reveled in the material, and printed all sorts of wild scenarios for the eventual outcome of Bulkeley's stolen term as governor.[6]

For Bulkeley, this new folk-hero status was sweet nectar from the gods, but he was smart enough to realize the risk. If he couldn't get a popular majority when he ran for governor in 1888, his odds of getting a majority in the eight towns of the First Congressional District were probably even lower now. Not to put too fine a point on it, but probabilities might be *considerably* lower. Bulkeley had been manipulating elections far too long to delude himself. That left only the seats of Connecticut's two U.S. senators—Orville Platt of Meriden, who was so loved that voters elected him five times in a row, and the deeply respected and incorruptible Joe Hawley of Hartford.

Platt stood tall at six foot four and looked as homely as a man could get, but he had no equals when it came to good judgment and fidelity to his constituents. Consequently, he held his Senate seat longer than any Connecticut politician before him. He served for twenty-six years, from 1879 until his death in 1905.[7] When Morgan Bulkeley first became governor in January 1889, he knew that Connecticut Chief Justice John Park would be forced to retire on March 26, 1889, at age seventy.[8] Thus, in an attempt to free up a Senate seat, Bulkeley offered Judge Park's job to Platt, but he quickly turned it down.[9] Bulkeley then named ex-Gov. Charles B. Andrews to the position.

Joe Hawley held tight to Connecticut's other Senate seat. Even if Hawley hadn't been so entrenched, Bulkeley would have had a tough time taking the post from a bona fide Civil War hero and legendary Republican like "Fighting Joe." It has been said Morgan Bulkeley had a soft spot in his heart for Gen. Joe Hawley, Connecticut's First Soldier, but in truth, it was the other way around. Except in the case of criminal ineptitude—such as that of Gen. Ben Butler—Joe Hawley would never say a bad word about another soldier.

Hawley's father, Rev. Francis Hawley, a native of Farmington, spent the early years of his ministry in North Carolina. It was there that he married Mary McLeod of Fayetteville, and where Joseph was born in 1826. Eleven years later, the family returned to Connecticut where young Joe attended the local grammar schools in Bristol, Colebrook, Wallingford, and finally the Hartford Grammar School. In 1842, the family moved to Cazenovia, New York, a hotbed of the abolitionist movement; and Joe received an abbreviated secondary education at Oneida Conference (Cazenovia) Seminary. After receiving his diploma in 1843, Hawley enrolled in Hamilton College, and graduated in 1847 with special distinction as a speaker and debater.[10]

Upon returning to Connecticut, Joe Hawley studied law with John Hooker in Farmington, after which time the two men opened a practice in Hartford. In 1855, Hawley married one of Hooker's relatives, Harriet Ward Foote. With paternal roots in Guilford, Harriet Foote was related to the Wards and the Beechers on her mother's side. In fact, she was the cousin of three Nook Farm notables—Harriet Beecher Stowe, Isabella Beecher Hooker, and Mary Beecher Perkins.[11]

Joe Hawley was a brilliant attorney, but his first love was newspapers. He contributed regularly to the *Hartford Evening Press* until February 1857, when he became editor-in-chief. Another Hamilton College graduate and an old friend, Charles Dudley Warner, joined him in 1860, and the two men continued happily in the newspaper business until the outbreak of hostilities in April 1861. (The *Press* was a Free-Soil newspaper founded by some of the same men who founded the new Republican Party of Connecticut in February 1856. After the war, the Free-Soil ideal became meaningless, and the city wasn't big enough for two Republican newspapers. In 1867 the *Press* and the *Courant* merged.)[12]

Never an idle talker, Hawley was a doer. Remember, it was in the law offices of Hooker & Hawley that the first organizational meeting of the Republican Party of Connecticut was held in 1856.[13] Also, the day after President Lincoln called for 75,000 volunteers to serve for three months in the Union army, Joe Hawley was the first enlistee from Connecticut. After three months with the First Connecticut Infantry Volunteers, he reenlisted as a Lt. Colonel with the Seventh Connecticut and eventually was brevetted a Major General. "Fighting Joe" engaged in thirteen major battles, including Bull Run. His horse Billy once took a musket ball meant for him.[14] Hawley had guts.

In the years following the war, Gen. Hawley resumed his editorial work and was elected governor, representative, and finally senator. He represented the people of Connecticut in Washington, with a few minor interruptions, from 1872 until his death in 1905. The *New York Herald* wrote,

> There is a dash of romance in [Hawley's] career, and when we crown it all with an uninterrupted record for personal honesty, wherever placed and however tempted, my hand goes to the head and removes its covering. . . . From that point of view, it seems a very small thing that letters are left oftentimes unanswered for weeks, and one's address is forgotten; that the arts of the practical politician are uncultivated and that many things in the creed of public affairs are left undone that ought to be done. . . . Count them as weaknesses . . . but they are not the rules men use to weigh the worth of a man—a real man.[15]

According to Charles Clark of the *Courant*, Gen. Hawley was unsurpassed as a political speaker.[16] In his prime, he would scribble a few notes on the back of an old coal bill and spellbind a crowd with an unobstructed stream of fire and eloquence, delivered in his inimitable basso profundo voice. At about five foot six inches tall, he "had the brusque imperious manner of a feudal lord but, at other times, the tender heart of a woman." His only potentially serious fault was "he wasn't over-fond of work."[17]

Perhaps the greatest blessing in Joe Hawley's life was his wife, Harriet. She was "of slight frame and delicate organization," but what she lacked in physical presence she more than made up for in character. She was an iron butterfly.[18]

Sadly, Harriet never carried Joe Hawley's child, though the couple adopted Harriet's orphaned niece, Margaret, after the Civil War in 1885. When Joe enlisted in the First Connecticut Volunteer Infantry, Harriet too helped in the war effort, first as a teacher, then as a hospital visitor and later as a nurse. From 1862 on, she taught and then worked as a visitor in the Beaufort and Hilton Head General Hospitals, and the post hospital at St. Helena. Later, she nursed the wounded soldiers at the Armory Square Hospital in Washington. In her ninety-seven-bed ward, forty-eight severely wounded men from the Battle of the Wilderness died on just a single day in May 1864. Women with far tougher constitutions could not match Hattie Hawley's devotion.[19]

Naturally, the Hawley name was highly esteemed. In addition to Joe's father, the minister, Gen. Hawley's uncle, "Father" David Hawley, head of the City Mission Society, devoted most of his working life to Hartford's poor.[20] "Fighting Joe" hailed from a family that placed service to others among life's highest callings.

Bulkeley's biggest competitor for a U.S. Senate seat was Samuel Fessenden of Stamford. A member of a distinguished Maine family and a graduate of Harvard, Fessenden sported a reputation as a political organizer of rare ability and energy.[21] At the start of the Civil War, he joined the Seventh Maine Battery and served under Ulysses Grant at the Battle of the Wilderness, Spotsylvania, Cold Harbor, and Petersburg, retiring from service after Appomattox as a captain of the Union army. Despite a bumptious streak, Fessenden was enormously popular, not only for his brains and talent but also for his halo of gallant service during the war. On the less positive side, one newspaper editor quipped, "No one who knew him would say that modesty was his besetting weakness."[22]

Legend holds that Fessenden and Bulkeley made an agreement whereby the former would go after Orville Platt's seat and the latter would take Hawley's. Whether true or not, Fessenden soon decided Platt was unbeatable and broke the deal. Twice in the 1890s Bulkeley and Fessenden engaged in a fierce competition to steal Joe Hawley's seat—once in 1893 and again in 1899.[23] Since U.S. Senators were not elected by popular vote until the passage of the Seventeenth Amendment in 1913, there were no senatorial elections in November of 1892 or 1898. Instead each party put forth its best candidate and, in January, the General Assembly made its choice. The oath of office was administered in Washington on March 4.

Thanks to this insuperable bottleneck, Morgan Bulkeley spent the 1890s building up Aetna Life and attending Civil War reunions, parades, and campfires, while Sam Fessenden tended to his law practice in Stamford.

Meanwhile, Bulkeley's nemesis, Francis Goodwin, the shrewd and cagey land speculator, kept busy protecting and expanding his family's real estate business.[24] Bulkeley and Goodwin spent their whole lives trying to determine which of them exuded more machismo.

The Long Depression of the 1870s generated a 14 percent unemployment rate, and clogged the center of the city with the downtrodden. These bad times extended into the 1880s for the average workingman and created a whole new underclass loitering around City Hall Square. Obviously, this hurt businessmen who owned rental property in the area. (For example, James and Francis Goodwin inherited the United States Hotel on the north side of State Street when their father, James M. Goodwin, died in 1878.)[25] In response, Francis Goodwin convinced the city to allow Christ Church to organize the Open Hearth Mission in the old Kilbourne mansion at 135 Front Street. For the down-and-out, breakfast, dinner, and supper could be worked off by chopping wood behind the house. Basically, this kept unemployed men pinned to the mission and away from City Hall Square.[26]

The Open Hearth simply solved a small problem, but the city's park system piqued Goodwin's attention. A ring of parks around Hartford would increase the value of his land and building lots manifestly. Goodwin's campaign to convince Hartford's wealthiest citizens to leave their estates to the city for parks yielded two outstanding successes.

Charles Pond, president of the Hartford Trust Company, and hopeless alcoholic and morphine addict, lived on the 106-acre Prospect Hill Farm straddling the Hartford-West Hartford line.[27] Goodwin talked to Pond for years and finally won him over. The result brought forth Elizabeth Park, named for Pond's late wife. While Goodwin gently nudged the dissolute Charlie Pond, he also courted Henry and Walter Keney, who owned the largest wholesale grocery business in the state. Goodwin convinced the brothers to entrust a large part of their estate to establish Keney Park, a 680-acre Eden on the north side of the city.[28]

Here's the rub. True, parks provide a pleasing and environmentally important green-preservation to Hartford's cityscape, and bravo to Goodwin for securing the space. However, when Francis Goodwin died in 1923, he left an estate worth

$6.6 million, but did not bestow one thin dime or single piece of real estate on the City of Hartford.[29] Francis Goodwin's park-project scheme augured only to swell his own personal bankroll.

⮞ If there was one quality Morgan Bulkeley's friends could count on, it was his loyalty. In fact, sometimes he was loyal to a fault. In his career, Bulkeley often supported Republican candidates about whom he was lukewarm. So when he bolted on a Republican candidate, there had to be a pretty good reason. In 1894, such a case arose.

During Morgan Bulkeley's first year as governor, he convinced the members of the legislature that the toll on the Morgan Street Bridge to East Hartford should be abolished. By so doing, shopping and business traffic to Hartford would increase and congestion at the bridge would end. Plainly, this was in the best interest of the city. As mentioned previously, the purchase of the charter and the bridge itself ran $210,000. The bill passed the General Assembly, Governor Bulkeley signed it into law, and the toll was history by September 10, 1889.[30]

Here's the legislative problem. The Free Bridge Bill needed more than just the elected officials of the five towns closest to the bridge to support it in order to have a chance of winning favor in the General Assembly. Even though the free bridge would be good for the capital city, votes had to be bought. Typically, Republicans were paid for their votes, while Democrats were paid to stay home and not vote.[31] The total expense amounted to about $35,000—dubbed "legal expenses"—with East Hartford paying $10,000.[32] The matter slipped by quietly until an East Hartford auditor, Henry L. Goodwin (a distant relation to the Hartford Goodwins) stood up at a town meeting and asked, "Where is this $10,000 that East Hartford has paid out? Who's got it?"[33] His fellow townsmen took him aside and said conspiratorially, "East Hartford got good value for that money, so drop it." But Goodwin refused. He was such a straight arrow that, when he represented East Hartford in the 1871 General Assembly, he refused to accept full pay for the session because he missed a few days, even though he was still entitled to the money.[34] Henry Goodwin could be so forceful in his righteousness that the *Courant* once called him "the tedious Mr. Goodwin."[35]

Instead of letting the matter drop, Goodwin hired an attorney, Francis H. Parker, to get an injunction from Hartford Judge Elisha Carpenter, enjoining East Hartford from paying the yet-to-be-disbursed $5,000. Parker took the matter all the way to the Connecticut Supreme Court. Eight years after Bulkeley signed the Bridge Bill, the court found for Goodwin, so East Hartford never had to pay the extra $5,000.[36]

Henry Goodwin and Francis Parker's lawsuit shone an unwelcome light on this $35,000 bribery scheme, which soon enough became known as the "Free

Bridge Scandal." During preliminary hearings into the matter, Morgan Bulkeley flatly stated that as long as it was for a good purpose, he didn't care if the expenditure was legal or not.[37] Oddly perhaps, Bulkeley expected everyone to think like him. When someone—like Francis H. Parker—hewed to a higher moral standard, Bulkeley had little patience. Therefore, in 1894 when Bulkeley found out Parker wanted to run for the state Senate, he swung into action.

Morgan Bulkeley was a complex man, who more than once in his political career displayed a vindictive streak. Since Parker almost single-handedly stripped him of the crowning jewel of his first term as governor—the free bridge—it would not have been out of character for Bulkeley to hang Parker out to dry.

However, the matter was far more complex. When a legislator was described as loyal to Bulkeley, it meant he was a team player and that his vote could be counted on when difficult legislation came up—perhaps for a price, perhaps not. Each case was different. So said, every time Bulkeley allowed a seat in the statehouse to go to an incorruptible man like Parker, his base effectively eroded. With enough men like Parker in the statehouse, Bulkeley's power would have quickly vanished.

Parker's résumé read as fine as any to come before the Republican State Committee—Wesleyan University, Yale Law School, and five years as a prosecuting attorney.[38] In truth, Parker looked so good on paper, and in person, that he obliged the committee to let him run. Unfortunately, the high-minded attorney wasted his time, because Morgan Bulkeley had already marked him for political oblivion.

Instead of backing Parker, Bulkeley threw all his support behind the malleable Democrat, John H. Hall. Bulkeley was endlessly inventive when it came to getting his way in politics. He knew elections were like courtships. Voters needed time to get used to a candidate. Deviously, Bulkeley announced that he was running for the state Senate and kept insisting he was a better candidate than Parker all the way into November.[39] Only after the Republican State Committee sent him a letter, begging him to step aside *for the good of the party* did Bulkeley relent.[40] Still, he managed to deprive Parker of that all-important courtship period.

Just to be on the safe side, Bulkeley also made an effort to steer voters away from Parker at the polls. According to the *Hartford Post*, longtime Bulkeley crony and fixer, Gideon Winslow, passed out Republican ballots on which friendly Democrats John H. Hall and Daniel Markham neatly replaced the Republican Party candidates for state senator and judge of probate respectively.[41]

Parker had come face-to-face with an ugly reality. At least while Morgan Bulkeley was around, his political career was a nonstarter. Six years later, with the recommendation of another incorruptible, Senator Joe Hawley, Parker was appointed U.S. attorney for Connecticut in the McKinley administration. Then in 1909—with Bulkeley nearing the end of his single term as U.S. senator and his political life almost over—Parker was finally able to represent Hartford in the General Assembly.[42]

≫ Bulkeley's life quieted down after the madness of his last two years in the governor's office. Almost fifty-six now, he was as healthy as a horse. Considering the tremendous burdens Bulkeley assumed—in business, in politics, and in his family obligations—it's quite remarkable that he enjoyed healthiness all of his life. Other than missing one council meeting because of some mysterious fever while he was mayor, he was never ill.[43] He nourished a hearty appetite. His mood was fairly uniform—although he became increasingly short tempered with reporters—and from time to time, associates alluded to a bit of insomnia.

He was out of politics for the moment, but Bulkeley still wasn't able to devote all his time to Aetna Life. Hartford had a problem that cried out for an able administrator. Bulkeley's ability to get things done—the *action* component of his winning formula—had become legendary, and now the city needed him.

Once again, it was the bridge to East Hartford. On a Friday night in May 1895, the covered bridge caught fire and burned madly until nothing was left save the stone piers in the river.[44] For the first time in fifty years, ferries began running from the shoreline in front of the River House—the biggest whorehouse in the city.[45] Two ferryboats were brought in to help shuttle passengers across the river—the *F.C. Fowler* from Goodspeed's Landing in East Haddam and the *Gildersleeve* from Portland.[46]

Within a few weeks, Governor Morris appointed a new Hartford Bridge Commission, which met in the tollhouse of the old bridge company on the banks of the river. Despite the best of intentions, the bridge commission got off to a poor start. Some members demanded an investigation of the fire, while others aspired to forge ahead. Some wanted the new bridge made of iron, while others wanted stone. It was a snarl.[47]

At last a meeting was held in Morgan Bulkeley's office at Aetna Life and he was elected president of the new commission. At the same time, straws were drawn to determine the length of service for each member of the group. It hardly mattered. Opinions on the materials and architecture of the new bridge mounted and completely stalled the committee's efforts to keep the project moving forward.[48]

Negotiations on the details of the new Hartford Bridge continued for the rest of 1895, testing everyone's patience and causing a number of commissioners to quit in disgust. Meanwhile, the committee sanctioned a temporary bridge, but just before Christmas of 1895, ice jams broke it up and sections of the bridge floated away with the rising freshet. As a temporary measure, Bulkeley arranged once again for the ferryboat *Gildersleeve* to ferry people back and forth to East Hartford.[49]

After the holidays, a flood carried away what remained of the temporary bridge and constituents pressed Bulkeley even harder to solve the problem. There were four ferries and steamers—two for animals and two for passengers—trying to negotiate the very small section of water between Hartford and East Hartford, and the weather wasn't cooperating. Accidents were numerous, and one by one, the ferries were forced into dry dock. The action component of Bulkeley's public persona was tarnished a bit but he eventually delivered a fabulous stone bridge. However, not before this mess dogged the city for years.[50]

In January 1899, the Republicans held a caucus to determine who would occupy Joe Hawley's Senate seat for the next six years. These caucuses always caused a great deal of excitement because almost anything could happen. "Fighting Joe" wanted to keep his seat, but the state Speaker of the House, Sam Fessenden, had run out of patience. His intention was to steal the seat from both Hawley and Morgan Bulkeley, and he came up from Stamford with a platoon of supporters and a ravenous appetite for victory.[51]

The atmosphere at the Capitol was perfect for a nasty political fight. The shades were pulled in the great Hall of the House, and the doors were bolted. No one could enter or leave the caucus. Not even a scrap of paper was allowed out of the room. Quickly the temperature in the hall soared, but the legislators were too preoccupied to remove their coats, allowing the smell of perspiration to waft over the grand chamber. Every other sentence out of the legislators' mouths was constructed around the word "chances." "What are Hawley's chances?" "What are the chances Fessenden has the votes?" "What are the chances Bulkeley and Hawley have made a deal?" "What are the chances Hawley will win on the first ballot?"[52]

The caucus began in the early afternoon and went through seven ballots with still no clear victor. After each ballot, the results were scribbled on a piece of paper and held up to the glass on the door for the reporters out in the lobby. Hawley only needed a few more votes, but they simply couldn't be found. Fessenden was in second place, but still twenty votes short. Bulkeley had put out the word that he did not want to unseat Hawley, but still received twenty-one votes from loyal friends.[53]

The balloting dragged on until eight in the evening and the possibility of an all-night session was in the air. In the eighth round, Bulkeley realized he had to head off Fessenden, so he told his supporters to vote for Hawley.[54] It was the smart thing to do. Fessenden was a relatively young man—only fifty-one—and, if elected now, could serve for the next two decades. By bowing out now, Bulkeley could have Hawley's seat in 1905, and his dream of "rounding out his career" with a term in the U.S. Senate would be achieved.

When the results of the eighth ballot were announced, Hawley had 117 to Fessenden's 69. "Fighting Joe" had just won a fourth term. A few days after his victory, he wrote a letter to Morgan Bulkeley:

> Dear Governor—
> I learn by the tabulated vote and by the telegrams from my friends that I am very greatly indebted to you for my success. I thank you most heartily and shall perhaps have the pleasure of doing so in person within a week.
> Excuse my brevity, for I have a bushel of letters and telegrams, more or less, to answer.
> Yours truly,
> J. R. Hawley[55]

In 1899, a man who would later betray Bulkeley surfaced. His name was George P. McLean, and he was a founding partner of the law firm of Sperry & McLean in Hartford.[56]

McLean was twenty years younger than Bulkeley and could trace his roots all the way back to Governor Bradford of *Mayflower* fame. He was born on a farm in Simsbury but came to Hartford at a young age, graduating from Hartford High School in 1877. Thereafter he went to work as a reporter for the *Hartford Post*. Then he was given the opportunity to study law with one of Hartford's leading attorneys, Henry C. Robinson, and was admitted to the bar in 1882. McLean represented his native Simsbury in both chambers of the General Assembly and was later appointed U.S. attorney for Connecticut during the Harrison administration.[57]

In March 1899, he represented Aetna Life in a General Assembly battle with James G. Batterson, the founder and president of Travelers Insurance. Morgan Bulkeley had purchased 1,000 shares of Travelers' stock as an investment for Aetna Life and had made it clear to Batterson—or thought he had—that the shares were strictly an investment. Aetna Life had no designs on Travelers.[58]

Batterson, with his flowing white beard and enormous girth, looked like central casting's idea of Santa Claus, however misleading. Batterson had begun his working life as a stonecutter in his father's quarry in Bloomfield, but eventually drifted into the insurance business. He was a genius and a true autodidact, a man who taught himself to read and write Greek and Latin.[59] Unfortunately, he didn't like Bulkeley, and had taken to calling him "Caesar" behind his back. Perhaps because he realized this little insult had reached Bulkeley's ears, and unaware that Bulkeley actually relished the epithet, Batterson became paranoid, fancying his life's work, Travelers Insurance, would be swallowed whole by Aetna Life. To head off this fate, Batterson petitioned the General Assembly for a law forbidding insurance companies from buying other insurance firms in the same business. Since Aetna Life had been writing accident insurance since 1891, such a law would protect Travelers.

Morgan Bulkeley had taken George McLean under his wing politically and also made sure the younger man's law firm got a good chunk of Aetna Life's legal work. In this case, McLean convinced the legislature that the new law Batterson had in mind was not only unnecessary, but probably unconstitutional. Nevertheless, Morgan Bulkeley would rue the day he steered Aetna Life's legal work to McLean, and even more so the day he helped "Gentleman George" McLean become governor.[60] As the nineteenth century came to a close though, the two men's friendship remained intact.

 By 1900, Connecticut's "rotten boroughs" system of representation at the General Assembly had become a disgrace. Both the Senate and the House were malapportioned. However, the problems in the Senate were nothing compared to the grossly unfair representation in the House of Representatives. Each town in Connecticut—regardless of size—received two votes in the House. Therefore, New Haven, with a population of 108,000, and little Union, with 428 citizens, each had two Representatives. Forty-four towns supported populations under 1,000, and seven of these numbered under 500. In short, forty-four towns—with an aggregate population of only 30,000—could easy overrule the four largest cities—with a combined citizenry of 300,000.[61] Something had to be done.

By the spring of 1901, even though he was personally opposed to a Constitutional Convention, newly elected Governor McLean sustained sufficient pressure to call for one. Not just Democrats, but many Republicans recognized the inequities as indefensible.[62]

At issue were three things. The first was the little technicality that had allowed Morgan Bulkeley to sit through two extra years as governor. A simple amendment to the state constitution giving the race to the candidate with the highest number of votes seemed long overdue. This was called the *plurality* issue. The second matter was the unfair representation in the state, referred to as the "rotten boroughs" system of government. The third item simply asked that a constitutional convention be convened to address these matters. This sparked a spell of wrangling that lasted several months.

The real showdown featured a back-and-forth debate between James Batterson and Morgan Bulkeley.[63] It is difficult to assess the true relationship of these two men because they were so dissimilar and traveled in completely different worlds. Batterson was a Baptist, very unusual in the upper reaches of Hartford society. Also, he was extremely well read, self-taught in geology, physics, engineering, painting, sculpture, sociology, economics, Greek, and Latin, and he could speak all of the modern languages of Europe. Batterson eschewed elective politics, but was a member of numerous scientific clubs in New England and New York. During his lifetime, Yale and Williams Colleges conferred honorary degrees on him.[64] It is fair to say that Batterson's intellectual abilities were unsurpassed in the Hartford area, and probably far beyond.

Batterson's grandmother was a Goodwin, and he married the former Eunice Goodwin, a first cousin of Francis Goodwin. Every member of this clan that Bulkeley became acquainted with caused him trouble in one way or another. Is this the reason he and Batterson were never close? Possibly.

In any event, Batterson argued forcefully in favor of a constitutional convention, while Morgan Bulkeley argued against it. Bulkeley's many friends in the legislature wouldn't be his friends long if he couldn't maintain the status quo. The Republicans from the small towns held a disproportionate amount of power in the state. Only by killing this attempt to change the "rotten boroughs" system of government would they be able to hold on to the power they had. Morgan Bulkeley's moment of truth presented itself.

As the sessions at the Capitol wore on, Bulkeley took the position that the state Senate was at the heart of the problem, claiming the state had failed in its responsibilities to redistrict properly.[65]

When he was asked to comment on the plurality election of governors and other state officials, he said the matter didn't even warrant discussion. Though he was in over his head debating Batterson, Bulkeley did make one cogent point. Since the state constitution provided the means for its own amendment, why did the legislators think they needed a constitutional convention? Moreover, the constitution did not give them the power to call a convention. Bulkeley felt the General Assembly should simply abide by the constitution and make the changes it saw fit. Thereafter, the people of Connecticut could vote to accept or reject the changes.[66]

It was James Batterson's turn. As expected, Batterson was erudition itself. Quoting from many different texts, he gave the whole chamber a lesson in the history of the state constitution and also the history of representation in Connecticut. He gently scolded members of the legislature who said political power was inherent in the towns. In point of fact, the towns had no rights. The only rights they had, they received from the legislature. Lastly, he made a stinging point that even Morgan Bulkeley was at a loss to dispute. He said it was not right for the legislature to pass on matters in which its members had a personal interest. Only by holding a constitutional convention would personal interest be removed from the equation.[67]

In his second day of testimony, Batterson took special aim at Bulkeley's point that the state Senate was redistricted poorly. The Senate was never supposed to be based on population, he pointed out, but the House was. Therefore, the crux of the matter was that the representation of the towns in the House had to be based more fairly on population.[68]

In rebuttal to one of ex-Governor Bulkeley's speeches, Batterson bellowed, "[Bulkeley] held aloft a verbatim record of my [so-called] errors and I watched for the gubernatorial 'crowbar' with which I and mine were to be speedily demolished . . . but . . . at that point, he dexterously slid away from the 'errors.' Why did he not point out the errors one by one if he could, and stick a pin through them, instead of shaking his rusty old 'crowbar' at me and leaving the errors alone?"[69]

Batterson's stylish rhetoric flowed scholarly, precise and logical. While the other speakers were reduced to tired, hackneyed prose, Batterson's understanding of the intent of the founding fathers of Connecticut was as awe-inspiring as his words were elegant.

Bulkeley's arguments, when held against Batterson's spellbinding discourse, fell flat. Batterson's golden "disinterested party" premise carried the day. Bulkeley lost the first round, as the legislature voted to hold a constitutional convention the following year.[70] Still, Bulkeley fought. He didn't mind losing the first battle as long as he won the war. (Evidently, James Batterson had not been in the best of health during this period. In September, he died in his sleep. He was seventy-eight.)[71]

In October 1901, the people of Connecticut voted in favor of adopting a plurality amendment, by which governors and other state officials would no longer need a majority to win.[72] This effectively reduced the power of the Republicans in the House. For another dozen years, the General Assembly would still have complete control over the appointment of U.S. senators, but the popular vote would now determine who governed the state. As things stood, Bulkeley's friends at the statehouse could still put him in the U.S. Senate, and he was determined to make sure it stayed that way.

In the same election, the voters decided to hold a constitutional convention. Bulkeley was really under the gun now. His job was clear. He had to muddy the waters enough to make certain voters would reject any proposed changes to the existing constitution. If the representation in the General Assembly were altered, it would dilute the power of his friends and possibly jeopardize his own political career.

Just as 1902 began, the constitutional convention got underway with recently retired chief justice of the state, Charles Andrews of Litchfield acting as president.[73] The convention lasted five months and produced some rather dramatic results—in truth, too dramatic.

The proposed changes would realign the Senate so there were forty-five districts, with similar populations in each.[74] Meanwhile, the House would be filled as follows—towns with less than under 2,000 citizens, one vote; town with populations between 2,000 and 50,000, two votes; towns with populations between 50,000 and 100,000, three votes; and lastly, towns of 100,000 or more would get four votes—plus one more vote for each extra 50,000 of population.[75]

The result was precisely as Morgan Bulkeley had hoped. The cities didn't think the changes went far enough, and the small towns were wary of any changes at all. While the voters called for a constitutional convention two-to-one, they barely showed up at all to vote on the proposed changes. In a gubernatorial race, for example, about 150,000 votes were cast, while only 31,000 voters weighed in on the changes to the constitution, *and 66 percent voted against it*.[76] Bulkeley won. (The "rotten boroughs" system of government in Connecticut remained uncorrected for another six decades.)

〰 The whole ruckus about changes in Connecticut's constitution lasted for over six months and ended with a dull thud on June 16, 1902, when the people said "No," and then made their summer vacation plans. As usual, Morgan Bulkeley took his small family to Fenwick. However, on August 22, 1902, he found a special reason to be in Hartford. The new president, Teddy Roosevelt, as part of a getting-to-know-you tour of New England, was scheduled to be in town.[77]

Roosevelt rose early and sailed on the *Sylph* to New Haven, where he boarded his private train for the trip to Hartford. Unfortunately for Morgan Bulkeley, Roosevelt's tour was a brief one and the welcoming committee was composed of the men in office at the time. Lt. Governor Keeler stood in for Governor McLean—on vacation because of an attack of nervous prostration—and Mayor Ignatius Sullivan did Irish-Americans proud by greeting the president as soon as he arrived.[78]

Roosevelt traveled a long parade route through the streets of Hartford in Pope's new Columbia Grand Victoria, an electric carriage, capable of carrying two passengers in the middle of the car.[79] The chauffeur rode high in the back, as with a hansom cab.[80] Traveling with the president in the automobile was Col. Jacob Greene, the welcoming committee chairman. Teddy Roosevelt was the first president to greet crowds from an automobile.

〰 Just before Thanksgiving 1902, Morgan Bulkeley's brother Billy, his closest friend, died of Bright's disease and other complications. He was only sixty-two. He had been an invalid for three years, although he managed to continue as president of Kellogg & Bulkeley up until a year before he died. The funeral took place at Bulkeley's home on Washington Street with Rev. Parker of South Congregational Church officiating. He was later interred in the Bulkeley family plot at Cedar Hill.[81]

Billy was the most affable of men, but lacking the stone heart that politics demanded, he could not succeed as his brother did in the games of power and at last stuck to business matters instead. Besides Kellogg & Bulkeley, he also was a partner in the Bee Hive dry goods store and he bought and sold land in Hartford as often as he could find the time. Thanks to his natural hustle, Billy managed to leave an estate of $1.1 million.[82]

Trouble never travels alone. On January 31, 1903, Fannie Bulkeley's father died at his Franklin Street mansion in San Francisco. Gen. James F. Houghton had been in declining health for about six months, and a case of pneumonia finally took him. He was seventy-five. At the time of her father's death, Fannie's mother survived, but her brother, Harry, had passed away in 1901 at age forty-three.[83] Fannie may or may not have headed west for the funeral—the record is unclear—but Governor Bulkeley remained in town.

There were so many contradictions in Bulkeley's life that one is often hard pressed to understand some of his choices. For example, he was elected Department Commander of the Grand Army of the Republic in May 1903 and he appointed his great rival, Sam Fessenden, as his advocate general.[84] Since he and Fessenden were such fierce rivals for the U.S. Senate seat of Joe Hawley, one has to wonder what Bulkeley was up to. Did he want Fessenden close by so he could keep an eye on him? Did he intend to saddle Fessenden with duties designed to get him out of town at opportune times? Or was this a sincere effort to extend an olive branch to his rival? Unfortunately, Bulkeley's real motive will forever remain a mystery. However, one thing must be remembered. Bulkeley actually liked Fessenden as a person. This could never be said of a man like Francis Goodwin. Beyond that, we are left to wonder.

As the Department Commander of the Grand Army of the Republic, Bulkeley had the right to decide where the national encampment would be held. Although it made no sense to hold a Civil War reunion in San Francisco—California wasn't involved in the Civil War—that's exactly where he organized one.

About six weeks before the national encampment, he made the necessary arrangements with the railroad and had the particulars of the trip printed in the newspaper. Engineers engaged a special train that included five sleepers, an observation car, baggage car, and dining car for the two hundred veterans. Best of all, this train ran straight through without a break—past Denver and Salt Lake City—from the shores of the Atlantic to the piers in San Francisco. The trip cost each man $78.50, and from existing accounts, it was worth every penny. The old

CROWBAR GOVERNOR

soldiers spent a fun-filled week in San Francisco and then returned home.[85] The Bulkeleys stayed on, spending a few extra weeks at Caroline Houghton's summer home in San Jose.

Bulkeley's correspondence with Joel English, the acting president of Aetna Life, shows the Bulkeleys leaving San Francisco sometime around September 5, this time choosing the Shasta Route—from San Francisco through Portland, Oregon; east from Seattle to Spokane and other places on the Northern Pacific railway; then to Minneapolis; down to Chicago; on to Buffalo; and through the Lehigh Valley route to New York. From there, they caught the New York, New Haven, and Hartford road to Fenwick. In a letter to Joel English at Aetna Life, written September 3, Bulkeley, now sixty-five wrote, "I have been in the best of health during my stay here, but shall be exceedingly glad once again to put myself in the harness in good old Connecticut."[86]

After returning to work, Bulkeley gathered a few reporters one day and said, "What the West wants—and I told them—is men and young men, those not burdened with many ties and with the energy and ability to succeed. They have plenty of land, arid and in need of irrigation, and the climate is splendid."[87]

As early as 1882, Bulkeley had been thinking about underwriting accident insurance. Of course, these things take time and this new line was not added to Aetna Life until 1891. Thereafter, the addition of new lines came more quickly. In 1899, health insurance was added, followed in 1902 by liability insurance. Automobile insurance came a little later, with a complete auto policy—covering fire, theft, collision, and bodily injury—in 1913. As one can easily see, by the turn of the twentieth century, Aetna Life was no longer simply another life insurance company. Instead, it had morphed into a full-line insurance conglomerate—and one that needed more space.[88]

Since the Charter Oak Life building that Morgan Bulkeley practically stole in 1888 occupied the most desirable location in the city, a move to another site didn't generate a whole lot of enthusiasm. Aetna Life had bought some land in the western part of the city, but then decided simply to remodel the existing building, work that was completed in 1904. Bulkeley took the north front office on the top floor.[89]

Aetna Life's building on the northeast corner of Main and Atheneum streets underwent a far more serious metamorphosis in 1913–14. In order to almost double the office space available to the firm, the officers and directors decided to add four floors atop the existing six, but in a most peculiar way. Eight massive steel columns would run from bedrock up to the top of the future ten-story building. From these columns, a steel truss work would be built and the new masonry stories added by building the top one first and working down to the existing building. When all of the construction was completed, even if the original floors of the building were removed, the top four fl urs uld still be hanging on these enormous columns. The work was completed in late 1914.[90]

≈ As a young man, Morgan Bulkeley was not troubled by the lack of a plan or the fact that he was going nowhere. For eighteen years, he sold household goods in Brooklyn with nary a complaint, but as he got older, these periods of political inactivity grated on him. Once he had a taste of power, he missed it when he was sidelined. The years from 1893 to 1905 were particularly frustrating because Senator Joe Hawley proved such an immovable obstacle.

Hawley was Mr. Republican in Connecticut, a war hero, a well-educated and well-read man with a remarkable gift for oratory. People admired Hawley; many envied him. Although Bulkeley and Fessenden fought desperately to pry Hawley out of his Senate seat in 1893 and 1899, Morgan Bulkeley might have been more surprised than anyone had he succeeded. Sam Fessenden held a higher self-opinion, and could have taken Hawley's seat without a backward glance. Bulkeley was different. Had he unseated Hawley, he probably would have sensed a certain inappropriateness in the move. Ultimately, he waited for Joe Hawley to run out of steam.

Chapter Ten

FENWICK

Although Morgan Bulkeley was not one of the first cottagers at Fenwick, he became so inextricably linked to this upscale beach community that writing about his life without including something about it would be like writing about Teddy Roosevelt without mentioning Oyster Bay. When Bulkeley first returned to Hartford as a young bachelor, he would take a room for the weekend at the Fenwick Hall hotel, in order to be with his sister, Mary; his brother Billy; and his other relatives. It doesn't seem likely that Bulkeley envisioned the day when he would be the grand potentate of this little settlement by the sea. Then again, who's to say?

Based on the exclusivity of twenty-first-century Fenwick, it tasks the imagination to know that this lovely Shangri-La was once just another failed real estate speculation, but that's exactly what it was.

In 1870, three friends, Daniel Spencer and Richard and John Bushnell, bought the old Pratt Farm and a few other parcels on Lynde's Neck and then resold all 250 acres to a group of Hartford investors for $41,780. This group of speculators, the New Saybrook Company, was the brainchild of Leverett Brainard, G. Wells Root, and C. S. Weatherby, among others.[1]

Immediately, the partners sold shares in the company to one hundred of their closest friends for $1,000 apiece. For that price, the lucky buyer received a building lot plus a single share of the New Saybrook Company. Soon thereafter, the principals commissioned Hartford architect Seneca Lincoln to draw plans for an ultraluxurious hotel, Fenwick Hall, which was completed by the builder Amander Hurlbut in July 1871.[2]

Nelson Hollister of Hartford, William Patton of Springfield, and Julius Eldridge, also of Springfield, built the first three cottages.[3] A few years later, the Brainards bought the Eldridge place and relocated it nearer the waterfront on the west side of Fenwick Avenue.[4] Originally a small cottage for four, the Brainards added to their home as their ten children arrived, and soon the cottage was a truly grand dwelling.[5] Unlike most of their friends, the Brainards preferred the waterfront area to the more convenient lots near Fenwick Hall's dining facilities.

The original owners of the Fenwick building lots included Elizabeth Colt,

R. W. H. Jarvis, president of Colt's Patent Fire-Arms; George Day of the Weed Sewing Machine Company; G. Wells Root of A. & C. Day Dry Goods; Hiram Bissell of H & S Bissell; Thomas Enders of Aetna Life; A. P. Pitkin of Pitkin Brothers; Henry Keney of Keney Brothers Grocers; Billy Buckley, now with Kellogg & Bulkeley; and several others.[6]

When it first opened in 1871, Fenwick Hall generated a booming business with 150 paying guests staying there at any time during the summer. Another 100 showed up on Saturday nights for the entertainment. There were times when cots had to be set up in the downstairs parlors to accommodate all the guests.[7]

On the first floor of Fenwick Hall, there were bedrooms, parlors, a reading room, and a grand saloon on the south side. On the east side, looking out to the Connecticut River and the Sound, sprawled a massive dining room—eighty by forty-four feet. A twelve-foot-wide corridor led to the first and second floor bedchambers—suites of two, three, four, and six rooms. The entire hotel was gas lit. A sixteen-foot-wide, four-hundred-foot-long veranda wrapped almost completely around the building.[8]

For the more active set, the hotel offered sailing, rowing, fishing, swimming, croquet, and tennis. On the northeastern part of the Fenwick property, guests could find bowling alleys and a "casino" for the kids.

The most affluent families of Hartford were buying lots like mad and looking forward to building cottages, but the Panic of 1873 changed all that. By the end of the Long Depression of the 1870s, Charter Oak Life had foreclosed on Fenwick Hall's mortgages and the New Saybrook Company was defunct.[9]

Each season, Charter Oak Life rented the hotel to an outside proprietor who thought he could make a go of it. In the first eight years, three different managers gave it a try, remodeling as needed, introducing new entertainments and enhancing the menu—whatever it took. Despite some truly noble efforts, one by one these entrepreneurs lost money and were forced to give up. Some seasons Fenwick Hall didn't open at all; others, it ran out of paying guests by the first week of August. The managers even cut the rate to three dollars a day in an attempt to keep the place full.[10] All for naught.

Smart Yankees that they were, most of the wealthy families who had purchased lots took a wait-and-see approach. They would build a cottage only after they were convinced the place had a future. Ten years after the first lots went up for sale, only eighteen cottages dotted the land at Fenwick. Some of the cottagers would eventually have big families—Mary and Leverett Brainard delivered their ten children; Billy and Emma Bulkeley raised six; G. Wells Root and his wife Paulina brought five; and Francis and Mary Goodwin added eight.[11]

Nevertheless Fenwick seemed melancholy. The hotel and all the cottages sat

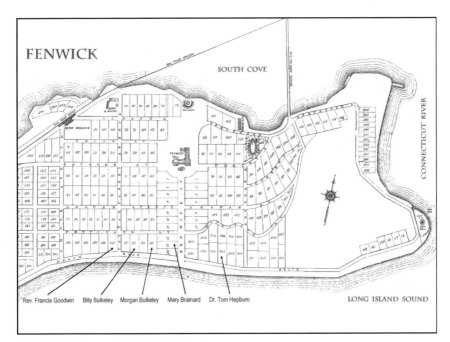

SOUTH COVE

CONNECTICUT RIVER

Rev. Francis Goodwin   Billy Bulkeley   Morgan Bulkeley   Mary Brainard   Dr. Tom Hepburn

LONG ISLAND SOUND

Map of Fenwick

on what had once been a cow pasture. There were no trees, no shrubbery, no bushes and very little grass. It was just a windswept piece of barren land with a mammoth, bankrupt hotel in the middle of it—and that was boarded up much of the time.[12]

Around 1880, Rev. Francis Goodwin, weary of the three-mile trip to Grace Episcopal Church in Old Saybrook, started fabricating Sunday services in the front parlor of his cottage. Soon, neighbors asked to sit in. Five years later, he asked carpenters to build a small chapel in his back yard.[13]

Sensing that the little chapel needed a home of its own—and knowing full well Francis Goodwin would rather ingest Paris Green than part with any of his extra building lots—G. Wells Root donated a lot for the Fenwick Chapel.[14] Ultimately, Goodwin's chapel was moved, enlarged, renovated, and given the name St. Mary's by the Sea.[15]

In the 1880s, the guest list at Fenwick Hall often included mayors, governors, captains of industry, and some just plain—albeit wealthy—folks.

By the summer of 1886, Mayor Bulkeley was a married man with a child and had more interest in Fenwick than ever before. Usually Morgan and Fannie stayed at Fenwick Hall for most of August. The Valley Railroad proved an enormous blessing for the cottagers—and also Mayor Bulkeley—as they all used the train well into the twentieth century to get back and forth to their summer places at Fenwick. At the end of each summer's workday, some of the most prominent businessmen in Hartford walked down to a little station on State Street by the river and boarded the 3:55 train to Saybrook. Early the next morning, they caught the northbound train at Fenwick station.[16]

One not so welcome guest at Fenwick Hall was Edward "Ned" Stokes, who arrived on his steam yacht *Fra Diavolo* with twenty-five New Yorker friends.[17] Stokes's reputation preceded him, and the society families at Fenwick were not at all pleased to have a murderer staying at Fenwick Hall. Besides his unsavory reputation, Stokes attracted a strange collection of Tammany Hall politicians, like Richard Croker, John J. Scannell, and Police Commissioner Jacob Hess. As if that weren't bad enough, he invited an eccentric group of New York theater people, like matinee idol Richard Mansfield and his paramour and future wife, Beatrice Cameron.[18]

The cottagers pondered a whole other set of perplexities in addition to avoiding the transient guests at Fenwick Hall. The families who decided to spend the summer at the shore needed their carriages and teams with them. Most cottagers opted to ship their horses and carriages downriver on a steamer. The Brainards were an exception because their coachman, Frank Wallace, didn't approve. Instead, he and the Brainard boys drove the carriages and teams the forty-five miles to Old Saybrook and back.[19]

In the days leading up to the transfer, the horses were exercised sparingly. (Mary Brainard always thought Frank Wallace used this as an excuse so he wouldn't have to drive her around the city.)[20] When the departure day came, Frank packed the carriages with extra harnesses in burlap bags, water buckets, lanterns, feed, and cottage goods for the summer.[21]

The Brainards often brought along a cow, with the expectation that Frank Wallace would care for her. Assumedly, Wallace approved of steam-shipping her, and he didn't drive the cow down the coast too.

By eight o'clock on the morning of departure, Frank and the boys got the grueling trip underway. The roads, often muddy and deeply rutted, were torturous. The horses got a break and took some food and water at the stable of the Higganum Inn. A little later, the drivers ate lunch on a hill overlooking the East Haddam ferry.[22]

Fenwick Hall's stables were on the north side of the settlement—near South Cove—where ocean breezes whipped away the stall smells. Spreading out in both directions, were private carriage sheds. Many of these sheds had sleeping quarters above for the coachmen.[23] Once safely settled at the shore, the teams—and the family's carriages—were used daily in the same fashion they were used back in Hartford.

〰 After the collapse of Charter Oak Life in 1887, Fenwick Hall and the New Saybrook Company had to be auctioned off to satisfy its receivers. Truth be told, the hotel was such a white elephant that nobody wanted it. Or almost nobody. There was one person in the whole Northeast who was just brainless enough to purchase Fenwick Hall—the murderer Ned Stokes.

In connection with this sale, a story—although suspect—was printed in the *Courant* and repeated regularly through the years, the details changing much too often for comfort. Apparently, the Sisters of Charity, who hoped to use the hotel as a convent, sent a representative to the auction. Obviously, Stokes didn't want the competition, so he cooked up a scheme to shanghai the young man. Sure enough, the morning of the auction, a friend of Stokes convinced the bidder to accept a quick ride on Stokes's steam yacht, *Fra Diavolo*.

Conveniently the steamer broke down during the excursion, ensuring that the young man missed the auction. Another newspaper claimed Bishop Lawrence McMahon of the Archdiocese of Hartford desired the hotel for an orphanage, and his bidder was conveniently delayed. Newton Brainard tells still a third version. In his memory, a Catholic order wanted to start a school at Fenwick Hall, and their representative, a young priest, mysteriously missed the bidding.[24]

In any case, when the bidding started at one o'clock on Wednesday, August 21, 1887, only two parties bid—John W. Brooks of Torrington, a shill bidder, since his brother was one of the receivers, and Elizur Foote, a proxy bidder for Stokes.[25]

Lester Phillips of New London conducted the auction, a lifeless affair akin to begging for volunteers to shovel manure. In no time at all, Stokes took Fenwick Hall and the remains of the New Saybrook Company for $16,500. Added together, the original cost of the hotel, the furnishings, the stables, the bowling alleys, and the casino amounted to $250,000.[26] It looked like a steal, except that no one else had been able to make a go of it. Would Ned Stokes be the first?

To understand what the Bulkeleys, Brainards, Goodwins, and others were facing, a quick word about Ned Stokes is in order. The cottagers had good reason to be wary of him. Ned Stokes was the one who shot and killed Jubilee Jim Fisk when Morgan Bulkeley lived in Brooklyn Heights.

Fisk, then thirty-eight, was married, but his wife, Lucy, lived in Boston.[27] Footloose in New York, Fisk became a corpulent voluptuary, leading a completely dissolute lifestyle. One upper-class New York lawyer described Fisk as an, "illiterate, vulgar, unprincipled, profligate . . . always making himself conspicuously ridiculous by some piece of flagrant ostentation."[28] Fisk wholeheartedly sought attention when he should have gladly embraced the sweet mercy of anonymity.

Fisk bought Pike's Theatre, at Twenty-third Street and Eighth Avenue, where he fitted the upstairs offices for his Erie Railroad and his Fall River & Bristol steamship lines, while producing stage shows and French operas on the old stage downstairs. Alternately, he dressed and swaggered around as an admiral of the Fall River & Bristol steamship line or a colonel of the Ninth Regiment of the New York Militia, a title he purchased along the way.[29]

Not to argue that Fisk deserved hell before death, but he wasn't exactly pure of heart. Together with Jay Gould, he tried to corner the gold market in 1869. The scheme culminated on Black Friday, September 24, 1869, when President Ulysses Grant dumped $3 million of gold on the market and pricked the bubble. Gould and Fisk managed a small profit, but thousands of speculators were ruined. In addition to this disastrous foray, Fisk ran a printing press in the basement of Pike's Theatre and spun off counterfeit shares of Erie Railroad stock whenever he needed money.[30]

In his spare time, Fisk fornicated with a succession of showgirls, but he fell madly in love with Josie Mansfield, a pudgy brunette with a baby-doll face, whose acting talent was, to put it charitably, diminutive.[31]

While at first the meretricious Josie thought Jubilee Jim a fine paramour, she later fell under the spell of the handsome New York socialite Ned Stokes, who was married and had a small child. Stokes's family was indeed wealthy, but his free-spending ways had forced them to keep him on a short financial leash. Added to his lack of respect for money loomed a certain mental instability—though obviously the latter contributed to the former.[32]

Always short of cash, Stokes skimmed money off an oil business in which he partnered with Fisk. The fleshy financier found out about this deceit and instigated a lawsuit. The legal costs were more than Stokes could bear, and he snapped. As if the tangled affairs of these three weren't convoluted enough, Josie Mansfield instigated a suit against Fisk for money she claimed he was holding for her in a fiduciary account. Observably, the machinations between Fisk, Stokes, and Mansfield were something right out of an Edgar Allen Poe story and difficult to follow, much less understand.[33]

What is not in dispute is that at four o'clock in the afternoon of Saturday, January 6, 1872, Ned Stokes arrived at the Grand Central Hotel, mounted the ostentatious main staircase and shot Jubilee Jim Fisk twice at point-blank range.[34] Living long enough to give the police a bullet-by-bullet account of the shooting, Fisk died the following day. Local newspapers pounced on Josie Mansfield and wallowed in the sordid details of "the adventures of a strumpet as notorious in her way as the chief actors in theirs. . . . The association of the assassin with the assassinated, as in cash it began, so through cash did it find its dismal end."[35] Stokes was such a dolt he hadn't even planned an escape route for himself. The police nabbed him in front of the hotel moments after the shooting.

In the ensuing years, Stokes negotiated three trials. At length, his family's money bought him a sweet verdict—guilty of third-degree manslaughter. All told, he served almost five years in the Tombs, Sing Sing, and Auburn prisons, and was released in October 1876.[36]

When the cottagers found out who purchased Fenwick Hall, they became heart-sick. Although Stokes carried a decent reputation as a hotelier at New York's Hoffman House, there was no getting around the fact he was a cold-blooded murderer.[37] In New York, Stokes became a pitiful curiosity among acceptable society, while his wife and son continued to live in Europe.[38] Rather than inspiring the belief that a whole new day had dawned at Fenwick, Stokes's purchase added just another layer of uncertainty to an already very "iffy" beach community.

Stokes spent a fortune trying to get his new real estate venture off to a good start. He completely remolded Fenwick Hall and then reduced the daily rate to three dollars a day for the season. Everyone who had ever vacationed at Fenwick Hall wondered how Stokes planned to offer a Hoffman House table for such a low price. By the end of May, many guests had already made reservations, including Mayor Root of Hartford and Mayor Grant of New York.[39]

The new manager, Elizur Foote, previously managed the Hoffman House in New York. Stokes engaged a cornet player, and a magician named Herrmann—an enigmatic showman who exchanged a nightly display of his talents for his room and board.[40] (The steamer *Fra Diavolo* eventually wound up with Herrmann.)[41]

Although he didn't realize it at the time, Stokes blundered badly just after buying Fenwick Hall. Thinking he had outwitted the denizens of Old Saybrook, he—along with the cottagers—forced the town to build and maintain a 2,800-foot-long wooden bridge across South Cove to Saybrook Point.[42] Situated so close to the sound, the maintenance costs of this bridge were just as staggering as they were never-ending. A dispute developed between the Town of Old Saybrook and Stokes's new Fenwick Hall Company. The matter soon found its way into court, and Stokes lost the first round. He still refused to pay his end, and in protest, shuttered the hotel for the whole 1894 season. The cottagers were resigned to the unpredictable situation at Fenwick Hall and went about their business as usual. However, the hulking, boarded-up hotel was an irksome eyesore. Community children rode the now popular bicycles up and down the huge porches and snuck into the hotel regularly. They darted through the spooky corridors, whispering to each other, as if the echoes of their full voices might come back to harm them.[43]

∽ The summer of 1894 started typically for the ex-governor and his family. They had been renting cottages for some time, mostly the Giraud place.[44] After considerable packing and a short train ride, they arrived at Fenwick by the end of June, ready to relax and enjoy the warm months. At the time, Morgan Jr. was nine and daughter Elinor was one. As was often the case, Fannie Bulkeley's sister, Minnie Houghton, spent much of the summer with them. Minnie, the more athletic of the two women, chose love carefully and remained single until she was fifty-three.[45]

Minnie died just a few years after her marriage. It had been rumored that she married a young stud and then died in a mysterious hunting accident while the two were alone in Canada. The truth, while just as sad, is less dramatic. Minnie married a divorced Norwegian immigrant, Calion Beacon (Adolph Bikjend), who was almost sixty. About three years after their marriage, the couple went rafting on the Mackenzie River in far northern Canada. They were back in Edmonton, preparing for their return to San Francisco, when Minnie suffered a cerebral hemorrhage. She died on October 4, 1923, at the Royal Alexandria Hospital. She was fifty-five.[46]

∽ Owing to Fenwick Hall's continuing woes, there were plenty of unsold lots, so Minnie Houghton and her friend, Lucy Brainard, began sewing flags and laid out the first three holes of a golf course. Using soup cans for the holes, they started playing golf on the unsold building lots. Any notion that this three-hole layout resembled a golf course—except for the flags—was way off base. Still, the amateurish efforts of these two young women should not be discounted out of hand, for they did plant the seed of an idea. The following year, a nine-hole course—winding its way around and among the cottages—opened for play.[47]

The summer of 1894 may have begun in the usual way, but it turned out a sad one for the Bulkeleys and Brainards. In August, the Bulkeleys received a telegram. Morgan Bulkeley's mother, eighty-seven-year-old Lydia, passed on the night of August 9. Besides bearing six children—only three of whom were still alive—she gave her time to many charities and served as president of the Hartford Orphan Asylum. Lydia Bulkeley's pastor, the Rev. William De Loss Love of the Pearl Street Congregational Church, returned from his vacation to conduct a simple service at the Bulkeleys' Hartford home the following Sunday. Lydia was laid to rest next to Judge Bulkeley in the family plot at Cedar Hill Cemetery.[48]

Ned Stokes's Fenwick investment blossomed into his worst investment in a lifetime of bad investments. Although Stokes finally got some good news in his fight with the town—he won the second round of the wooden bridge battle in an appellate court—the ecstasy didn't last long. A few years later, the Connecticut Supreme Court of Errors handed down its decision. The court held that the Fenwick community was responsible for the costs associated with the maintenance of the bridge. Stokes's share, with interest, had mushroomed to over $7,000. He was livid.[49] It was August 1898 and he was at the end of his rope.

Morgan Bulkeley had been around Fenwick enough by this time to know Stokes fairly well. Stokes "suffered from the horrors affecting some killers, fearing Fisk's ghost and Fisk's friends. He always left a light burning when he slept, and his manner was often described as that of a haunted man."[50] Bulkeley didn't like Stokes or the boisterous crowd he brought from New York, but Stokes probably never knew it. If Bulkeley could hoodwink the General Assembly and the Connecticut Supreme Court, Stokes was easy work. Another important point—Bulkeley had become an astute businessman, buying and selling vast tranches of stocks and bonds with aplomb. If such an instinct is a gift from the Almighty, then Bulkeley was blessed indeed. He now focused this laserlike intuition on Stokes's Fenwick Hall Company, for the time was nigh.

Without question, Governor Bulkeley had been negotiating with Stokes for some time, but on Saturday, August 6, 1898, when the town clerk at Old Saybrook received a check of $7,043.97 for back taxes from Stokes, word spread quickly that something was afoot.[51] Five days later, the deed to the Fenwick Hall Company was transferred to Morgan Bulkeley. For $22,725, he bought "the hotel . . . barns, sheds, farm house and bowling alley . . . the grove and all unplanted land . . . the depot grounds east from the centerline of the railroad . . . all the streets . . . all interest in the bathing pavilion and any bath houses, wharfs . . . and also 136 lots and three larger pieces, 8 acres, 8 acres and 2.5 acres, respectively."[52] Stokes's original investment (without renovations) and his back taxes came to about $23,544, and Bulkeley only gave him $22,725.[53] Also, since people were stunned that Stokes had lowered rates to only $3 a night, he couldn't possibly have been making a profit. Thus, Stokes lost every dime he sunk into Fenwick Hall. For better or for worse, Fenwick was now Morgan Bulkeley's summer barony to do with as he pleased.

As for Ned Stokes? His troubles were soon over. He sold his interest in the Hoffman House in 1897, and thanks to numerous lawsuits with his cousin, W. E. D. Stokes, Ned was almost penniless when he died of Bright's disease in 1901. His mistress, Josie Mansfield, although abandoned by fortune, managed to relocate to Paris and live to age seventy-eight. She was buried in the historic Montparnasse Cemetery.[54]

As Bulkeley saw it, a number of problems at Fenwick begged to be addressed before anything good could happen. First, the boisterous Tammany Hall political hacks and the theater folks had to be thrown out. Secondly, all cottagers would be obliged to pay their fair share. As things stood, some made small improvements, while others contributed nothing. Lastly, since Fenwick was so far from the center of Old Saybrook, it demanded self-governance in order to supply water; to control swill or "night soil;" to regulate or prohibit trade, manufacturing, or commercial enterprises; and to suppress gambling houses, houses of ill repute, and so forth.[55]

Bulkeley knew Connecticut law well and decided the best way to handle the problem was to incorporate Fenwick as a separate entity. In April 1899, he enticed the state legislature to pass a bill incorporating the borough of Fenwick. With this one piece of legislation, he was able to address all of the problems in one fell swoop. The obnoxious New Yorkers were excluded because the right to vote on borough matters was restricted to Connecticut residents. With a separate borough tax, the cost of improvements would be borne by everyone equally. Lastly, the borough's charter addressed every other matter of importance.[56]

Humorously enough, when the bill incorporating the borough of Fenwick was brought to the floor of the General Assembly eight months after Bulkeley purchased the property, it passed the House "without discussion" and the Senate without mention of any debate.[57] At last Bulkeley had complete control of Fenwick.

Meanwhile, he set about acquiring the exact piece of land he wanted for Beaumaris. His original purchase included Fenwick Hall, 136 building lots, and about thirty acres of assorted land—but not the piece he wanted for his cottage. Bulkeley had to have the waterfront land just west of his sister Mary. The fact that there were already cottages on the land meant nothing to him. He simply bought the owners out and then set about rearranging the buildings to suit his needs. First, he bought the Giraud cottage he and Fannie had been renting for many years.[58] Then he purchased the Stokes and Holley cottages that were on the waterfront land he wanted. These were moved back to higher ground. Finally, he moved the Giraud cottage about seventy-five feet to the east, where the west and north sides of it could be added to, creating one monstrous, but elegant, cottage—Beaumaris. While the movers were at it, they slid a number of old barns back from the waterfront, giving the whole place a much-needed facelift.[59]

With her husband busy moving heaven and earth, Fannie met with the architect Willis Becker, who was a great favorite of society women because he did all of his preliminary drawings free of charge.[60] The women could change their minds a hundred times and the easy-going Becker would appease them. Beaumaris was the first home Fannie Bulkeley could really call her own, so she undoubtedly spent many hours ruminating over the layout and details of the "cottage."

Carpenters worked throughout the winter months of early 1900, so Beaumaris would be completed for the coming season. Prior to Beaumaris, Fenwick cottages tended to be smaller, more utilitarian affairs. The Goodwin's cottage—on the waterfront, west of Pattaquasset Avenue—was probably the biggest of them all. Then again, the Goodwins had eight children. They needed a big cottage.

As the summer wore on, a crew of laborers raked out truckloads of the richest loam on the land, and then, of course, seeded it with the finest grass seed available.[61] Beaumaris boasted a rich, plush lawn in an otherwise rustic—some would say ramshackle—low-key vacation colony.

In the years after Governor Bulkeley built Beaumaris, a fantastic "cottage envy" took wing. Lucius Barbour, who had been Governor Bulkeley's adjutant-general, was one of the first to catch the bug, moving Billy Bulkeley's old place back from Lot #25 and building a large new cottage—almost as big as Beaumaris—on the site.[62] (This was in 1907 when, five years after Billy Bulkeley's passing, his widow Emma "gave up the cottage" and moved into Fenwick Hall.)[63] Barbour knew it was a waste of time to build a place bigger than Beaumaris because Bulkeley would add on to his cottage faster than you could say "Sachem." Soon, new construction boomed at Fenwick.

Once Bulkeley controlled Fenwick, he began picking his neighbors carefully. For instance, the ex-governor convinced Hartford resident Charles Buckley—who had served in the Thirteenth Regiment with Morgan Bulkeley during the war—to build a cottage at Fenwick.[64] And so it went.

Still, Bulkeley wasn't sure what to do with Fenwick Hall. He rented it out to the same manager who ran it so successfully the year before, John E. Chatfield of the Jefferson House in New York. Just as in previous years, Chatfield was able to book an almost endless number of get-togethers for the Connecticut chapter of the DAR, the Connecticut Army and Navy Club, and the Connecticut Association of Fire Insurance Agents. Typically, there were hundreds of guests staying at the hotel at any given time. Once in a while, even J. P. Morgan stayed there for a few days.[65] Despite its checkered past, odds now favored a long run for the troubled Fenwick Hall.

Morgan Bulkeley helped too. Aetna Life Men's Club started holding their annual outings at Fenwick. Just as he had hired a train for Hartford's poor in the 1880s, Morgan hired a special train to bring his employees to Fenwick for a field day. More than 700 clerks boarded the Valley Railroad each year. Others went down by boat, mooring and staying the night at the Hotel Champion in East Haddam, which was far cheaper than Fenwick Hall.[66] Besides the usual cookout and swimming, employees played golf, tennis, and baseball. The Fenwick Station of the Hartford Yacht Club opened to the employees, a nice way for the club's members to thank Morgan Bulkeley for their use of his land. At 5:30 in the afternoon, President Bulkeley presided over the presentation of awards and prizes for the winners in each of the different field activities.

As a final salute to their host, the Governor's Foot Guard Band marched along Fenwick Avenue to Long Island Sound, turned west onto Beach Road and then came to a halt in front of Beaumaris. As Morgan and Fannie Bulkeley stood on their porch, the band played a number of selections for their pleasure. Twenty minutes later, the musicians reversed their route and caught the train back to Hartford. These annual outings were held at Fenwick from 1911 through 1916. The Great War brought them to an end.[67] Just prior to the United States' involvement, electricity became generally available to the cottagers. Six electric streetlights brightened Beach Road.[68]

There were many from Hartford who simply didn't long to vacation at Morgan Bulkeley's little summer colony. Samuel Colt's widow, Elizabeth, was one of the first people to buy a lot at Fenwick in 1871, but never built there.[69] When searching for a reason why she never garnered much love for Fenwick, one important fact stands out. Her late husband, Samuel Colt, was a Democrat and had a hatred of Hartford's merchant-banker class bordering on the irrational. Elizabeth Colt would never have been able to bed down beside the Republicans at Fenwick, so she sold her waterfront lot to Francis Goodwin in 1879.[70]

Irish immigrant Pat McGovern, who for thirty-eight years was considered joined-at-the-hip to Morgan Bulkeley, had done well for himself—amassing a huge fortune. He certainly could afford a place at Fenwick, and since he and Bulkeley were purportedly close friends, it would seem natural for him to have one, but he never did.[71] True, McGovern was a Republican, but let's not forget he was an Irish Catholic and an immigrant. In July 1908, he entertained friends at Long Brothers Farm in West Hartford, and the guests were almost exclusively Irish—Coyle, Ahern, Costello, Nolan, Murray, Mullen, Bailey, Keefe, and Kennedy.[72] As such, McGovern would not have fit in with Republican Protestants like Dr. Tom Hepburn who held Roman Catholics in low regard.[73]

At the Republican mayoral caucus of 1892, Bulkeley nominated McGovern, whose most cherished dream was to become mayor of Hartford. Unhappily the Republicans would have none of it and went with the sitting mayor, Henry C. Dwight, instead. Out of allegiance to McGovern, Bulkeley had no choice but to back the Gold Democrat, William Waldo Hyde, helping him to unseat Henry Dwight.[74] Since Hyde was a weak candidate—polling lowest of all the candidates on the Democratic city ticket in 1892—perhaps the Bulkeley-McGovern camp envisioned a McGovern-Hyde race in 1894, culminating in victory and the fruition of Pat McGovern's dream.[75] However, no matter how high the hope or powerful the dream, it never happened.

Ex-Mayor William Waldo Hyde graduated from Hartford High, went on to Yale—Skull & Bones, 1876—and then joined his father's law firm, Waldo, Hubbard & Hyde.[76] He was a member of The Hartford Club and simply did not let his political affiliation keep him from joining Republicans in matters where their interests dovetailed. Hyde would never have become mayor in 1892 without Morgan Bulkeley's help, and he was forever in the older man's debt. In the course of helping Hyde in his mayoralty bid, Bulkeley took a shine to the man and convinced him to purchase at Fenwick.[77]

Like Pat McGovern, another immigrant who never owned a Fenwick cottage was Gideon Winslow, the alderman whose butcher shop was key to Bulkeley controlling the river wards in the mayoral races of the 1880s. Winslow was an English immigrant, a Protestant, and his son Fred Winslow even worked at Aetna Life, but he still wasn't Fenwick material. Curiously enough, the two immigrants who did the most to get—and keep—Morgan Bulkeley in the mayor's office in the 1880s, never mixed with him socially. He used these immigrants for his own purposes, but seems to have drawn the line at the water's edge.[78]

〜 In the end, Morgan Bulkeley reaped no better luck with Fenwick Hall than any of his predecessors. The massive hotel, just like the Valley Railroad, was incapable of turning a profit. The proliferation of resort hotels on the Connecticut shore spawned a fierce competition. In 1895, rates at Fenwick Hall started at $17.50 a week, but by 1913, they had dropped to $12.50.[79] Even with Fenwick on the rise and the place booked solid most summers, the taxes, maintenance costs, and operating expenses made the hotel a money pit. Bulkeley decided to retrench.

In April 1917, he sold Fenwick Hall to Abe Goldberg of the Hartford Wrecking Company.[80] The firm would strip the hotel of its valuable mantle pieces, moldings, cabinets, stair parts, windows, doors, and chandeliers. However, Hartford Wrecking did not get the land. Bulkeley kept that.

The dismantling work commenced almost immediately, and by the middle of May, most of the really valuable items had been removed. On Saturday, May 19, while the workmen were having lunch, the place suddenly caught fire. In no time at all, the flames were out of control.

Worse still, an offshore breeze sent sparks east toward the yacht club and south toward Beaumaris. In short order, Fenwick Hall and the yacht club burned to the ground, while the wrecking crew saved Beaumaris and other cottages by putting out the small fires as they began. Fenwick Hall was not insured; the yacht club was.[81]

Word got back to Hartford as soon as the fire began. The Bulkeleys had their chauffeur, Arthur, take them to the shore in their Pierce Arrow. They arrived at four o'clock, just in time to see the hotel and the yacht club in ruins and to inspect a few small burn marks on Beaumaris.[82]

There has always been speculation Morgan Bulkeley had something to do with the fire at Fenwick Hall. Facts don't support this. Once Bulkeley sold the hotel to Hartford Wrecking, he no longer had an insurable interest. To be sure, Bulkeley wanted it gone, but since Hartford Wrecking was removing it, he didn't need to burn it down. Lastly, Bulkeley's lawlessness was confined to corrupt election practices; arson for profit was beyond him. The items making up the shell of the building—studs, yellow pine sheathing, clapboards, plaster, lath and roof shingles—had no resale value, so it's certainly possible Abe Goldberg of Hartford Wrecking set fire to the hotel, but no proof exists to support that theory either.

And what of the sagging wooden bridge to Saybrook Point at the epicenter of all the trouble? After Bulkeley managed to reroute auto traffic to the abandoned railroad causeway, storms dismembered the wobbly bridge haphazardly. Soon enough, even in the minds of old timers, it was nothing but a distant memory.

In July 1917, Morgan Bulkeley bought the largest farm in Old Saybrook.[83] Like everything Bulkeley did at the beach, thirty-two-acre Arrowhead Farm served as part fun, part practicality, part whim, part folly, and part genius. The farmhouse was a white colonial home built in 1773 by Samuel Hart, the grandson of Yale student Rev. John Hart, whose hornbook Bulkeley had purchased a few years before. Samuel's father headed a church in Old Saybrook and married Lucy Bushnell, a young resident of the area and the owner of the land at Fenwick. During those years, it was called "Neck Farm," and after Samuel Hart married Lucy Bushnell, the granddaughter of Nathaniel Lynde—whose family owned Lynde's Neck—he joked, "I married my wife for her beautiful 'Neck.' "[84]

Bulkeley installed Walter Schults, of the Connecticut Agricultural School at Storrs as caretaker for Arrowhead Farm.[85] The plan was to cultivate only twelve acres at first—eight for potatoes and four for tomatoes, beans, and rhubarb. Another eight acres featured wild berries and five were set aside for the pasturage of horses, cows, chickens, and pigs. The rest remained salt meadow for hay fertilizer.[86]

Mary Brainard provided even more fresh fruits and vegetables when she purchased a farm in West Hartford. Since she closed her Hartford home for the summer, and her two sons, Morgan and Newton, needed to stay in the city to work, she purchased a farm on Albany Avenue (just west of Renbrook School). Her sons had a place to stay, and on weekends they drove to the shore, bringing fresh fruits and vegetables for the Brainards and their neighbors.[87]

Chapter Eleven

SENATOR BULKELEY

When 1904 rolled around, Morgan Bulkeley's biggest political dream began to snowball into a reality. He waited twelve years for the sainted Joe Hawley to give up his Senate seat and much had changed in the interim.

In that time, the population of Hartford had grown by 50 percent.[1] The waves of Irish Potato Famine immigrants that had washed into Hartford beginning in the middle of the nineteenth century had now been replaced by an equally powerful surge of Northern Europeans and Italians. Since 1892, the Democrats, harnessing the new-immigrant votes, managed to win half of the mayoral races.[2]

Due to a still-high infant mortality rate and workplace accidents, the average life expectancy held stubbornly below fifty years, yet the amenities of life had expanded greatly.[3] Even people of limited means now had safety bicycles, enabling young women to get about freely and allowing factory workers to zip home for a hot lunch. Wealthier people used electric vehicles.[4]

Speaking of upper-income families, 18 percent of all the homes in the United States hired a domestic servant of some kind. Budgets needn't be stretched, because the national average wage was twenty-two cents an hour, and offering meals and lodging effectively cut that rate in half.[5]

City folks enjoyed indoor toilets, but only 14 percent of Hartford's homes featured bathtubs. In a wealthy city like Hartford, a great many people hooked up telephones, but nationwide only 8 percent would answer them. There were 8,000 cars driving on 144 miles of paved roads in the United States. Still, hygiene lagged, and four decades away from the common availability of antibiotics, people died mostly from pneumonia and tuberculosis.[6]

Life was good for the Bulkeleys of Washington Street. Morgan turned sixty-six while Fannie celebrated forty-four. Their three children, Morgan Jr., Elinor, and Houghton, were eighteen, ten, and seven, respectively. As for creature comforts, no mortals had it better. There were domestic servants, cooks, coachmen and nannies.[7] The Bulkeleys socialized extensively and threw lavish parties for prominent guests from all over the United States. Morgan and Fannie Bulkeley knew almost every person worth knowing in the country and one or both of them had made the acquaintance of every president since Ulysses S. Grant.

Their son, Morgan Jr., graduated from Hartford Public High School in 1902 and now attended Yale University.[8] Naturally, Elinor and Houghton would be afforded all the same educational opportunities as their older brother.

On the not-so-pleasant side, many of the lodestones of Morgan Bulkeley's life were gone—his mother and father; his brothers Charlie and Billy; his brother-in-law Leverett Brainard; his political touchstone, Marshall Jewell; and his first real boss and mentor, Uncle Henry Morgan. However, just as Bulkeley wielded a heft of fortitude when it came to politics, he heaped an even greater amount of denial when it came to the grim reaper.

While temporarily out of the political arena, Bulkeley busied himself overseeing Aetna Life and enjoying his family, Republican Party meetings, military encampments, parades, horse racing, antique collecting, and traveling. He could never have spent so much time in politics or at play if it hadn't been for the loyal and talented executives at Aetna Life. Chief among them was Vice President Joel English, whom shareholders regarded so highly that they offered him the top job after Morgan Bulkeley's passing in 1922. By then, however, English was seventy-six, and poor health forced him to decline.[9]

In May 1904, one of the biggest celebrations ever held in Hartford was scheduled to take place—the National Encampment of the members of the Grand Army of the Republic (GAR). Fifteen thousand soldiers and spectators from all over the East Coast were expected to attend.[10]

While the event was still in the planning stages, Morgan Bulkeley visited Fitch's Old Soldiers Home in Noroton (a section of Darien, Connecticut) to issue a general invitation to the elderly veterans.[11] As a result of this little courtesy, almost 400 soldiers from Fitch's Home chartered a special train to Hartford for the encampment.

While Bulkeley walked the grounds at Fitch's Home, an old soldier approached him. The man handed Bulkeley a small item, carefully wrapped in tissue paper. When Bulkeley opened it, he beheld a picture of his brother, Capt. Charles Bulkeley, who died during the Civil War forty years earlier. "That's a picture of my Captain," the soldier offered, "and your mother gave me the picture herself. I'm going up to Hartford next month with the Grand Army to put a bouquet on his grave."[12]

On the east side of Bushnell Park, organizers pitched a sizeable tent for use as a dining hall. They erected a second big tent as a kitchen and set up forty wall tents for headquarters of the different Grand Army posts.[13] As if there weren't enough tents, they raised three more for the chief marshal and his aides. The infrastructure list went on and on.[14]

Many different groups in the city assisted the National Encampment by offering money, food, tents, and other materials for the veterans. However, one small hitch surfaced. Some of Hartford's puritanical grand dames collected a sum of money that they contributed to Bulkeley's committee, with one stipulation—none of the money could be used to buy alcoholic beverages. Without missing a beat, Bulkeley reassured them, "I should say not. . . . No indeed. Not one penny of this money shall be spent that way. I reserve that privilege and pleasure for myself. I shall personally see that those old heroes have all the liquor they want while they're here." And they did.[15]

All told, the committee raised $7,000 for the entertainment of the veterans. President Roosevelt's new secretary of war, William Howard Taft, planned to attend, but canceled at the last minute due to illness.[16] Prominent guests included Gen. Oliver Otis Howard (who lost his right arm at Fair Oaks), Gen. Dan Sickles, Gen. S. L. Woodford, Connecticut's Senator Orville Platt, and hundreds of other dignitaries and military men. (Senator Joe Hawley's health had failed in 1902 and he was too ill to show.)[17]

Over 7,000 men marched in the parade, while thousands more lined the parade route. Unhappily, the weather refused to cooperate. The day grew chilly and a drizzling rain followed the parading soldiers like a mourning cloak. All over Bushnell Park there were stations for veterans to get sandwiches and coffee. For the crowd's amusement, Morgan Bulkeley, at his own expense, commissioned an orgiastic light show to flash around the pond in Bushnell Park. Because the *Courant*'s reporter described the events best, Bulkeley ordered memorial copies mailed to every member of the GAR in the state as soon as the two-day affair ended.[18] Interestingly, a few days later, he found that these newspapers were being held up for insufficient postage, so he raced to the post office and paid the necessary funds himself—textbook Morgan Bulkeley.[19]

Summertime brought a nice surprise. The Aetna Life employees threw a big party at the Putnam Phalanx Armory honoring their boss for his twenty-five years at the helm.[20] During this tenure, Aetna Life's assets almost tripled from $25 million to $68 million. Annual income went from $4 million to $14 million, and insurance coverage in force skyrocketed from $79 million to $225 million.[21] Impressive indeed. All employees took the afternoon off to attend the party, where they presented Bulkeley with a gorgeous silver service. After lunch, a receiving line formed, allowing each employee to meet and talk individually with the boss.[22]

In the fall, the political air was as thick as a spectral fog on a Connecticut lake. At seventy-eight, "Fighting Joe" Hawley, Connecticut's U.S. senator and

First Soldier fell gravely ill, and declared his lengthy career over. Bulkeley waited so long for Hawley's Senate seat, that he was now almost sixty-seven. There was a bright side. Though he usually had to build backfires to keep Sam Fessenden at bay, Lady Luck intervened. While both candidates waited in the wings, Fessenden blundered badly. Eighteen months earlier, when the State of Connecticut finally received Civil War reparations of $606,000 for monies advanced during the conflict, U.S. attorney for Fairfield County, Samuel Fessenden, took 25 percent as his fee.[23] That $151,000 amounted to an enormous sum for legal work that "any good lawyer would have gladly performed for $5,000," and public indignation knew no bounds.[24] Greed had done him in. Now, Fessendon plus a small band of supporters were the only people who thought his political career was salvageable.

When word spread regarding Fessenden's outrageous commission, Senator Orville Platt took Connecticut's U.S. Representative from the Third District, Frank Brandegee, under his wing. Brandegee accepted this gesture by remarking at the Republican State Convention at New Haven in May, "Senator Platt of our state is the real leader in the Senate."[25] This verbal embrace sent a signal to the legions of voters who knew and loved Orville Platt. As a result, Fessenden understood once and for all that he had no chance for Platt's seat. His only hope was to outflank Morgan Bulkeley for Joe Hawley's seat.

All eyes now focused on the November 1904 Republican caucus at the Capitol. Opinions ran strongly in favor of Bulkeley, but not surprisingly, the newspapers stoked the fires shamelessly. Meanwhile, Fessenden's supporters did what they could to derail Bulkeley's bid.

Morgan Bulkeley owed a great part of his political career to the secret ballot, but intuited he wouldn't need it this time. In fact, by claiming that he favored the transparency of a roll call vote, he picked up some extra supporters.[26] Conversely, Fessenden needed a secret ballot, hoping this would allow some legislators to vote for him without the need to explain their decision.[27] On the night of the balloting, Bulkeley's roll call vote won out over Fessenden's secret ballot preference and the legislators rose and shouted their choice for senator like traders in an open-outcry commodity pit.[28]

Fessenden was cooked. In the state Senate, Governor Bulkeley's friends outnumbered both the Fessenden men and the Democrats combined, and in the House, the situation tipped even more toward Bulkeley. In a particularly brazen move, Fessenden slipped into a vacant seat in the state Senate so that he could vote for himself.[29] This backfired, striking everyone as particularly bad form. In the end, Fessenden lost because colleagues perceived him as a greedy opportunist. He should have paid more attention to Morgan Bulkeley's maxim, "As a general rule, I think the people rather prefer those who wait until honors come to them."[30] In the final vote, Bulkeley beat Fessenden by 29 to 6 in the Senate and 219 to 36 in the House.[31]

Now that the Republicans had nominated Morgan Bulkeley, the General Assembly still needed to pick between Bulkeley and the Democrat, A. Heaton Robertson, for U.S. senator. Since the General Assembly voted overwhelmingly Republican, this was strictly a formality. Reportedly, "It [was] Bulkeley's turn."[32] Some newspapers stated openly that the Republican legislators from the smaller towns in Connecticut were thanking Morgan Bulkeley for helping them maintain power. Had he not torpedoed the proposed changes at the 1902 Constitutional Convention, they would have considerably less sway now. When asked later about the vote, Bulkeley replied, "The members were simply ratifying the judgment rendered by the people at the polls in November."[33]

And what was the odds-on favorite doing while the General Assembly trudged hip-deep in all this political intrigue? Morgan Bulkeley worked in his office at Aetna Life until three o'clock in the afternoon, and then he simply walked in a misting rain along Main Street, up Capital Avenue and down Washington Street to his home. A big walker all his life, Morgan routinely strode around the city chewing a Havana cigar in his inimitable fashion.[34] Reporters were dumbfounded to see him pay so little attention to the proceedings at the Capitol. Morgan Bulkeley was sometimes unreadable, and at others, completely inscrutable.

In the weeks following his election to the U.S. Senate, Bulkeley received hundreds of congratulatory telegrams and letters from all over the country.[35] Just responding to these well-wishers constituted a full-time job. It would have to wait, though, for Morgan and Fannie needed to get to Washington.

On Wednesday, January 25, the Bulkeleys boarded a private parlor car attached to the rear of the early morning New York, New Haven, and Hartford train.[36] Service had improved markedly by 1905, but the ride to Washington was still a twelve-hour affair. When they got there, night had fallen and the air temperature was only few degrees warmer than Hartford. Snow covered the roads, and horses with sleighs transported people around the city under streetlights. The senator-elect and his bride quickly slid to the Arlington Hotel and settled in.[37]

The next day, they called on Senator Joe Hawley and his wife, Edith, at their home on N Street. Senator Hawley was terribly sick, and Edith Hawley returned the visit to the Bulkeley's Arlington suite alone. Both Morgan and Fannie admired Edith Hawley, and she coached Fannie on all the ins and outs of Washington.[38]

Next, they stopped by the office of Senator Orville Platt, who received them graciously. After a bit of conversation, he escorted them over to the White House to meet President Roosevelt.[39] Much has been written about Teddy Roosevelt's gruff side, describing him as a "steam engine in pants," among plenty of other metaphors designed to capture the man's raw energy. But in the presence of women, Teddy was gentle—even shy. He particularly liked Fannie Bulkeley, and there may have been a good reason.

Fannie Bulkeley looked very youthful at age forty-four, and she bore a striking resemblance to the ill-fated Alice Lee, Roosevelt's first wife. Alice died tragically at twenty-two.[40] Roosevelt never discussed Alice Lee. As hard as it is to believe, he never even mentioned her (by name) in his autobiography. Could Fannie Bulkeley's likeness to Alice Lee have been something President Roosevelt was drawn to?

After their visit to the White House, Platt and the Bulkeleys visited the Capitol Building, where Morgan presented his credentials and conferred with a number of future colleagues—many of whom he already knew.[41]

On the morning of February 1, the Bulkeleys left Washington and traveled through to Hartford. They still needed to find a place to live in Washington, among other things, but they had time.

At the beginning of the twentieth century, newly elected senators traveled to Washington to take the oath of office in early March. In Bulkeley's case, there was a short special session from March 4 to March 18, but the first session of the Fifty-ninth Congress didn't actually begin until December 4, 1905. It continued to June 30, 1906. The second session began on December 3, 1906, and ended the following March 3.[42]

The brevity of these sessions may have been because there was infinitely less to do in Washington in the days before the government had anything to do with education, Social Security, Medicare, Medicaid, farm subsidies, interstate highways, environmental protection, and on and on. There wasn't even a federal income tax for the average wage earner in 1905, and the Federal Reserve wasn't created until 1913. In truth, the real power had not moved to Washington yet. The great industrialists of the Northeast and Midwest and the big financial houses on Wall Street still amassed it.[43]

Based on his congressional schedule, Senator Morgan Bulkeley spent most of his time from March 18 to December 4 in Connecticut, tending to the business of Aetna Life. In his spare time, he dedicated monuments, marched in parades, and summered at Fenwick.

~∞ Less than a fortnight after Senator Joe Hawley's term expired on March 4, he died. He was first waked at his home on N Street in Washington and then at the State Capitol in Hartford. From there, his remains were carried to Rev. Joseph Twichell's Asylum Hill Congregational Church for a traditional religious service and then to Cedar Hill for internment.[44]

Senator Orville Platt traveled on the funeral train to Hartford. At Union Station, a long wait befell the platform while bearers offloaded the general's casket and commenced the funeral procession. Some say that Platt caught a chill. Nonetheless, he delivered a moving eulogy at the Capitol and then immediately returned to Washington. After two or three days, he traveled back to Kirby Corner (in Washington, Connecticut) where he died of pneumonia on Good Friday, April 21.[45]

Joe Hawley and Orville Platt served like a matched set of Belgian draft horses. Platt had already been in the Senate for two years when Hawley joined him in 1881 and then the two men served together for almost a quarter of a century. In 1905, they died within a month of each other. Many contend—not without merit—that Connecticut has never been so faithfully represented.

When Platt passed away, he was in his fifth term in the Senate, a term that was not scheduled to end until 1909. Thus, a mad scramble erupted in the General Assembly to appoint a successor. The usual cast of characters emerged, but with a twist. Sam Fessenden, realizing the delegates in the statehouse would not support him, threw all his weight behind his longtime lieutenant, the forty-year-old bachelor, Frank Brandegee.[46] (Fessenden died in January 1908 after a long fight with kidney disease, so he may also have had an intuitive lack of interest.)[47]

Ex-Governor George McLean, who was embarrassingly ambitious in his own right, was just recovering from another attack of "nervous prostration," but his friends, led by Bulkeley, insisted he run. For a long time, he led. However, in a classic late-night caucus—thirty-six ballots—Brandagee took the nomination.[48]

Bulkeley would have breathed much easier if McLean had landed Platt's seat because, among other benefits, it would have eliminated one of the most serious and popular contenders for his own seat. It just wasn't meant to be.

In November 1905, the Bulkeleys rode back to Washington and found a place to live. Brigadier Gen. Henry Corbin owned a house at 1701 Twenty-second Street NW, on the corner of R Street. The location was ideal—a block from Massachusetts Avenue and close to Dupont Circle. William McKinley's biggest supporter, Senator Mark Hanna of Ohio and his wife, Charlotte, rented the house. Hanna died in February 1904, and his widow was finally ready to return home. The Bulkeleys assumed the rental and immediately hired contractors to completely remodel the place to their tastes. During the six months that they lived and worked in D.C., they closed their Hartford home and brought their household staff with them. The rental house stood four stories tall and spread four times longer than it was wide. Its size and interior layout easily qualified it as a mansion, but neighbors dubbed it "the Corbin jail" due to its unwelcoming façade.[49]

Although the nation's capitol city displayed plenty of luxurious homes and eye-popping public buildings and monuments, it felt like a pleasant, little village.

Traveling about the city's streets, observers were just as likely to see an expensive brougham carriage pulled by a jet-black driving pair as a broken-down plow horse leading a shabby coupe.

The city fostered a blithe spirit, like the day when Quentin Roosevelt ushered Algonquin the pony up the White House elevator to his brother Archie, who was in bed with the measles. The Roosevelt children also roller-skated in the White House hallways. There wasn't even a fence around the White House, and government workers and tourists alike walked across the mansion's sweeping lawns as if the grounds belonged to a public park. Despite wars and assassinations, good times and bad, Washington renewed itself as often as the faces changed in Congress, and now the Bulkeleys arrived to take in the city and its incomparable social whirl.

When Morgan Bulkeley joined the Senate, an unwritten rule declared that no new member should give a floor speech in his first year. It was just the kind of rule Bulkeley loved to break, but he held his tongue. Senators basically faced a choice—they could either be a center-stage personality like Nelson Aldrich of Rhode Island or a quietly effective man like Senator W. Murray Crane of Massachusetts. Bulkeley chose the latter. Judging by the number of pensions he secured for Connecticut's old soldiers and their widows, he played the role well.[50] Bulkeley even managed to secure a fifty-dollar-a-month pension for Senator Joe Hawley's widow, Edith, a pension he had to fight like a street thug to get.[51] Edith Hawley was English and had $50,000 worth of property (mostly her husband's interest in the Courant); therefore, some senators felt she shouldn't get a dime. Bulkeley persuaded them otherwise.[52]

Bulkeley served on a number of standing committees—on Canadian Relations, the Coast and Insular Survey, Cuban Relations, Civil Service Examinations, Fisheries, Military Affairs, and Railroads.[53] Nevertheless, Bulkeley's years in Washington frustrated him because he had become accustomed to running matters himself. As a conservative Republican, he often found himself at odds with Teddy Roosevelt's progressive agenda. While Roosevelt wanted a massive national parks system, a canal across the Isthmus of Panama, and all sorts of new governmental programs, the tight-fisted administrator and free-enterprise man, Morgan Bulkeley, didn't think the government should take the lead in these endeavors.

One of the most important relationships Bulkeley forged in Washington had little to do with Congress. It had to do with the lovable, obese Will Taft. Teddy Roosevelt pulled Taft back from his post as governor-general of the Philippines to be his secretary of war in 1904. In the early part of the twentieth century when the United States enjoyed peace, there was precious little for Taft to do, so the job was made to order. Each day, Will Taft went up to Capitol Hill to kibitz with congressmen and reporters.[54] They all loved Taft. He was always good for a humorous story and didn't take himself—or life—too seriously.

Taft's eyes were blue, his skin fair, and like Bulkeley, his mustache made him look a little walruslike. Easily the most conspicuous feature of Will Taft was his 335-pound body larded onto a six-foot-two-inch frame. Accounts disagree, but it is generally accepted: Taft once ballooned to 360 pounds—fat but jolly. Taft hated politics. He once wrote, "Politics, when I am in it, makes me sick."[55] He also suffered obstructive sleep apnea, which caused him to sleep long periods of time yet wake up exhausted. After a good twelve-hour snore, he used to say, "I really did some great work at sleeping last night."[56]

Morgan Bulkeley met Taft at Republican conventions, and the two men got along famously. Both were conservative Republicans, in stark contrast to Teddy Roosevelt, who was so progressive his wealthy contributors groused, "We bought the son-of-a-bitch, but he didn't stay bought."[57]

The Tafts lived at 5 Dupont Circle, only a few blocks from the Bulkeley's place, and the two couples socialized regularly.[58] Fannie Bulkeley was about the same age as Nellie Taft, and the perfect friend for such an ambitious woman. Nellie aspired to be the first lady, and since Morgan Bulkeley would be seventy-three by the time his first term in the Senate ended, competition really wasn't an issue.

Just after the Fifty-ninth Congress got underway, President Roosevelt held a dinner at the White House on December 8. Among the guests at the Bulkeley's table were Speaker of the House "Uncle Joe" Cannon and his wife, Mary; Senator and Mrs. Joseph Foraker of Ohio; Representative and Mrs. Charles Grosvenor of Ohio; and Alice Roosevelt (Theodore and the late Alice Lee's daughter); and Major McCarley.[59]

One suspects twenty-year-old Alice Roosevelt was seated with the Bulkeleys because Fannie, at forty-four, was one of the youngest of the political wives. The two women had nothing in common. Alice was a trial. She smoked, drank, drove her own automobile, and even played the horses. To top it off, she had a caustic wit that could shrink concrete. When she thanked her stepmother, Edith, for organizing her wedding party, the older woman replied, "I want you to know I am glad to see you leave. You have never been anything but trouble."[60]

The Marine Band played their scores, and the menu listed huitres (oysters), potages (soups), poisson (fish), releve (fruits and vegetables), entrée (main), sorbet, roti (roast), salade, and dessert. Get-togethers at private residences could be every bit as elaborate.[61]

At the end of January 1906, the Bulkeleys threw a party for Vice President Charles Fairbanks and his wife, Cornelia. The group included Secretary of Commerce and Labor Victor Metcalf and his wife Emily; Senator Warren of Wyoming; Senator Kean of New Jersey; and a dozen other couples. The Bulkeleys served caviar, green turtle soup, tribbles, sweet bread pate, filet with mushrooms, aspic de fois gras, quail; Waldorf salad, and ice cream.[62]

Life was sweet in Washington. The work on Capitol Hill consumed a few hours a day. Socializing made the job full-time. Congress accommodated some of the richest men in America—or their proxies—passing laws that profited them (and their benefactors) the most. This has always been the case, but it rang especially true in the years Morgan Bulkeley served in the Senate. Across the nation, citizens referred to it as the "Millionaire's Senate," or the "Millionaire's Club."[63]

So said, in February 1906, William Randolph Hurst's *Cosmopolitan* magazine created a national sensation when it printed a nine-part series of articles, "Treason of the Senate," by David Graham Phillips. The opening sentence offers a good taste, "Treason is a strong word, but not too strong to characterize the situation in which the Senate is the eager, resourceful, and indefatigable agent of interests as hostile to the American people as any invading army could be." From there Phillips spells out exactly how big corporations and corrupt state legislators played too large a role in selection of senators. Phillips was particularly incensed by a group of senators called "the interests." When this group banded together, almost anything was possible. With great care, Phillips lists the fifty senators who were part of "the interests." Senator Morgan G. Bulkeley made that list.[64]

These articles had everyone on the defensive. Teddy Roosevelt himself thought the articles were an attempt to smear his administration, and he fought back, using the term "muckraker" for the first time.[65] As a rule, the people of Connecticut did not hold Bulkeley's wealth against him. He was a pleasant enough man and had done much for Hartford, but when Phillips and *Cosmopolitan* rubbed their noses in it, bad feelings took root. It is difficult to say exactly when the bloom came off the rose for Morgan Bulkeley, but this defamatory piece by David Graham Phillips may well have started it.

Just as an example of the type of men who populated the Fifty-ninth Congress, consider this—the most powerful member of the Senate was Nelson Aldrich of Rhode Island, whose daughter, Abby, married John D. Rockefeller, Jr., the only child of the wealthiest man in America. Other senators were Henry A. du Pont, the grandson of the founder of E. I. du Pont de Nemours and Company (DuPont); W. Murray Crane of Crane Paper Company in Massachusetts, the sole supplier of paper to the United States Bureau of Printing and Engraving; John F. Dryden, founder of Prudential Insurance Company of America and the Fidelity Trust

Company of New Jersey; Thomas C. Platt, president of Tioga National Bank and Southern Central Railroad; Chauncey Depew, chairman of the board of the entire Vanderbilt Railroad System; Philander Knox, who was general council of Carnegie Steel Company and was instrumental in the formation of United States Steel; and Joseph Millard of Nebraska, president of the Omaha National Bank and incorporator of Omaha & Northwestern Railroad.[66] The term "Millionaire's Senate" was not a misnomer.

Just as the Bulkeleys were beginning to enjoy Washington, they were brought up short by an astounding event a continent away. At 5:12 A.M., local time on April 18, 1906, an earthquake ruptured the northernmost 296 miles of the San Andreas Fault and tore through San Francisco. The earthquake began a series of fires that almost wiped the "Paris of the Pacific" from the face of the earth. In all, the fires destroyed 500 city blocks.[67]

Of immense concern to the Bulkeleys were Fannie's mother and sister, living in the shadow of Nob Hill. Caroline and Minnie Houghton, and their servants, came up lucky. Although it is not recorded, most likely they took refuge at the Houghton's summer home in San Jose, or went to the Stanfords' weekend retreat at Palo Alto. In any event, the fires in San Francisco traveled west to Van Ness Avenue and then were contained—just a single block east of the Houghton mansion on Franklin Street.[68] They were extremely lucky.

The earthquake and the fires left tens of thousands of families homeless, and many of them pitched tents in the city's parks, including Lafayette Square, a two-by-two-block city park easily visible from the Houghton mansion.[69]

In May 1906, the House Committee on the Judiciary listened to a witness, Miles M. Dawson, an actuary on New York's Armstrong Committee, who said, "Not one of America's fire insurance companies knows today whether they would or would not be solvent after they pay their San Francisco losses."[70]

The following day, Morgan Bulkeley appeared before the same committee and set the record straight. "There is no foundation for such a statement. . . . I know of no American company that does not know just where it stands financially. . . . Years from now, these great insurance corporations existing today, will own the major portion of the investment securities of the country. . . . They will control absolutely the finances of the United States and the world."[71]

A little later, in response to a question from Democratic representative David De Armond of Missouri about campaign contributions, and Aetna Life's in particular, Bulkeley admitted that he had indeed given $5,000 of Aetna Life's money to the McKinley campaign and added, "[I]t might as well have been $20,000, which was a 'flea-bite' compared to what he had given personally. . . . If you men of the House of Representatives, who disburse millions of the people's money, disbursed it as honestly as money is handled by insurance companies of this country, you need have no fear of going before your constituents."[72]

~ As early as 1907, there was talk back in Hartford as to who would take Frank Brandegee's Senate seat in 1909. Since Brandegee was appointed by his friends in the state legislature to finish out Orville Platt's term, it was uncertain whether or not the same friends would let Brandegee have a term of his own. Of course, such talk quickly led to speculation about who would take Morgan Bulkeley's seat in 1911. Sure, everyone felt that it was "Bulkeley's turn" in 1905, but would they feel the same way in 1911?

The Fifty-ninth Congress met for six and a half months in its first session and two and a half months in its second, allowing each of its members plenty of time to take care of business back home. In early March 1907 all the legislators packed their bags and went home.

When the Bulkeleys returned to Washington in the first week of December 1907 for the Sixtieth Congress, the senator was quickly engrossed in one of the most memorable investigations of his career. As a member of the Military Affairs Committee, he was charged with gathering the details of an event that occurred two and a half years before.[73]

During the nighttime hours of August 13–14, 1906, African American soldiers of the Twenty-fifth United States Infantry, stationed at Fort Brown, allegedly staged an attack on Brownsville, Texas. This regiment was composed of former slaves and Civil War veterans. During this alleged gun battle, bartender Frank Natus was killed, and the arm of police lieutenant M. Y. Dominguez was badly injured.[74]

A cursory investigation took place, at which time the soldiers denied any involvement in the raid. Nevertheless, President Roosevelt dishonorably discharged all 167 men. This shocked Roosevelt's African American constituency and immediately turned the whole affair into a sensation.

Things quickly began to spiral out of control to the point where the presidential aspirations of Will Taft, secretary of war, were in jeopardy. Stoking the fires of this public relations fiasco was Senator Joseph Foraker of Ohio, who had presidential ambitions of his own. He insisted on a congressional investigation.

The Senate Military Affairs Committee conducted hearings and issued a majority report in March 1908, concurring with the official White House version. A minority report, submitted by Senators Foraker and Bulkeley, asserted the soldiers' innocence, and presented evidence that the townspeople had staged the raid to banish the black troops.[75]

Morgan Bulkeley always felt Roosevelt and Taft had treated the soldiers badly, as evidenced by their half-hearted attempts to allow a few of the soldiers to reenlist. Bulkeley wanted the soldiers reinstated and each given a year's back pay.[76] Taft's election slammed the lid on this matter, and it stayed closed for the next sixty years. Finally, in 1972, Congress asked for a final settlement of this ugly chapter of American military history. The Nixon administration obliged by changing all the discharges to the status of "honorable," but refused to issue any back pay.[77] Senator Bulkeley may have been right, and he may have been the senior senator from Connecticut, but his findings were obviously not validated during his lifetime.

Morgan Bulkeley was like a magnet when it came to honorary commissions and assignments. For many years, baseball fans had been clamoring for the answer to a very simple question—"Who invented baseball?" The who, what, where, when, and why never had been satisfactorily recorded, and by 1904, the time to address it had arrived. Following an article by Henry Hardwick, an early baseball writer who contended that the game was a spin-off from the English game of "rounders," Albert Spalding urged the formation of a commission. Accordingly, seven prominent men were asked to join Col. A. G. Mills to settle the issue once and for all. In addition to Mills, the Mills Commission consisted of Senator Morgan Bulkeley; Senator Arthur P. Gorman of Maryland; Alfred J. Reach of Philadelphia; George Wright of Boston; James E. Sullivan of New York; and Nicholas E. Young of Washington, D.C.[78]

For three years, the men collected testimony and finally issued their definitive report on December 30, 1907: "The first scheme for playing baseball, according to the best evidence obtainable to date, was devised by Abner Doubleday at Cooperstown, N.Y. in 1839." Ardent baseball fans have been arguing about the conclusion of the Mills Commission ever since. The largest faction contends that Abner Doubleday was attending West Point at the time, without even an overnight pass to explain his presence in Cooperstown. The best evidence to date concurs with Hardwick that the game was based on the English game of rounders—the first rules of American baseball having been established by Alexander Joy Cartwright of New York City in 1845.[79]

The Baseball Hall of Fame in Cooperstown offers the following: "[S]uch a finding will not diminish the Mills Commission's contribution. . . . By collecting the memories of many early fans and players while they were still living, the committee created a treasure trove of early Baseball history that would otherwise have been lost. Moreover, by identifying a site for Baseball's origin, the Mills Commission initiated the process that ultimately established a home for the sport—the National Baseball Hall of Fame and Museum."[80] Suffice it to say, the Baseball Hall of Fame is unlikely to ever relocate to Manhattan.

In February 1908, Will Taft quietly launched his presidential campaign by fulfilling a promise to speak at Foot Guard Hall in Hartford. Taft arrived at Union Station in the late afternoon, where Mayor William Henney and a brand new Pope-Hartford presidential automobile greeted him.[81]

After Taft had settled in at Foot Guard Hall, Alderman Charles Goodwin, the son of Francis Goodwin, called the meeting to order. On the dais were Pat McGovern, Lucius Barbour, and Morgan Bulkeley's nephews, W. E. A. Bulkeley and Morgan B. Brainard. (Senator Bulkeley was still in Washington.)[82] Taft thanked everyone for the invitation, delivered one of his least memorable speeches, and soon departed the Charter Oak City for Washington.

The Republican National Convention for 1908 commenced in the Chicago Coliseum on July 16 and concluded on July 19. Teddy Roosevelt, still wildly popular with Americans, had pledged in a moment of weakness not to run in 1908 if the voters gave him a term of his own in 1904. It was a terrible mistake, but a promise he felt duty-bound to keep. Thus, Will Taft had Teddy Roosevelt's endorsement and received the nomination. After hearing the news, Bulkeley sent a telegram to Taft congratulating him, and Taft returned the cable with his thanks.[83] He still needed to win the general election, but these were the days when the Republicans controlled the country.

Taft, often cited as one of our ten worst presidents, had enormous potential. He had graduated second in his class at Yale and was an eminently capable jurist. The problem, of course, was that Taft had no real interest in the presidency, yet his wife, Nellie, and his half-brother, Charlie, practically insisted on it. The results were dismal. As Roosevelt once remarked, "He means well and he'll do his best, but he's weak. They'll get around him."[84]

Taft has been designated the "automobiling president," although, as we have seen, Teddy Roosevelt first campaigned from a horseless carriage. During his campaign for the presidency, trains took Taft on wide swings through the West, the Midwest, and New England, but automobiles showcased him to the American public. Taft disliked the limelight and regarded his campaign for the presidency as "the most uncomfortable four months of my life."[85] All told, he gave 418 speeches in forty-one days—real snoozers too.[86] When election day finally rolled around, Taft beat William Jennings Bryan by a comfortable margin to become the twenty-seventh president of the United States. Bulkeley, of course, sent another congratulatory telegram to Taft and again received a thank-you cable in return.[87]

As fall came to New England, Hartford prepared for an enormous celebration as the new bridge across the Connecticut River drew to completion. The old bridge had burned in 1895 and thirteen long years passed before a permanent structure spanned the river. In the process of construction, eight caissons had to plunge thirty feet to hit bedrock, and secure the pier foundations in the river.[88] Now, four years later, the bridge—first called the Hartford Bridge but renamed for Bulkeley after his death in 1922—opened.

The dedication party lasted three days—October 6, 7, and 8, 1908, and attracted over 200,000 revelers. There were reenactments of Thomas Hooker's landing at Hartford in 1634, plenty of food and beverages, and endless parades. At one point, Senator Bulkeley's youngest child, Houghton, fourteen at the time, removed a flag from one of the dedication plaques, instigating a huge round of applause from the spectators.[89]

When the town fathers appointed Morgan Bulkeley to chair the Bridge Committee, few realized that a direct descendant of his had been on the three-man committee to build the first wooden bridge across the river in 1810.[90] His name was John Morgan and he was from the same New London line of Morgans from which Bulkeley's mother Lydia descended.

The Vanderbilt Cup race, held on Long Island (Garden City, New York) was about as close as Morgan Bulkeley got to the exciting new field of automobiles in the first decade of the new century. It began in the middle of October each year and was cutting-edge stuff.[91]

One year, Senator Bulkeley attended with his older son and nephews. The race had become the biggest draw among auto enthusiasts, and yet no one in Senator Bulkeley's party thought to make room reservations. When they got to the raceway, everything was booked solid. With some effort, bunks were located. One of the hotels offered to remove extra coffee pots, and assorted cups, saucers, and silverware from a closet for the senator. An old cot was brought in and wedged into place. This small closet became the overnight accommodations of Connecticut's elder statesman—United States Senator Morgan Gardner Bulkeley.[92]

The dovetailing of the horse-and-buggy era with that of the automobile was by no means seamless. By 1900, there were about twenty electric and gasoline-powered automobiles negotiating the streets of Hartford. Most of these vehicles were owned by Pope's Motor Carriage Division and driven by the company's officers and engineers. Dr. Edward K. Root—Senator Bulkeley's physician—purchased a Pope for use on his daily rounds, and thus became an early proponent.[93]

As late as 1910, horses still pulled some fire-fighting equipment, and trash collection happened entirely by horse and wagon. As late as 1920, there were still many livery stables with horses for hire and twenty blacksmiths still plied their trade in the city[94]

When automobile dealers began to open showrooms in 1903 on Allyn and Asylum Streets, Morgan Bulkeley hardly took notice. In fact, Sam Miner sold Pierce-Arrows, Knoxes, and Oldsmobiles for five years before Morgan Bulkeley paid him a visit.[95]

The wealthy people of Hartford preferred the horse-drawn carriage for all formal occasions until almost 1920. Since the earliest autos didn't have heaters, carriages were every bit as comfortable. Besides, car tires behaved poorly in the snow because they were so thin, making sleighs preferable during New England winters.

Another reason for Bulkeley's slow shift to the automobile was his love of horses. As first vice president of the National Trotting Association, he not only used horses for basic transportation, he enjoyed nothing better than an afternoon spent watching, or judging races at Charter Oak Park.

Beyond all other considerations, rural roads were wretched. The roads to and from Fenwick, for example, were still so poor that Bulkeley and his family were better off taking the train. The senator actually preferred taking the Valley Railroad back and forth to Beaumaris, as he could sit in the "smoker" and play cards or just watch the world go by.

In October 1908, Bulkeley finally broke down and ordered his 1909 Pierce-Arrow limousine from Sam Miner.[96] It arrived from the Buffalo factory three months later and was the most luxurious auto on the road. Two years after the senator's purchase, Francis Goodwin ordered the same model Pierce-Arrow limousine.[97]

Around the time Bulkeley bought his first automobile, he addressed the Automobile Club of Hartford at a luncheon at the Allyn House, "The subject of automobiles is relatively unfamiliar to me. . . . I have never tried to run any machine except a voting machine and of that machine I am hardly in favor."[98] (The paper ballot—or rather the misuse thereof—made Morgan Bulkeley.)

In the summertime, Bulkeley left the Pierce-Arrow and his chauffeur at Fenwick so Fannie and her friends could go out driving. There were special occasions when Bulkeley needed it in the city, but these were rare. Besides, Connecticut's speed limit for automobiles topped out at twenty-five miles per hour while the Valley Railroad usually managed twice that.[99]

In common with most of the summer homes at Fenwick, Beaumaris did not feature a garage. The Bulkeleys sheltered their Pierce-Arrow in one of the old carriage sheds by the railroad station, and Arthur Stone slept in a room above. This was fine for a while, but as people started driving themselves, it was too big a nuisance to walk across the golf course to get to the cars. To remedy this, everyone started adding garages to their cottages.

Even though there were less than two thousand automobiles in Connecticut, in September 1909 Bulkeley, with Arthur Stone at the wheel, suffered a car accident in Chester, the tiny river town just north of Deep River. It wasn't actually a fender-bender as such, more of an accident caused by trying to avoid an accident. When Arthur crested a hill, he applied the Pierce-Arrow's brakes to hold the automobile back on the down slope. The car behind them, driven by Perley Keeney, came over the hill too fast and had to go off the road and up an embankment to avoid a crash. Unfortunately, the car rolled over, and Keeney; his father, Charles; and two women in the back seat were tossed out.[100]

Bulkeley asked Arthur to turn around and the two men returned to the scene to help the people in the other auto. Some of them were seriously hurt. Two months later, sixty-two-year-old passenger Charles Keeney, the purchasing agent for the Hartford Life Insurance Company died as a result of his injuries.[101]

Bulkeley was involved in another accident a few years later, a fender bender, in Deep River.[102] Considering that there were still only a couple thousand automobiles in the whole state, one wonders if the actuaries at Aetna Life were scratching their heads in disbelief, raising premiums, or both.

For Morgan Bulkeley, the months of April and November were like a couple of stiff drinks. Politics got his juices flowing like nothing else. In April, the city elections kept him busy. As Connecticut's undisputed Republican boss, no one got very far in politics without Bulkeley's approval. Sometimes, he would acquiesce to a candidate if the man had enough friends, but further advancement was out of the question unless Bulkeley warmed to him.

Even though Morgan Bulkeley was still the leading Republican politician in Connecticut, young aggressors were amassing behind his back. At Christmastime in 1908, Morgan turned seventy-one, and local newspapers referred to him as the "aged Senator Bulkeley." One would expect this from the *Hartford Times*, the Democratic organ, but now Charles Clark of the *Courant* had begun to slam him.[103] It should be remembered that Morgan Bulkeley never cared for the moderate Republican Ezra Clark, the president of the Board of Water Commissioners back in the 1870s and 1880s. Now Clark's son was using his position as editor-in-chief of the *Courant* to exact a little revenge.

Combined with these assaults from the newspapers, the closer Bulkeley's 1911 Senate reelection campaign got, the bolder the young Republicans became. The biggest challenge to Bulkeley's position as party boss and powerbroker came from a thirty-eight-year-old attorney, J. Henry Roraback, of North Canaan in Litchfield County.[104] The brother of Connecticut Supreme Court Judge Alberto T. Roraback, this young lawyer was the rising star in Republican circles. Although he eschewed elective office for himself, he loved to play puppet master.

In the senatorial nomination process of January 1909, Frank Brandegee wanted badly to win a term of his own. Fine, but Roraback and his followers were pushing hard for the nomination of Representative Ebenezer Hill of the Fourth Congressional District.[105]

The Brandegee-Hill face-off illustrates beautifully the subtleties of politics. Brandegee, the son of United States Representative Augustus Brandegee of New London, was a decent man, but let's not forget he had been Sam Fessenden's biggest supporter. Naturally, he never did anything to help Morgan Bulkeley. However, a Hill win now would be a disaster for Bulkeley. It would mean he had already lost all his power to J. Henry Roraback. Under the circumstances, he couldn't possibly keep his Senate seat in 1911.

Sensing the importance of Brandegee's nomination, Bulkeley began work in Washington to line up support for Connecticut's junior senator and got back to Hartford just in time for the big vote. His long-distance persuasions—as well as the tireless efforts of men like Pat McGovern—proved effective.

On January 12, 1909, at 2:10 P.M., Chairman Michael Kenealy of the Republican State Central Committee stepped to the podium in the great Hall of the House at the Capitol and called the meeting to order. A caucus chairman was chosen, and voting commenced soon thereafter. On the first ballot, Frank Brandegee won with a majority of fifteen votes.[106] (Brandegee barely kept his seat in 1908, but he managed to stay in the Senate until October 14, 1924, when, as a result of bad real estate investments and ill health, he took his own life.)[107]

Frank Brandegee's win over Ebenezer Hill was good news indeed, and the first person in Washington Morgan Bulkeley told was his secretary, Loyal Thompson, who dutifully forwarded the contents of the telegram to other interested parties.[108] When Bulkeley sent the telegram to Thompson, was he letting his secretary know that his own reelection looked secure? Was he signaling to Thompson that his services would be needed at least until March 1917? Quite possibly.

In the aftermath of all the senatorial intrigue, one final piece of business lingered. Postmaster George Allen of Middletown had read the situation incorrectly and supported Ebenezer Hill in the Brandegee-Hill face-off. Now he had to pay the price. Both Bulkeley and Brandegee rejected his reappointment in the Senate, and he was out. Postmaster jobs around the state were considered the sweetest of political plums. They paid well and required little or no work, but without good political instincts, they could be very short sinecures.[109]

Taft's presidency was so full of bizarre incidents that it seems more like opéra bouffe than official United States history. The first order of business was to replace his bathtub with a jumbo model. When Nellie Taft found out she and her husband had to pay for state dinners, she fired the caterers. Thereafter all dinners were prepared in the White House kitchens. Nellie replaced the frock-coated ushers with liveried servants. Lincoln's double bed went next, and in its place twin beds with canopies were installed—a first in the White House.[110] Apparently, size does matter.

The whirlwind personified by Nellie Taft proved too much even for her. Two months after Will Taft took the oath of office, the forty-seven-year-old Nellie Taft suffered a stroke. Though she was able to take her first automobile ride a month later, the stroke robbed her of her speech and her ability to walk for a year.[111]

Upon hearing of her friend's medical problems, Fannie Bulkeley sent a dozen American Beauty roses. Nellie Taft wrote her a nice thank-you card, noting they "filled the room so nicely" and wished the Bulkeleys a pleasant summer.[112]

Even without this personal hardship, Taft's presidency was doomed. One critic called him "an amiable island completely surrounded by men who knew exactly what they wanted."[113] Among his other problems, he hated "Uncle Joe" Cannon, whose vulgarities grated on Taft's Midwestern sensibilities. When a president can't get along with the Speaker of the House of Representatives, things can go downhill quickly.

In March 1909, Bulkeley was back in Hartford working at Aetna Life when President Taft called a special session of Congress to revise the tariff (an upgrade of the Dingley Act, which would protect labor and industry from the difference in the cost of production in the United States and overseas). Before he left for Washington, Bulkeley told a close friend, Railroad Commissioner Andrew Gates, that he *would* be a candidate for reelection in 1911.[114] The city's newspapers were quick to point out that Bulkeley said he would only serve one term on a number of occasions and reminded readers that the senator would be in his seventy-fourth year when his present term expired.[115]

Another matter of consternation was Bulkeley's friend and protégé, ex-governor George McLean. He had supported Ebenezer Hill in the Brandegee-Hill face-off and claimed he was undecided about challenging Bulkeley. McLean owed a great deal to Morgan Bulkeley, but now their friendship was on the line.

Politically, Senator Bulkeley got caught in a number of mishaps that played badly in Connecticut. One involved the Speaker of the House, "Uncle Joe" Cannon, who was as polarizing a figure as ever served in the House. "Uncle Joe" was difficult to love, but Bulkeley always stood up for Cannon—probably because he needed his help with legislation—and the voters of Connecticut didn't like this at all.[116]

Then Bulkeley insulted Republican Senator Weldon Heyburn of Idaho on the floor of the Senate. Heyburn was an easterner and an attorney who had moved to Shoshone County, Idaho. He complained about the postal system, claiming some maps he had mailed out never got to the people back home. Bulkeley suggested the problem might be peculiar to Idaho. Not to be gainsaid, Heyburn became indignant with this attempt at levity and challenged the senator from Connecticut on the matter.[117]

Bulkeley replied, "The mere presence in the Senate of the senator from Idaho is a cause for mirth." This caused a flap, and Bulkeley, sensing he'd made a terrible mistake, managed to get his remarks expunged from the Congressional Record, but it was too late. The press caught his remarks and printed them both in Washington and in Hartford. Bulkeley appeared insensitive, and even arrogant.[118]

Then in May, Bulkeley wrote to the Mattatuck Rod & Gun Club in Waterbury, explaining he would like their input as to where a fish hatchery should be located in their area. Apparently, he had appropriated $25,000 for the hatchery, but didn't realize the hatchery had to have access to both fresh and salt water. Since Waterbury is about twenty-five miles from the nearest salt water, they obviously were excluded from the program.[119]

By early June 1910, Bulkeley's Senate reelection bid began to draw fire. The not-to-be-denied J. Henry Roraback was backing ex-governor George McLean as a successor to Morgan Bulkeley. Incidentally, Roraback was an attorney, but he was also the postmaster of little Canaan-Four-Corners in Litchfield County.

Since Roraback had to get Bulkeley out of the way to become the Republican boss of Connecticut, his backing of McLean wasn't exactly a shock. Still, for Bulkeley, it brought up the question of the legality—or the appearance of impropriety—for a postmaster to use his office to openly campaign for a candidate for the Senate. Bulkeley decided to clip Roraback's wings and called for his dismissal. By July, Roraback was removed as postmaster of Canaan-Four-Corners and Bulkeley was at Fenwick enjoying life.[120] Power—use it or lose it.

Newspapers print stories, and all summer long they made hay with the McLean-Bulkeley confrontation. Did Bulkeley tell McLean he only wanted to serve one term, as McLean claimed? Did Bulkeley tell McLean he might not even finish his first term, that he might quit at any time?" There was plenty of innuendo and lots of seemingly good reasons for McLean to turn on Bulkeley without remorse.

Bulkeley had been in politics a long time and liked everyone to believe he was unmoved by such sniping. This was difficult now, as even the New York journalists suggested that times had changed—Bulkeley's type of politics was a thing of the past. Even the all-powerful Senator Nelson Aldrich of Rhode Island had withdrawn from the coming Senate race, because he "could see the handwriting on the wall."[121] (This might not have been true, because Aldrich had served five terms in the Senate and may have been ill, since he died a year after his retirement.)

On Thursday, August 11, 1910, Senator Bulkeley completed his work at Aetna Life in time to catch the 3:55 P.M. train to Fenwick. The trip usually took one hour and sixteen minutes. As was his custom, the senator took a seat in the smoker and began to play whist with Andrew Breughel and Charles Ware of Hartford and Aseph Hale of Portland.[122]

Everything went according to schedule until the train was a few miles south of Middletown and approaching the Maromas Station. There was a bend in the track just before Maromas, and conductor Fred Bosworth couldn't see that another crew had allowed four freight cars on a siding to roll back down onto the main tracks. Bosworth slammed on the brakes as soon as he could, but it was too late. The Valley train slammed into the four cars at forty miles an hour. Sadly, the wreck pinned Bosworth in his cab and he died instantly.

Bulkeley was tossed over his seat, but unharmed. The placement of the baggage car ahead of the smoker car saved him. The unpeopled luggage car took the brunt of the blow, lessening the impact on the smoker's passengers.[123]

By the end of August, Bulkeley was fighting all out for his political life. Early caucuses favored McLean, and it was only a question of time before he would be in the race for Bulkeley's Senate seat up to his collar buttons.[124] Adding insult to injury, Morgan Bulkeley sensed voters' moods in Connecticut. When Manchester, West Hartford, and Middletown held their caucuses, they turned him down flat.[125]

As if the public knew Morgan Bulkeley only too well, a groundswell of support for a roll call vote in the Republican caucus began to rise within the state.[126] Bulkeley remained silent. A roll call vote couldn't possibly help him; a secret ballot might. He had many friends who could be counted on in a secret ballot, but in a roll call vote, they had to honor their constituency or be voted out of office.

When a reporter finally caught up with Bulkeley and asked whether or not he was in favor of a roll call vote, Bulkeley snapped, "It makes no difference if I am or not." The reporter continued, "You won't tell us what you think?" Bulkeley raised his voice, "It's none of their business what I think."[127] In the Republican caucuses around the state, McLean was outpolling Bulkeley consistently and the older man's frustration grew.[128] Where were all those friends who used to toast him at political dinners? Besides McLean, where were all the men who owed their political careers to him?

In caucus after caucus, Bulkeley lost ground to McLean. Things got so uncomfortable that Bulkeley began denying that he had anything to do with the firing of postmasters while he was a senator.[129] Desperately, Bulkeley tried to herald his achievements in Washington, but his junior colleagues felt that he had too much power. One Democratic politician wrote, "Of course he owns both of the Connecticut seats of the Senate, for did he not deliver the goods to Brandegee after Ebenezer [Hill] had the seat all bought and paid for?"[130]

By the time of the general elections in November 1910, Bulkeley realized his Senate career was over. He would not be reelected. In January, when the delegates in the statehouse voted, he would lose his seat and all of his political power. His seat would pass to George McLean, and his political power to J. Henry Roraback without a courtesy call from either of them.

When it came to settling scores, Bulkeley sometimes struck like a bow hunter and at other times had the patience of an ice fisherman. Whether bolting on an undeserving candidate or settling up with an ungrateful postmaster, on any number of occasions, he proved he was up to the job. So it's not surprising he chose this moment to settle the oldest score of them all.

Bulkeley had managed fairly well to keep Francis Goodwin at arm's length, even with both of them living and working in Hartford and vacationing at Fenwick. Sure, Goodwin could be the Parks Commissioner if he wanted, but if he ever tried to enter elective politics, he would have had a rude awakening. From time out of mind, the Goodwins had been a thorn in Bulkeley's side. Now, Charles Goodwin, Francis's son, wanted to be governor. Bulkeley had had enough.

Charles Goodwin began his gubernatorial race as Hartford's golden boy— Yale undergrad, Harvard Law, good-looking, wealthy, and erudite. Bulkeley watched him grow up at Fenwick, saw him become a championship sailor and near-scratch golfer. Charles was a founder and senior partner at Bennett & Goodwin and had served as executive secretary to two governors, George Lilley and Frank Weeks. Additionally, Charles sat on the boards of a dozen Hartford institutions and corporations. In short, Charles Goodwin's future seemed unlimited.[131]

Charles Goodwin, however, made a costly mistake. Sensing that Bulkeley's renomination was in jeopardy, he tried to straddle the fence. Typical of his campaign rhetoric, he delivered this nugget at a campaign function held in the ballroom of the Garde Hotel in Hartford, "[I] would say of Senator Bulkeley, what [I have] said in public and private before, the senator deserves the vote of the City of Hartford for whatever he wants."[132] Unhappily for the young lawyer, Bulkeley knew Goodwin wasn't in his corner. Charles Goodwin's dilemma was simple. He didn't want to cross Morgan Bulkeley because of his political power, but neither could he alienate soon-to-be U.S. Senator George McLean.[133]

Given the demise of his own career and his intense dislike of everything Goodwin, Bulkeley threw all his support to the Democratic candidate, Judge Simeon Baldwin of New Haven. Bulkeley's campaign against Charles Goodwin may have even included some really nasty trickery. For example, there was a story about Francis Goodwin's first cousin J. P. Morgan coming to Connecticut for secret meetings with young Charles Goodwin, implying Morgan money would be used to buy votes.[134] One writer referred to talk of "Morgan's 'private car,' Morgan's 'steam yacht' and Morgan's 'little black valise.' "[135] Coupled with this, the Democratic candidate, Simeon Baldwin of New Haven, claimed the Democratic nomination came to him "unsought and unbought," as if Goodwin could claim neither.[136] Bulkeley knew better than anyone that the stink of corruption could be deadly.

Sure enough, in the gubernatorial election in November, Charles Goodwin lost to Simeon Baldwin by 4,000 votes.[137] This ended Charles Goodwin's political career. He never ran for public office again. The Goodwin family, bitter about this whole sordid affair, cemented their grudge against Morgan Bulkeley.

Thereafter, Charles Goodwin avoided Fenwick. When he got married in 1912 and the children started to arrive, the Goodwins built a cottage on Fisher's Island and summered there for the next thirty-five years. Goodwin licked his wounds for a long time. Only after World War II, with Morgan Bulkeley twenty-five years in the grave, did Charles Goodwin return to Fenwick.[138]

Chapter Twelve

TWILIGHT

By 1911, Hartford had changed so much that it is hard to believe seventy-three-year-old Morgan Bulkeley was able to keep up with it all. Just the city's makeup seemed eye opening. Two-thirds of the city's residents were first- or second-generation immigrants, and composed 90 percent of the population in the river wards. Italian-Americans constituted the single biggest ethnic group relocating to the city, and by the end of World War I, Hartford's African American population had more than doubled.[1]

The conflicts between automobiles and horse-drawn wagons had become so contentious that the General Assembly finally set a speed limit of twelve miles per hour within city limits.[2] This, of course, increased regularly.

Since Morgan Bulkeley helped ensure the election of Democratic governor Simeon Baldwin, he wasn't about to miss the Governor's Ball. He and Fannie were accommodated in the first row of Foot Guard Hall's spectators' gallery for the January 4, 1911, gathering. Bulkeley was seated right next to ex-governor George McLean, the traitor who would slip into his Senate seat just six days hence.[3] Though McLean obviously disgusted Bulkeley, in public the senator never uttered a bad word about him, and even wished him well on several occasions. Of course, Bulkeley had a right to resent such perfidy. McLean's episodes of "nervous prostration" alone were enough to exclude him from higher office except for the fact that Morgan Bulkeley always stood by him.[4] As long as McLean had Bulkeley's confidence, the public went along. Ultimately, McLean used this priceless backing to unseat his old friend and political patron. It would be delightful to report that seventy-three-year-old Morgan Bulkeley took all of this philosophically, realizing that some days you're the pigeon and some days you're the statue, but he was made of different stuff. Perhaps the person in charge of seating for the Governor's Ball knew such a pairing would cause uneasiness; then again maybe such a cynical view is unwarranted.

In his last month of office, Bulkeley used his influence to hold up George Schleuter's nomination in the U.S. Senate for Darien postmaster.[5] Fairly quickly, though, he was overpowered by Connecticut congressman Ebenezer Hill and others, so he withdrew his opposition. Schleuter won reappointment. Such a small thing, but a poignant example of how fast Bulkeley's domination had slipped away.

In September, President Taft visited Hartford again. It was another one of his lightning-fast visits. His train pulled into Union Station at 1:21 in the afternoon and departed at 5:00 sharp. Attorney General George Wickersham accompanied the president, and Governor Baldwin and the First Company of the Governor's Foot Guard met Taft at the station.[6]

Lunch was served at Memorial Hall in the new State Library building, where a swarm of local dignitaries flocked to greet the president. Morgan Bulkeley was there and had a nice conversation with his old friend. The Connecticut Fair Association actually invited Taft to Hartford, so right after lunch, the group headed for Charter Oak Park. While there, in addition to watching a few races, Taft spoke to 30,000 people about national peace and peace treaties in general.[7]

In late 1911, Bulkeley came face-to-face with a delicate problem. His daughter, Elinor, was to make her Hartford society debut. The obvious venue for this party was The Hartford Club, except that it didn't have a room big enough for such a gathering. Other young women celebrated their coming-out parties at The Hartford Club, but other families didn't do things on the scale the Bulkeleys did. Instead they organized the party in their home on Washington Street. On Wednesday, November 8, 1911, Morgan and Fannie hosted 300 people for Elinor's coming-out party, which lasted from suppertime until late in the evening.[8] Even with such a lengthy guest list, some relatives and friends had to be held over to a second coming-out party a week later. On November 15, a shorter party reveled between the hours of 5 and 7 P.M.[9]

Now that Morgan Bulkeley was back at Aetna Life full-time, his first move in 1912 involved taking some profits on bank stocks the company had been holding for years.[10] However, simply calling a broker and making the trade proved far too straightforward for him. Bulkeley wanted to boost the price first, so he began to buy shares of Phoenix Bank like a madman. Word of these purchases got around quickly, and rumor spread that Bulkeley sought to effect a merger between Aetna National Bank and Phoenix Bank or perhaps even a triple merger with Aetna National, Phoenix, and American National. On the face of it, either of these propositions made infinite sense because it would effectively reduce the power of Hartford National Bank, the biggest bank in town.[11]

After getting everyone riled up and out of their minds with merger mania, presumably, Bulkeley quietly sold all of Aetna Life's bank stocks. Two months later, a little talk about a Phoenix-American Bank merger lingered, but nothing ever came of it and whispers of any other mergers were nonexistent.[12]

Bulkeley's method of pumping up the price of these bank shares before unloading them brings up the question of insider trading, a very gray area. To begin, Nathan Rothschild used carrier pigeons to perfect this market-manipulation method just after the Battle of Waterloo. As soon as one of his pigeons dropped a note announcing Napoleon's loss to Wellington, he feigned panic and sold everything. Naturally, other investors followed suit. Then, very quietly he bought back his original shares plus many more.[13] This is more or less what Bulkeley did with his bank shares in 1912—except in reverse.

A more important consideration is that insider trading was not illegal in 1912. The Securities and Exchange Commission, which polices insider trading, wasn't created until 1934, and by its own admission, it has a very difficult time enforcing insider-trading laws.[14]

In addition to jumping back into Aetna Life, Bulkeley also indulged in some fun he couldn't afford while he was a U.S. senator. In the April city elections, Bulkeley got word that a Park Street shoe store owner, Nathan Spiegel, couldn't get out to vote because he had no one to mind the store. Bulkeley sent for his limousine.

Arriving at Spiegel's store, he said, "Mr. Spiegel, we want your vote."

"But I can't leave. I have no one to watch the store for me while I am gone," countered Spiegel.

"That's what I'm here for," said Bulkeley, "Now get your coat and I'll tend store for you while you're gone. All I want is to be allowed to smoke."

Spiegel grabbed his coat and got into the limousine. Bulkeley wriggled out of his topcoat, lit a cigar, and waited for customers to appear. Presently, a would-be shoe buyer stopped in.

"Mr. Spiegel has just run out for a minute and I'm tending the store. I wouldn't lose a customer for him, not for a city block. I want you to wait."

The customer was stunned at the sight of Senator Bulkeley, but waited. In about twenty minutes, Nathan Spiegel returned.

"All right, Senator?"

"All right, Mr. Spiegel. I've saved a customer for you."

With that, Bulkeley got into his limousine and left.[15]

Also in April 1912, J. Henry Roraback was elected to the chairmanship of the Republican State Central Committee.[16] Morgan Bulkeley kept Roraback at bay for a couple of years, but once Bulkeley lost his Senate seat to George McLean in 1911, the young lion took over. This wasn't an easy thing to accept, but Bulkeley did better than most. There was never any reason for J. Henry Roraback and Morgan Bulkeley to be close, and they never were, but the ex-senator never spoke badly of the new Republican boss.

Even though he was a very capable attorney, Roraback was also involved in a lime-fertilizer business in Canaan and subsequently became president of the

Connecticut Light and Power Company.[17] This was a figurehead position, enabling him to travel the state freely on Republican Party business yet still draw a handsome paycheck. Roraback controlled the Republican Party in Connecticut until he took his own life in 1937.[18]

❧ Morgan Bulkeley was quick to spot opportunities. Up to this time, automobile insurance policies were bare-bones contracts, and an automobile policy in 1912, for example, didn't even include fire insurance. By reviving Manufacturers Fire and Marine Insurance Company, Aetna Life finally offered "all-risk" automobile insurance that included loss by "accident, fire, etc." The company introduced the complete policy in 1913.[19]

❧ Meanwhile, the Hartford YMCA needed new headquarters and staged a building drive the same year. Despite Herculean efforts by its staff, the fundraising fell short of its goal. At the last moment, the call went out to Morgan Bulkeley, who came up with an unusual solution to the problem. He gave everyone at Aetna Life a raise, which they in turn donated to the YMCA building fund.[20] This was far cleverer than it sounds, because Bulkeley could have simply taken the money out of petty cash. However, the new YMCA was much bigger than the old facility and would need new members. By involving the employees of Aetna Life, he created interested parties—young people who might become members— as well as donors.

❧ Although Bulkeley was not the type of man to complain about cold weather, judging by the time he scheduled his vacations, he may well have been trying to escape New England's winters as he got older. At seven o'clock on a cold February evening in 1915, Morgan Bulkeley and his party boarded the Independence, a private Pullman car, for a trip to the American West. The group included Morgan and Fannie Bulkeley; their daughter, Elinor; a friend of Elinor's, Miss Anna English; Minnie Houghton; Minnie's maid; and Mr. and Mrs. T. Belknap Beach. (The Beaches were fellow Fenwick cottagers.) Bulkeley's spirits were high and his eyes were sparkling, so the idea he needed a vacation wasn't even close to the mark.[21]

Upon arrival in Washington, the whole group moved onto the Rocket, the most luxurious parlor car in the United States. The Independence collected them at Hartford because there were several bridges between Hartford and Washington under which the Rocket could not pass.

The rear section of the Rocket functioned as an observation room, which could be changed to a two-berth sleeping room at a moments notice. Four opulently furnished sleeping rooms took up the left side of the car from the observation room up to the dining room, which was about ten feet square and contained a large mahogany table and eight chairs. There were pictures and flowers adorning the walls and tables, making the car quite homey. Attending the Bulkeleys and their friends were a steward, a waiter and George Richards, a consummate railroad chef, who ran the galley and prepared the meals.[22]

The train traveled the Pennsylvania route to New Orleans for Mardi Gras week. By March 6, they stopped in San Antonio, arriving on a Monday morning and leaving a day later. From there, the train continued on the southern route west and then north through California to San Francisco, where they dropped off Minnie Houghton and her maid.[23]

Three weeks later, they were at the Hotel Huntington in Pasadena, where a local reporter interviewed Senator Bulkeley. Regarding World War I, Bulkeley held, "The war is all right, so long as it stays on the other side of the Atlantic. . . . Let them fight it out." Concerning the new Federal Reserve, he dismissed it by saying, "I never saw any need for it."[24] The party visited the Grand Canyon and then returned to San Francisco. At about this point, the Beaches had to get back to Hartford and left by train from San Francisco.

The week of April 17, the Bulkeleys joined in a six-day observance of the San Francisco earthquake, which had leveled the city nine years earlier. When they were finally ready to return to Connecticut, the Bulkeleys boarded the Rocket and took the Canadian-Pacific route, pulling into Hartford at eight o'clock on the morning of May 6. They were gone for seventy-three days.[25]

Life wasn't exactly serene with World War I raging in Europe. President Woodrow Wilson ran for reelection in the fall of 1916 on the slogan "He kept us out of war," but less than ninety days after his swearing in, he asked Congress for a declaration of war against Germany. The response in the nation was tepid. The American people felt, even though we had declared war on Germany, the country would never be forced to send an army overseas. A military draft quickly changed their minds. Ultimately the United States dressed 4.3 million men under arms and suffered 364,000 casualties in the war.[26]

For the Bulkeleys, life took a shaky turn in the middle of June 1916, when Pancho Villa raided New Mexico, causing a national emergency. President Woodrow Wilson called on each state to send National Guard units to the Mexican border in an abortive military operation.

Troop B was a cavalry unit of the Connecticut National Guard and included Morgan Bulkeley's two sons and three of his nephews.[27] The soldiers had almost no time for training and were poorly equipped. One of the leaders of the unit, Capt. J. H. Kelso Davis, a West Point graduate, had a son, Jack, who married Mary

Brainard's daughter, Edith. The biggest problem for Capt. Davis was horse-flesh. There were 120 cavalry soldiers in the troop, but only thirty-seven horses. What to do?

Davis went to see Morgan Bulkeley at Aetna Life and explained the situation. Bulkeley said, "Get back to me tomorrow, Kelso. I'll see what I can do."[28] After Davis left, Bulkeley went into action. Locally, he managed to have fifty-three horses brought in from Meriden at a cost to him of $13,000.[29] Then, by telephone he found an Aetna Life agent in the tiny railroad town of Mexico, Missouri. He asked the man if he could have thirty horses with saddles and bridles at the train station in three days. The agent said he could do it, and Bulkeley wired the necessary funds. The next day, the senator told Kelso, "When you make train reservations, be sure the train stops in Mexico, Missouri, because there will be thirty horses waiting there for you."[30] (The train depot is actually in the nearby town of Columbia.)

Troop B arrived in Nogales, Arizona, in the first week of July. Of course, Pancho Villa wasn't stupid enough to attack the United States with so many troops pouring in from all over the country, so Troop B's stay in the Southwest was uneventful. After a sleepy four-month deployment, they arrived back in Hartford on October 28.[31]

These were turbulent times, and President Woodrow Wilson completely de-stroyed Elinor Bulkeley's wedding plans. Instead of a large church wedding, Elinor settled for quite a bit less. Her fiancé, John Ingersoll—employed in the New York office of Aetna Life—was a member of New York's Squadron A and waited for an Arizona deployment too.

Rather than waiting until he got back from fighting Pancho Villa, the couple decided to marry. Ingersoll got a twenty-four-hour pass and they exchanged vows on June 27, 1916, in the chapel of St. Thomas Church in New York City. Following the ceremony, the family threw a reception at the Waldorf-Astoria. Although everyone had a good time, the bride's two brothers were absent because they were already on a train to Arizona. To make matters worse, Elinor's new husband was due back in camp at Van Cortland Park that night.[32]

Elinor Bulkeley was only one of the thousands of young women whose sons, boyfriends, and husbands were off guarding the southwestern border of the United States from an assault by Pancho Villa, but she had one thing the others did not—a father who was wealthy and resourceful.

Two weeks before Thanksgiving, Morgan, Fannie, and Elinor (Mrs. John Ingersoll) piled into another richly appointed parlor car and headed for the Pacific Coast. On the way out, they stopped for three days at Camp McAllen where Elinor spent some time with her new husband.[33]

This trip was a short one, but on the way back from California, the group stopped in Brownsville where the infamous "Brownsville Raid" had taken place back in 1906. Bulkeley had visited when he and Senator Joseph Foraker were tasked with investigating the raid, but hadn't been back since. En route to Hartford, the Bulkeleys also stopped in Tennessee and Georgia to visit a number of Civil War battlefields. Early in the evening of December 7, Morgan, Fannie, and Elinor arrived back at Union Station in Hartford. By Morgan Bulkeley's standards, this three-week hop was one of his shortest trips to the West Coast.[34]

≈ Hartford had been in need of a more modern municipal building for some time when plans were finally approved for a massive new structure on Main Street. The new City Hall was completed in 1915. As a result, the former seat of municipal government, the Old State House, faced a bleak future. By this time, it housed restrooms for those awaiting trolleys at the Isle of Safety, and that was about it. Meetings to determine the building's future were held at City Hall—the Old State House—as early as 1906.[35] Many wanted the old building demolished. A certain simple-minded logic buttressed this option because all of the land at the center of the city could then be given over to the Federal Building and post office, sitting directly east of the Old State House.[36]

Happily, many argued that it was the post office that ought to go, leaving the Old State House to be restored. Morgan Bulkeley favored the restoration. At one meeting, Bulkeley told stories of his childhood in and around the Old State House. He had spent much of his boyhood in State House Square and had watched his father preside as Hartford Court Judge in 1849 and Speaker of the House of Representatives in 1855.[37] As mayor, Morgan Bulkeley occupied an office in the building for eight years.

Typically, Bulkeley didn't like the idea of spending $20,000 for a minor face-lift. Instead, he wanted to spend $100,000—or more if necessary—to bring the building back to its original condition. He also wanted to spend $500,000 to buy the post office building, raze it, and restore the land to its original appearance.[38]

One can imagine the slacked-jaws of those in the meeting as the former senator laid out his magnificent vision for the future of the Old State House and Hartford's center. Say what one may, Morgan Bulkeley always thought big.

The Old State House, designed by the great architect Charles Bulfinch and built in 1796, was the oldest statehouse still standing in the United States. Bulkeley announced in May 1917 that he would give $5,000 toward the restoration of the landmark if nine others would donate equal amounts. Within ten days, donors had subscribed over $100,000—twice the amount needed.[39]

During the restoration, Bulkeley visited the building many times, but one visit stands out. A disagreement had arisen about some architectural details, and he was asked to stop by. The stairs had been removed and three inches of broken plaster littered the floor. As Bulkeley stood in the east end of the hall, he was asked where the stairs had been in the original layout. He walked forward, made a mark in the debris with the heel of his shoe, and said, "Here." The foreman said, "Senator, you are only eighteen inches off. We found the traces of it this morning."[40]

Bulkeley also remembered a small door on the stair landing, leading to the courtroom gallery. It too had been revealed when the plaster was torn away. He went on to explain that the bell rope—used to signal a fire alarm—hung in the center of the spiral balustrade.[41]

≫ For Morgan and Fannie Bulkeley, the summer and fall of 1917 bore difficulties, since both of their sons, Capt. Morgan G. Bulkeley Jr. and Corporal Houghton Bulkeley, were called to fight in the Great War.[42] Under the command of Gen. John J. Pershing, ultimately 50,069 young Connecticut men served during the war.[43]

Troop B, with the Bulkeleys and their Brainard cousins aboard, was converted to a Machine Gun Battalion of the 101st. They were ordered to Niantic for machine gun training and remained there through September.[44]

Because of this training, the wedding plans of Houghton and his fiancée, Margaret Whitmore, were in turmoil. Finally on September 5, 1917, he was given a twenty-four-hour pass to wed. The ceremony took place at 5 P.M. in Niantic's St. John's Church. Shortly thereafter, the 101st Machine Gun battalion boarded a troop ship to France. By May of 1918, they were traveling with General Pershing in northern France, where Houghton Bulkeley was promoted first to sergeant and later lieutenant. At roughly the same time, Capt. Morgan Bulkeley Jr. was promoted to major.[45]

Hartford organized a big Liberty Loans drive—government bond issues—in the spring of 1918 to finance the war. Fannie Bulkeley acted as state chair of the Women's Liberty Loan Committee, while her husband manned booths at the rallies. In his most persuasive tones, he told listeners to, "Get what is left in your vest pockets and turn them inside out; search your trousers' pockets and take what's left; even go into your stockings and give of your saving. Contribute liberally in this campaign that we are about to enter." He spoke feelingly of, "our boys now living in the trenches and fighting to help the Allies. . . . We have sent some of the best blood of Connecticut."[46] During the World War I Liberty Loan drives, Aetna Life and affiliated companies subscribed to $23,992,500 in bonds.[47]

≫ An unpleasant contretemps manifested in 1918, centering on Bulkeley's old political aide-de-camp, Pat McGovern. Morgan Bulkeley may have recognized McGovern's usefulness as far back as the mid-1870s, but in the end, he dis-

missed him like an incompetent domestic servant. Though the two had a dis-
agreement over a mayoral candidate, the falling out went deeper. They met at the
Allyn House to talk. Morgan Bulkeley wanted a witness, so he made sure that
Mayor Kinsella joined them.[48]

Very often, it took a cascade of events to bring out Bulkeley's dark side. In this
case, McGovern backed a mayoral candidate who would not allow the senator's
nephew, Morgan B. Brainard, to stay on as a police commissioner. As time
passed, the conversation got so heated that Bulkeley finally blurted, "I want your
resignation immediately." McGovern replied, "You can have it, and you can have
it right now. I have shares in Aetna Life . . . and that's all I want."[49] Their
friendship was over.

Bulkeley's feelings about Pat McGovern may have been skewed by the tremendous wealth this Irish immigrant had amassed. In 1887, the top twenty-four
shareholders in Aetna Life were listed in the *Courant*. The record included: Lydia
Bulkeley, Billy Bulkeley, Mary (Bulkeley) Brainard, Morgan Bulkeley, Leverett
Brainard, and nineteen others. Among this group, the largest shareholder was
the Judge's widow with 1,081 shares. Morgan Bulkeley had 700. Pat McGovern
wasn't even on the list, although he had been with Aetna Life for eight years.[50]

In the ensuing decades, McGovern made up for lost time. When Morgan
Bulkeley demanded McGovern's resignation, the shrewd Irishman was well on
his way to piling up 70,000 shares of Aetna Life, which is what he had when he
died in 1941.[51] When Fannie Bulkeley died in 1938, she left 10,260 shares of stock
in Aetna Life, so most probably, Morgan Bulkeley never had much more than that
amount in his lifetime.[52] Could this have been a sore point for Bulkeley? Without
question.

Bulkeley had a fascinating life and never wanted for anything, but he was
more generous than he was personally wealthy. Even his younger brother, Billy,
left a larger estate.[53] Aetna Life did phenomenally well under Bulkeley's leader-
ship and he was paid handsomely, but he never pyramided his stock holdings in
the company the way he could have. Money was never a great motivator for him.

≫ On January 4, 1919, a small band of people in heavy coats waited aboard the
platform at Union Station for the train from Boston. They looked like any other
family awaiting the return of a soldier, but this group included Morgan Bulkeley;
his wife, Fannie; his daughter, Elinor Ingersoll; and his granddaughter, Elinor.
Also huddled on the platform were Morgan's sister, Mary Brainard, and some of
her children.[54]

By and by, the train pulled in, and Major Morgan G. Bulkeley Jr. disembarked.
Loud cheering and whooping ensued, and as he came toward the group, he saw
his father, the happiest man in town.

Later it all came out. At Verdun alone, the 101st pelted the Germans with over a million rounds of machine gun fire and slept in trenches with gas masks on. During the war, their unit suffered over 100 casualties. Morgan Bulkeley had always embellished his own military service—or let others do it for him—but he knew that his hitch in the Civil War was a joke compared to what his two sons and their cousins survived in Europe.[55]

Bulkeley's nephew, Newton Brainard, was elected mayor in 1920, and Hartford continued to change. Increasingly, financial companies rose to the fore. Elm Street, running along the south side of Bushnell Park was called "Insurance Row." Scottish Union and National Insurance, Phoenix Insurance, Phoenix Mutual Life, and Connecticut General Life all occupied buildings on Elm Street. Around the corner on Trinity Street, Orient Insurance operated its headquarters.

Aviation was all the rage, and airmail pilots touched down in Goodwin Park (south end) because Hartford had no airport. This convinced the city fathers to build one. Mayor Brainard set aside land in the south meadows for the purpose. Hartford Airport (later renamed Brainard Field) was dedicated on June 21, 1921, and commercial airline service began almost immediately.[56]

Hartford's wealthiest families migrated to the West End or into West Hartford. A number of Morgan Bulkeley's children, including Maj. Morgan Bulkeley and nephews and nieces already lived on Prospect Avenue (city line) or in West Hartford. For the moment, Morgan and Fannie Bulkeley; Billy Bulkeley's widow, Emma; and Mary Brainard remained on Washington Street, but not for long.[57]

While the Bulkeleys were enjoying another long, lazy summer at Fenwick in 1921, Morgan's sister, Mary Brainard, died in her cottage. She suffered from heart disease for a number of years before it finally took her. She was seventy-eight.[58]

Bulkeley still puttered around Fenwick as the unofficial royal potentate of the small band of cottagers. He loved to walk about his little community in the summertime, greeting newcomers like Dr. Tom Hepburn and sharing stories with old friends. He and Fannie returned to Hartford later and later each fall.

In mid-October of 1922, Morgan Bulkeley began fighting off a cold and serious cough.[59] He also suffered from what doctors then called "tobacco heart." By November 2, Bulkeley's personal physician, Dr. Edward K. Root, put him to bed as a precaution.

A few years earlier, on January 8, 1919, the day Governor Holcomb was inaugurated for his third term, Bulkeley had "an acute attack of indigestion in the barber shop of the Heublein Hotel." He was laid up for eight days.[60]

This most recent downturn struck hard. In the early evening hours of November 6, a drizzling Monday evening, he took a turn for the worse, and all of the Bulkeley and Brainard clans were called to his Washington Street home. The family had known all along he was sick, but did not disburse the information to the public. At eight o'clock in the evening of Monday, November 6, Morgan Bulkeley breathed his last. Officially, he died of "old age and heart disease."[61]

The funeral was held at 2:30 P.M. on Thursday at the Bulkeley home with the Rev. Warren Archibald of the South Congregational Church conducting the service. The funeral mirrored simplicity itself.[62]

Flags were flown at half-staff throughout the city, and on November 9, the day of the funeral, the offices of Aetna Life closed. A most unusual honor was accorded Morgan Bulkeley on the day of his funeral—businesses throughout the city came to a complete standstill for fifteen minutes, beginning at 2:30 P.M.[63]

The day before the funeral, the family announced the honorary pallbearers, including Governor Lake, Senator Brandegee, Mayor Kinsella, and nineteen other close friends and dignitaries. There was one honorary pallbearer Morgan Bulkeley never would have picked had he been handling his own arrangements. Francis Goodwin.[64] If Goodwin had ever been to the Bulkeley home before, it must have been a very quick visit, for it is not recorded anywhere. The Bulkeleys were big entertainers all their lives, and thousands of people crossed their threshold, but Francis Goodwin wasn't one of them.

The actual bearers were Bulkeley's nephews and son-in-law, allowing Morgan Jr., Elinor and Houghton to stay with Fannie Bulkeley throughout the service. Morgan Bulkeley was interred in the family plot at Cedar Hill next to the Judge, Lydia, Charlie, Billy, and Mary. At some point along the way, the remains of Mary Morgan Bulkeley, the ill-fated first child of the Judge and Lydia was brought up from East Haddam and reinterred in the family plot in Cedar Hill. Lastly, E. A. Bulkeley, Jr., the child who died a year after the Bulkeleys relocated to Hartford in 1847, was reinterred at Cedar Hill too. When Morgan Bulkeley died in 1922, the Judge and Lydia, for the first time, had all of their six children with them. (The Bulkeley and Brainard family plots at Cedar Hill abut one another and together include about forty remains.[65])

In the days after Bulkeley's death, notes, letters, telegrams, and floral arrangements came in from every corner of the United States. Even the National Baseball League sent a seven-foot-tall floral piece, and John Heydler, the president of the league, attended the funeral.[66]

A short time after Morgan Bulkeley's death, the *Courant* reprinted a story from the *Wall Street Journal* called "Jimmy and the Financier." Bulkeley had visited New York one July in order to dine at the Waldorf with a newspaperman, who was running late. To keep Bulkeley occupied, the reporter sent a copyboy, Jimmy, who had obviously been crying. Bulkeley, concerned about the boy, announced that he had waited long enough and that the two of them would enjoy dinner instead. Come to find out, Jimmy's mother was deathly ill and Jimmy had been nursing her every spare minute. The poor kid hadn't had a decent meal for days. Bulkeley was aghast, exclaiming, "Starving for mother's sake. My God, I didn't know they could do such things in New York." Bulkeley summoned the parish priest and the chief of staff from a nearby hospital and they all descended on the squalid tenement where Jimmy and his mother lived. Despite all of his efforts, Bulkeley received word the following week of the woman's death. Worse, a few days later, he got a telegram from the newspaperman saying, "Fever, acquired nursing mother, took Jimmy today." The parish priest received funeral expenses plus a sizable check for charity. The letter accompanying the check was on the stationary of the Aetna Life Insurance Company and signed—Morgan G. Bulkeley.[67]

One of the intriguing mysteries surrounding Morgan Bulkeley's death is that he died intestate.[68] Most wealthy men leave wills, and inasmuch as he was completely surrounded by lawyers his whole life, one has to wonder why Bulkeley did not. There are three possibilities.

First, rather than think about death, Bulkeley preferred to think about the future. This comes across loud and clear when considering his Arrowhead Farm purchase when he was seventy-nine. Second, the State of Connecticut had strict inheritance guidelines in place for those who died intestate, so he really didn't need a will. Lastly, Bulkeley had built up a large collection of very valuable antiques. His failure to make out a will—and an inventory—gave his children plenty of time to spirit these items to their homes. These antiques were not included in Morgan Bulkeley's final inventory. True, this isn't exactly above board, but it's a common practice all the same.

Whatever the real reason for the lapse, Fannie Bulkeley completed an inventory of Morgan Bulkeley's worldly possessions, a document accepted by the probate court the following May. The final inventory was interesting to say the least.[69]

To begin, only one piece of land in West Hartford—near his older son's home—was listed in his estate. His beautiful home on Washington Street and his huge cottage at Fenwick were in Fannie's name, and therefore did not appear among his possessions. Also, building lots and some other land in Fenwick bore Fannie's name and weren't listed either. The inventory makes no mention of jewelry of any kind, although Bulkeley was always nattily turned out, as evidenced by any number of photographs revealing gold watch chains, tie pins, cuff links and other expensive jewelry.

Beyond these omissions, he left $692,300 almost completely in the stock of Hartford firms—Aetna Life, Aetna Fire, Hartford Steam Boiler, Phoenix Insurance, Colt's Patent Fire-Arms, and Standard Screw. There were also U.S. Liberty Bonds and $10,000 in cash. When Fannie died sixteen years later, her estate—

including all of the real estate, her jewelry and furniture, and Pierce Arrow limousine—came to almost a million dollars, a good guess as to Morgan Bulkeley's *actual* estate.

In the forty-three years that Morgan Bulkeley presided over Aetna Life, the company's annual income increased from $6 million to $80 million, and the number of employees rose from 29 to 2,000.[70] The firm also branched out into every kind of insurance imaginable.

During his time at the helm, it is almost humorous to note the level of nepotism Bulkeley employed at Aetna Life. By 1922, Mary Brainard's son, Morgan Bulkeley Brainard, served as vice president of the company. Aetna Life's chief auditor was his brother Billy's son, William E. A. Bulkeley, and Maj. Morgan Bulkeley Jr. held the treasurer post. Through the years, Bulkeley also brought his brother Billy; his brother-in-law, Charles Houghton in San Francisco; and his son-in-law, John Ingersoll in New York—just to mention the most obvious relatives—into the company. A number of other cousins and grandchildren joined the company after Bulkeley's death.[71]

In January 1922, there were ten directors at Aetna. Four of them counted as direct relations: Morgan G. Bulkeley, Morgan B. Brainard, Morgan Bulkeley Jr., and William E. A. Bulkeley. Samuel Dunham and J. O. Enders were the sons of longtime Aetna stalwarts. The seventh member of the board was Bulkeley loyalist, Joel English. The final three men were hired hands.[72] In short, Aetna remained a tight company until Morgan B. Brainard died in 1957 and Henry S. Beers became CEO. In over one hundred years—not counting Thomas Enders's seven-year term in the 1870s—Beers was the first outsider to head the company.[73]

✍ Fannie Bulkeley could not stand living in the Washington Street house after Morgan's passing. By Christmas, she purchased a brick home at 6 Woodside Circle in Hartford's West End.[74] She moved into the house a few months later, keeping all of her domestic servants with her. Fannie Bulkeley outlived her husband by sixteen years, dying on June 22, 1938, at the age of seventy-seven.[75]

Contractors from West Hartford bought the Bulkeley home on Washington Street and then leased it to the Connecticut State Police. In 1937, the owners tore it down to make way for a modern State Police building.[76]

Sadly, Morgan and Fannie's oldest child, Morgan Jr., lived a shortened life as a result of World War I. In the eighteen months he spent in Europe, Bulkeley commanded Company B of the 101st Machine Gun Battalion on many French battlefields, and a few days before the Armistice, he was gassed badly at Verdun and hospitalized at Limoges. Released from the service in January 1919, he rejoined Aetna Life. Doctors discovered a brain tumor in 1925, and he underwent surgery in Boston. He never regained his health and died in 1926. He was forty when he left his wife, Ruth, and their three children—Morgan G. Bulkeley III, William E. C. Bulkeley, and Edward Root Bulkeley.[77]

Elinor Bulkeley Ingersoll—predeceased by her husband, John, who headed his own Hartford insurance agency—died at her Prospect Avenue home in West Hartford in 1964, at age seventy-one. She left four children—John A. Ingersoll Jr., Elinor Bulkeley Ingersoll Jr., Lydia Ingersoll Ely, and Frances Ingersoll Staniford.[78]

The Bulkeley's youngest child, Houghton, died of a self-inflicted gunshot wound at his Terry Road home in May 1966 at the age of sixty-nine. Houghton Bulkeley, a stockbroker-partner with Putnam & Co. and later Cooley & Co., retired in 1953. After he left the work-a-day world, he studied and catalogued all the antique furniture he inherited from his parents. He liked to say that an old clock was the only major piece of antiquity he ever purchased. His wife, Virginia, and three children—Hope Bulkeley Friedberg, Nancy Houghton Bulkeley, and Peter Bulkeley—were left behind.[79]

Morgan Bulkeley's competitor, nemesis, sparring partner, touchstone, bad penny, and a hundred other things, Francis Goodwin, died a year after Bulkeley, in October 1923.[80] Though he was alleged to have heart trouble, Goodwin nevertheless managed to father eight children and work as a cleric and a real estate magnate all his long life. In fact, he was at his real estate office until the day before his death in 1923, when a case of bronchitis felled him. His physician, Dr. William Porter, gave the primary cause of death as "bronchial asthma—(very severe)."[81] He was eighty-four.

One last piece of business—after the 1936 Veterans Election Committee neglected to name any nineteenth-century baseball standouts, the Hall of Fame opted to ask a small committee to select inductees "for outstanding service to baseball apart from playing the game." At the December 1937 winter meeting in Chicago, National League President, Ford Frick, announced that the Commission had elected Connie Mack, John McGraw, George Wright, Byron "Ban" Johnson (first president of the American League), and Morgan G. Bulkeley (first president of the National League).[82]

Since Bulkeley served only one year as president of the National League, his induction hasn't proven a popular choice among serious baseball fans. However, he remains enshrined at Cooperstown—and probably always will.

ACKNOWLEDGMENTS

First, I would like to once again acknowledge the great debt that I owe my parents, Bob and Mary Murphy, for giving me life, a first-class education, and a million incidentals along the way. Too late, we realize that childhood is the most outrageous theft of services.

Also, a special thanks goes to Bill and Rosalie Rishar, who, through their great generosity, gave me a fabulous place to write, with luxurious quiet and freedom from financial worries.

This book is a testament to the patience and professionalism of Suzanna Tamminen, the director and editor in chief of Wesleyan University Press, who extended herself completely to an unknown author. A big thank-you goes to assistant director and marketing manager Leslie Starr, whose tenacious belief in this book defies description. I am beholden to acquisitions editor Parker Smathers, who was courteous and encouraging throughout the process. Lastly, a hearty thank-you to publicist Stephanie Elliott for her hard work. I would also like to thank Victoria Stahl for her help in the final editing of the manuscript.

I must thank Peter Bulkeley, grandson of Morgan Bulkeley, who filled in many gaps and put me in touch with J. H. Kelso Davis, who actually knew his grandfather.

Many thanks to West Hartford resident Tony Lettere, who was the biggest supporter of my first book, *Water for Hartford*, and a huge help in preproduction matters related to *Crowbar Governor*.

Thanks are also due Dr. Karl Stofko and Charles Farrow of East Haddam for their help in understanding the town during the years that the Bulkeleys lived there. In piecing together the details of Governor Bulkeley's secondary education, a tip of the hat goes to Jeffrey Mathieu of Bacon Academy, Colchester town historian Stanley Morash, and Colchester town clerk Nancy Bray.

Regarding Morgan Bulkeley's years in Brooklyn Heights, a word of appreciation goes to Linde Aseltine for her research. Along the same lines, Joy Holland, division manager of the Brooklyn Collection at the Brooklyn Public Library was of incalculable help in making sense of Morgan Bulkeley's years in Brooklyn as well.

The sections of the book dealing with the Bulkeleys' many trips to California—and especially San Francisco, including information on the Houghton mansion at 2018 Franklin Street—were made possible through the efforts of Fanny Truong, Matthew Thomas, and Concepcion Vindell at the San Francisco Assessor and Recorder's Office. Another person in California who was very helpful was researcher Sandra Harris at the San Francisco Public Library. Many thanks. For the details of Minnie Houghton Beacon's death in Canada, I must reach across our northern border to thank Colleen Andriats and Patti Sherbaniuk, research librarians at the Edmonton Public Library in Alberta.

The information on Bulkeleys' property dealings is extensive, and I am indebted to the staffs of the Halls of Records in East Haddam and Hartford. Most of all, I would like to thank town clerk Sarah Becker of Old Saybrook, who was helpful in uncovering the ownership of building lots at Fenwick.

At the Probate Records Office of the State of Connecticut, many thanks to Julie Winiarski, who dug out a great many wills, inventories, and probate records.

The able staff of the Connecticut Historical Society—Judith Ellen Johnson, Barbara Austen, Nancy Finlay, Cindy Harbeson, Sierra Dixon, Diane McCain, Susan P. Schoelwer, Jill Davis Adams, Sharon Steinberg, and Richard C. Malley—made many historical and genealogical contributions. For their help, I will always be indebted.

At the Connecticut State Library, I would like to thank Cheryl Schutt, Debra Pond, Dick Roberts, Mel Smith, Carol Ganz, Carolyn Picciano, Jeannie Sherman, Bonnie Linck, Steve Rice, Kristi Finnan, Kevin Johnson, Bruce Stark, and Dave Corrigan.

Lastly, I reach out in the darkness to offer a humble thank you to the Connecticut historians who vetted the original manuscript of *Crowbar Governor*. Among these historians, I must express deep respect and gratitude to Professor Matthew Warshauer of Central Connecticut State University and editor of the professional journal *Connecticut History*. He vetted the original manuscript and gave freely of his time and insights into the writing of historical works.

This, I'm afraid, is only a representative collection of the people who contributed to *Crowbar Governor*. For those I may have inadvertently failed to mention by name, rest assured that this book would never have come together without your help. Many thanks.

NOTES

Undoubtedly some readers and historians will fault me for leaning too heavily on the newspapers of New England, New York, Washington, and San Francisco. Ideally, a biographer draws from a treasure trove of diaries, letters, official documents, and personal papers. Sadly, this was not possible with Morgan Bulkeley. One can assume that he wrote to his mother and his Aunt Eunie during the Civil War, but only one letter survives. Bulkeley did not keep a diary, so his inner life remains a mystery. The Connecticut State Library has a collection of Morgan Bulkeley's gubernatorial papers, but it is fairly small and casts almost no light on the major events of his two terms as governor. The Connecticut Historical Society has some scrapbooks of Bulkeley's years as Hartford mayor and as U.S. senator, but again, they offer little of substance. Beyond these limitations, virtually all historians—even the most respected ones—have perpetuated myths and outright falsehoods about Morgan Bulkeley, going back a century or more. Lastly, even a fantastic collection, like the Hawley Papers (over 13, 000 documents in the Library of Congress), makes little or no mention of Morgan Bulkeley. Based on this, I have had to evaluate each piece of data carefully against direct quotes from Morgan Bulkeley, those of his contemporaries, and newspaper accounts of the day. Only then was I able to assign a value to the information and use it accordingly.

1. THE MAN

1. When the Bulkeleys hired Willis Becker in 1899 to draw Beaumaris, he was a struggling—albeit pleasant—thirty-five-year-old architect with a wife and a three-year-old child. As noted in Chapter 10, Becker did all the preliminary drawings for free.

2. Marion Hepburn Grant, *In and Around Hartford: Its People and Places* (Hartford: Connecticut Historical Society, 1989), 100.

3. Ibid., 104–5.

4. "Former Senator Morgan Bulkeley Now a Farmer," *Hartford Courant*, July 1, 1917, X5.

5. U. S. Census Records, 1910, 1920; Grant, 104–5.

6. U. S. Census Records, 1910, 1920; Grant, 105.

7. When James II ascended to the English throne in 1685, he authorized Sir Edmund Andros to seize Connecticut's Charter of 1662. To thwart such a move, Captain Joseph

Wadsworth secreted the charter in a hollowed-out section of an oak tree on the Wyllys estate. The tree was thereafter referred to as the Charter Oak. Sadly, it was felled during a great storm on August 21, 1856. Naturally, Hartford became the Charter Oak City.

8. Richard Hooker, *Aetna Life Insurance Company: Its First Hundred Years* (Hartford, CT: Aetna Life Insurance Co., 1956), 100.

9. "Brer Rabbit Bulkeley," *Hartford Times*, November 15, 1890, 4 (repr. from the *Springfield Republican*).

10. Grant, 102.

11. Grant, 97.

12. "Leverett Brainard: Death of Substantial Public-Spirited Citizen . . . ," *Hartford Courant*, July 3, 1902, 13; Grant, 97. The Brainard children—in no special order—were Albert, Robert, Charles, Helen, Mary, Ruth, Edith, Lucy, Morgan, and Newton. The first five died in childhood or early adulthood, including ten-year-old Helen, who died after an emergency appendectomy on the Brainard's kitchen table at their Washington Street home. Billy and Emma Bulkeley's children—from the oldest to the youngest—were Mary Morgan, William E. A., Grace Chetwood, John Charles, Sally Taintor, and Richard Beaumaris.

The Brainards kept the same cottage on Lot #18 from 1877 until long after Mary Brainard's death in 1921. Likewise, Morgan and Fannie Bulkeley's children kept Beaumaris in the family. However, Billy and Emma Bulkeley built their fist cottage on Lot #299 in 1877, but only kept it four years. About 1881, they built a nicer place on waterfront Lot #25, just west of where Morgan and Fannie built Beaumaris in 1900. Five years after Billy's death in 1902, Emma Bulkeley let that cottage go and began spending summers at Fenwick Hall.

13. *Atlas of the City of Hartford and the Town of West Hartford* (New York: Sanborn Map Co., 1921), 1; Old Saybrook Land Records, vol. 7, p. 152, Old Saybrook Town Hall, Old Saybrook, CT.

14. "Common School Report," *Hartford Daily Courant*, February 20, 1845, 4. Some of Hartford's common schools were little more than a couple of rented rooms in an office building, but the Centre School was first-class, boasting separate playgrounds for the boys and girls, each with its own outhouse. A "Brick School House" shows up in the newspapers as early as 1790 when the *Courant* wrote, "A Meeting of the Inhabitants of the First or Middle School District will be held this evening at the Brick School House, agreeable to adjournment." (*Connecticut Courant*, April 19, 1790, 3). The school that the Bulkeley children attended was a stone school with a brick front built in 1816. (*Hartford Daily Courant*, February 20, 1845, 2) It was located on Dorr Street, undoubtedly named after Rev. Dr. Edward Dorr, pastor of the First Church from 1748 until his death in 1772. See George Leon Walker, *History of the First Church in Hartford* (Hartford, CT: Brown & Gross, 1884), 332. However, in 1829—eighteen years before the Bulkeleys moved to Hartford— the name of this narrow lane was changed to Market Street because of the huge town

market in the basement of City Hall on the corner of Temple and Market Streets. F. Perry Close, *History of Hartford's Streets* (Hartford: The Connecticut Historical Society, 1969), 73.

15. Grant, 9–10.

16. Ibid., 173; Marion Grant describes in great detail Morgan Bulkeley's first meeting with Dr. Tom Hepburn in *The Fenwick Story*. Since the Hepburns did not own a cottage at Fenwick until September 1921 and Morgan Bulkeley died in November 1922, the only time this meeting could have taken place was in the early summer of 1922.

17. "Three Men with One Wish," *New York Sun*, August 8, 1886, 3.

18. Grant, 30.

19. "Fenwick Hall Settles," *Hartford Courant*, August 9, 1898, 4; Newton C. Brainard, *Fenwick* (Hartford, CT: Case, Lockwood & Brainard Co., 1944), 33–35.

20. Grant, 30.

21. J. H. Beers & Co., *Commemorative Biographical Record of Hartford County* (Chicago: J. H. Beers & Co., 1901), 69.

22. Old Saybrook Land Records, vol. 17, p. 598, September 30, 1921; Grant, 173.

23. Grant, 99–102; tel. interview with Morgan Bulkeley's grandson, Peter Bulkeley, September 11, 2002.

24. U. S. Census Records, 1870, 1880; Grant, 99–100.

25. Rootsweb, "Houghton/Haughton Project, Houghton Genealogy," #8850, http://freepages.genealogy.rootsweb.ancestry.com/houghtonfamily/p132.htm (accessed 12/08/2008); Rootsweb, "Houghton/Haughton Project, Houghton Genealogy," #8853, http://freepages.genealogy.rootsweb.ancestry.com/houghtonfamily/p132.htm (accessed 12/08/2008).

26. Rootsweb, "Houghton/Haughton Project, Houghton Genealogy," #8864, at http://freepages.genealogy.rootsweb.ancestry.com/houghtonfamily/p132.htm (accessed 12/08/2008).

27. Old Saybrook Land Records, Morgan B. Brainard to Dr. Donald Hooker, vol. 17, p. 437, June 21, 1918; Donald Hooker to Katharine Martha Hepburn, vol. 17, p. 598, September 30, 1921, Lots 305 and 306. Most of the Fenwick lots were about a half acre, so these two lots gave the Hepburns an acre. However, the property also came with a deed restriction, so a second cottage could not be built on Lot #306.

28. "Dr. Hepburn's Son, 15, Hangs Himself while Visiting in New York," *Hartford Courant*, April 4, 1921, 1; "Hepburn Says—Died as a Result of Boyish Prank," *Hartford Courant*, April 5, 1921, 15.

29. State of Maryland, Certificate of Death #5594, Sewell S. Hepburn, Jr., April 5, 1921.

30. Old Saybrook Land Records, vol. 17, p. 598, September 30, 1921.

31. Grant, 173; Old Saybrook Land Records, vol. 17, p. 598, September 30, 1921; U. S. Census Records, 1910, 1920, 1930.

32. Tudor Place, "Sir Richard of Beaumaris and Anglesey, Knight," at http://www.tudorplace.com.ar/Bios/RichardBulkeley1.htm (accessed 3/12/2008); Beers, 71.

33. Archives and Records Council Wales, "Bangor University, Baron Hill Manuscripts," at http://www.archivesnetworkwales.info/cgi-bin/anw/search2?coll_id=11114&inst_id=39&term=heneglwys (accessed 3/12/2008).

34. Donald Lines Jacobus, *The Bulkeley Genealogy: Rev. Peter Bulkeley, Being an Account of His Career, His Ancestry.* . . . (New Haven: Tuttle, 1933), 92–118.

35. Jacobus,117, 263, 264, 277, 284, 289, 292, 296. Peter Bulkeley's son, Gershom Bulkeley, enlisted as a surgeon and was wounded in King Philip's War. Capt. John Bulkeley—and his brother Thomas—served in the French and Indian War; Giles Bulkeley, Lexington Alarm 1778; Lt. Solomon Bulkeley, Lexington Alarm, 1775; Capt. Stephen Bulkeley, Col. Webb's Regiment, 1777; Col. Eliphalet Bulkeley, Lexington Alarm, 1775; Capt. Daniel Bulkeley, Lexington Alarm, 1775; Lt. Charles Bulkeley, War of 1812.

36. Beers, 68–69.

37. Bulkeley High School is now on Wethersfield Avenue. Bulkeley Stadium was the home of semiprofessional baseball in Hartford from 1921 to 1952 and was located on George Street (east of Goodwin Park). Bulkeley Avenue is in the extreme west end of the city. Bulkeley Bridge, of course, spans the Connecticut River, and tiny Bulkeley Park (now gone) was next to the western approach to the bridge.

2. THE JUDGE'S WORLD

1. State of Connecticut, "Connecticut Population by Town, 1756–1820," at http://www .ct.gov/ecd/cwp/view.asp?A=1106&Q=250670 (accessed 5/01/2009).

2. Richard Hooker, *Aetna Life Insurance Company: Its First Hundred Years* (Hartford, CT: Aetna Life Insurance Co., 1956), 20.

3. Ibid., 21; Nathaniel H. Morgan, *Morgan Genealogy: A History of James Morgan, of New London, Conn., and His Descendants; from 1607 to 1869* (Hartford, CT: Case, Lockwood & Brainard, 1869), 17–18.

4. Hooker, 21; Ellsworth Grant, *Yankee Dreamers and Doers* (Chester, CT: Pequot Press, 1983), 25.

5. Ellsworth Grant, *Thar She Goes: Shipbuilding on the Connecticut River* (Old Saybrook, CT: Fenwick Productions), 2000, 52, 64–68; Karl Stofko and Rachel I. Gibbs, *A Brief History of East Haddam* (East Haddam, CT: East Haddam Historical Society), 1977, 1–3, 18–28.

6. Horse-powered ferries employed a rotating treadmill slightly below the boat's deck. As a horse walked in place on this treadmill, power was delivered to paddles on the sides or back of the ferry. Institute of Nautical Archaeology, "Lake Champlain Horse Ferries," http://inadiscover.com/projects/all/north_ america/lake_champlain_projects/lake _champlain_horse_ferries/(accessed 5/01/2009).

7. Edmund Delaney, *The Connecticut River: New England's Historic Waterway* (Chester, CT: The Globe Pequot Press, 1983), 119–20.

8. Grant (2000), 105–6.

9. U. S. Census Records, 1830. Ann Morgan, an East Haddam widow, had ten children.

George Morgan of East Haddam had five children. Besides these Morgans, Mary Bulkeley and Noah Bulkeley also lived in East Haddam. The odd spelling of Bulkeley ensures that all parties were related, and undoubtedly the Morgans of East Haddam were somehow connected to the same James Morgan line of New London from which Lydia (Morgan) Bulkeley descended.

10. J. H. Beers & Co., *Commemorative Biographical Record of Hartford County* (Chicago: J. H. Beers & Co., 1901), 68.

11. Eliphalet Bulkeley, "Eliphalet Bulkeley's Daybook, 1832–1850" (No file number) (Hartford: Connecticut Historical Society), 15, 41.

12. Hooker, 21.

13. Hooker, 21; Hartford Probate District, "Eliphalet A. Bulkeley" (no catalog or file number), April 25, 1872, *Hartford: History and Genealogy*, Connecticut State Library.

14. Beers, 68.

15. Albert E. Van Dusen, *Connecticut: A Fully Illustrated History of the State from the Seventeenth Century to the Present* (New York: Random House, 1961), 189.

16. About 1860, the Bulkeley's house became the north section of the Maplewood Musical Seminary, a school that lasted until 1880. There is nothing left of the school or building today. East Haddam Land Records, Property of Lester Pasco, vol. 23, p. 383, June 12, 1835. East Haddam Town Hall, East Haddam, CT; tel. interview with Dr. Karl Stofko, East Haddam Town Historian, April 11, 2002.

17. Ibid.

18. Other losses included the death of Eliphalet Adams Bulkeley Jr., who was born at Hartford in 1847 but died at eighteen months. The Bulkeleys' oldest son, Charles Edwin, died during the Civil War, and the Judge and Lydia Bulkeley had to sit by helplessly as five of their ten Brainard grandchildren died young.

19. Beers, 69–70; tel. interview with Dr. Karl Stofko.

20. The Bulkeley's were in East Haddam from 1830 to 1847, and all the children were born there save Eliphalet Adams Bulkeley Jr., who was born at Hartford on July 11, 1847, and died in December of the following year. By the beginning of 1849, there were only four Bulkeley children left: Charlie, Morgan, Billy, and Mary.

21. Stofko and Gibbs, 9–12.

22. East Haddam Land Records, Property from Gideon Wiggins, vol. 23, p. 640, June 8, 1838; Property of Fred Greene, vol. 25, p. 54. December 13, 1869; Property of Fred Greene, vol. 25, p. 223, May 1, 1841; Property of Richard Miller, vol. 25, p. 541, April 15, 1845; Property of Gamaliel Tracy, vol. 26, p. 421, June 19, 1848; Beers, 68.

23. Beers, 69.

24. "Assistant Commissioner," *Hartford Daily Courant*, July 10, 1845, 2.

25. Eliphalet A. Bulkeley, 33 Items, MS 79246, Governor Roger Baldwin to Eliphalet Bulkeley: "Appointment as Assistant School Fund Commissioner," July 18, 1845, Connecticut Historical Society, Hartford; Eliphalet A. Bulkeley, 33 Items, MS 79246, General

Assembly, May Session 1845, $1000 annual salary plus expenses for Assistant School Fund Commissioner, Connecticut Historical Society, Hartford.

26. Printers had a difficult time keeping up with the changes in building numbers on State Street during this transition period. Simply put, even numbers are universally assigned to buildings on the north and east sides of streets. This was Hartford's attempt to bring the older buildings on State Street into compliance (Hooker, 19); For example, the first of Hartford's City Directories was published by Ariel Ensign in 1828 and contained the following addresses—Hartford Bank, 16 State Street; Exchange Coffee-House, 33 State Street; and Aetna (Fire) Insurance, 35 State Street. Later, Gardner's City Directory, published in 1838 by Case, Tiffany & Co., shows the same businesses at 24, 36, and 38 State Street, respectively. Keep in mind, in the Geer's City Directory of 1847, published by Elihu Geer, the final address for Aetna Fire Insurance was 58 State Street. The renumbering of the businesses on north side of State Street was an irksome process.

27. Hartford Land Records, vol. 80, p. 94, November 27, 1850, Hartford City Hall, Hartford, CT.

28. "President Taft Sends Greetings to Dr. Parker, Senator Bulkeley Presides," *Hartford Courant*, January 12, 1910, 10; Beers, 68; In 1899, the Pearl Street Congregational Church moved and became the Farmington Avenue Congregational Church. In 1914, they invited the Park Church (corner Asylum and High Streets) to merge with them as Immanuel Church of Farmington Avenue.

29. Beers, 68–69; Bulkeley, "Daybook," 253.

30. Hartford Board of Trade, *Hartford, Conn., as a Manufacturing, Business and Commercial Center; with Brief Sketches of Its History, Attractions, Leading Industries, and Institutions* (Hartford: Author, 1889), 46–48.

31. William Cahn, *A Matter of Life and Death: The Connecticut Mutual Story* (New York: Random House, 1970), 26.

32. Hooker, 23. Dr. Guy Phelps was always considered the "great manager" behind Connecticut Mutual, although he ultimately held no titles of moment. He was secretary early on, but stepped down to save the company money. He died in 1869 (Beers, 32–34).

33. Hooker, 23, 28–29.

34. Cahn, 31, 44.

35. Cahn, 4.

36. Cahn, 44; Junius Morgan was the son of Joseph Morgan who removed to Hartford from West Springfield in November 1816, when he bought Morgan's Tavern on State Street. James Goodwin worked for Joseph Morgan when he was young and even bought the older man's stagecoach business in the 1820s. Goodwin also married Joseph Morgan's daughter Lucy in 1832.

37. Cahn, 44.

38. Cahn, 44. In 1848, James M. Goodwin petitioned the General Assembly to amend Connecticut Mutual's charter so that board meetings could be called at any time.

39. James Junius Goodwin, *The Goodwins of Hartford, Connecticut: Descendants of William and Ozias Goodwin* (Hartford, CT: Brown & Gross, ca. 1891), 702. James M. Goodwin married Lucy Morgan on July 30, 1832.

40. U.S. Census Records, 1860.

41. Hartford Land Records, vol. 35, p. 360, November 21, 1816. Ransom then sold the property to William Hitchcock. Next in line was Hitchcock's son, Eliakim Hitchcock, with his partner, Joseph Norton. These two men kept it for a few years and then sold it to Joseph Morgan, and it was referred to regularly in the papers as Morgan's Tavern or Morgan's Coffee-House. Selah Treat bought the property from Joseph Morgan in 1829, and it became Treat's Coffee-House.

42. Goodwin, 701–4. After stagecoaches left Morgan's Tavern, they proceeded over the section of State Street later known as the Isle of Safety.

43. Henry R. Gall and William G. Jordan, *One Hundred Years of Fire Insurance: Being a History of Aetna Insurance Company* (Hartford, CT: Aetna Insurance Co., 1919), 26–36. Joseph Morgan, in addition to owning Morgan's Coffee-House, was on the first board of directors of Aetna Fire Insurance in 1919. After selling his stage business to James M. Goodwin in the 1820s, he bought City Hotel, but later sold it to devote all his time to Aetna Fire. He was particularly active in the company from the early 1830s until his death in July 1847.

44. Glenn Weaver, *Hartford: An Illustrated History of Connecticut's Capital* (Woodland Hills, CA: Windsor Publications, 1982), 58.

45. Ibid.; Hartford Board of Trade, 20–21.

46. Gall and Jordan, 70–71; "Aetna Insurance Company," *Connecticut Courant*, June 3, 1837, 4; "Aetna Insurance Company," *Daily Courant*, November 4, 1837, 4.

47. "Aetna Insurance Company," *Connecticut Courant*, June 3, 1837, 4; "Aetna Insurance Company," *Daily Courant*, November 4, 1837, 4.

48. Goodwin, 703–4.

49. Goodwin, 701; Appleton Morgan, *The Family of Morgan* (Westfield, NJ: The Shakespeare Press, 1892), 74.

50. Beers, 68–71, 1391–93.

51. "Two Mean Schemes," *Hartford Courant*, November 3, 1910, 8; "Unsought and Unbought," *Hartford Courant*, October 22, 1910, 1. It is inconceivable Morgan Bulkeley could have generated this much hate for James M. Goodwin's grandson, Charles, without some previous history. See chapter 11.

52. Hooker, 23–24.

53. Ibid.

54. Weaver, 87.

55. Hooker, 34.

56. Ibid., 26–28.

57. Ibid., 26.

58. Hooker, 26.

59. Ibid., 28–31.

60. Ibid., 26–28.

61. Hooker, 31–33.

62. Ibid., 33–34.

63. Hooker, 45.

64. Beers, 68–69.

65. Hooker, 14–15.

66. Ibid., 12–13.

67. Newton C. Brainard, *The Hartford State House* (Hartford: Connecticut Historical Society 1964), 63.

68. Ellsworth Grant, *The Miracle of Connecticut* (Hartford: Connecticut Historical Society and Fenwick Productions, 1992), 107–8.

69. Charles W. Burpee, *The History of Hartford County, 1633–1928* (Chicago: The S. J. Clark Publishing Co., 1928, 16–21.

70. Hooker, 97.

71. "Three Men with One Wish," *New York Sun*, August 8, 1886, 3.

72. "The Water Works," *Hartford Daily Times*, February 26, 1856, 2.

73. "The Granite State," *Hartford Daily Courant*, April 19, 1853, 2; Weaver, 101.

74. "Lord's Hill, 1840–1850: An Interesting Sketch," *Hartford Daily Courant*, June 14, 1887, 1. Ann Street, where the young sledders gathered, was "[n]amed after Ann Sheldon Goodwin by her sons, James and Nathanial Goodwin, who opened the street through their land in 1814." F. Perry Close, *History of Hartford's Streets* (Hartford: Connecticut Historical Society, 1969), 73.

75. Brainard, 2.

76. Brainard, 63. Hartford's fire alarm was the bell atop the Old State House until September 1867, when the city's seventy-five-foot-high Old Bell-Tower was erected behind the Old Sack & Bucket Company on Pearl Street. It had "a steel bell weighing two tons" that cost $9,091. It struck for the last time on May 25, 1921, when sirens came into use ("Fire Alarm Tower," *Hartford Daily Times*, September 7, 1867, 2).

77. Margaret Fay, ed., *Memories of Hartford: A Project of the Seniors Jubilee 350 Committee* (Hartford: Phoenix Mutual Life Insurance Co., 1986), 14; Kevin Murphy, *Water for Hartford: The Story of the Hartford Water Works and the Metropolitan District Commission* (Wethersfield, CT: Shining Tramp Press, 2004), 160.

78. Morgan Bulkeley to Lydia Bulkeley, Civil War Letters of William H. Bulkeley, July 24, 1861, MS 66554, Connecticut Historical Society, Hartford; "Governor Bulkeley's Correspondence, Outgoing Letters," RG 5, Box #78, Connecticut State Library, Hartford.

79. Morgan Bulkeley to Lydia Bulkeley, MS 66554.

80. Internet Archive, "Obituary Record of Graduates, Yale University, July 1859–July 1870, 1856," at http://www.archive.org/ stream/1860t700obituaryooyaleuoft/1860t700obitu aryooyaleuoft_djvu.txt (accessed 12/14/2008).

NOTES

81. Van Dusen, 349.

82. Beers, 69–70. The Centre School was nicknamed the "Old Stone Jug" by its young pupils, although references to this colloquialism are rare. William Larkum, a classmate of Morgan Bulkeley, celebrated his eightieth birthday in January 1919 and reference is made to the "Old Stone Jug" in "William Larkum Has 80th Birthday," *Hartford Courant*, January 24, 1919, 9.

83. "From Grocery Store to the U.S. Senate," *Hartford Courant*, April 13, 1908, 2 (repr. from the *Brooklyn Daily Eagle*).

84. Ibid.

85. "Bacon Academy, Centennial Celebration of Colchester School," *Hartford Courant*, August 29, 1903, 12.

86. The Centre School was on Market Street at the foot of Kingsley. In 1868, the new F. A. Brown School was completed on the southeast corner of Market and Talcott Streets. The Brown School, nicknamed the "Brown Jug," was still going strong when Bulkeley made these remarks in 1919. By then, however, the student body was 90 percent Italian ("Morgan G. Bulkeley Recalls the Old Days at Brown School," *Hartford Courant*, June 21, 1919, 12). It is a fascinating etymological curiosity that "jug" referred to the whole school in the nineteenth century, but in the twentieth century the word was saved exclusively for detention.

87. "Bacon Academy Students to Celebrate Anniversary," *Hartford Courant*, May 10, 1953, E1.

88. "Dry Goods," *Brooklyn Daily Eagle*, April 15, 1854, 3. Uncle Henry Morgan's advertisement for help coincides nicely with young Morgan's removal to Brooklyn Heights. It seems logical that he started in the dry goods business in spring 1854 when he was sixteen.

89. Ibid.

90. Nathaniel H. Morgan, *Morgan Genealogy: A History of James Morgan, of New London, Conn., and His Descendants; from 1607 to 1869* (Hartford, CT: Case, Lockwood & Brainard, 1869), 17–18; Hooker, 96; U.S. Census Records, 1860, 1870. Avery and Jerusha Morgan's children from the oldest to the youngest were: Lyman Gardner, Lydia Smith, Jedidiah Stark, William Avery, Mary Gardner, Nathan Denison, and Henry Packer.

91. "The Funeral of Major Day," *Hartford Daily Courant*, June 14, 1884, 1.

3. BROOKLYN HEIGHTS

1. Clay Lancaster, *Old Brooklyn Heights* (Rutland, VT: Charles E. Tuttle Co., 1961, reprinted, Gillon, Edmund V. Jr., ed. New York: Dover Publications, 1979), 13–20.; "Brooklyn News," *New York Times*, October 31, 1860, 5.

2. U.S. Census Records, 1860. "State of New York, Table 3, Population of Cities and Towns, etc.," Brooklyn, King's County, Wards 1 and 2, p. 335, at http://www2.census.gov/prod2/decennial/documents/1860a-10.pdf (accessed 12/12/2008).

3. Lancaster, 18.

4. "From Grocery Store to the U.S. Senate," *Hartford Courant*, April 13, 1908, 2.

5. "The Water Works, A Final Triumph," *Hartford Daily Times*, October 24, 1855, 2; "Assessment Notice," *Brooklyn Daily Eagle*, December 21, 1854, 4.

6. "The Water Bill as It Passed into Law," *Brooklyn Daily Eagle*, April 21, 1859, 2.

7. "Common Council, September 13," *Hartford Daily Courant*, September 14, 1847, 2; "Office of the Board of Sewer Commissioners," *Brooklyn Daily Eagle*, January 15, 1858, 3.

8. Some of New York's newspapers included the *Daily Times*, *Daily Tribune*, *Evening Express*, *Herald*, *Morning Express Observer*, *Spectator*, *Sun*, *Albion*, *Christian Intelligencer*, *Evening Mirror*, *Evening Post*, *Home Journal*, *Morning Courier & Enquirer*, *National Anti-Slavery Standard*, *Irish American*, plus other ethnic papers.

9. Masthead of the *Brooklyn Daily Eagle* with comments following, particularly, "This paper has the largest circulation of any evening newspaper published in the United States, and as a medium for business and general advertising is not surpassed by any other journal."

10. Lancaster, 20.

11. Nathaniel H. Morgan, *Morgan Genealogy: A History of James Morgan, of New London, Conn., and His Descendants; from 1607 to 1869* (Hartford, CT: Case, Lockwood & Brainard, 1869), 141.

12. "Obituary," *Brooklyn Daily Eagle*, September 29, 1853, 2; U.S. Census Records, 1860, 1870.

13. Richard Hooker, *Aetna Life Insurance Company: Its First Hundred Years* (Hartford, CT: Aetna Life Insurance Co., 1956), 96.

14. "Schoomaker & Hicks," *Brooklyn Daily Eagle*, April 30, 1850, 2.

15. U.S. Census Records, 1860. In 1860, the census taker visited the Morgan's house on June 28, 1860. At that time, Eunice was twenty-eight. Thus, she would have turned eighteen in 1850, almost assuredly before she married Henry P. Morgan.

16. U.S. Census Reports, 1860, 1870.

17. "From Grocery Store to the U.S. Senate."

18. "Rich Fancy and Staple Dry Goods," *Brooklyn Eagle*, May 27, 1850, 2; "Cranky but Honest Mayor," *Brooklyn Daily Eagle*, June 4, 1896, 7.

19. "The Early Closing Movement," *Brooklyn Daily Eagle*, April 21, 1863, 3.

20. "Obituary," *Brooklyn Daily Eagle*, April 9, 1894, 5. Uncle Henry Morgan's obituary lists better than most sources all of his far-flung activities in Brooklyn Heights during his lifetime.

21. Charles W. Burpee, *The History of Hartford County, 1633–1928* (Chicago: The S. J. Clark Publishing Co., 1928), 16–21; J. H. Beers & Co., *Commemorative Biographical Record of Hartford County* (Chicago: J. H. Beers & Co., 1901), 69. It is important to remember that men paid twenty-five dollars (Joseph Hawley, Papers of Joseph R. Hawley, 1638–1906, Library of Congress, 29 reels, Connecticut State Library) to have their biographies pub-

lished in the 1901 J. H. Beers book, so naturally the information is sometimes self-serving and unreliable. For example, Morgan Bulkeley claimed to have been a partner in H. P. Morgan & Co., but would Uncle Henry give or sell his nephew a piece of the business only to be forced to buy it back if the young clerk ever returned to Hartford? Probably not—and the details are lost to history—so we're forced to use our own judgment.

22. Bruce Catton, *The American Heritage New History of the Civil War* (New York: Viking, 1996), 16.

23. [No title] *Brooklyn Daily Eagle*, May 26, 1856, 2.

24. Barbara A. White, *The Beecher Sisters* (New Haven, CT: Yale University Press, 2003), 205; "Beecher," *Brooklyn Daily Eagle*, May 20, 1875, 1.

25. U. S. Census Records, 1870, 1880, 1900; Beers, 70–71.

26. Stephen Lendman, "Excess Debt and Deflation = Deflation," *Baltimore Chronicle & Sentinel*, December 12, 2008, at http://baltimorechronicle.com/2008/121208 Lendman .shtml (accessed 12/12/2008).

27. Catton, 18.

28. John Niven, *Connecticut for the Union: The Role of the State in the Civil War* (New Haven, CT: Yale University Press, 1965), 15. The two leading abolitionists in Connecticut were Leonard Bacon, pastor of the First Ecclesiastical Society of New Haven, and the attorney Joseph R. Hawley of Hartford.

29. Catton, 16.

30. "An Interesting Find, Call for the Formation of the Republican Party in Connecticut," *Hartford Courant*, October 16, 1896, 6. Hooker and Hawley were two of the fiercest abolitionists in Hartford, and the free-soil, antislavery beliefs of Welles, Day, and Howard can be found in John Niven's *Connecticut for the Union* and also in their autobiographical sketches in J. H. Beers. Nat Shipman's beliefs are rarely discussed, but in the Hawley Papers, his beliefs surface and they are very much like those of Welles, Day, and Howard.

31. "From Grocery Store to the U.S. Senate." In fact, Bulkeley claimed that Brooklyn was Democratic by 30,000 votes at the time.

32. "Another Republican Rally, City Hall—Friday Evening Next," *Hartford Daily Courant*, February 29, 1860, 2.

33. Abraham Lincoln Online, "Letter to Horace Greeley," August 22, 1862, at http://showcase.netins.net/web/creative/lincoln/speeches/greeley.htm (accessed 09/10/2008).

34. David Morris Potter, *The Impending Crisis 1841–186* (New York: Harper Collins, 1976), 442.

35. Ibid.

36. Catton, 26.

37. Catton, 32.

38. "The War Excitement," *Brooklyn Daily Eagle*, April 23, 1861, 2.

39. William H. Bulkeley to Lydia Bulkeley, Civil War Letters of William H. Bulkeley," n.d., MS 66554, Connecticut Historical Society, Hartford.

40. "The War Excitement, the Feeling in the City," *Brooklyn Daily Eagle*, April 19, 1861, 2.

41. Ibid.

42. Donald Lines Jacobus, *The Bulkeley Genealogy: Rev. Peter Bulkeley, Being an Account of His Career, His Ancestry, . . .* (New Haven, CT: Tuttle, 1933), chap. 1, n.28.

43. William H. Bulkeley to Lydia Bulkeley, May 7, 1861, MS 66554.

44. "War Excitement: A Meeting to Organize a Home Guard to Protect the City," *Brooklyn Daily Eagle*, April 23, 1861, 2; "Brooklyn City Guard," *Brooklyn Daily Eagle*, April 26, 1891, 20. One of Brooklyn's fire companies offered itself as a "Home Guard." While it was a nice gesture, one councilman suggested that the city not be too quick to accept the offer, "as there is a "Home Guard" being formed in nearly every ward of the city for its protection." In a word, things were chaotic.

45. William H. Bulkeley to Lydia Bulkeley and Morgan Bulkeley, MS 66554.

46. Morgan Bulkeley to Lydia Bulkeley, July 24, 1861, MS 66554.

47. "History of the Thirteenth Regiment," *Brooklyn Daily Eagle*, February 17, 1864, 2.

48. Ibid.

49. "News Items," *Brooklyn Daily Eagle*, April 23, 1861, 2.

50. "The War Excitement," *Brooklyn Daily Eagle*, April 19, 1861, 2. While Billy Bulkeley was with the Thirteenth at Annapolis in 1861, he and fifty other soldiers traveled down Chesapeake Bay about ninety miles by steamer to Smith Point, Virginia. Their mission was to destroy the Smith Point Lightship, a beacon used to direct marine traffic to the mouth of the Potomac River. Some musket fire was exchanged—although no one was hit—and the Thirteenth headed for home, leaving the lightship intact. The Smith Point Lightship Affair was the most serious fighting the Thirteenth Regiment ever saw.

51. "War Excitement: The 13th and 28th Regiments," *Brooklyn Daily Eagle*, April 23, 1861, 2. "History of the Thirteenth Regiment," *Brooklyn Daily Eagle*, February 17, 1864, 2.

52. Ibid.

53. Glenn Weaver, *Hartford: An Illustrated History of Connecticut's Capital* (Woodland Hills, CA: Windsor Publications, 1982), 78.

54. R. L. Wilson, *The Book of Colt Firearms* (Minneapolis, Blue Book Publications, 1993), 120.

55. "The War Excitement," *Brooklyn Daily Eagle*, April 25, 1861, 2.

56. "War Intelligence: Melancholy Affair at Annapolis," *Brooklyn Daily Eagle*, June 12, 1861, 2.

57. "War Intelligence: Military Funeral," *Brooklyn Daily Eagle*, June 15, 1861, 2; Field Drums, "In Memory of a Young Civil War Drummer," at http://www.fielddrums.com/2008/05/in-memory-of-young-civil-war-drummer.html (accessed 12/12/2008).

58. "War Intelligence: Military Matters at the Seat of War . . . ," *Brooklyn Daily Eagle*, June 29, 1861, 2.

59. "War Intelligence: Col. Smith Re-Instated," *Brooklyn Daily Eagle*, August 3, 1861, 2.

60. Morgan Bulkeley to Lydia Bulkeley, July 24, 1861, MS 66554.

61. "Return of the Thirteenth Regiment," *Brooklyn Eagle*, July 30, 1861, 2; New York State Military Museum, "Unit History Project: 13th Regiment, New York State Militia, New York National Guard, Civil War," at http://www.dmna.state.ny.us/ historic/reghist/civil/ infantry/13thInfNYSM/13thInfNYSMMain.htm (accessed: 12/12/2008).

62. "Thursday Evening, May 29," *Brooklyn Eagle*, May 29, 1862, 3.

63. "Local and Miscellaneous War News," *Brooklyn Daily Eagle*, October 22, 1861, 2.

64. "The Thirteenth Regiment in Virginia," *Brooklyn Daily Eagle*, June 19, 1862, 3.

65. "Departure of the Thirteenth Regiment," *Brooklyn Daily Eagle*, May 29, 1862, 3.

66. "Miscellaneous War News," *Brooklyn Daily Eagle*, June 7, 1862, 2.

67. "Miscellaneous War News," *Brooklyn Daily Eagle*, June 9, 1862, 2.

68. William H. Bulkeley to Morgan Bulkeley, (n.d.), MS 66554.

69. "War Intelligence: Col. Smith Re-Instated."

70. William Stone Hubbell et al. (comp.), *The Story of the Twenty-First Regiment, Connecticut Volunteers* (Middletown, CT: Stewart Printing Co., 1900), 102–16. Though Suffolk was of limited military importance, a desultory four-week battle took place there in April–May 1863 as the Union armies fought to keep their shipping routes open.

71. "Our Brooklyn Regiments, The Thirteenth Regiment in Camp," *Brooklyn Daily Eagle*, June 28, 1862, 2.

72. Ibid.

73. Ibid.

74. "Our Brooklyn Regiments, The Thirteenth Regiment in Camp," *Brooklyn Daily Eagle*, June 28, 1862, 2.

75. Ibid.

76. Ibid.

77. John Formby, *The American Civil War: A Concise History of Its Causes, Progress and Results* (London: John Murray, 1910), 189.

78. Catton, 63–64.

79. "The Thirteenth at Suffolk, Va.," *Brooklyn Daily Eagle*, July 3, 1862, 2.

80. "Life in Virginia," *Brooklyn Daily Eagle*, August. 4, 1862, 2.

81. Ibid.

82. Ibid.

83. "Letter from the Thirteenth Regiment," *Brooklyn Daily Eagle*, August 19, 1862, 2.

84. Ibid.

85. Ibid.

86. "The Thirteenth Regiment at Suffolk," *Brooklyn Daily Eagle*, July 8, 1862, 2.

87. "The Regiment Left Suffolk, Va.," *Brooklyn Daily Eagle*, September 5, 1862, 2; "The Detachments of the Thirteenth Regiment," *Brooklyn Daily Eagle*, September 6, 1862, 2.

88. "The Burial of a Soldier at Suffolk, Va.," *Brooklyn Daily Eagle*, August 7, 1862, 2; "The Detachments of the Thirteenth Regiment," *Brooklyn Daily Eagle*, September 6, 1862, 2. Guy Holt was returning from picket duty along a set of railroad tracks when, a short

distance away, the Fourth Regiment guard fired their muskets at some trees. One of the musket balls went through the stand of trees and hit Holt in the head. He died instantly. "Letter from the 13th Regiment . . . ," *Brooklyn Daily Eagle*, August 18, 1862, 2.

89. "Local Military Matters," *Brooklyn Daily Eagle*, September 5, 1862, 2.

90. Ibid.

91. Ibid.

92. Ibid.

93. New York State Military Museum, "Unit History Project, 13th Regiment."

94. Beers, 70–71.

95. Ibid.

96. Beers, 69.

97. Internet Archive, "Obituary Record of Graduates of Yale College, Deceased from July 1859 to July 1870," at http://www.archive.org/stream/1860t700bituaryooyaleuoft/ 1860t700bituaryooyaleuoft_djvu.txt (accessed 12/14/2008).

98. William H. Bulkeley to Lydia Bulkeley," June 8, 1861, MS 66554

99. Internet Archive, "Obituary Record of Graduates of Yale College."

100. Robert N. Scott, *The Official Records of the War of the Rebellion*, prepared under the direction of the Secretary of War (Washington, DC: Government Printing Office, 1880), at http://www.civilwarhome.com/records.htm (accessed 3/17/2008).

101. Internet Archive, "Obituary Record of Graduates of Yale College."

102. Ibid.

103. Hooker, 78.

104. "The Late Capt. Charles E. Bulkeley," *Hartford Daily Courant*, February18, 1864, 2; Records of Cedar Hill Cemetery, Maple Avenue, Hartford, CT.

105. William H. Bulkeley to Lydia Bulkeley, March 2, 1864, MS 66554.

106. "Bread for the Soldier's Families," *Brooklyn Daily Eagle*, February 10, 1866, 1; "Medicine for the Poor," *Brooklyn Daily Eagle*, May 15, 1868, 2; "Municipal Salaries," *Brooklyn Daily Eagle*, July 7, 1868, 2; "Working Men under Martial Law," *Brooklyn Daily Eagle*, February 28, 1870, 2; "Failure in the Saloon Business," *Brooklyn Daily Eagle*, March 10, 1870, 14.

107. Prospect Park Alliance, "About Prospect Park," at http://www.prospectpark.org/ about (accessed 12/14/2008).

108. American Dialect Society, at http://listserv.linguistlist.org/cgi-bin/wa?A2=indo4 12A&L=ADS-L&P=697 (accessed 5/23/2008). Bulkeley reference to "one o'cat licks" found in "Men of Note Talk Baseball Lore," *Hartford Courant*, October 31, 1913, 1.

109. "The Early Closing Movement," *Brooklyn Daily Eagle*, July 6, 1867, 2.

110. "The New Republican General Committee," *Brooklyn Daily Eagle*, December 23, 1870, 3.

111. "Gen. Bulkeley's Comrades," *Brooklyn Daily Eagle*, November 14, 1902, 8.

112. "Republican Primaries," *Brooklyn Daily Eagle*, May 6, 1870, 3.

113. "A Pawnbroking Bank," *Brooklyn Daily Eagle*, April 5, 1870, 7.

114. Ibid.

115. "Pawnbrokery in New York," *Brooklyn Daly Eagle*, June 25, 1868, 4.

116. "A Pawnbroking Bank."

117. Ibid.

118. "The East River Bridge," *Brooklyn Daly Eagle*, February 19, 1868, 2; David Mc-Cullough, *The Great Bridge: The Epic Story of the Building of the Brooklyn Bridge*, (New York: Simon & Schuster, 2001), 88–91; U.S. Census Records, 1870, 1880.

119. "From Grocery Store to the U. S. Senate."

120. "The Lesson of the Death and Life of Fisk," *Brooklyn Daily Eagle*, January 8, 1872, 2.

4. RETURN TO HARTFORD

1. Hartford Land Records, vol. 129, p. 482, February 1, 1870 Hartford City Hall, Hartford, CT.

2. *Connecticut Quarterly*, vol. 1, January 1895–December 1896, 295–97.

3. "Streets and Governors," *Hartford Courant*, December 24, 1920, 10.

4. *Atlas of the City of Hartford and the Town of West Hartford, Connecticut* (New York: Sanborn Map Co., 1921) 1.; U. S. Census Reports, 1860, 1870; Hartford Land Records, vol. 129, p. 544, March 10, 1870.

5. Richard Hooker, *Aetna Life Insurance Company: Its First Hundred Years* (Hartford, CT: Aetna Life Insurance Co., 1956), 49.

6. Ibid., 49.

7. Ibid., 58.

8. Ibid., 58.

9. Ibid., 60.

10. "Financial Matters . . . ," *Hartford Daily Courant*, October 7, 1857, 2.

11. [No title], *Hartford Daily Courant*, February 2, 1858, 2.

12. Hooker, 60; "Money and Business," *Hartford Daily Courant*, August 20, 1857, 2; "Local Affairs," *Hartford Daily Courant*, September 4, 1857, 2.

13. *Geer's City Directory* (Hartford CT: Hartford Printing Company), 1869, 1870, 1871; Hartford Land Records, vol. 168, p. 656; Release of mortgage by *Aetna Life* on Washington Street property, September 29, 1877.

14. J. H. Beers & Co., *Commemorative Biographical Record of Hartford County* (Chicago: J. H. Beers & Co., 1901), 70–71.

15. The Philadelphia Print Shop, Ltd., "Popular Lithographs by the Kellogg Brothers of Hartford," at http://www.philaprintshop.com/kellogg.html (accessed 12/14/2008). John Comstock's biography is included in this article.

16. "Kellogg & Bulkeley Lithographers," *Hartford Daily Courant*, April 30, 1870, 2; "A Busy Hartford Concern," *Hartford Courant*, June 11, 1889, 1.

17. "Death of Judge Eliphalet Adams Bulkeley," *Hartford Daily Courant*, February 14, 15, 1872, 2.

18. Ibid.

19. "Last Inventory and Distribution of Eliphalet A. Bulkeley," Hartford Probate District, April 25, 1872 (no catalog or file number), Connecticut State Library, Hartford.

20. U. S. Census Records, 1870.

21. Hooker, 98.

22. Beers, 30–31.

23. Hooker, 88.

24. Ibid., 89.

25. *Geer's City Directory*, 1854, 1855.

26. Gravestone of Bridget McCormick, Cedar Hill Cemetery; Obituaries: "Daniel T. Wallace," *Hartford Courant*, September 24, 1906, 2; "Frank M. Wallace," *Hartford Courant*, April 19, 1939, 4.

27. Photo: "Klondike Hotel on Gold Street," CD 3153, Img. 0092.pcd, Connecticut Historical Society, Hartford.

28. "Hartford and Vicinity Brief Mention," *Hartford Daily Courant*, August 9, 1877, 2.

29. "The Telephone," *Hartford Courant*, October 28, 1911, 8.

30. "Going," *Hartford Daily Courant*, March 31, 1863, 2; "The Horse Cars," *Hartford Daily Courant*, June 2, 1863, 2.

31. "Shipped to New York," *Hartford Courant*, February 26, 1896, 3; "Hartford at Last Has the Jitney," *Hartford Courant*, March 28, 1915, 1. Hartford's last horse car was retired in 1896 and the electric trolley ran for a fairly short period of time—until 1915. Slowly they were replaced by what were called "jitney buses." Over the next few years, these vehicles morphed into the buses of today.

32. "Important Postal Arrangement, Letter Boxes to Be Put Up," *Hartford Daily Courant*, December 13, 1865, 2.

33. Oliver Jensen, *The American Heritage History of Railroads in America* (New York: American Heritage Publishers, 1975), 105.

34. *Resolutions and Special Laws of Connecticut*, vol. VII, pp. 389–91, charter approved July 31, 1872, State Archives, Connecticut State Library, Hartford.

35. "The Legislature: The Work of the Session," *Hartford Daily Courant*, August 3, 1872, 2.

36. Gergely Baics, "The Saloons of Hartford's East Side, 1870–1910," report written with an award by the U. S. Department of Housing and Urban Development, Trinity College, Hartford, at http://www.trincoll.edu/depts/tcn/Research_Reports/60.htm (accessed 3/21/2008).

37. Ibid.

38. Ibid.

39. U. S. Census Records, 1860, 1870, 1880.

40. "Wills Probated," *Hartford Daily Courant*, February 23, 1880, 2; U.S. Census Records, 1870.

41. Andrew Walsh, "Contesting the City: Catholic Assertings and Protestant Responses in Late 19th Century Hartford," A paper presented to the New England Religious Discussion Society, September 1999, at http://64.233.169.104/search?q=cache:ctDLaxVqO7YJ:hi rr.hartsem.edu/bookshelf/Andrew%2520Walsh%2520paper.pdf+Contesting+the+City& hl=en&ct=clnk&cd=2&gl=us (accessed 3/21/2008).

42. Albert E. Van Dusen, *Connecticut: A Fully Illustrated History of the State from the Seventeenth Century to the Present* (New York: Random House, 1961), 260.

43. Glenn Weaver, *Hartford: An Illustrated History of Connecticut's Capital* (Woodland Hills, CA: Windsor Publications, 1982), 93–94.

44. *Connecticut Quarterly*, 297. Virtually all manufactories of this period had power transferred from a waterwheel or steam engine to a large overhead shaft that ran the length of the building. Jewell's continuous leather belting transferred power down to the individual lathes, drill presses, and other machines on the floor. Without these belts, manufactories would never have been able to operate.

45. Beers, 373–74; "The Death of Governor Jewell," *Hartford Daily Courant*, February 13, 1883, 2.

46. "The Death of Governor Jewell," *Hartford Daily Courant*, February 13, 1883, 2.

47. "Recollections of Forty Years in Connecticut Politics," *Hartford Courant*, October 25, 1914, E21–23.

48. Ibid.

49. Ibid.

50. Ibid.

51. Ibid.

52. Jensen, 108.

53. James Ford Rhodes, *History of the United States: From the Compromise of 1850 to the McKinley-Bryan Campaign of 1896*, vol. VII (New York: The MacMillan Co., 1920), 100–117.

54. "Review of the Market: Bank Stocks," *Hartford Daily Courant*, October 22, 1875, 4; *Hartford Daily Courant*, December 6, 1878, 4; *Hartford Daily Courant*, February 18, 1881, 4. Since newspapers at the time often gave only the bid and not the ask price, one of these prices had to be recalculated from the bid.

55. "Three Men with One Wish," *New York Sun*, August 8, 1886, 3; "Morgan G. Bulkeley Political Scrapbook, 1885–88," MS 93631, Connecticut Historical Society, Hartford.

56. "Election Frauds in Hartford," *Hartford Daily Courant*, November 4, 1878, 2.

57. "Recollections of Forty Years in Connecticut Politics."

58. Ibid.

59. "The Charter Oak Life, Change in Management of the Company," *Hartford Daily Courant*, November 29, 1875, 2.

60. "The City Election," *Hartford Daily Courant*, April 4, 1876, 2.

61. Beers, 1510.

62. Ibid, 177.

63. "Recollections of Forty Years in Connecticut Politics."

64. Ibid.

65. Ellsworth S Grant and Marion H. Grant, *The City of Hartford 1784–1984: An Illustrated History*. Hartford: Connecticut Historical Society, 1986, 16; "Former Mayor I. A. Sullivan Dies in West," *Hartford Courant*, February 14, 1928, 1; Beers, 177. Democratic Mayor Ignatius Sullivan was born in Canton, Massachusetts, while Mayor Alexander Harbison was born in County Armagh, Ireland.

66. "Recollections of Forty Years in Connecticut Politics," *Hartford Courant*, October 25, 1914, E21–23.

67. Beers, 343; "Recollections of Forty Years in Connecticut Politics."

68. Ibid.

69. "Death of J. Ella Gallup Sumner," *Hartford Daily Courant*, March 3, 1875, 2.

70. "The City Election," *Hartford Daily Courant*, April 2, 1878, 2.

71. Weaver (1982), 98–100.

72. Ibid.

73. Ibid.

74. Ibid.

75. "The Return of the Flags," *Hartford Daily Courant*, September 18, 1879, 2.

76. Weaver (1982), 100.

77. Ibid., 100–101.

78. Ibid., 100.

79. "The Willimantic Linen Company: A Visit to the Factories," *Hartford Daily Courant*, March 14, 1878, 2.

80. Glenn Weaver, *The Hartford Electric Light Company* (Hartford, CT: The Hartford Electric Light Company, 1969), 5.

81. "Twisting the Figures: A Republican Defeat Anyway," *Hartford Daily Courant*, April 4, 1878, 2.

82. "Local Politics: Republican City Nominations," *Hartford Daily Courant*, March 29, 1880, 2.

83. *General Statutes of Connecticut, and Public Acts from 1875 to 1882*, "Bribery Laws of Connecticut 1875–1882; 1877," 244, 518, State Archives, Connecticut State Library, Hartford.

84. "Corrupt Practices: Gov. Bulkeley's Views . . . ," *Hartford Courant*, May 12, 1893, 1.

85. "Hartford and Vicinity: The Election in Hartford," *Hartford Daily Courant*, November 5, 1884, 2; November 13, 1884, 1. Hiram Buckingham's arrest for buying votes happened in 1884, and he was bailed out by former Lt. Governor Billy Bulkeley, who had served under Governor Hobart Bigelow from 1881 to 1883.

86. "Recollections of Forty Years in Connecticut Politics."

87. "Thayer Writes to Alec Harbison," *Hartford Courant*, August 13, 1910, 12.

88. "Sudden Death of Ex-Mayor Thayer," *Hartford Courant*, April 27, 1915, 1.

89. "Gideon D. Winslow Dead, Age 68 Years," *Hartford Courant*, September 18, 1914, 11.

90. Ibid.

91. Ibid.

92. "Commissioner Winslow Criticized," *Hartford Courant*, April 8, 1891, 2; "Commissioner Winslow Reappointed," *Hartford Courant*, May 3, 1892, 2.

93. "The Situation at Hartford," *New York Times*, April 8, 1891, 5.

94. "Corrupt Practices: Gov. Bulkeley's Views . . . ," *Hartford Courant*, May 12, 1893, 1.

95. "The Vote on the Water," *Hartford Daily Times*, July 25, 1865, 2.

96. "Election Frauds in Hartford," *Hartford Daily Courant*, November 4, 1878, 2.

97. "A Bad Day for Cheaters," *Hartford Daily Courant*, November 6, 1878, 2.

98. Kevin Murphy, *Water for Hartford: The Story of the Hartford Water Works and the Metropolitan District Commission* (Wethersfield, CT: Shining Tramp Press, 2004), 91.

99. Ibid. 97–98.

100. "From Grocery Store to the u.s. Senate," *Hartford Courant*, April 13, 1908, 2.

101. "The Law on Bribery," *Hartford Daily Times*, Apr. 3, 1880, 2.; "The Election," *Hartford Daily Times*, Apr. 5, 1880, 2. With a mountain of circumstantial evidence, it can be "proved" Morgan Bulkeley was a vote buyer. However, once the cash was passed to his fixer, Pat McGovern, Bulkeley had plausible deniability. He was careful about this.

102. Morgan Bulkeley to Lydia Bulkeley, Civil War Letters of William H. Bulkeley, July 24, 1861, MS 66554, Connecticut Historical Society, Hartford.

103. When Morgan Bulkeley became president of Aetna Life in July 1879, he stayed on as a figurehead president at the United States Trust Company for two years while Thomas Enders regained his health. On June 20, 1881, Enders accepted the presidency of u.s. Trust and remained in that position until 1891, three years before his death (*Hartford Daily Courant*, June 20, 1881, 2; Beers, 30–31).

104. "Afternoon Session: Some Interesting Questions and Answers," *Hartford Daily Courant*, May 7, 1879, 2.

105. Ibid.

106. "Bulkeley on Corruption," *New York Times*, May 23, 1893, 4.

107. "Three Men with One Wish"; "Morgan G. Bulkeley Political Scrapbook, 1885–88," MS 93631, Connecticut Historical Society, Hartford.

108. "The Election," *Hartford Daily Times*, April 3, 1880, 2; "The City Election," *Hartford Times*, April 7, 1884, 8; "The Election," *Hartford Times*, April 6, 1886, 5; "The City Election: Mr. Bulkeley Re-Elected," *Hartford Times*, April 6, 1886, 5.

109. Hooker, 91.

110. Ibid., 98.

111. Ibid.

112. Ibid.

113. Ellsworth Grant, *The Club on Prospect Street: A History of the Hartford Club* (Hartford, CT: The Hartford Club, 1984), 24.

114. David Arcidiacono, *Grace, Grit, and Growling: The Hartford Dark Blues Base Ball Club, 1874–1877* (Author: 2003), 12.

115. "The Base Ball Nine," *Hartford Daily Courant*, February 23, 1874, 2. Though most of the money was put up by the men in the meeting, the subscription books were then opened to the public and the last few shares were sold over the next couple of weeks.

116. "Three Men with One Wish"; "Morgan G. Bulkeley Political Scrapbook, 1885–88."

117. Friends of Vintage Baseball, at http://www.friendsofvintagebaseball.org/coltmead ows_sked.html (accessed 5/17/2009); Hog River Journal, "The Hartford Dark Blues," at http://www.hogriver.org/issues/vo1no3/dark_blues.htm (accessed 5/17/2009).

118. "Contest His Seat?" *Hartford Courant*, May 23, 1910, 1.

119. Arcidiacono, 28.

120. Hog River Journal, "The Hartford Dark Blues."

121. Arcidiacono, 65.

122. Ibid., 47–50, 70–71, 74–75; National Baseball Hall of Fame, "The Hall of Famers," at http://www.baseballhalloffame.org/enterworkflow.do?flowId=playerDetails .playerDetails (accessed 12/14/2008).

123. Arcidiacono, 68.

124. Ibid., 82.

125. "Men of Note Talk Baseball Lore," *Hartford Courant*, October 31, 1913, 1.

126. National Baseball Hall of Fame & Museum.

127. "Morgan G. Bulkeley," *Hartford Times*, November 7, 1922, 10.

128. West Hartford Land Records, West Hartford City Hall, West Hartford, CT. Burdette Loomis's land acquisitions comprise thirty-nine documents over three years, vol. 5, pp. 165–504; vol. 6, pp. 72–165; vol. 7, pp. 57–170; vol. 8, pp. 28–138.

129. "Charter Oak Exhibition Hall Crashes Under Snow," *Hartford Courant*, January 15, 1923, 1; "Health Board Will Act on Charter Oak," *Hartford Courant*, September. 15, 1930, 18; Charter Oak Foreclosure Is Entered, *Hartford Courant*, May 12, 1931, 6; Charter Oak Park Chosen for Factory," *Hartford Courant*, January 1, 1937, 1.

5. MAYOR BULKELEY: PART ONE

1. Glenn Weaver, *Hartford: An Illustrated History of Connecticut's Capital* (Woodland Hills, CA: Windsor Publications, 1982), 102–3.

2. Colt, "Colt History," at http://www.colt.com/mil/history.asp (accessed 12/10/2008).

3. Charles R. Morris, *The Tycoons: How Andrew Carnegie, John D. Rockefeller, Jay Gould, and JP Morgan Invented the American Supereconomy* (New York: Times Books, 2005), 101, 182. Pope's

bicycles, then his electric cars, and finally the Pope-Hartford gasoline-powered automobiles were increasingly successful.

4. Weaver (1982), 74–75, 80–81, 104–5, 109, 101, 75; Hartford Board of Trade, *Hartford, Conn., as a Manufacturing, Business and Commercial Center; with Brief Sketches of Its History, Attractions, Leading Industries, and Institutions* (Hartford, CT: Author, 1889), 101–4, 116–18, 120–23, 123–25, 126–30; Ellsworth Grant, "The Miracle on Capital Avenue," *Hog River Journal*, at http://www.hogriver.org/issues/v02n03/miracle.htm (accessed 21 May 2009).

5. Hartford Board of Trade, 95–97.

6. Weaver (1982), 101.

7. State of Connecticut, Secretary of the State, "Nineteenth Century Hartford," at http://www.ct.gov/sots/cwp/view.asp?a=3188&q=392624

8. Mark Twain, "Hartford: The Blue Laws," *Alta California*, San Francisco, September 6, 1868.

9. J. H. Beers & Co., *Commemorative Biographical Record of Hartford County* (Chicago: J. H. Beers & Co., 1901), 69–70.

10. Bulkeley's portrait first hung in the Capitol but was eventually moved to the State Library, which was completed in 1910.

11. "City Election: Mayor Bulkeley Re-Elected," *Hartford Daily Courant*, April 4, 1882, 2.

12. Beers, 12–13.

13. "The Revolution in Hartford," *Hartford Daily Courant*, April 2, 1872, 2.

14. "The Mayoralty," *Hartford Daily Courant*, April 2, 1880, 2. The Democratic Party needed badly to reform, but chose instead to cater to its lowest element. This was a godsend for Morgan Bulkeley, although his vote buying left nothing to chance.

15. "The City Election," *Hartford Daily Courant*, April 2, 1880, 2. "Bummer" was a pejorative term for a Democrat who refused to reform after the war and refused to admit that the Democratic Party had been wrong and badly shamed by its states' rights stance during the conflict.

16. "St. Patrick's Day," *Hartford Daily Courant*, March 18, 1879, 2.

17. "The City Election," *Hartford Daily Courant*, April 2, 1880, 2.

18. "City Election," *Hartford Daily Courant*, April 4, 1882, 2.

19. "The Waterloo," *Hartford Daily Courant*, April 6, 1880, 2; "City Election," *Hartford Daily Courant*, April 4, 1882, 2; "The City Election," *Hartford Daily Courant*, April 8, 1884, 2; "Mayor Bulkeley Re-Elected," *Hartford Times*, April 6, 1886, 5. Bulkeley's numbers (first) in the Fifth and Sixth Wards against those of his opponents are as follows: 1880, Fifth, 280–276, Sixth, 398–265; 1882, Fifth, 231–308, Sixth, 275–40; 1884, Fifth, 290–286, Sixth, 306–421; 1886, Fifth, 211–376, Sixth, 297–486. Morgan Bulkeley's majorities in the elections of 1880, 1882, 1884, and 1886 were: 1,369; 229; 830; and 328, respectively.

20. "Election Today, Voting Places," *Hartford Daily Courant*, April 3, 1882, 2.

21. Ibid.

22. "Hezekiah Gaylord, Death of a Long-Time Resident and Businessman," *Hartford Daily Courant*, May 3, 1909, 7; Hartford Land Records, vol. 200, p. 553, October 2, 1887; vol. 210, p. 710, December 6, 1887; vol. 207, p. 392, October 19, 1888; vol. 207, p. 423, November 15, 1888 (Morgan St. property); and vol. 200, p. 560, October 24, 1887; vol. 203, p. 630, November 3, 1887; vol. 207, p. 424, November 15, 1888 (Girard Ave. property).

23. Not only was the *Courant* silent because it was the Republican organ, but also because Gen. Joe Hawley was the paper's overlord. Except where there was criminally inept behavior—as in the case of Gen. Ben Butler—Joe Hawley would never say a bad word about another soldier. Even though Hawley knew Bulkeley "never smelled powder" during the Civil War, he still wouldn't criticize him. Gen. Hawley's stance smacks of nobility, but veterans were the only ones who gave him universal love and respect for his sacrifices during the war.

24. "The Law on Bribery," *Hartford Daily Times*, April 3, 1880, 2.

25. "The Election," *Hartford Daily Times*, April 5, 1880, 2.

26. "News of the State: The Mayor's Salary at Waterbury," *Hartford Daily Courant*, December 2, 1886, 4.

27. "Salaries Paid Insurance Men," *Hartford Courant*, May 12, 1906, 13.

28. Weaver (1982), 102.

29. "The New Reservoir," *Hartford Daily Courant*, April 17, 1880, 2.

30. Kevin Murphy, *Water for Hartford: The Story of the Hartford Water Works and the Metropolitan District Commission* (Wethersfield, CT: Shining Tramp Press, 2004), 143.

31. "The Water Question," *The Hartford Daily Times*, September 26–27, 1873, 2; Murphy, 144–46.

32. Murphy, 143.

33. Biographical Directory of the United States Congress, "Ezra Clark, Jr.," at http://bioguide.congress.gov/scripts/biodisplay.pl?index=C000429 (accessed 3/27/2008).

34. Beers, 72.

35. Beers, 1392.

36. Herbert Mitgang, "Books of The Times; Making the Civil War Real with Pictures and Essays," review of Geoffrey C. Ward, *The Civil War: An Illustrated History*, *New York Times*, September 5, 1990, at http://query.nytimes.com/gst/fullpage.html?res=9C0CE4D71330F 936A3575AC0A966958260 (accessed: 12/14/2008).

37. Beers, 1393.

38. James Junius Goodwin, *The Goodwins of Hartford, Connecticut: Descendants of William and Ozias Goodwin* (Hartford, CT: Brown & Gross, ca. 1891), 124, 627–694. Farmers William Goodwin (1733), Allyn Goodwin (1756); tavern-keepers: Samuel Goodwin (1781), James Goodwin (1777); tailors: John Goodwin (1819), Erastus Goodwin (1795); cabinetmaker: William Goodwin (1789); saddler: John E. Goodwin (1811); sea captains: Ozias Goodwin (1755), Asher Goodwin (1768); coffee importer: Eliza Goodwin (1854); real estate speculators: James M. Goodwin (1803).

39. Beers, 1393; "Trinity Graduates," *Hartford Courant*, June 26, 1902, 9.

40. Marion Hepburn Grant, *In and Around Hartford: Its People and Places* (Hartford: The Connecticut Historical Society, 1989), 138; Marion Hepburn Grant, *The Fenwick Story* (Hartford: The Connecticut Historical Society, 1974), 115–19; "Trinity Church-Fifty Years Old," *Hartford Courant*, May 16, 1910, 12. Francis Goodwin stepped down as rector of Sigourney Street's Trinity Church on November 20, 1871.

41. Francis Goodwin had enormous success talking Charles Pond, Henry and Walter Keney—Walter was married to Francis Goodwin's aunt Mary Jeannette Goodwin Keney—and others into leaving their land to the city for his "ring of parks." Besides these bequests, he also convinced the city fathers to buy the land for Riverside and South (Goodwin) Parks. Lastly, he talked his cousin, J. P. Morgan, into underwriting an addition to the Wadsworth Atheneum in honor of the latter's father, Junius Spencer Morgan. Francis Goodwin was persuasive indeed.

42. "Reminiscenses and Studies," *Hartford Courant*, March 27, 1873, 2; From an exhibition *The Goodwin's Parlor* at the Wadsworth Atheneum, Hartford.

43. Bushnell Park Foundation, "Park History" at http://www.bushnellpark.org/Content/Park_History.asp (accessed 3/27/2008).

44. Beers, 1393.

45. Because Francis Goodwin was the biggest individual taxpayer in Hartford, thanks to his real estate holdings, one would expect Mayor Bulkeley and Goodwin to have a great many business dealings, but they had almost none. Goodwin showed up at common council meetings as needed, but that was about the only time the two men crossed paths. "Large Tax-Payers," *Hartford Daily Courant*, April 10, 1866, 2; "Largest Taxpayers," *Hartford Courant*, January 2, 1900, 14.

46. "The Mayoralty," *Hartford Courant*, March 21, 1900, 10.

47. "Personals," *Hartford Daily Courant*, May 26, 1880, 2.

48. Chicago Historical Society, "Parades, Protests and Politics in Chicago, The 1880 Republican Convention," at http://www.chicagohs.org/history/politics/1880.html (accessed 12/23/2008).

49. "General Bulkeley Serenaded," *Hartford Daily Courant*, August 18, 1880, 2.

50. Ibid.

51. "The Excursion for the Children," *Hartford Daily Courant*, July 29, 1878, 2; August 16, 1879, 2. Fenwick Grove was a piece of land north of the Shore Line Railroad tracks, a pleasant grove that included a beach on South Cove.

52. "The Children's Excursion," *Hartford Daily Courant*, August 25, 30, 1880, 2; M. H. Grant, (1974), 102.

53. The Mayor's Excursion," *Hartford Daily Courant*, August 23, 1881, 2.

54. "The Mayor's Excursion," *Hartford Daily Courant*, August 30, 1880, 2; "The Mayor's Excursion," *Hartford Daily Courant*, August 23, 1881, 2.

55. Ibid.

56. Ibid.

57. Ibid.

58. Robert Owen Decker, *Hartford Immigrants: A History of the Christian Activities Council (Congregational) 1850–1980* (New York: United Church Press, 1987), 78.

59. "Union Veteran's Meeting: Meeting Tonight at Whittlesey's Hall," *Hartford Daily Courant*, September 20, 1880, 1.

60. "Orders for the Parade," *Hartford Daily Courant*, October 16, 1880, 2; "Grant: His Reception in Hartford," *Hartford Daily Courant*, October 18, 1880, 2.

61. "Bulkeley Defends Campaign Gifts," *Hartford Courant*, May 17, 1906, 1.

62. "Welcome Grant!" *Hartford Daily Courant*, October 16, 1880, 2.

63. "Grant: His Reception in Hartford," *Hartford Daily Courant*, October 18, 1880, 2.

64. Ibid.

65. Ibid.; Ron Powers, *Mark Twain* (New York: Simon and Schuster, 2005), 506.

66. "Grant: His Reception in Hartford."

67. Ibid.; "Gen. Grant in New York," *Hartford Daily Courant*, October. 18, 1880, 3.

68. "City Government Last Evening," *Hartford Daily Courant*, December 28, 1880, 2.

69. "City Government Last Evening," *Hartford Daily Courant*, May 24, 1881, 2.

70. "Horse Railroad Extension: Final Action of the City Council," *Hartford Daily Courant*, June 20, 1881, 3.

71. Richard Hooker, *Aetna Life Insurance Company: Its First Hundred Years* (Hartford: Aetna Life Insurance Co., 1956), 100. These figures are extrapolations.

72. "McGovern's Career Ends at Age of 91," *Hartford Courant*, February 6, 1941, 1.

73. Ibid.

74. Ibid.

75. Ibid.

76. Ibid.

77. "Obituary: Sudden Death of Mrs. Patrick McGovern at Bristol," *Hartford Courant*, August 25, 1902, 8.

78. U.S. Census reports, 1910.

79. "Visiting the Willimantic Mill," *Hartford Daily Courant*, February 4, 1881, 3.

80. Ibid.

81. "The Forgotten Home Team in Hartford," *New York Times*, April 13, 2003, (n.p.).

82. Justin Kaplan, *Mr. Clemens and Mark Twain* (New York: Simon and Schuster, 1991), 162.

83. Mark Twain, "Hartford: The Blue Laws," *Alta California*, San Francisco, September 6, 1868.

84. "Visiting the Willimantic Mill," *Hartford Daily Courant*, February 4, 1881, 3.

85. Glenn Weaver, *The Hartford Electric Light Company* (Hartford, CT: The Hartford Electric Light Company, 1969), 10–13.

86. Ibid., 10.

87. Ibid., 14.

88. Ibid., 10.

89. Ibid., 11.

90. "Senate Joint Resolution No. 81," *Special Acts and Resolves of the State of Connecticut*, IX (Hartford 1885), 212–14.

91. Weaver (1969), 12–13.

92. Ibid., 14–15.

93. Ibid., 16–17.

94. Ibid., 17.

95. Ibid. Glenn Weaver inserts the following comment in his notes on page 222 of *The Hartford Electric Light Company*: "If Bulkeley was concerned with 'conflict of interest,' his attitude was unusual for the time. . . . There seems, however, no other way to explain his reluctance to participate actively in the affairs of *The Hartford Electric Light Company*."

96. "Army of the Potomac: Its Thirteenth Annual Reunion," *Hartford Daily Courant*, June 9, 1881, 1.

97. "A Bulkeley Story," *The Hartford Daily Courant*, August 22, 1924, 10. The spoken word and the written word are not always compatible, so Gen. Sherman's remarks were edited for the good of the story. His original speech is as follows: " What on an occasion like this uplifts the spirit, what is exhilarating, making one glad to be among you thoroughbreds, is the fact that every one of you exemplifies the fact that being an American is to be self-forgetful, self-assessing, whenever and wherever the chance shows to advance national good feeling. American sportsmanship just boils down into making sport better, making the public wholesomely happy. And as such men develop in their recreations it can be depended they show in every one of life's relations, in politics, in business, everywise. Your president—I speak from long affectionate acquaintance—reaches in this the utmost ideal. Can any man think of Bulkeley of Connecticut as a seeker after or an acceptor of self-advancement, self-glorification? Impossible!"

98. Ibid.

99. Roger Matuz, *The Presidents Fact Book* (New York: Black Dog & Leventhal, 2004), 322–30.

100. "The Day of the Funeral," *Hartford Daily Courant*, September 23, 1881, 2.

101. Ibid.

102. Ibid.

103. "The Atlanta Excursionists," *Hartford Daily Courant*, October 31, 1881, 2.

104. "The Governor's Message," *Hartford Daily Courant*, January 6, 1881, 2.

105. "The Connecticut Campaign," *Boston Daily Globe*, September 22, 1882, 2.

106. University of Connecticut, "The UConn Story," at http://www.uconn.edu/history/yesteryear/archives/founding/founders.php (accessed 3/29/2008).

107. "The Great Fires: Destruction of the High School Building," *Hartford Daily Courant*, January 25, 1882, 2.

108. Ibid.

109. "Hartford Public High School," *Hartford Daily Courant*, February 7, 1882, 2.

110. Harriet Beecher Stowe, Isabella Beecher Hooker, and Mary Beecher Perkins were daughters of Rev. Lyman Beecher, and they had seven cleric brothers. Harriet Beecher Stowe's husband was Rev. Calvin Stowe. John Hooker was sixth in descent from Rev. Thomas Hooker, the founder of Hartford. Henry "Eugene" Burton—married to John and Isabella Hooker's daughter Mary—was the son of Rev. Henry Burton of Washington Street, Middletown, and Eugene's brother, Rev. Nathaniel J. Burton, was pastor of Park Church (Congregational). Samuel Clemens's best friend, Rev. Joseph Twichell, was pastor of the Asylum Hill Congregational Church. Gen. Joseph Hawley's father was Rev. Francis Hawley and the General's favorite Civil War chaplain was Rev. Henry Clay Trumbull, a frequent speaker at the Fourth Congregational Church. Logically, the Nook Farm group could not vote for Morgan Bulkeley after his vote buying (lawbreaking) came to light.

111. "City Election: Mayor Bulkeley Re-Elected." *Hartford Daily Courant*, April 4, 1882, 2.

112. "The City Election," *Hartford Daily Times*, April 4, 1882, 2.

113. "City Campaigns in the Olden Days," *Hartford Courant*, March 17, 1908, 4.

114. "Mayor Bulkeley," *New Haven Register*, August 25, 1882, 2.

115. "For Alleged Libel: The New Haven Register Sued by Morgan G. Bulkeley for $25,000," *Boston Daily Globe*, August 26, 1882, 1.

116. "Hartford and Vicinity: City Briefs," *Hartford Daily Courant*, July 4, 1884, 2.

117. "Celebrating the Fourth," *Hartford Daily Courant*, June 17, 1882, 2.

118. "The Glorious Fourth: The Celebration in Hartford," *Hartford Daily Courant*, July 6, 1866, 8.

119. Ibid.

120. "Recollections of Forty Years in Connecticut Politics," *Hartford Courant*, October 25, 1914, E21–23.; National Governor's Association, "Governor's Information: Connecticut Governor Thomas MacDonald Waller," at http://www.nga.org/portal/site/nga/menuitem.29fab9fb4add37305ddcbeeb50101oao/?vgnextoid=1eba224971c81o1oVgnVCM10000o1ao1o1oaRCRD&vgnextchannel=e449aocaqe3f1o1oVgnVCM10000o1ao1o1oaRCRD (accessed 3/29/2008).

121. Joseph Hawley to Charles Warner, May 27, 1884, in Papers of Joseph R. Hawley, 1638–1906, Library of Congress, 29 reels, Connecticut State Library.

122. "Three Men with One Wish," *New York Sun*, August 8, 1886, 3; "Morgan G. Bulkeley Political Scrapbook, 1885–88," MS 93631, Connecticut Historical Society, Hartford.

123. "The Vote Count," *Hartford Daily Times*, November 10, 1882, 2. The total vote count was 114,165, with Waller garnering 59,180, while Billy Bulkeley got 54,526. The Prohibitionist candidate and a fourth party hopeful got 1,459 between them.

124. "A Letter from Chairman Cole," *Hartford Daily Courant*, December 15, 1882, 1. From the drawings of the ballots ("The Black Ballots," *Hartford Daily Courant*, December 15,

1882, 1), it is clear that black paper was not actually used. Instead a printer's block was engraved with the candidates' names, inked and then pressed onto white ballot paper. The result was a ballot completely covered with black ink except for the white-lettered names of those running for office.

125. "A Question for Mr. Waller," *Hartford Daily Courant*, December 9, 1882, 2.

126. "The Black Ballots," *Hartford Daily Courant*, December 28, 1882, 2.

127. "Gen. W. H. Bulkeley, Death of a Prominent Business Man," *Hartford Courant*, November 8, 1902, 2.

128. "Current Comment," *Hartford Courant*, December 18, 1882, 1.

129. Weaver (1969), 15; "Electric Light at Hartford," *Boston Daily Globe*, July 22, 1884, 2.

130. Weaver (1969), 28.

131. Ibid., 34.

132. "The Waterloo," *Hartford Daily Courant*, Apr. 6, 1880, 2.; "The Revolution in Hartford," *Hartford Daily Courant*, Apr. 2, 1872, 2.

6. WEDDING BELLS

1. See the Bulkeleys' mustaches in this book's photos.

2. Gergely Baics, "The Saloons of Hartford's East Side," report written with an award by the U. S. Department of Housing and Urban Development, Trinity College, Hartford, at http://www.trincoll.edu/depts/tcn/Research_Reports/60.htm (accessed 3/21/2008).

3. J. H. Beers & Co., *Commemorative Biographical Record of Hartford County* (Chicago: J. H. Beers & Co., 1901), 68.

4. Telephone interview with Morgan Bulkeley's grandson, Peter Bulkeley, September 11, 2002.

5. Marion Hepburn Grant, *The Fenwick Story* (Hartford: Connecticut Historical Society, 1974), 99; *California Historical Society Quarterly*, vol. 26: 240–41; vol. 30: 134–35.

6. California State Lands Commission, "James F. Houghton, 1862–66," at http://www .slc.ca.gov/Misc_Pages/Historical/Surveyors_General/Houghton.html (accessed 05/31/ 2009).

7. Ibid.

8. Ibid.

9. *National Cyclopedia of American Biography* (New York: J. T. White, 1897), 146.

10. Ibid.

11. Ibid.

12. National Park Service, "Golden Spike," at http://www.nps.gov/gosp (accessed 12/23/2008).

13. *California Historical Society Quarterly.*

14. Rootsweb, "Houghton/Haughton Project," Person Page 155, at http://freepages .genealogy.rootsweb.ancestry.com/houghtonfamily/p155.htm#i9982 (accessed 3/29/ 2008).

15. U.S. Census Records, 1860, 1870, 1880, 1900.

16. *California Historical Society Quarterly.*

17. J. P. Munro-Fraser, *History of Santa Clara County, California.* San Francisco: Alley, Bowen & Co., 1881, 420.

18. U.S. Census Records, 1900, 1910, 1920.

19. Stanford University, "History of Stanford," at http://www.stanford.edu/about/history (accessed 12/15/2008).

20. "Hartford and Vicinity, City Briefs," *Hartford Daily Courant*, July 21, 1884, 2.

21. "Morgan G. Bulkeley Political Scrapbook, 1881–89," MS 93631, Connecticut Historical Society, Hartford.

22. Francis E. Hyde, *Cunard and the North Atlantic, 1840–1973: A History of Shipping and Financial Management* (Atlantic Highlands, NJ: Humanities Press, 1975), appendix, 328–29.

23. Norway-Heritage, "Hands Across the Sea: SS *Servia*, Cunard Line," at http://www.norwayheritage.com/p_ship.asp?sh=servi (accessed 12/15/2008).

24. "Aetna Insurance Co. of Hartford" (advt.), *Hartford Daily Courant*, September 22, 1884, 4.

25. "Lord's Hill, 1840–1850: An Interesting Sketch," *Hartford Courant*, June 14, 1887, 1.

26. Nathaniel H. Morgan, *Morgan Genealogy: A History of James Morgan, of New London, Conn., and His Descendants; from 1607 to 1869.* (Hartford, CT: Case, Lockwood & Brainard), 1869, 17–18.

27. "Obituary, Junius S. Morgan," *The Hartford Courant*, April 9, 1890, 1; "The Early Life and the Rise to Power of J. Pierpont Morgan," *The Hartford Courant*, April 1, 1913, 10. These two obituary articles, particularly the latter, explain J. P. Morgan's childhood in Hartford. He was born on Asylum Street (opposite the Allyn House) and later lived in the Morgan Homestead at 108 Farmington Avenue (the site of St. Joseph's Cathedral today) until he was fourteen years old. At that time, 1851, the family relocated to Boston, where he got his secondary education at the English High School on Bedford Street. This article also states that J. P. Morgan attended the West Middle (Lord's Hill) School—located on the land created by the fork of Asylum Street and Farmington Avenue. Lastly, it documents the Morgan connections with George Peabody & Co.; J. S. Morgan & Co.; Dabney, Morgan & Co.; and finally Drexel, Morgan & Co.

28. "City Personals," *The Hartford Courant*, August 19, 1884, 3. The *Grand Hotel News* noted, "Leander Hall, superintendent of the Hartford Hospital, accompanied by his wife and friends, Mr. and Mrs. E. S. Kibbe and Mrs. Wadsworth are with us. We welcome them to our new mountain home."

29. "City Briefs," *The Hartford Daily Courant*, September 13, 1884, 2.

30. Barney Warf, *Time-Space Compression* (Milton Park, UK: Routledge, 2008), 107.

31. "The *Alaska*'s Rapid Voyage," *New York Times*, September 22, 1884, 8.

32. Bulkeley, Morgan, Envelope of Memorabilia, MS 72426, Connecticut Historical

Society, Hartford. In September 1884, Morgan Bulkeley was forty-six (b. December 26, 1837), Caroline Houghton was fifty-two (b. March 29, 1832) and Fannie Houghton was twenty-four (b. July 3, 1860).

33. "Marine Intelligence, New York, Sunday, Sept. 21," *New York Times*, September 22, 1884, 8.

34. "City Briefs," *Hartford Daily Courant*, September 18, 1884, 2.

35. "Hartford and Vicinity, City Briefs," *Hartford Daily Courant*, November 17, 1884, 2.

36. "Hartford and Vicinity, City Briefs," *Hartford Daily Courant*, January 12, 1885, 1.

37. Lucius Beebe, *Mr. Pullman's Elegant Palace Car* (New York: Doubleday & Co., 1961), 351–61.

38. Central Pacific Railroad Photographic History Museum and History, "Palace Hotel" at http://cprr.org/Museum/Palace_Hotel_SF (accessed 3/30/2008).

39. Bruce C. Cooper, "A Brief Illustrated History of the Palace Hotel," at http://the palacehotel.org (accessed 12/23/2008).

40. "Mary Morris Scrapbook Collection" (social), Vol. II, Connecticut Historical Society, Hartford.

41. Ibid.

42. Ibid.

43. Ibid.

44. Ibid.; Stanford University, "History of Stanford." There is no mention of Billy and Emma Bulkeley in attendance.

45. "McCauley-Bulkeley, Chrysanthemum Wedding at the Pearl Street Church," *Hartford Courant*, November 8, 1895, 6.

46. "Mary Morris Scrapbook Collection."

47. Ibid.

48. Ibid.

49. Louis Quinze refers to French Classical, Rococo and early Neo-Classical architecture, furniture and decorations of the reign of King Louis XV (1715–74), characterized by its charm, lightness, and elegance.

50. Ibid.

51. John Kendall, *History of New Orleans* (Chicago: The Lewis Publishing Company, 1922), 457–67.

52. Ibid.

53. Matriculation Records, 1885, Miss Porter's School, Farmington, CT.

54. M. H. Grant (1974), 100.

55. Ibid., 100.

56. Ibid., 102.

57. *Connecticut Quarterly*, vol. 1, no. 1, January, February, March, 1895, 296.

1. "The City Elections," *Hartford Times*, April 7, 1884, 8.

2. "The Fifth Ward," *Hartford Times*, April 8, 1884, 8.

3. "The City Elections: A Mixed General Ticket," *Hartford Daily Courant*, April 8, 1884, 2.

4. "The Mayor's Message," *Hartford Daily Courant*, April 21, 1885, 2.

5. "Entertainments: 'The Bohemian Girl,' " *Hartford Daily Courant*, May 15, 1885, 2.

6. The actor Karl Malden played the Gypsy King in *The Bohemian Girl* while he was in high school and delivered this harsh assessment of the aria. (Karl Malden, *When Do I Start? A Memoir* (New York: Simon & Schuster, 1997), 32.

7. "Gen. Grant's Death," *Hartford Daily Courant*, July 24, 1885, 2.

8. "The Grant Memorial," *Hartford Daily Courant*, August 7, 1885, 2.

9. "Mayor Bulkeley Renominated," *Hartford Daily Courant*, April 1, 1886, 2.

10. "All Sorts of Tickets," *Hartford Daily Courant*, April 5, 1886, 2.

11. Ibid.

12. Ibid.

13. "Hartford City Election," *New York Times*, April 6, 1886, 2.

14. "Mayor Bulkeley Re-Elected," *Hartford Times*, April 6, 1886, 5.

15. Ibid.

16. "A Satisfactory Result," *Hartford Daily Courant*, April 5, 1886, 2.

17. Glenn Weaver, *The Hartford Electric Light Company* (Hartford: The Hartford Electric Light Company, 1969), 37.

18. "Naphtha Condemned," *Hartford Daily Courant*, September 10, 1883, 1. Hartford's naphtha streetlight contract was in the hands of Boston Globe Gas Light Company at the time this article was written. Since the city started using naphtha in 1877—to augment coal gas—different suppliers bid on the work. Naphtha lamps ran about 60 percent of what coal gas lamps cost, and there was considerable interest in them. However, they gave off less light and blew out more often than the coal gas models.

19. J. Hammond Trumbull, *The Memorial History of Hartford County: 1633–1884* (Boston: Edward L. Osgood, Publisher, 1886), 462. When the gas company first went into operation in 1849 they were getting about $4 per thousand cubic feet for their coal gas. This price slid to $2.40 on the eve of the Civil War, but was driven back up to $4 by wartime inflation. In its fierce battle with Morgan Bulkeley's Hartford Electric Light Company, Hartford Gas Company's price eventually plummeted to $1.60 in 1885. Efforts to keep the city's street-light contract proved an exercise in futility for the gas company.

20. Ibid., 15.

21. "Hartford News, City Briefs," *Hartford Daily Courant*, April 22, 1886, 2.

22. "Visiting the Reservoirs," *Hartford Daily Courant*, June 5, 1886, 2.

23. "Mr. Garvie's Injunction," *Hartford Daily Courant*, March 26, 1886, 2.

24. "The Garvie Case Decided," *Hartford Daily Courant*, February 4, 1887, 2.

25. "An Execution against the City," *Hartford Daily Courant*, June 16, 1886, 2.

26. "Hartford News, Sale of the Black Maria," *Hartford Daily Courant*, July 22, 1886, 3.

27. "The Republican Convention," *Hartford Daily Courant*, September 8, 1886, 2.

28. [No title], *The Springfield Republican*, August 28, 1886, 2.

29. National Governor's Association, "Governor's Information: Connecticut Governor Phineas Chapman Lounsbury," at http://www.nga.org/portal/site/nga/menuitem.29fab9f b4add37305ddcbeeb50101oa0/?vgnextoid=32ca224971c81010VgnVCMI000001a01010aRC RD&vgnextchannel=e449a0ca9e3f1010VgnVCMI000001a01010aRCRD (accessed 4/3/2008).

30. "Recollections of Forty Years in Connecticut Politics," *Hartford Courant*, October 25, 1914, E21–-23.

31. "Lounsbury and Howard," *Hartford Daily Courant*, September 10, 1886, 1.

32. "Gen. Hawley," *Hartford Courant*, March 18, 1905, 1; "Recollections of Forty Years in Connecticut Politics."

33. "The Campaign: Mayor Bulkeley's Congratulations," *Hartford Daily Courant*, September 11, 1886, 2.

34. "Reception by Mayor Bulkeley," *Hartford Daily Courant*, September 16, 1886, 1.

35. "Reception at Mayor Bulkeley's," *Hartford Daily Courant*, January 15, 1887, 1.

36. "Mr. Lounsbury's Winter Residence," *Hartford Daily Courant*, November 22, 1886, 2; "A Winter Residence," *Hartford Daily Courant*, November 2, 1887, 5.

37. Connecticut State Library, "Raymond Earl Baldwin, Governor of Connecticut," at http://www.cslib.org/gov/baldwinr.htm (accessed 12/17/2008).

38. Connecticut Historical Society, "Civil War Monuments of Connecticut," at http://www.chs.org/ransom/049.htm (accessed 3/30/2008). Connecticut sent about 45,000 young men off to war, and as a result of the conflict, 12,350 were dead or wounded; still others were missing. Hartford alone supplied 4,000 soldiers, of which 400 died. John Niven, *Connecticut for the Union: The Role of the State in the Civil War* (New Haven, CT: Yale University Press, 1965), 87–91, 262–63; Glenn Weaver, *Hartford: An Illustrated History of Connecticut's Capital* (Woodland Hills, CA: Windsor Publications, 1982), 82–83).

39. "The Memorial Arch: The Structure Dedicated," *Hartford Daily Courant*, September 18, 1886, 1.

40. Ibid.

41. Ibid.

42. J. H. Beers & Co., *Commemorative Biographical Record of Hartford County* (Chicago: J. H. Beers & Co., 1901), 1393.

43. "Rev. J. H. Twichell Dies at Four Score," *Hartford Courant*, December 21, 1918, 2.

44. "The Bridge Ordered: The Overhead Plan Unanimously Adopted," *Hartford Daily Courant*, March 12, 1887, 2.

45. "Asylum Street Bridge: A Thoroughly Satisfactory Test Yesterday," *Hartford Courant*, December 6, 1888, 4.

46. "City Intelligence," *Hartford Times*, May 23, 1887, 5.

47. Ibid.

48. Papers of Morgan Bulkeley, Boxes #82, #84, State Archives, Connecticut State Library, Hartford.

49. Ellsworth Grant, *The Club on Prospect Street: A History of the Hartford Club* (Hartford, CT: The Hartford Club, 1984), 29.

50. Albert E. Van Dusen, *Connecticut: A Fully Illustrated History of the State from the Seventeenth Century to the Present* (New York: Random House, 1961), 218.

51. [No Title] *New Haven Union*, March 25, 1888, 2.

52. "The Electric Lights: Mayor Vetoes . . . ," *Hartford Courant*, January 24, 1888, 2.

53. "A Great Storm: A Genuine Blizzard," *Hartford Courant*, March 13, 1888, 1.

54. "Relieving the Poor," *Hartford Courant*, March 13, 1888, 2.

55. "A Republican Victory: Result of the City Election," *Hartford Courant*, April 3, 1888, 1.

56. Beers, 192–93.

57. "Gen. Dwight Elected," *Hartford Courant*, April 8, 1890, 1.

58. "Citizen's Rally," *Hartford Daily Courant*, April 13, 1858, 2; "City Intelligence: The City Election," *Hartford Daily Courant*, April 12, 1864, 2; "The Election: A Glorious Result," *Hartford Daily Courant*, April 2, 1872, 2.

59. "Mayor Root: The New Mayor Sworn In," *Hartford Courant*, April 4, 1888, 8.

60. Ibid.

61. "Ex-Gov. Morgan Bulkeley's Rare Horn Book," *Hartford Courant*, November 7, 1915, X8. A hornbook was a piece of board with a handle. On the face of the hornbook was a piece of paper upon which a pupil's lesson was inscribed. A sheet of translucent horn protected the paper from a student's dirty fingers.

62. "President Morgan Bulkeley of Aetna Life," *Hartford Courant*, February 8, 1916, 1.

63. "The Connecticut Valley Railroad," *Hartford Courant*, January 21, 1870, 2. The sad story of Charter Oak Life can be found in almost any book about Fenwick or Hartford, including those of Albert Van Dusen, Glenn Weaver and Marion Hepburn Grant.

64. "Connecticut Valley Railroad: Contract Awarded," *Hartford Courant*, March 21, 1870, 2.

65. Kevin Murphy, *Water for Hartford: The Story of the Hartford Water Works and the Metropolitan District Commission* (Wethersfield, CT: Shining Tramp Press, 2004), 99.

66. Marion Hepburn Grant,. *The Fenwick Story* (Hartford: Connecticut Historical Society, 1974), 19.

67. Ibid., 18.

68. Ibid., 21.

69. "The Charter Oak Life," *Hartford Daily Courant*, January 30, 1883, 2.

70. "Charter Oak Building," *Hartford Courant*, March 9, 1888, 8.

71. "The Charter Oak Building," *Hartford Courant*, April 9, 1888, 8.

72. Ibid.

73. "The Charter Oak Life Building," *Hartford Courant*, April 26, 1888, 8. Foreclosure

laws differ from state to state, but most offer a "right of redemption," allowing the party whose property has been foreclosed to reclaim that property by making payment in full of the sum of the unpaid loan plus costs (prior to sale or auction). Obviously, Charter Oak Life, as a bankrupt corporation, could not raise the necessary funds and the building went to the first mortgage holder, Aetna Life.

74. "The Proposed Charter Oak Block," *Hartford Daily Courant*, April 9, 1868, 2.

75. "Hits States' Demands for Federal Aid," *Hartford Courant*, May 31, 1933, 3. The shift of power from the Northeastern and Midwestern industrialists and Wall Street bankers to Washington, D.C., was a slow and subtle process. In the Panic of 1907, it was J. P. Morgan and other Wall Street bankers who brought order out of chaos. However, with the Income Tax Act of 1913, the Federal Reserve Act of 1913, and the Volstead Act of 1919, the stage was quietly set for Washington to assume greater power over the states. The above-cited article quotes Dr. William Morgan, regent of Georgetown University and former president of the American Medical Association who stated, "The gradual usurpation of the functions of the individual states by the Federal Government is advancing so insidiously that the great masses of the people are unaware of the extent to which it has already gone."

76. "The Charter Oak Life Building," *Hartford Courant*, April 26, 1888, 8.

77. Richard Hooker, *Aetna Life Insurance Company: Its First Hundred Years* (Hartford, CT: Aetna Life Insurance Co., 1956), 120.

8. CROWBAR GOVERNOR

1. Ellsworth Grant, *The Club on Prospect Street: A History of the Hartford Club* (Hartford, CT: The Hartford Club, 1984), 31.

2. "Recollections of Forty Years in Connecticut Politics," *Hartford Courant* October 25, 1914, E21–23.

3. "The "Allies" of Prohibition," *Hartford Daily Courant*, August 28, 1886, 2; "The Democrats Backing Prohibition," *Hartford Courant*, July 30, 1888, 1.

4. "The Election," *Hartford Daily Courant*, Apr. 7, 1874, 2.

5. "Old Connecticut," *Hartford Times*, November 7, 1888, 4. The *Times* gave the makeup of the General Assembly in 1888 as Democrats 8, Republicans 16 in the Senate, and Democrats 105, Republicans 144 in the House, ensuring that any race tossed into the legislature would be decided in favor of the Republicans.

6. [No title], *The Gazette & Courier* (Franklin County, Massachusetts), August 10, 1874, n.p. In Birdsall's obituary, Mrs. Troubee is mentioned as Birdsall's widow.

7. "City Briefs," *Hartford Daily Courant*, November 2, 1883, 2.

8. "The Hartford Telegram: A New Haven Opinion of It," *Hartford Courant*, July 4, 1888, 5.

9. Ibid.

10. "Arrested for Embezzlement: Daniel C. Birdsall . . . ," *Hartford Daily Courant*, May 7, 1887, 1.

11. "Judge Birdsall's Taste for Fingers," *Hartford Daily Courant*, April 2, 1886, 2; "Judge Birdsall Arrested for Assault," *Hartford Daily Courant*, April 5, 1886, 2.

12. "D. C. Birdsall Arrested, Charged with Printing Abusive Matter," *Hartford Courant*, July 4, 1888, 5.

13. Richard Hooker, *Aetna Life Insurance Company: Its First Hundred Years*. (Hartford, CT: Aetna Life Insurance Co., 1956), 108.

14. Hooker, 109.

15. Ibid.

16. Ibid.

17. Ibid.

18. "D. C. Birdsall Arrested," *Hartford Courant*, July 4, 1888, 2.

19. "Birdsall Again Arrested, Condemned by Business Men," *Hartford Courant*, July 6, 1888, 5.

20. "Birdsall Arrested Again: A Civil Suit by the Aetna Life for $25,000," *Hartford Courant*, October 6, 1888, 8.

21. Hooker, 110.

22. "A Specimen Birdsall Fabrication," *Hartford Courant*, October 31, 1888, 1.

23. "D. C. Birdsall Dead," *Hartford Courant*, December 5, 1891, 8.

24. "Three Men with One Wish," *New York Sun*, August 8, 1886, 3; "Morgan G. Bulkeley Political Scrapbook, 1885–88," MS 93631, Connecticut Historical Society, Hartford.

25. Connecticut State Library, "Obituary Sketch of Luzon B. Morris," at http://www.cslib.org/memorials/morrisl.htm (accessed 4/5/2008).

26. "The Republicans: A Good Day's Work," *Hartford Courant*, August 16, 1888, 2.

27. "In Connecticut, Bulkeley Will Be Governor," *Hartford Courant*, November 7, 1888, 1.

28. "Old Connecticut," *Hartford Times*, November 7, 1888, 4.

29. "The Great Democratic Fizzle," *Hartford Courant*, November 7, 1888, 8.

30. Ibid.

31. Ibid.

32. Ibid.

33. "Gov. Bulkeley's Staff," *Hartford Courant*, January 11, 1889, 5.

34. Samuel Hart et al., *Encyclopedia of Connecticut Biography* (Boston: American Historical Society, 1917), 225.

35. J. H. Beers & Co., *Commemorative Biographical Record of Hartford County* (Chicago: J. H. Beers & Co., 1901), 58–59.

36. "The Changes of Today," *Hartford Courant*, January 10, 1889, 4.

37. Ibid.

38. "The Governor's Message," *Hartford Courant*, January 11, 1889, 4.

39. Ibid.

40. "The Governor's Message." In Morgan Bulkeley's inaugural message to the Gen-

eral Assembly, he said of the state's indebtedness, "Provisions should be in my judgment be made for the redemption of this debt at maturity by the creation of a sinking fund." He also stated that "the rate of state taxation can be reduced to one mill . . . [and] this tax can be still further reduced and eventually eliminated entirely." Solid proposals to reduce state spending are conspicuously absent from the inaugural messages of Bulkeley's nearest Democratic predecessor, Thomas Waller (1883), or his closest Democratic successor, Luzon Morris (1893). The complete text of these messages can be found in the *Hartford Courant*, January 4, 1883, 1; and the *Hartford Courant*, January 5, 1893, 8.

41. "The Governor's Message."

42. *Connecticut Public Acts 1915–1919*, "An Act Concerning the Retirement of State Employees," 189, Connecticut State Library, Hartford.

43. "The Inaugural Reception: A Success . . . ," *Hartford Courant*, January 11, 1889, 1.

44. Ibid.

45. "Governor Bulkeley's Correspondence, Incoming Letters," RG 5, Box #46, Connecticut State Library, Hartford.

46. Ibid.

47. Ibid.

48. Ibid.

49. Ibid.

50. "Governor Bulkeley's Correspondence, Outgoing Letters," RG 5, Box #78, Connecticut State Library, Hartford.

51. "Yale Alumni Assoc., Banquet in Foot Guard Hall," *Hartford Courant*, February 7, 1889, 8.

52. Ibid.

53. "Charter Oak Park," *Hartford Courant*, February 6, 1889, 8.

54. "The General Assembly," *Hartford Courant*, February 16, 1889, 8.

55. "He Has Painted Five Governors: Charles Noel Flagg . . . ," *Hartford Courant*, January 16, 1905, 3.

56. "The General Assembly, 1889," *Hartford Courant*, February 21, 1889, 3; "The General Assembly, Session 1889," *Hartford Courant*, March 13, 1889, 2.

57. "The General Assembly, Session of 1889," *Hartford Courant*, May 29, 1889, 2.

58. "On to Washington," *Hartford Courant*, March 1, 1889, 5.

59. William Manners, *TR and Will: A Friendship That Split the Republican Party* (New York: Harcourt, Brace & World, 1969), 29.

60. Ibid.

61. "Wide Awakes at Washington," *Hartford Courant*, March 8, 1889, 1.

62. Ibid.

63. Ibid.

64. "Obituary, Mrs. Gen. Hawley," *Hartford Courant*, March 4, 1886, 2.

65. Agnes Repplier, *J. William White, MD* (New York: Houghton Mifflin, 1919), 49.

66. "Senator Hawley Married," *New York Times*, November 16, 1887, 1.

67. W. T. Sherman to J. R. Hawley, November 6, 1888, Papers of Joseph Hawley, L.C., Accessed at Connecticut State Library, Hartford.

68. "Senator Hawley Married"; "Their Wedding Day, Hawley-Horner," *Boston Globe*, November 16, 1887, 8.

69. "The General Assembly," *Hartford Courant*, March 22, 1889, 3; "The General Assembly," *Hartford Courant*, March 30,1889, 3; "The General Assembly," *Hartford Courant*, April 4, 1889, 3.

70. "General Merwin for Governor," *Hartford Courant*, May 21, 1890, 4. The legislature adjourned before May 21 in 1890 with very little accomplished.

71. "Swift's Reprieve," *Hartford Courant*, April 5, 1889, 5.

72. "The Swift Case," *Hartford Courant*, April 16, 1889, 8.

73. Ibid.

74. "The Law Is Appeased, John H. Swift Is Hanged," *Hartford Courant*, April 19, 1889, 1.

75. "He Has Painted Five Governors: Charles Noel Flagg."

76. "Connecticut's Delegation," *Hartford Courant*, May 1, 1889, 1.

77. "Gov. Bulkeley's Reception," *Hartford Courant*, May 29, 1889, 1.

78. Ibid.

79. "The Secret Ballot Bill," *Hartford Courant*, June 8, 1889, 4.

80. Ibid.

81. "The Hartford Toll Bridge," *Hartford Courant*, February 8, 1889, 8; "The General Assembly," *Hartford Courant*, June 4, 1889, 2.

82. "Yale Commencement," *Hartford Courant*, June 27, 1889, 1.

83. "From Grocery Store to the U.S. Senate," *Hartford Courant*, April 13, 1908, 2.

84. "Governor Bulkeley's Papers, Incoming Letters," RG 5, Box #46, State Archives, Connecticut State Library, Hartford.

85. Ibid.

86. "The President Coming," *Hartford Courant*, July 2,1889, 1.

87. "Connecticut's Greeting," *Hartford Courant*, July 4, 1889, 1.

88. "The Glorious Fourth," *Hartford Courant*, July 5, 1889, 1.

89. Ibid.

90. Ibid.

91. "President Harrison, His Journey . . . ," *Hartford Courant*, July 6, 1889, 1.

92. Ibid.

93. Ibid.

94. "Horses and Horsemen," *Hartford Courant*, March 8, 1890, 1.

95. Ibid.

96. Ibid.

97. Ibid.

98. "Harry Houghton, Superintendent Agencies, Pacific Div., Aetna Life Insurance Co., 511–13, Safe Deposit Bldg," *San Francisco City Directory*, 1890, 1901.

99. Biographical History of the United States Congress, "Stanford, Leland," at http://bioguide.congress.gov/scripts/biodisplay.pl?index=S000793 (accessed 4/6/2008).

100. U.S. Supreme Court, 75 U. S. (8 Wall) 168 (1869).

101. David P. Currie, *The Constitution in the Supreme Court* (Chicago: University of Chicago Press, 1985), 352; Insurance Data Management Association, at http://www.idma.org, (accessed 12/26/2008). One of the small advantages the government still allows the insurance industry is the right to share information. In theory, this leads to more competitive pricing of insurance products.

102. "Talcott v. Philbrick: The Seventh Ward Case in Court Again," *Hartford Courant*, May 16, 1890, 1.

103. Ibid.

104. "The Ballots Void," *Hartford Courant*, October 9, 1890, 1.

105. "Recollections of Forty Years in Connecticut Politics."

106. "The State Vote," *Hartford Courant*, November 6, 1890, 1.

107. Ibid.

108. "Morris Not Elected," *Hartford Courant*, November 7, 1890, 4.

109. Ibid.

110. "Three Men with One Wish"; "Morgan G. Bulkeley Political Scrapbook, 1885-88."

111. Albert E. Van Dusen, *Connecticut: A Fully Illustrated History of the State from the Seventeenth Century to the Present* (New York: Random House, 1961), 244, 260.

112. "The Governor's Proclamation," *Hartford Courant*, January 20, 1891, 4.

113. "Brer Rabbit Bulkeley," *The Springfield Republican* (repr. in the *Hartford Times*, November 15, 1890, 4).

114. "Crazy Politicians . . . ," *Hartford Courant*, January 14, 1891, 1.

115. Ibid.

116. Ibid.

117. Ibid.

118. Ibid.

119. Ibid.

120. "The Governor's Proclamation."

121. "Recollections of Forty Years in Connecticut Politics."

122. Ibid.

123. "Electing Senators from 1887–1891," *Hartford Courant*, December 21, 1913, 12.

124. "The Governor Opens the Door," *Hartford Courant*, March 23, 1891, 1.

125. Ibid.

126. Ibid.

127. "Former Sheriff's Funeral Today, James Price Used Crowbar at State Capitol in Bulkeley's Time," *Hartford Courant*, October 10, 1923, 11.

128. Ibid.

129. "To the Courts at Last," *Hartford Courant*, April 14, 1891, 1.

130. "The Senate's Future Action," *Hartford Courant*, April 2, 1891, 4; "Another Refusal," *Hartford Courant*, April 30, 1891, 1; "In the Senate: A Proposition . . . ," *Hartford Courant*, May 15, 1891, 4.

131. "Afternoon Session, Some Interesting Questions and Answers . . . ," *Hartford Courant*, May 7, 1879, 2.

132. "Money to Be Furnished," *Hartford Courant*, May 9, 1891, 1.

133. Hooker, 125.

134. "Political Notes," *New York Times*, November 16, 1891, 4 (repr. from the *New Bedford Journal*, November 3, 1891).

135. "The Courant: The Oldest Newspaper in the United States," *Hartford Courant*, December 10, 1892, 1. There are many articles in the *Courant* over the years telling the story of the newspaper's different owners. When the *Evening Press* merged with the *Courant* in 1867, the five owners were Joseph Hawley, Charles Dudley Warner, William Goodrich, Thomas M. Day, and Able N. Clark. In 1888, Charles Hopkins Clark bought the late Able Clark's one-fifth share. In 1891, a new corporation, the *Hartford Courant Company*, was formed with Charles Hopkins Clark as president. By then, Charles Dudley Warner was dead and Gen. Hawley was no longer involved in the paper's day-to-day management.

136. "The Great Case, Bulkeley Governor De Jure . . . ," *Hartford Courant*, January 6, 1892, 1.

137. "Is Ready for Business," *Hartford Courant*, February 26, 1891, 1; "The Comptroller Yields, Mr. Brainard Can Have His Salary," *Hartford Courant*, January 7, 1892, 8.

138. "Hartford's Heavy Vote: A Quiet Election . . . ," *Hartford Courant*, November 9, 1892, 4.

139. "Ready for Business, Connecticut's Legislative Machinery . . . ," *Hartford Courant*, January 5, 1893, 1.

140. Ibid.

141. "Corrupt Practices: Bulkeley's Views," *Hartford Courant*, May 12, 1893, 1.

142. "Edward Spicer Cleveland," *Hartford Courant*, September 3, 1886, 1; *Hartford Courant*, September 30, 1886, 1.

143. "Corrupt Practices: Bulkeley's Views."

9. ON THE SIDELINES

1. "Governor Bulkeley Gives a Dinner," *Hartford Courant*, January 11, 1894, 4.

2. "Recollections of Forty Years in Connecticut Politics," *Hartford Courant*, October 25, 1914, E21–23.

3. "The Latest Figures," *Hartford Courant*, November 11, 1892, 4.

4. "Nutmeg Republicans," *Boston Daily Globe*, September 21, 1882, 5; "General Assembly: Liquor Matters," *Hartford Daily Courant*, April 15, 1881, 1. Reporting directly from the

Republican State Convention at New Haven in 1882, the *Boston Daily Globe* printed an article, "The Following Is a Text of the Platform." In it, the newspaper noted, "[The Republican Party] therefore declares itself in favor of submitting to the people, at a special election to be held for the purpose, the Amendment to the Constitution proposed at the last session of the General Assembly, relative to the prohibition of the sale and manufacture of intoxicating liquors." (*Boston Daily Globe*, September 21, 1882, 5).

5. The twenty presidents who were governors first include: Thomas Jefferson, James Monroe, Martin Van Buren, John Tyler, James Polk, Rutherford Hayes, Grover Cleveland, William McKinley, Theodore Roosevelt, Franklin Roosevelt, Woodrow Wilson, Calvin Coolidge, Jimmy Carter, Ronald Reagan, William Clinton, and George W. Bush; There were three territorial/military governors: Andrew Jackson, Andrew Johnson, and William H. Harrison. Lastly, William H. Taft was governor-general of the Philippines.

6. "The Constitution," *Hartford Courant*, April 17, 1901, 8; Brer Rabbit Bulkeley, *Springfield Republican* (repr. in *The Hartford Times*, November 15, 1890, 4).

7. "Recollections of Forty Years in Connecticut Politics."

8. "Chief Justice Park: He Retired Yesterday," *Hartford Courant*, April 27, 1889, 4.

9. Louis A. Coolidge, *Orville H. Platt of Connecticut* (New York and London: G. P. Putnam's Sons, 1910), 537.

10. J. H. Beers, & Co., *Commemorative Biographical Record of Hartford County* (Chicago: J. H. Beers & Co., 1901), 34–35.

11. Barbara A. White, *The Beecher Sisters* (New Haven: Yale University Press, 2003), 83.

12. "History of 'The Courant' . . . ," *Hartford Courant*, October 25, 1914, E2.

13. "An Interesting Find: Call for Formation of the Republican Party in Connecticut," *Hartford Courant*, October 16, 1896, 6.

14. J. R. Hawley to Charles W. Warner, *Hartford Times*, November 9, 1929 (repr. of 200 surviving Hawley letters); "Obituary, J. R. Hawley," *Hartford Courant*, March 18, 1905, 3.

15. "Senator Hawley: The Man and His Career," *New York Herald* (repr. in the *Hartford Courant*, July 25, 1898, 8.

16. "Recollections of Forty Years in Connecticut Politics."

17. Ibid.

18. "Obituary, Mrs. General Hawley," *Hartford Daily Courant*, March 4, 1886, 2.

19. L. P. Brockett and M. C. Vaughan, *Women's Work in the Civil War: A Record of Heroism, Patriotism and Patience*. (Philadelphia: Zeigler, McCurdy & Co., 1867), 416–19.

20. Robert Owen Decker, *Hartford Immigrants: A History of the Christian Activities Council (Congregational) 1850–1980* (New York: United Church Press, 1987), 5, 12–13.

21. Connecticut State Library, "Obituary Sketch of Samuel Fessenden," at http://www.cslib.org/memorials/fessendens.htm (accessed 4/7/2008).

22. "Recollections of Forty Years in Connecticut Politics."

23. "Election of Senator," *Hartford Courant*, January 19, 1893, 1; "The Senatorial Contest," *Hartford Courant*, January 11, 1899, 11.

24. "Largest Taxpayers," *Hartford Daily Courant*, April 10, 1866, 2; *Hartford Courant*, January 2, 1900, 14. Anytime a grand list was compiled for the City of Hartford, the Goodwins were always at the top of the list for individuals. In 1900, for example, Aetna Fire's assessed property value was $3.2 million and Aetna Life's was $2.5 million, but the assessed value of Francis Goodwin's real estate holdings was $948,000. His brother, James J. Goodwin, owned property assessed at $450,000.

25. [Editorial article 2–no title], *Daily Courant*, September 29, 1838, 2; "United States Hotel," *Hartford Courant*, May 23, 1901, 5.

26. *The Open Hearth, No. 135 Front Street* (in-house pamphlet), 1888, Connecticut State Library, Hartford; *Special Laws of Connecticut*, 1896, 713. Senate Resolution No. 289, incorporating The Open Hearth Corporation . . . Francis Goodwin, et al., approved June 14, 1896.

27. "Charles Pond's Mind," *Hartford Courant*, February 14, 1896, 4; Charles Pond's Habits," *Hartford Courant*, February 18, 1896, 4; "Charles Pond's Mind," *Hartford Courant*, February 25, 1896, 4.

28. "Mr. Keney's Will," *Hartford Courant*, November 23, 1894, 6.

29. Hartford Probate Court Records, Francis Goodwin's Will, vol. 331, p. 145 (admitted for probate October 9, 1923), Hartford Probate Court, Hartford, CT.

30. "A Free Bridge at Last," *Hartford Courant*, June 11, 1889, 1.

31. "Recollections of Forty Years in Connecticut Politics." In the matter of buying votes in the statehouse, the editor-in-chief of the *Courant*, Charles Clark, once claimed he had heard of "payments of $500 for legislators votes in governors' races . . . and once he heard of $18,000 for a single vote."

32. "Will Not Investigate," *Hartford Courant*, October 24, 1893, 1.

33. "Who's Got the Money?" *Hartford Courant*, October 10, 1893, 2.

34. "Hartford and Vicinity, Brief Mention," *Hartford Courant*, July 31, 1871, 2.

35. [Editorial article 2—no title], *Hartford Courant*, February 10, 1883, 2.

36. "The Injunction Stands," *Hartford Courant*, December 1, 1897, 6. Though Henry L. Goodwin and his attorney chased the matter through the courts, the Bridge Bill passed and was signed by Governor Bulkeley, making the Morgan Street Bridge free to all on September 10, 1889.

37. "Will Not Investigate," *Hartford Courant*, October 24, 1893, 1.

38. Beers, 247.

39. "M'Govern's Comedy . . . Ex-Gov. Bulkeley Nominated for Senator," *Hartford Courant*, October 20, 1894, 5.

40. "Republican Nominees . . . Ex-Gov. Bulkeley Withdraws from the McGovern Ticket," *Hartford Courant*, November 5, 1894, 6.

41. "Bulkeley and McGovern," *Hartford Courant*, November 8, 1894, 6 (repr. of story in the *Hartford Post*, November 7, 1894).

42. Beers, 247.

43. "Hartford and Vicinity, City Briefs," *Hartford Daily Courant*, April 28, 1881, 2.

44. "The Bridge Fire," *Hartford Courant*, May 20, 1895, 3.

45. Gergely Baics, "The Saloons of Hartford's East Side," report written with an award by the U.S. Department of Housing and Urban Development, Trinity College, Hartford, at http://www.trincoll.edu/depts/tcn/Research_Reports/60.htm (accessed 3/21/2008).

46. "Ferrying on the River," *Hartford Courant*, May 20, 1895, 4.

47. "Bridge Legislation," *Hartford Courant*, May 29, 1895, 10.

48. "The Bridge Commission, Morgan G. Bulkeley Elected President," *Hartford Courant*, July 4, 1895, 4.

49. "To Start the Ferries," *Hartford Courant*, December 24, 1895, 6.

50. "The Ice Breaking Up," *Hartford Courant*, February 8, 1896, 8.

51. "The Senatorship," *Hartford Courant*, January 9, 1899, 8.

52. "Gen. Hawley for Senator," *Hartford Courant*, January 12, 1899, 1.

53. Ibid.

54. Ibid.

55. "Letter from Gen. Hawley," *Hartford Courant*, January 21, 1899, 3.

56. Beers, 80.

57. Ibid.

58. "Committee Hearings, James G. Batterson . . . ," *Hartford Courant*, March 3, 1899, 7.

59. Beers, 23.

60. "Recollections of Forty Years in Connecticut Politics."

61. Albert E. Van Dusen, *Connecticut: A Fully Illustrated History of the State from the Seventeenth Century to the Present* (New York: Random House, 1961), 260–61; "Favor a Convention," *Hartford Courant*, October. 4, 1901, 1; "Governor's Advice," *Hartford Courant*, April 20, 1901, 2.

62. Ibid.

63. "General Assembly," *Hartford Courant*, April 4, 1901, 5; *Hartford Courant*, April 10, 1901, 8; *Hartford Courant*, April 12, 1901, 8; *Hartford Courant*, Apr. 17, 1901, 8; *Hartford Courant*, April 18, 1901, 8.

64. Beers, 23; "Obituary, James G. Batterson," *Hartford Courant*, September 18, 1901, 1.

65. "The Constitution," *Hartford Courant*, April 12, 1901, 8.

66. "At the Coliseum: Constitution Discussed at Meeting Last Night," *Hartford Courant*, July 14, 1902, 7.

67. "The Constitution," *Hartford Courant*, April 10, 1901, 8.

68. "Debate Closed," *Hartford Courant*, April 18, 1901, 8.

69. "Mr. Batterson," *Hartford Courant*, April 12, 1901, 8.

70. "Convention Assured," *Hartford Courant*, June 14, 1901, 3.

71. "James G. Batterson: Death Came at an Early Hour," *Hartford Courant*, September 18, 1901, 1.

72. "What the People Did on Monday: Reform Certain," *Hartford Courant*, October 9, 1901, 10; "Reform Certain," *Hartford Courant*, October 8, 1901, 1.

73. "In Convention," *Hartford Courant*, January 2, 1902, 1.

74. Van Dusen, 260–61.

75. Ibid.

76. "State Says, 'No.'" *Hartford Courant*, June 17, 1902, 1.

77. "President Roosevelt City's Guest," *Hartford Courant*, August 23, 1902, 1. While President McKinley was attending the Pan-American Exposition in Buffalo, he was gunned down by the anarchist, Leon Czolgosz. When he finally expired, it catapulted Teddy Roosevelt—who many Republican leaders regarded as a madman—into the presidency.

78. Ibid.

79. Ibid.

80. A low-hung, two-wheeled, covered vehicle drawn by one horse, for two passengers, with the driver being mounted on an elevated seat behind and the reins running over the roof.

81. Beers, 70–71; "Gen. W. H. Bulkeley: Death of Prominent Business Man," *Hartford Courant*, November 8, 1902, 2.

82. "Gen. Bulkeley's Estate," *Hartford Courant*, December 20, 1902, 4.

83. "Gen. James F. Houghton: Death in San Francisco," *Hartford Courant*, February 2, 1903, 9; Rootsweb, "Houghton/Haughton Project," Harry Bertram Houghton, #11,469, at http://freepages.genealogy.rootsweb.ancestry.com/houghtonfamily/p184.htm#i11468 (accessed 6/14/2009).

84. "State Commander, Ex-Gov. Bulkeley Chosen," *Hartford Courant*, May 9, 1903, 14.

85. "G.A.R. Encampment," *Hartford Courant*, June 11, 1903, 8; "Off for California, Department Officials G.A.R. and Guests," *Hartford Courant*, August 8, 1903, 4.

86. "City Personals, Social Gossip," *Hartford Courant*, September 9, 1903, 7.

87. "Enjoyed His Trip: Gov. Bulkeley Talks about West Coast," *Hartford Courant*, September 15, 1903, 4.

88. Richard Hooker, *Aetna Life Insurance Company: Its First Hundred Years* (Hartford, CT: Aetna Life Insurance Co., 1956), 103–4; 101.

89. "President Bulkeley's Office," *Hartford Courant*, July 8, 1904, 7.

90. "First Picture of Aetna Life's Remodeled Building," *Hartford Courant*, October 19, 1913, A11; "Cleaning Up on Aetna Life Building," *Hartford Courant*, October 13, 1914, 6.

10. FENWICK

1. Marion Hepburn Grant, *The Fenwick Story* (Hartford: Connecticut Historical Society, 1974), 16–18.

2. Ibid.

3. Newton C. Brainard, *Fenwick* (Hartford, CT: Case, Lockwood & Brainard Co., 1944), 18.

4. Grant, 94.

5. Grant, 93; Burial Records of Cedar Hill Cemetery (Section 1), Hartford CT.

6. Grant, 16–18.

7. "Fenwick Hall Notes," *Hartford Daily Courant*, August 1, 1871, 2.

8. Brainard, 12–13.

9. Grant, 22.

10. "Fenwick Hall," *Hartford Daily Courant*, May 24, 1875, 2. Though the daily rate before the cut to three dollars cannot be ascertained, based on weekly rates and other items in the newspapers, one can assume the daily rate was around four dollars.

11. U.S. Census Reports, 1870, 1880, 1900.

12. Photo CD2821, file: img.0001.pdg, Fenwick Hall (1871), Connecticut Historical Society, Hartford.

13. Grant, 37–38.

14. Paris Green—a very poisonous green copper and arsenic compound—was an extremely popular way of committing suicide in the nineteenth century. The powder was used as an insecticide and also as a pigment in Paris green oil paint. The powder was so toxic that newspapers constantly hammered the public with warnings like this one: "Paris green will rid any house of cockroaches or children" (*Hartford Daily Courant*, October 10, 1872, 2). Unfortunately for those with a death wish, it was officially banned for use as an insecticide in the United States on August 1, 1988. The renovations to the chapel were done by Barrett Brothers of Hartford, and completed about July 1, 1883 (*Hartford Daily Courant*, July 2, 1883, 2). G. Wells Root was a partner in the dry goods firm Root & Childs and was a well-respected member of the Hartford business community. Sadly, it was discovered after his death that he had taken $75,000 from the firm without the knowledge of his partners. This error in judgment made his "will . . . altogether bankrupt" (*Hartford Daily Courant*, April 13, 1897, 8).

15. Grant, 38.

16. "Hartford News, City Briefs," *Hartford Daily Courant*, August 16, 1886, 1; tel. interview with J. H. Kelso Davis, March 2, 2002.

17. Grant, 24–25;

18. Ibid. Richard Mansfield was a controversial German-American actor-producer of the late nineteenth century whose career took off with his popular adaptation of Robert Lewis Stevenson's *Dr. Jekyll and Mr. Hyde* (1887). His greatest success was in *Beau Brummel*. In 1892, Mansfield married Susan Hegeman, who had appeared with his company under her stage name, Beatrice Cameron. Her outstanding portrayals were Portia in *The Merchant of Venice* and Nora in *A Doll's House*.

19. Brainard, 41.

20. Ibid.

21. Ibid.

22. Ibid.

23. Ibid.

24. "The Sale of Fenwick Hall," *Hartford Courant*, September 10, 1887, 2; Grant, 23; Bill

Ryan, "Victoriana in the Fenwickian Tradition," *New York Times*, June 11, 1995, CN1; Brainard, 26.

25. "New York Letter, Fenwick Hall Sold," *Hartford Courant*, September 1, 1887, 1.

26. Ibid.

27. John Steele Gordon, "To a Speculator Dying Young," at http://www.americanheritage.com/articles/magazine/ah/1992/7/1992_7_18.shtml (accessed 4/9/2008).

28. W. A. Swanberg, *Jim Fisk: The Career of an Improbable Rascal* (New York: Charles Scribner & Sons, 1959), 1.

29. Gordon, "To a Speculator Dying Young."

30. Swanberg, 4, 41, 253.

31. Ibid., 4–10, 196–98.

32. Ibid., 120–21.

33. Ibid., 196, 254–58.

34. Gordon, "To a Speculator Dying Young."

35. "The Lesson of the Death and Life of Fisk," *Brooklyn Daily Eagle*, January 8, 1872, 2.

36. "The Stokes Case," *Brooklyn Daily Eagle*, October 24, 1872, 4; "Stokes: An Eagle Reporter Visits Him . . . ," *Brooklyn Daily Eagle*, February 8, 1873, 4; "Stokes Sentenced," *Brooklyn Daily Eagle*, October 30, 1873, 2; "Stokes Released," *Brooklyn Daily Eagle*, October 28, 1876, 2.

37. "New York Letter," *The Hartford Courant*, September 1, 1887, 1.

38. "Stokes Released," *The New York Times*, October 28, 1876, 2; Gordon, "To a Speculator Dying Young."

39. "Saybrook: Work in and about Fenwick Hall," *The Hartford Courant*, May 2, 1888, 6.

40. Grant, 24.

41. "Magician Herrmann Dead," *New York Times*, December 18, 1896, 5.

42. "Fenwick Hall Settles," *The Hartford Courant*, August 9, 1898, 4.

43. Brainard, 28.

44. "News of Fenwick," *Hartford Courant*, October 12, 1899, 10; "Improvements at Fenwick," *Hartford Courant*, June 12, 1900, 12; Grant, 100.

45. Grant, 100; U.S. Census Reports, 1920; *San Francisco City Directories*, 1920, 1921.

46. Grant, 100; U.S. Census Reports, 1880, 1900, 1910, 1920; *San Francisco City Directories*, 1920, 1921; "Obituary, Minnie Houghton Beacon," *Edmonton Journal*, October 6, 1923, 24; Province of Alberta, Medical Certificate of Cause of Death, October 4, 1923, Minnie Houghton Beacon.

47. Grant, 100; Newton Brainard recalled, "The course was the natural grass land full of blackberry vines . . . and each stroke was followed by a long hunt for the ball. Money enough was raised to have the grass cut twice a year with a farmer's hay-mowing machine" (Brainard, 44).

48. "Mrs. E. A. Bulkeley, Death of the Mother of Ex-Gov. Morgan Bulkeley," *Hartford Courant*, August 10, 1894, 1.

49. "Fenwick Hall Settles," *Hartford Courant*, August 9, 1898, 4.

50. Swanberg, 291–92.

51. "Fenwick Hall Settles," *Hartford Courant*, August 9, 1898, 4.

52. Old Saybrook Land Records, vol. 10, p. 162, August 11, 1898, Old Saybrook Town Hall, Old Saybrook, CT.

53. Stokes's purchase price in August 1887 was $16,500. His bill for back taxes to the Town of Old Saybrook by August 1898 was $7,043.97, a total of $23,543.97. Bulkeley's payment of $22,725 put Stokes's losses at $818.97 plus all other taxes, utilities, improvements, and repairs he made from 1887 to 1898.

54. "Death Ends E. S. Stokes' Years of Suffering," *Brooklyn Daily Eagle*, November 3, 1901, 8; "Fisk Murder in 1872 Recalled by Death, Josie Mansfield . . . ," *New York Times*, October 29, 1931, 14; "Only 3 Mourners at Josie Mansfield Bier," *New York Times*, October 30, 1931, 23.

55. Grant, 28.

56. "The General Assembly, Fenwick Borough," *Hartford Courant*, April 14, 1899, 7; "The General Assembly, Fenwick Borough," *Hartford Courant*, April 20, 1899, 7; "The General Assembly," *Hartford Courant*, April 28, 1899, 9.

57. Ibid.

58. Grant, 100; "News of Fenwick," *Hartford Courant*, October 12, 1899, 10; "Improvements at Fenwick," *Hartford Courant*, June 12, 1900, 3.

59. Grant, 100; "News of Fenwick"; "Improvements at Fenwick."

60. Willis Becker's advertisements in *Geer's Hartford City Directory*, 1899, 1900.

61. Grant, 100.

62. Ibid., 110.

63. Brainard (1944), 28; "Fenwick Predicts Successful Season," *Hartford Courant*, June 21, 1907, 17.

64. Brainard (1944), 185.

65. "Guests at Fenwick," *Hartford Courant*, July 13, 1912, 12.

66. "Aetna Life Club at Fenwick Today," *Hartford Courant*, June 20, 1914, 4; "Aetna Life Men in Annual Outing," *Hartford Courant*, June 21, 1914, 10.

67. Grant, 102; "Annual Outing, Aetna Life Club . . . ," *Hartford Courant*, June 12, 1911, 11; "Four Insurance Outings Today," *Hartford Courant*, June 17, 1916, 5.

68. Grant, 9.

69. Ibid., 17.

70. Old Saybrook Land Records, Elizabeth Colt's purchase from New Saybrook Company, vol. 4, p. 264, September 30, 1871. Elizabeth Colt's sale to Francis Goodwin, vol. 7, p. 264, August 29, 1879.

71. Old Saybrook Land Records. Between the years 1854 and 1934, no one by the name of McGovern owned property at Fenwick.

72. "Senator McGovern Entertains Friends," *Hartford Courant*, July 9, 1908, 7.

73. Anne Edwards, *A Remarkable Woman: A Biography of Katharine Hepburn* (New York: William Morrow & Co., 1985), 46.

74. "Mayor Dwight, Choice of Hartford Republicans," *Hartford Courant*, March 31, 1892, 1.

75. "The Election: William Waldo Hyde Chosen Mayor," *Hartford Courant*, April 5, 1892, 1.

76. J. H. Beers & Co., *Commemorative Biographical Record of Hartford County* (Chicago: J. H. Beers & Co., 1901), 1505.

77. Grant, 81.

78. Old Saybrook Land Records. Between the years 1854 and 1934, no one by the name of Winslow owned property at Fenwick; "Gideon D. Winslow Dead, Age 68 Years," *The Hartford Courant*, September 18, 1914, 11.

79. "Fenwick Hall," *Hartford Courant*, June 28, 1895, 11; "Fenwick Hall," *Hartford Courant*, July 9, 1913, 19.

80. "Fenwick Hall Sold, to Be Demolished," *Hartford Courant*, April 23, 1917, 13.

81. "Building Burned, but Not for 'Movies,' " *Hartford Courant*, May 21, 1917, 1. There had been a rumor—without foundation—that Francis Goodwin had paid for the Fenwick Station of the Hartford Yacht Club. The club was built with funds collected from all the members and was built on land leased from Morgan Bulkeley at Folly Point on the Connecticut River side of Fenwick (*Hartford Courant*, February 24, 1900, 9; *Hartford Courant*, June 21, 1900, 10).

82. "Building Burned, but Not for 'Movies.' "

83. "Former Senator Morgan Bulkeley Now a Farmer," *Hartford Courant*, July 1, 1917, X5.

84. Grant, 4.

85. "Former Senator Morgan Bulkeley Now a Farmer."

86. Ibid.

87. Tel. interview with J. H. Kelso Davis, March 2, 2002. The Newton Brainards left a large portion of their abundant estate to the Hartford Foundation for Public Giving, and they left a large parcel of land connected with Brainard Farm to the MDC for public use (Grant, 97).

11. SENATOR BULKELEY

1. Connecticut Population Statistics, Secretary of State's office, Hartford.

2. Ellsworth S. Grant and Marion H. Grant, *The City of Hartford 1784–1984: An Illustrated History* (Hartford: Connecticut Historical Society, 1986), 23.

3. *Institute for Historical Study Newsletter* vol. 27, no. 4, Spring 2007: 7, at http://www.tihs.org/IHS%20Spring%202007%20Newsletter.pdf (accessed 12/24/2008).

4. "An Electric Carriage," *Hartford Courant*, December 28, 1894, 9. These first electric vehicles could do "eleven miles per hour on the asphalt."

5. *Institute for Historical Study Newsletter*, 7.

6. Ibid.

7. U.S. Census Records, 1900, 1910.

8. "Maj. Bulkeley Dies after Long Illness at His Home Here," *Hartford Courant*, March 23, 1926, 1.

9. Richard Hooker, *Aetna Life Insurance Company: Its First Hundred Years* (Hartford, CT: Aetna Life Insurance Co., 1956), 144.

10. "No Blue-Grey Reunion, Says Connecticut G.A.R.," *Hartford Courant*, May 19, 1904, 11.

11. "His Brother's Picture," *Hartford Courant*, April 26, 1904, 5.

12. Ibid.

13. "Forty tents" can be misleading because there were ultimately eighty-seven GAR posts in Connecticut. The posts were named after war heroes, and the two in Hartford were the Nathaniel Lyon Post and the Robert O. Tyler Post.

14. "Dinner for the Vets," *Hartford Courant*, May 17, 1904, 8.

15. Hooker, 132–33.

16. "Taft Unable to Come," *Hartford Courant*, May 11, 1904, 11.

17. "Taft Will Be Here," *Hartford Courant*, May 10, 1904, 5.

18. "Memorial Edition in Great Demand," *Hartford Courant*, May 23, 1904, 1.

19. "Governor Bulkeley Paid Postage," *Hartford Courant*, May 30, 1904, 3.

20. "Many Honor Aetna Life's Head," *Hartford Courant*, July 8, 1904, 8.

21. "President 25 Years," *Hartford Courant*, June 29, 1904, 5.

22. Ibid.

23. "State Gets $450,000," *Hartford Courant*, March 17, 1903, 14.

24. "The Bulkeley-Fessenden Contest," *Hartford Courant*, October 24, 1904, 10.

25. "Brandegee Makes Ringing Speech," *Hartford Courant*, May 11, 1904, 11.

26. "Bulkeley Will Win on First Ballot," *Hartford Courant*, November 10, 1904, 5.

27. "Gov. Bulkeley on the First Vote," *Hartford Courant*, January 12, 1905, 1.

28. "Bulkeley's Vote Over Twice That of Fessenden's," *Hartford Courant*, January 13, 1905, 1.

29. Ibid.

30. "The Mayoralty," *Hartford Courant*, March 21, 1900, 10.

31. "Bulkeley's Vote Over Twice That of Fessenden's."

32. Ibid.

33. "Congratulations for Gov. Bulkeley," *Hartford Courant*, January 13, 1905, 2.

34. "Bulkeley's Vote Over Twice That of Fessenden's."

35. "Congratulations for Ex-Governor Bulkeley," *Hartford Courant*, January 14, 1905, 5.

36. "Bulkeley in Washington," *Hartford Courant*, January 30, 1905, 11.

37. Ibid.

38. Ibid.; "Pension for Mrs. Hawley," *Hartford Courant*, March 2, 1907, 1.

39. "Bulkeleys Back from Congress," *Hartford Courant*, February 1, 1905, 6.

40. TR's first wife, Alice Hathaway Lee Roosevelt, died of Bright's disease at age twenty-two. (TR's mother died the same day.) Their daughter, Alice, was the only child born of that union. She later became Alice Roosevelt Longworth when she married Congressman Nicholas Longworth of Ohio. In later life, Washington wags called her "the other Washington Monument."

41. "Bulkeleys Back from Congress."

42. Government Printing Office, "Fifty-Ninth Congress," at http://www.gpoaccess .gov/serialset/cdocuments/hd108-222/59th.pdf (accessed 12/19/2008).

43. Federal Reserve Bank of New York, "The Founding of the Fed: Federal Reserve Act of 1913," at http://www.newyorkfed.org/aboutthefed/history_article.html (accessed 12/24/2008).

44. J. H. Beers & Co., *Commemorative Biographical Record of Hartford County* (Chicago: J. H. Beers & Co., 1901), 34–35; "Gen. Hawley, He Died This Morning," *Hartford Courant*, March 18, 1905, 1.

45. Louis A. Coolidge, *Orville H. Platt of Connecticut* (New York and London: G. P. Putnam's Sons, 1910), 584.

46. "Fessenden Out of Senatorial Race," *Hartford Courant*, May 2, 1905, 1.

47. "Samuel Fessenden Dies at Stamford," *Hartford Courant*, January 8, 1908, 15.

48. "After the Caucus," *Hartford Courant*, May 6, 1905, 8.

49. "Senator Bulkeley Is Off for Washington," *Hartford Courant*, December 2, 1905, 5; "Washington Home of the Bulkeleys," *Hartford Courant*, March 17, 1906, 13.

50. "Pension for Old Naval Veteran," *Hartford Courant*, June 22, 1906, 8; "Thompsonville," *Hartford Courant*, December 21, 1906, 17; "Connecticut Pensions: Bills by Sen. Bulkeley," *Hartford Courant*, June 8, 1907, 14.

51. "Pension for Mrs. Hawley," *Hartford Courant*, March 2, 1907, 1.

52. *The Congressional Record*, Senate, March 1, 1907, 4327–29. Besides Joe Hawley's interest in the *Courant*, Edith Hawley also inherited the house at 147 Sigourney Street in Hartford, which had been rented out for years. The Hawleys also owned Lot #85 at Fenwick. Eighteen months after Senator Hawley's death, Edith Hawley sold the building lot to Senator Bulkeley (Old Saybrook Land Records, vol. 10, p. 506, October 11, 1906, Old Saybrook Town Hall, Old Saybrook, CT).

53. Biographical Directory of the United States Congress, "Bulkeley, Morgan Gardner," at http://bioguide.congress.gov/scripts/biodisplay.pl?index=B001044 (accessed 4/11/2008).

54. William Manners, *TR and Will: A Friendship That Split the Republican Party* (New York: Harcourt, Brace & World, 1969), 5–10.

55. Ibid., 5–10, 59.

56. Ibid., 63.

57. Nathan Miller, *Theodore Roosevelt: A Life* (New York: William Morrow & Co., 1992), 440.

58. Manners, 30; "Mary Morris Scrapbook Collection," (social), vol. II, Connecticut Historical Society, Hartford.

59. "Mary Morris Scrapbook Collection."

60. Carol Felsenthal, *Alice Roosevelt Longworth* (New York, G. P. Putnam's Sons, 1988), 107.

61. "Mary Morris Scrapbook Collection."

62. "Connecticut Pensions . . . Sen. Bulkeley Entertains," *Hartford Courant*, January 29, 1906, 13; "Mary Morris Scrapbook Collection."

63. Rodger Streitmatter, *Mightier Than the Sword* (Boulder, CO: Westview Press, 1998), 99; Hooker, 135–36.

64. United States Senate, "Historical Minute Essays: Treason of the Senate," at http://www.senate.gov/artandhistory/history/minute/Treason_of_the_Senate.htm (accessed 4/12/2008).

65. Ibid.

66. "Biographical Directory of the United States Congress," at http://bioguide.congress.gov/biosearch/biosearch.asp (accessed 4/12/2008).

67. The National Archives, "San Francisco Earthquake, 1906," at http://www.archives.gov/legislative/features/sf/ (accessed 12/20/2008).

68. National Park Service, "Presidio of San Francisco, 1906 Earthquake: Fire Fighting," at http://www.nps.gov/prsf/historyculture/1906-earthquake-fire-fighting.htm (accessed 12/20/2008).

69. Ibid.

70. "Would Cut Down Reserve Fund," *Hartford Courant*, May 16, 1906, 1.

71. "Bulkeley Defends Campaign Gifts, Says Work of Armstrong Committee Has Not Bettered Conditions," *Hartford Courant*, May 17, 1906, 1.

72. Ibid.

73. Hooker, 137–38.

74. "Senators Probing Brownsville Affair," *Hartford Courant*, February 5–7, 1907.

75. Ibid.

76. "Bulkeley Firm in Brownsville Case," *Hartford Courant*, March 12, 1908, 1; "Bulkeley to Speak on Brownsville Case," *Hartford Courant*, April 13, 1908, 2.

77. University of Texas at Brownsville, "Major Events: Brownsville Raid," at http://blue.utb.edu/localhistory/brownsville_raid.htm (accessed 4/12/2008).

78. The National Baseball Hall of Fame, at http://web.baseballhalloffame.org/museum/history.jsp (accessed 4/12/2008).

79. Ibid.

80. Ibid.

81. "A Fine Welcome for Secretary Taft," *Hartford Courant*, February 17, 1908, 13.

82. Ibid.

83. "Mary Morris Scrapbook Collection."

84. Manners, 5.

85. Manners, 59.

86. Manners, 60.

87. "Mary Morris Scrapbook Collection."

88. "To Bedrock by Caisson," *Hartford Courant*, March 12, 1904, 13.

89. "Civic Spirit Typified in Great Bridge," *Hartford Courant*, October 7, 1908, 11.

90. "At a Meeting of the Hartford Bridge Company . . . ," *Hartford Courant*, October 18, 1809, 1.

91. "Off for the Big Vanderbilt Race," *Hartford Courant*, October 13, 1905, 11; *Hartford Courant*, October 22, 1908, 15; *Hartford Courant*, October 24, 1908, 11.

92. "Personal Mention," *Hartford Courant*, October 22, 1908, 15.

93. "Automobiles in Town," *Hartford Courant*, February 6, 1900, 5.

94. Glenn Weaver, *Hartford: An Illustrated History of Connecticut's Capital* (Woodland Hills, CA: Windsor Publications, 1982), 106.

95. [Advertisements], *Hartford Courant*, April 27, 1903, 8; "Garage Gleanings," *Hartford Courant*, October 1, 1908, 12.

96. "Garage Gleanings," *Hartford Courant*, October 1, 1908, 12.

97. "Factory and Garage," *Hartford Courant*, December 22, 1910, 20.

98. "Automobile Club Discusses Law," *Hartford Courant*, November 7, 1908, 13.

99. "Bulkeley Thrown Out of His Seat in Wreck on Valley," *Hartford Courant*, August 12, 1910, 1.

100. "Personal Mention," *Hartford Courant*, September 20, 1909, 5.

101. "C. R. Keeney Dies of Auto Injuries," *Hartford Courant*, November 18, 1909, 1.

102. "Senator Bulkeley in Auto Mishap," *Hartford Courant*, September 23, 1919, 6.

103. "Two Senators Put Knife into Allen," *Hartford Courant*, January 22, 1909, 1.

104. "Hill Is Gaining Ground Steadily," *Hartford Courant*, January 4. 1909, 1; "Hill Spent . . . Roraback, Political Agent," *Hartford Courant*, January 29, 1909, 18.

105. "Hill Is Gaining Ground Steadily," *Hartford Courant*, January 4, 1909, 1.

106. "Brandegee Wins by Fifteen Votes," *Hartford Courant*, January 13, 1909, 1.

107. "Bad Investments And Ill Health Given as Causes," *Hartford Courant*, October 15, 1924, 1.

108. "Brandegee Wins by Fifteen Votes"

109. "Two Senators Put Knife into Allen."

110. Manners, 68, 83.

111. Manners, 86–88.

112. "Mary Morris Scrapbook Collection."

113. Manners, 59.

114. "Senator Bulkeley a Candidate," *Hartford Courant*, March 15, 1909, 1.

115. "The Senatorship, How Bulkeley's Announcement Is Received . . . ," *Hartford Courant*, March 17, 1909, 14.

116. "Uncle Joe's Fate, Where Senator Bulkeley Misjudges Connecticut Sentiment," *Hartford Courant*, January 25, 1910, 8.

117. Ibid.

118. Ibid.

119. "How It All Happened," *Hartford Courant*, May 11, 1910, 8.

120. "Name Successor to Roraback," *Hartford Courant*, June 24, 1910, 1.

121. "Bulkeley in Danger of Losing His Seat," *New York Times*, October 23, 1910, 6.

122. "Bulkeley Thrown Out of His Seat in Wreck on Valley."

123. Ibid.

124. "McLean, Goodwin at Bridgeport Outing," *Hartford Courant*, August 26, 1910, 14.

125. "Bulkeley Reverse: Three Towns Turn Senator Down Hard," *Hartford Courant*, September 2, 1910, 1.

126. "The Senatorship Campaign: No Bolt, No Roll Call . . . ," *Hartford Courant*, December 26, 1910, 8.

127. "It's None of Their Business What I Think," *Hartford Courant*, November 1, 1910, 1.

128. "Politics in Middletown," *Hartford Courant*, October 10, 1910, 1; "The Drift to McLean," *Hartford Courant*, October 13, 1910, 8; "Bulkeley's Chances," *Hartford Courant*, October 14, 1910, 1.

129. "56 Majority for Goodwin, Bulkeley Replies to the Man from Maine, That Is, in Part—Says He Did Not Decapitate Roraback," *Hartford Courant*, September 12, 1910, 1.

130. "Mayor Thayer out with Another Letter," *Hartford Courant*, July 19, 1910, 12.

131. "Charles A. Goodwin Dies," *Hartford Courant*, October 8, 1954, 1.

132. "Kenealy Predicts Republican Victory," *Hartford Courant*, October 24, 1910, 5.

133. "An Interesting Threat," Letter to *New Haven Union* (repr. *Hartford Courant*, October 3, 1910, 8); "Bulkeley Reverse: Three Towns Turn Senator Down Hard."

134. "Two Mean Schemes," *Hartford Courant*, November 3, 1910, 8.

135. "Chandler Declares for Roll Call Vote," *Hartford Courant*, November 3, 1910, 2.

136. "Unsought and Unbought," *Hartford Courant*, October 22, 1910, 1.

137. "Baldwin Elected by about 4,000," *Hartford Courant*, November 9, 1910, 1.

138. Marion Hepburn Grant, *The Fenwick Story*. (Hartford: The Connecticut Historical Society, 1974), 119.

12. TWILIGHT

1. Gergley Baics, "The Saloons of Hartford's East Side," report written with an award by the U. S. Department of Housing and Urban Development, Trinity College, Hartford, at http://www.trincoll.edu/depts/tcn/Research_Reports/60.htm (accessed 3/21/2008).

2. "Speed of Motor Vehicles," *Hartford Courant*, May 8, 1901, 4.

3. "Governor's Ball Crowns Glories of Inauguration Day," *Hartford Courant*, January 5, 1911, 1.

4. "Recollections of Forty Years in Connecticut Politics," *Hartford Courant*, October 25, 1914, E21–23.

5. "Darien Postmaster Finally Confirmed," *Hartford Courant*, February 11, 1911, 1.

6. "Hearty Welcome Here for Taft," *Hartford Courant*, September 8, 1911, 1.

7. Ibid.; "Climax of Races at Charter Oak, President Taft Smiles on Crowd . . . ," *Hartford Courant*, September 8, 1911, 15.

8. "Bulkeley Home the Scene of Merrymaking," *Hartford Courant*, November 9, 1911, 10.

9. "Reception for Miss Bulkeley," *Hartford Courant*, November 16, 1911, 2.

10. "Bulkeley Plans for a Big Bank," *Hartford Courant*, February 28, 1912, 1; "Phoenix-American Deal Up Next Week, Merger Scheme May Be Blocked by Bulkeley," *Hartford Courant*, April 5, 1912, 11.

11. "Bulkeley Plans for a Big Bank"; "Phoenix-American Deal Up Next Week . . ."

12. "Phoenix-American Deal Up Next Week." For the remainder of 1912, there was no bank merger activity reported in the papers.

13. Rumor Mill News, "Nathan Rothschild and the Battle of Waterloo," at http://www.rumormillnews.com/cgi-bin/archive.cgi/noframes/read/39506 (accessed 4/12/2008).

14. "Timeline of SEC and Securities History," at http://www.sechistorical.org/museum/timeline/index.php (accessed 12/26/2008).

15. "Ex-Senator Bulkeley "Kept Store" for Owner," *Hartford Courant*, April 3, 1912, 1.

16. "Roraback Succeeds Kenealy as Chairman," *Hartford Courant*, April 18, 1912, 10.

17. "Roraback Elected Head of Power Co.," *Hartford Courant*, December 22, 1925, 1.

18. "J. Henry Roraback Dies of Self-Inflicted Wound at Estate in Harwinton," *Hartford Courant*, May, 20, 1937, 1.

19. "Charter of Fire Co. Acquired by Aetna Life," *Hartford Courant*, January. 24, 1913, 1; Richard Hooker, *Aetna Life Insurance Company: Its First Hundred Years* (Hartford, CT: Aetna Life Insurance Co., 1956), 103–4.

20. Hooker, 133.

21. "The Bulkeley Party Will Leave Today," *Hartford Courant*, February 23, 1915, 12; "Bulkeley's Off to Golden Gate," *Hartford Courant*, February 24, 1915, 1.

22. "The Bulkeley Party Will Leave Today"; "Bulkeley's Off to Golden Gate."

23. Ibid.

24. "Ex-Senator Bulkeley Talks in Pasadena," *Hartford Courant*, April 4, 1915, 5.

25. Ibid.

26. James L. Stokesbury, *A Short History of World War I* (New York: William Morrow & Co., 1981), 221–27, 310.

27. Tel. interview with J. H. Kelso Davis, March 2, 2002.

28. Ibid.

29. "Troop B Fully Recruited . . . ," *Hartford Courant*, June 22, 1916, 2.

30. Tel. interview with J. H. Kelso Davis.

31. "Troop B to Leave Arivaca Wednesday," *Hartford Courant*, October 9, 1916, 11.

32. "Miss Bulkeley Bride of J. A. Ingersoll," *Hartford Courant*, June 28, 1916, 1.

33. Senator Bulkeley Back from West, *Hartford Courant*, December 8, 1916, 12.

34. Ibid.

35. "Sentiment Favors City Hall Repair," *Hartford Courant*, March 9, 1906, 11.

36. "The Post Office Question," *Hartford Courant*, May 17, 1917, 2.

37. "Many Appeal for Old State House," *Hartford Courant*, October 18, 1913, 1.

38. Ibid.

39. "State House Fund Open This Week," *Hartford Courant*, May 23, 1917, 8.

40. Newton C. Brainard, *The Hartford State House* (Hartford: Connecticut Historical Society, 1964), 63.

41. Ibid.

42. "Their Christmas in France Was a Great Success," *Hartford Courant*, January 24, 1918, 5.

43. Leonard P. Ayres, *The War with Germany* (Washington, DC: Government Printing Office, 1919), 22, diagram 7.

44. "They Strip Out Excess Baggage," *Hartford Courant*, August 30, 1917, 13.

45. "Social and Personal, They Command the 101st . . . ," *Hartford Courant*, September 9, 1917, X3; "Personal Words from Troop B Men," *Hartford Courant*, May 7, 1918, 13.

46. "Half of Quota Comes In," *Hartford Courant*, April 7, 1917, 1.

47. "Ex-Senator Morgan Bulkeley Dies . . . ," *Hartford Courant*, November 7, 1922, 1.

48. "As McGovern Tells It, His Resignation Was Demanded," *Hartford Courant*, May 21, 1918, 1.

49. Ibid.

50. "Largest Shareholders," *Hartford Courant*, November 28, 1887, 5.

51. "McGovern's Career Ends at Age of 91," *Hartford Courant*, February 6, 1941, 1.

52. Hartford Probate Court Records, Fannie Bulkeley's will, vol. 518, p. 384, probated June 28, 1938, Hartford Probate Court, Hartford, CT. Since Morgan Bulkeley kept many assets in Fannie's name, his inventory at death never told the whole story. Fannie's estate of almost $1 million gives a much better account of Morgan Bulkeley's true worth at the time of his passing.

53. "Gen. Bulkeley's Estate: Appraised at a valuation of, $1,145,993.50 . . . ," *Hartford Courant*, December 20, 1902, 4.

54. "All of 101st Deserve Distinguished Service Crosses, Says Bulkeley . . . ," *Hartford Courant*, January 4, 1919, 8.

55. Ibid.

56. Glenn Weaver, *Hartford: An Illustrated History of Connecticut's Capital* (Woodland Hills, CA: Windsor Publications, 1982), 116.

57. U.S. Census Records, 1920. Richard B. Bulkeley lived in the West End; Maj. Morgan Bulkeley Jr. lived on the Hartford side of Prospect Avenue; Elinor (Bulkeley) Ingersoll lived

on the West Hartford Side of Prospect Avenue; and, John Bulkeley lived on Walbridge Road, West Hartford.

58. "Mrs. Brainard Dies at Saybrook Point," *Hartford Courant*, July 24, 1921, 2.

59. "Ex-Senator Morgan G. Bulkeley Dies Following Brief Illness," *Hartford Courant*, November 7, 1922, 1.

60. "Morgan G. Bulkeley," *Hartford Times*, November 7, 1922, 10.

61. State of Connecticut, Bureau of Vital Statistics, Medical Certificate of Death, Morgan G. Bulkeley, November 6, 1922.

62. Ibid.

63. "Half-Mast Flags for Senator Bulkeley," *Hartford Courant*, November 8, 1922, 12.

64. "Bulkeley Funeral to Be Held Today," *Hartford Courant*, November 9, 1922, 2; "Final Tribute Is Paid to Bulkeley," *Hartford Courant*, November 10, 1922, 6.

65. "Bulkeley Funeral to Be Held Today"; "Final Tribute Is Paid to Bulkeley."

66. "Bulkeley Funeral to Be Held Today"; "Final Tribute Is Paid to Bulkeley."

67. "Jimmy and the Financier," *Wall Street Journal* (repr. *Hartford Courant*, July 4, 1923, 10).

68. Hartford Probate Court Records, vol. 324, p. 148, November 14, 1923, Hartford Probate Court, Hartford, CT. (Fannie Bulkeley accepts responsibility to build an inventory and probate Morgan Bulkeley's estate.)

69. Hartford Probate Court Records, vol. 329, pp. 546–47, May 14, 1923, Hartford Probate Court, Hartford, CT. Probate record accepted by the court, May 14, 1923.

70. Hooker, 95–139.

71. "Aetna Casualty Year Satisfactory," *Hartford Courant*, January 27, 1922, 15.

72. Ibid.

73. Hooker, 214–17.

74. "Mrs. Bulkeley Buys Woodside Road Home," *Hartford Courant*, December 22, 1922, 10.

75. "Mrs. M. G. Bulkeley Dies Suddenly in Sleep at Her Home," *Hartford Courant*, June 23, 1938, 8.

76. "Miss M'Grath Buys Bulkeley Home," *Hartford Courant*, March 31, 1923, 2; "Bulkeley Mansion New Home for State Police," *Hartford Courant*, July 19, 1924, 1.

77. "Maj. Bulkeley Dies after Long Illness at His Home Here, " *Hartford Courant*, March 23, 1926, 1.

78. "Mrs. E. B. Ingersoll Dies, Father Was Governor," *Hartford Courant*, October 6, 1964, 4.

79. "Houghton Bulkeley Found Shot Dead," *Hartford Courant*, May 4, 1966, 4A.

80. "Death of Rev. Dr. Goodwin Unexpectedly Takes City's Venerable Leading Citizen," *Hartford Courant*, October 6, 1923, 1.

81. State Of Connecticut, Bureau of Vital Statistics, Medical Certificate of Death, Francis Goodwin, October 5, 1923.

82. "To Honor Pioneers of Baseball," *Hartford Courant*, December 8, 1937, 12.

BIBLIOGRAPHY

NEWSPAPERS, JOURNALS, PERIODICALS

Connecticut: *Connecticut Quarterly; Evening Press; Bridgeport Standard; Hartford Times; Hartford Courant; Hartford Daily Courant; Hartford Daily Times; Hartford Post; Hartford Telegram; Hog River Journal; Journal Courier; New Haven Palladium; New Haven Register; New Haven Union; New London Telegraph; Norwich Bulletin; Springfield Republican.*

Massachusetts: *Boston Daily Globe, Boston Globe; Gazette and Courier* (Franklin County); *Springfield Republican.*

New York: *Cosmopolitan; New York Herald; New York Sun; New York Times; New York World; New York Post; Wall Street Journal; Brooklyn Daily Eagle.*

California: *Alta California; California Historical Society Quarterly; San Francisco Morning Call; San Francisco Examiner; San Francisco Daily Evening Bulletin; San Francisco Chronicle; San Francisco Observer; San Francisco Daily Evening Post.*

Washington, D.C.: Congressional Record; *Washington Post.*

HALLS OF RECORDS

Connecticut Historical Society, 1 Elizabeth Street, Hartford, CT

East Haddam Land Records, Town Hall, Main Street, East Haddam, CT

Hartford Land Records; City Hall, Main Street, Hartford, CT

Hartford Probate District, 250 Constitution Plaza, Hartford, CT

Maryland State Archives, 6550 Reisterstown Road, Baltimore, MD

Old Saybrook Land Records, Town Hall, Main Street, Old Saybrook, CT

West Hartford Land Records, Town Hall, Main Street, West Hartford, CT

WEB SITES

Various Web sites cited in endnotes.

Connecticut, State of. "State of Connecticut, Connecticut Population by Town, 1756–1820." http://www.ct.gov/ecd/cwp/view.asp?a=1106&q=250670 (accessed 12/12/2008).

Connecticut, State of. "General Statues of Connecticut." http://www.cga.ct.gov/LCO/Statute_Web_Site_LCO.htm (accessed 12/12/2008).

TELEPHONE INTERVIEWS
Peter Bulkeley, September 11, 2002
J. H. Kelso Davis, March 2, 2002
Dr. Karl Stofko, April 11, 2002

PERSONAL PAPERS

Bulkeley, Eliphalet. Eliphalet Bulkeley, Daybook, 1832–1850. (No file number). Hartford: Connecticut Historical Society.

Bulkeley, Eliphalet A. Eliphalet A. Bulkeley Papers. Connecticut State Library.

Bulkeley, Morgan. Morgan G. Bulkeley Political Scrapbook, 1885–88, MS 93631, Hartford: Connecticut Historical Society.

Hartford Probate District. "Eliphalet A. Bulkeley" (No catalog or file number). Hartford: History and Genealogy, Connecticut State Library. Apr. 25, 1872.

Hawley Joseph. Papers of Joseph R. Hawley, 1638–1906. Library of Congress. 29 Reels. Connecticut State Library.

BOOKS

Allis, Marguerite. *Connecticut River*. New York: G.P. Putnam's Sons, 1939.

Andrews, Kenneth R. *Nook Farm: Mark Twain's Hartford Circle*. Boston: Harvard University Press, 1950.

Arcidiacono, David. *Grace, Grit, and Growling: The Hartford Dark Blues Base Ball Club, 1874–1877*. Author, 2003.

Atlas of the City of Hartford and the Town of West Hartford. New York: Sanborn Map Co., 1921.

Ayres, Leonard P. *The War with Germany*. Washington, DC: Government Printing Office, 1919.

Beebe, Lucius. *Mr. Pullman's Elegant Palace Car*. New York: Doubleday & Co., 1961.

Beers, J. H. & Co., *Commemorative Biographical Record of Hartford County*. Chicago: J. H. Beers & Co., 1901.

Brainard, Newton C. *Fenwick*. Hartford, CT: Case, Lockwood & Brainard Co., 1944.

Brainard, Newton C. *The Hartford State House*. Hartford: Connecticut Historical Society, 1964.

Brockett, L. P., and M. C. Vaughan. *Women's Work in the Civil War: A Record of Heroism, Patriotism and Patience*. Philadelphia: Zeigler, McCurdy & Co., 1867.

Burpee, Charles W. *The History of Hartford County, 1633–1928*. Chicago: The S. J. Clark Publishing Co., 1928.

Burpee, Charles W. *A Century in Hartford: The History of the Hartford County Mutual Fire Insurance Company*. Hartford, CT: The Hartford County Mutual Fire Insurance Co., 1931.

Cahn, William. *A Matter of Life and Death: The Connecticut Mutual Story*. New York: Random House, 1970.

Catton, Bruce. *The American Heritage New History of the Civil War*. New York: Viking, 1996.

Chapman, Helen Post. *My Hartford of the Nineteenth Century*. Hartford, CT: Edwin Valentine Mitchell, 1928.

Close, F. Perry. *History of Hartford's Streets*. Hartford: Connecticut Historical Society, 1969.

Coolidge, Louis A. *Orville H. Platt of Connecticut*. New York and London: G. P. Putnam's Sons, 1910.

Crocker-Langley San Francisco City Directory, 1920, 1921.

Currie, David P. *The Constitution in the Supreme Court*. Chicago: University of Chicago Press, 1985.

Decker, Robert Owen. *Hartford Immigrants: A History of the Christian Activities Council (Congregational) 1850–1980*. New York: United Church Press, 1987.

Delaney, Edmund. *The Connecticut River: New England's Historic Waterway*. Chester, CT: The Globe Pequot Press, 1983.

DeVito, Michael C. *Connecticut's Timbered Crossings*. Warehouse Point, CT: DeVito Enterprises, 1964.

Edwards, Anne. *A Remarkable Woman: A Biography of Katharine Hepburn*. New York: William Morrow & Co., 1985.

Ensign, Ariel. *Hartford City Directory*, 1828, pub. by Ariel Ensign, 19 Front Street, Hartford (reprinted New Haven: Price, Lee Co., 1884).

Erving, Henry W. *The Connecticut River Banking Company, 1825–1925: One Hundred Years of Service*. Hartford: Connecticut River Banking Co., 1925.

Fay, Margaret, ed. *Memories of Hartford: A Project of the Seniors Jubilee 350 Committee*. Hartford, CT: Phoenix Mutual Life Insurance Co., 1986.

Felsenthal, Carol. *Alice Roosevelt Longworth*. New York: G. P. Putnam's Sons, 1988.

Formby, John. *The American Civil War: A Concise History of Its Causes, Progress and Results*. London: John Murray, 1910.

G. Fox and Co., *Highways and Byways of Connecticut*. Hartford, CT: G. Fox & Co., 1947.

Gall, Henry R., and William G. Jordan. *One Hundred Years of Fire Insurance: Being a History of Aetna Insurance Company*. Hartford, CT: Aetna Insurance Co., 1919.

Gardner, Melzar, ed. *Gardner's City Directory*, Hartford, CT: Case Tiffany & Co., 1838–1841 (copyright sold to Elihu Geer in 1841).

Geer's City Directory. Hartford, CT: Hartford Printing Co., 1838–1960.

Goodwin, James Junius. *The Goodwins of Hartford, Connecticut: Descendants of William and Ozias Goodwin*. Hartford, CT: Brown & Gross, ca. 1891.

Grant, Ellsworth. *Yankee Dreamers and Doers*, Chester, CT: Pequot Press, 1983.

Grant, Ellsworth. *The Club on Prospect Street: A History of the Hartford Club*. Hartford, CT: The Hartford Club, 1984.

Grant, Ellsworth. *The Miracle of Connecticut*. Hartford: Connecticut Historical Society and Fenwick Productions, 1992.

Grant, Ellsworth. *Thar She Goes: Shipbuilding on the Connecticut River*. Old Saybrook, CT: Fenwick Productions, 2000.

Grant, Ellsworth S., and Marion H. Grant. *The City of Hartford 1784–1984: An Illustrated History*. Hartford: Connecticut Historical Society with the support of Society for Savings, 1986.

Grant, Marion Hepburn. *The Fenwick Story*. Hartford: Connecticut Historical Society, 1974.

Grant, Marion Hepburn. *In and Around Hartford: Its People and Places*. Hartford: Connecticut Historical Society, 1989.

Hart, Samuel, et al. *Encyclopedia of Connecticut Biography*. Boston: American Historical Society, 1917.

Hartford Board of Trade. *Hartford, Conn., as a Manufacturing, Business and Commercial Center; with Brief Sketches of its History, Attractions, Leading Industries, and Institutions*. Hartford: Author, 1889.

Hawthorne, Daniel. *The Hartford of Hartford: An Insurance Company's Part in a Century and a Half of American History*. New York: Random House, 1960.

Hooker, Richard. *Aetna Life Insurance Company: Its First Hundred Years*. Hartford, CT: Aetna Life Insurance Co., 1956.

Hooper, Marion, and Lewis Browne. *Life along the Connecticut River*. Brattleboro, VT: Stephen Daye Press, 1939.

Hosley, William N. *Colt: The Making of an American Legend*. Amherst: University of Massachusetts Press, 1996.

Hubbell, William Stone, et al. (comp.). *The Story of the Twenty-First Regiment, Connecticut Volunteers*. Middletown, CT: Stewart Printing Co., 1900.

Hoyt, James B. *The Connecticut Story*. New Haven, CT: Reader's Press, Inc., 1961.

Hyde, Francis E. *Cunard and the North Atlantic, 1840–1973: A History of Shipping and Financial Management*. Atlantic Highlands, NJ: Humanities Press, 1975.

Jacobus, Donald Lines. *The Bulkeley Genealogy: Rev. Peter Bulkeley, being an account of his career, his ancestry, the ancestry of his two wives, and his relatives in England and New England, together with a genealogy of his descendants through the seventh American generation*. New Haven, CT: Tuttle, 1933.

Jensen, Oliver. *The American Heritage History of Railroads in America*. New York: American Heritage Publishers, 1975.

Kaplan, Justin. *Mr. Clemens and Mark Twain*. New York: Simon and Schuster, 1991.

Kendall, John. *History of New Orleans*. Chicago: The Lewis Publishing Company, 1922.

Lancaster, Clay. *Old Brooklyn Heights*. Rutland, VT: Charles E. Tuttle Co., 1961 (reprinted, Gillon, Edmund V. Jr., ed. New York: Dover Publications, 1979).

Love, William DeLoss. *The Colonial History of Hartford*. Hartford, CT: Case, Lockwood & Brainard, 1935.

Manners, William. *TR and Will: A Friendship That Split the Republican Party*. New York: Harcourt, Brace & World, 1969.

Matuz, Roger. *The Presidents Fact Book*. New York: Black Dog & Leventhal, 2004.

McCullough, David. *The Great Bridge: The Epic Story of the Building of the Brooklyn Bridge*. New York: Simon & Schuster, 2001.

Miller, Nathan. *Theodore Roosevelt: A Life*. New York: William Morrow & Co., 1992.

Mills, Lewis Sprague. *The Story of Connecticut*. New York: Exposition Press, 1953.

Morgan, Appleton. *The Family of Morgan*. Westfield, NJ: The Shakespeare Press, 1892.

Morgan, Nathaniel H. *Morgan Genealogy: A History of James Morgan, of New London, Conn., and His Descendants; from 1607 to 1869*. Hartford, CT: Case, Lockwood & Brainard, 1869.

Morris, Charles R. *The Tycoons: How Andrew Carnegie, John D. Rockefeller, Jay Gould, and JP Morgan Invented the American Supereconomy*. New York: Times Books, 2005.

Munro-Fraser, J. P. *History of Santa Clara County, California*. San Francisco: Alley, Bowen & Co., 1881.

Murphy, Kevin. *Water for Hartford: The Story of the Hartford Water Works and the Metropolitan District Commission*. Wethersfield, CT: Shining Tramp Press, 2004.

National Cyclopedia of American Biography. New York: J. T. White, 1897.

Nenortas, Thomas. *Victorian Hartford*. Mount Pleasant, SC: Arcadia Publishing, 2005.

Niven, John. *Connecticut for the Union: The Role of the State in the Civil War*. New Haven, CT: Yale University Press, 1965.

Potter, David Morris. *The Impending Crisis, 1848–1861*. New York: Harper Collins, 1976.

Open Hearth, No. 135 Front Street. Hartford: Connecticut State Library (pamphlet), 1888.

Powers, Ron. *Mark Twain*. New York: Simon and Schuster, 2005.

Resolves and Private Laws of the State of Connecticut, Vol. III, 1836-1857. Published under and by virtue of a resolution of the General Assembly, passed May session 1856. New Haven: Thomas J. Stafford, Printer, 1857.

Repplier, Agnes. *J. William White, MD*. New York: Houghton Mifflin, 1919.

Rhodes, James Ford. *History of the United States: From the Compromise of 1850 to the McKinley-Bryan Campaign of 1896*. Vol. VII. New York: The MacMillan Co., 1920.

Roth, David M. *Connecticut: A Bicentennial History*. New York: Norton, 1979.

Society for Savings. *Passbook to a Proud Past and a Promising Future*. Hartford, CT: Author, 1969.

Special Laws of Connecticut, 1896. Published under and by virtue of a resolution of the General Assembly, Hartford: State Law Library, 1896.

Stafford, Marshall P. *The Life of James Fisk, Jr.: A Full and Accurate Narrative of All the Enterprises in Which He Was Engaged*. Manchester, NH: Ayer Publishing, 1981 (originally published New York: Polhemus & Pearson, 1871).

Starr, Frank Farnsworth. *The Miles Morgan Family of Springfield, Massachusetts in the Line of Joseph Morgan of Hartford, Connecticut, 1780–1847*. Hartford, CT: Tuttle, Morehouse & Taylor Co., 1904.

Stofko, Karl, and Rachel I. Gibbs. *A Brief History of East Haddam*. East Haddam, CT: East Haddam Historical Society, 1977.

Stokesbury, James L. *A Short History of World War I*. New York: William Morrow & Co., 1981.

Streitmatter, Rodger. *Mightier Than the Sword*. Boulder, CO: Westview Press, 1998.

Swanberg, W. A. *Jim Fisk: The Career of an Improbable Rascal*. New York: Charles Scribner & Sons, 1959.

Trumbull, J. Hammond, *The Memorial History of Hartford County: 1633–1884*. Boston: Edward L. Osgood, Publisher, 1886.

Twitchell, Willis I., ed. *Hartford in History: A Series of Papers by Resident Authors*. Hartford, CT: Press of the Plimpton Manufacturing Co., 1907.

Van Dusen, Albert E. *Connecticut: A Fully Illustrated History of the State from the Seventeenth Century to the Present*. New York: Random House, 1961.

Van Why, Joseph S. *Nook Farm*. Hartford, CT: The Stowe-Day Foundation, 1975.

Walker, George Leon. *History of the First Church in Hartford*. Hartford, CT: Brown & Gross, 1884.

Warf, Barney. *Time-Space Compression*. Milton Park, UK: Routledge, 2008.

Weaver, Glenn. *The Hartford Electric Light Company*. Hartford, CT: The Hartford Electric Light Company, 1969.

Weaver, Glenn. *Hartford: An Illustrated History of Connecticut's Capital*. Woodland Hills, CA: Windsor Publications, 1982.

White, Barbara A. *The Beecher Sisters*. New Haven, CT: Yale University Press, 2003.

Wilson, R. L. *The Book of Colt Firearms*. Minneapolis, Blue Book Publications, 1993.

Wright, George E. *Crossing the Connecticut*. Hartford, CT: Smith-Linsley Co., 1908.

INDEX

Bulkeley, Morgan: abolishes Hartford
Bridge toll, 116, 133; *action* component,
50–51, 135; Aetna Life compensation
of, 64; as Aetna Life president, 55–56;
alcohol at GAR encampment, 162;
alderman seat, 49; antique collecting,
92, 101; automobile accidents, 176;
bachelor party in New York, 86; baseball, 56; Baseball Hall of Fame, 58;
birth of, 11; as Brer Rabbit Bulkeley,
121; bribery statute, 52; on buying
votes, 127; buys Arrowhead Farm, 1,
158; buys horses for Troop B, 188;
"Caesar," 128; campaign contributions,
70, 170; campaigns for Gen. Zachary
Taylor, 18; cigars, 2, 164; "citizen" ballot, 94, 119–20; Civil War, letter from,
31–32; comforts orphan children, 104;
common council seat, 48; conflict of
interest, 77, 81, 99; crowbar incident,
123; death of, 193; death penalty, stance
on, 115; dies intestate, 194; director,
Charter Oak Park, 59; electricity, fas-
cination with, 74, 90; entertains members of legislature, 115; estate, value of,
194; Federal Reserve, opinion of, 187;
final bill to legislature, 126; "grand
illumination," 51; gubernatorial address, 110; gubernatorial mail pro-
cedures, 112; gubernatorial proclamation (1891), 122; health, 135, 143; hiring
of Pat McGovern, 73–74; "holdover"
governor, 129; honorary Yale and Trinity degrees, 116; horse racing, 56;
inferiority, feelings of, 55; insufficient
postage, GAR, 162; legislation favoring
Aetna Life, 114; liquor interest ties, 80,
108; mayors' portraits collection, 101;
Mutual "nine," 57; National Commandery, GAR, 77, 142; *New Haven Register*
lawsuit, 80; oil portraits, 62, 113; opera,

93; pensioning judges, 110; physical
qualities, 2; private parlor cars, 186–87;
purchase of Black Maria, 96; raises railroad tracks at Union Station, 99; ringing State House bell, 19; salary as
mayor, 64; saving Old State House,
189; schooling, 16; state appropriations
stalled, 124; sweeping out Aetna Fire,
18; Valley Railroad wreck, 180; YMCA
building fund drive, 186
Bulkeley, Maj. Morgan G., Jr., 1, 91, 160–
61, 190–91, 195–96
Bulkeley, Rev. Peter, 7
Bulkeley, Richard Beaumaris, 7
Bulkeley, Sally Taintor (Billy's daughter),
90
Bulkeley, Sarah (Sally) Taintor, 8
Bulkeley, Sir Richard (of Beaumaris), 7–8
Bulkeley, Thomas, 7
Bulkeley, William H. (Billy): commissary
general, 62; death of, 141–42, 161; at
East Haddam, 11; elective politics, 62;
estate, value of, 142; at Fenwick, 2, 146,
155; gubernatorial race of 1882, 62, 80–
81, 105; Harrison inauguration, 113;
Helco investment, 95; lieutenant gover-
nor, 62, 68, 71, 75, 80; move to Brook-
lyn Heights, 26; relocation to Hartford,
62; schooling, 16
Bunce, Henry, 45, 56
Burnham, Atty. Frederick, 111
Bushnell (Memorial) Hall, 111
Bushnell, Lucy, 158
Butler, Gen. Ben, 129

California gold rush, 16
Cammeyer, William, 58
Cannon, "Uncle Joe," 168, 178
Capital City Electric Light Co., 76
Cartwright, Alexander Joy, 172
Case, Lockwood & Brainard, 61

Radcliffe College, 6
railroad bankruptcies, 47
Ransom, Amos, 15
Reithor, Morris, 125
Republican City Judiciary Convention, 38
Republican General Committee of Kings
    County, 38, 54
Republican National Committee, 46
Republican National Convention, 68, 173
Republican Party: first Connecticut organi-
    zational meeting, 27, 130; prohibition
    plank, 128
Republican State Central Committee, 93,
    105, 134, 177, 185
Republican State Convention (1886), 96
Republican Town (City) Committee, 52,
    62, 73, 94
Robertson, A. Heaton, 164
Robert's Opera House, 94
Robinson, Henry C., 82, 98, 100, 137
Robinson-Patman Act of 1936, 119
Rockefeller, John D. Jr., 169
Rockefeller, Mrs. John D. Jr., 169
Roebling, John A., 38
Roebling, Washington, 38–39
Roosevelt, Alice, 168
Roosevelt, Alice Hathaway Lee, 165
Roosevelt children, 167
Roosevelt, Edith Carow, 168
Roosevelt, President Theodore, 141, 145,
    162, 164–65, 167, 169, 173
Root, Capt. John G., 100–101, 151
Root, Dr. Edward K., 174, 192
Root, G. Wells, 146–47
Roraback, J. Henry, 177, 179, 185
Roseland Park, 117–18
"rotten boroughs," 121, 138
rounders, 172–73

St. Joseph's Cathedral, 45
St. Vitus' Dance (Sydenham's chorea), 6

San Francisco earthquake, 170
Saybrook Point, 4
Schleuter, George, 183
Schoomaker & Hicks, 24, 54
Second Landing District School, 12
Secret Ballot Bill, 116
Securities and Exchange Commission, 185
Servia, SS, 85
Seventeenth Amendment (1913), 132
Seventh Army Corps, 32
Seymour, Governor Thomas, 17, 40
Seymour, state Senator John W., 41, 122
Sharps Rifle Manufacturing Co., 30
Sheridan, General Philip, 114
Sherman Anti-Trust Act, 119
Sherman, Gen. William Tecumseh, 77–78,
    114
Shipman, Nathaniel, 27
Sickles, Gen. Dan, 162
Sluyter, Elizabeth, 100
Smith, Col. Able, 31, 33
Smith, Virginia Thrall, 70, 100
Soldiers and Sailors Memorial Arch, 97,
    117
South Congregational Church, 13, 193
Southern New England Telephone Co., 46
South Street Seaport, 23, 30
Spalding, Albert, 57–58
Sparhawk, Caroline. See Houghton,
    Caroline
Spencer, Christopher, 61
Sperry & McLean, 137
Spiegel, Nathan, 185
Sprague, Mayor Joseph, 48
Springfield muzzle-loader, 30
Stanford, Jane Lathrop, 6, 89
Stanford, Leland, 6, 84, 89, 119
Stanford, Leland, Jr., 89, 91
Stanford University, 6
State Police, Connecticut, 195
states' rights, 27, 103

Garnet Books

ABOUT THE AUTHOR

Kevin Murphy is an independent historian who lives in
Rocky Hill, Connecticut. He is the author of *Water for
Hartford: The Story of the Hartford Water Works and the
Metropolitan District Commission* (2004).

ABOUT THE DRIFTLESS CONNECTICUT SERIES

The Driftless Connecticut Series is a publication award
program established in 2010 to recognize excellent books with
a Connecticut focus or written by a Connecticut author. To be
eligible, the book must have a Connecticut topic or setting or
an author must have been born in Connecticut or have been a
legal resident of Connecticut for at least three years.

The Driftless Connecticut Series is funded by the
Beatrice Fox Auerbach Foundation Fund at the Hartford Foundation
for Public Giving. For more information and a complete
list of books in The Driftless Connecticut Series,
please visit us online at
http://www.wesleyan.edu/wespress/driftless.